THE CHRISTIAN PLATONISTS

OF

ALEXANDRIA

EIGHT LECTURES

PREACHED BEFORE THE UNIVERSITY OF OXFORD
IN THE YEAR 1886

ON THE FOUNDATION OF THE LATE REV. JOHN BAMPTON, M.A.
CANON OF SALISBURY

BY

CHARLES BIGG, D.D.

AMS PRESS
NEW YORK

Reprinted from a copy in the collections of Yale Univeristy
Library
From the edition of 1886, Oxford
First AMS EDITION published 1970
Manufactured in the United States of America

International Standard Book Number: 0-404-00799-6

Library of Congress Card Catalog Number: 75-123764

AMS PRESS, INC.
NEW YORK, N.Y. 10003

EXTRACT

FROM THE LAST WILL AND TESTAMENT

OF THE LATE

REV. JOHN BAMPTON,

CANON OF SALISBURY.

—— " I give and bequeath my Lands and Estates to the
" Chancellor, Masters, and Scholars of the University of Oxford
" for ever, to have and to hold all and singular the said Lands or
" Estates upon trust, and to the intents and purposes hereinafter
" mentioned ; that is to say, I will and appoint that the Vice-
" Chancellor of the University of Oxford for the time being shall
" take and receive all the rents, issues, and profits thereof, and
" (after all taxes, reparations, and necessary deductions made)
" that he pay all the remainder to the endowment of eight
" Divinity Lecture Sermons, to be established for ever in the
" said University, and to be performed in the manner following :

" I direct and appoint, that, upon the first Tuesday in Easter
" Term, a Lecturer may be yearly chosen by the Heads of Col-
" leges only, and by no others, in the room adjoining to the
" Printing-House, between the hours of ten in the morning and
" two in the afternoon, to preach eight Divinity Lecture
" Sermons, the year following, at St. Mary's in Oxford, between
" the commencement of the last month in Lent Term, and the
" end of the third week in Act Term.

vi *Extract from the Rev. John Bampton's Will.*

" Also I direct and appoint, that the eight Divinity Lecture
" Sermons shall be preached upon either of the following
" Subjects—to confirm and establish the Christian Faith, and
" to confute all heretics and schismatics—upon the divine
" authority of the holy Scriptures—upon the authority of the
" writings of the primitive Fathers, as to the faith and practice
" of the primitive Church—upon the Divinity of our Lord and
" Saviour Jesus Christ—upon the Divinity of the Holy Ghost—
" upon the Articles of the Christian Faith, as comprehended in
" the Apostles' and Nicene Creed.

" Also I direct, that thirty copies of the eight Divinity Lec-
" ture Sermons shall be always printed, within two months after
" they are preached ; and one copy shall be given to the Chan-
" cellor of the University, and one copy to the Head of every
" College, and one copy to the Mayor of the city of Oxford, and
" one copy to be put into the Bodleian Library ; and the
" expense of printing them shall be paid out of the revenue of
" the Land or Estates given for establishing the Divinity Lecture
" Sermons ; and the Preacher shall not be paid, nor be entitled
" to the revenue, before they are printed.

" Also I direct and appoint, that no person shall be qualified
" to preach the Divinity Lecture Sermons, unless he hath taken
" the degree of Master of Arts at least, in one of the two Uni-
" versities of Oxford or Cambridge ; and that the same person
" shall never preach the Divinity Lecture Sermons twice."

PREFACE.

NOT many words will be necessary by way of Prolegomena to this book. A glance at the Synopsis will explain what I have undertaken; and the Lectures themselves will prove with what means, in what spirit, and with what success, the undertaking has been achieved.

A Bampton Lecturer labours under some peculiar difficulties. His eight discourses—eight *Stromateis* or Carpet Bags, if I may use the quaint phrase of Clement —will not pack away more than a limited, if somewhat elastic, number of articles. I have preferred to omit what could not comfortably be included, rather than force things in, to the destruction of their proper shape and utility. It is better to travel *expeditus* than to carry about a mere collection of samples. But then it becomes necessary to keep to the main lines of country, and not wander off into every tempting nook, or down each shadowy lane. The voyager may do this with safety, if he makes careful note of the finger-posts and by-roads, which others with more leisure and ampler means may wish to investigate. I trust I have given such landmarks as may enable the reader to check my own aberrations from the king's highway, and to gather for himself any further information that he may desire.

The accomplished student will notice other deficiencies of a more serious kind ; and here again the high-sounding title of Bampton Lecturer entails a penalty. *Quid dignum tanto feret hic promissor hiatu?* I wish I could take for my motto the words of Clement (*Strom.* i. 1. 17), 'No book can be so fortunate, but that some will find fault; and that may be reckoned to have fared not ill, which none can with justice censure.' It was a wise as well as a graceful practice of older times to begin every preface with the address *Lectori Benevolo.* All I can hope is that my shortcomings are not due to slackness or indolence, to want of consideration for my readers, or of reverence for those bright stars of holiness, of wisdom, of erudition, whose names occur in the following pages. Here I may observe that the Bishop of Durham's monumental work on Ignatius did not come into my hands till too late to be of much service. I had deferred the perusal till the completion of my own task should have set me at freedom once more to become a learner, not anticipating (as I ought to have done) that it would n so many ways shed light upon my theme. It is necessary to mention this, lest the reader should suspect me, on one or two points, of a desire to controvert, without reason given, the opinion of so illustrious a scholar.

One such point arises out of a passage in the Epistle of Ignatius to the Romans (chap. 7): ζῶν γὰρ γράφω ὑμῖν ἐρῶν τοῦ ἀποθανεῖν. ὁ ἐμὸς ἔρως ἐσταύρωται, καὶ οὐκ ἔστιν ἐν ἐμοὶ πῦρ φιλόυλον, ὕδωρ δὲ ζῶν καὶ λαλοῦν ἐν ἐμοί, ἔσωθέν μοι λέγον· Δεῦρο πρὸς τὸν πατέρα. Origen (see Lecture V. p. 188) translated the words ὁ ἐμὸς ἔρως ἐσταύρωται

'Meus autem Amor crucifixus est.' Dr. Zahn objects
to this ; 'Non Christum, quem solum amet, crucifixum
esse dicit Ignatius, quemadmodum plerique post
Origenem intellexerunt, nec vero eum, qui crucifixus est
amorem suum vocavit, sicuti graecorum verborum ignari
nonnulli halucinati sunt, sed suam rerum terrestrium
cupiditatem quasi crucifixam esse profitetur (cf. Gal. vi.
14).' It did not appear to me that a comment, which
attributed ignorance of Greek to Origen, called for special
notice. But as Dr. Zahn's conclusion has been adopted
and supported by the high authority of the Bishop of
Durham, it is no longer safe or respectful to pass over
the matter in silence. It is not indeed a necessary part
of my task to consider whether Origen was right or
wrong. Nevertheless as the Commentary on the Song
of Songs fostered, if it did not initiate, a remarkable
change in the expression of Christian love, it is of interest
to trace this change as near the fountain-head as possible.

I do not quite understand the point of Dr. Zahn's
assertion that Origen's rendering is bad Greek. He
may mean that ἔρως ought not to be confounded with
ἀγάπη. Or he may mean that ἔρως, which signifies the
passion of love, or the god by whom the passion was
supposed to be inspired, does not signify the object of
the passion, the darling or beloved one.

To the first question it is almost sufficient to reply, that
whether the confusion of ἔρως and ἀγάπη ought to have
been made or not, it certainly was made, not only by
Origen but by Clement (ὁ ἐραστός of Christ, *Strom.* vi. 9.
72). And if by them why not by Ignatius? Origen, a

good Greek scholar *pace* Dr. Zahn, asserts that Ignatius
employed this hyperbole in the present passage. And
what other sense can the words convey? Can ἔρως,
when used without limiting additions, signify ' earthly
passions,' 'carnal appetites?' Like our 'love,' of which
it is almost an exact equivalent, it may be applied to
base uses, but it is not, like ἐπιθυμία, a base word. From
the time of Parmenides it had been capable of the most
exalted ▪signification; it is introduced here by the
participle ἐρῶν in the sense of ardent spiritual desire; it
is opposed in true Platonic fashion to πῦρ φιλόυλον (we
have other Platonic phrases in this same Epistle: chap.
iii, οὐδὲν φαινόμενον καλόν : chap. vi, μηδὲ ὕλη κολακεύσητε).

The second point is but a trivial one. It has been
remarked that ἔρως is almost an exact equivalent of
' love.' The exception is that in classical Greek it
perhaps never signifies 'the beloved.' Yet it may be
urged that all words indicative of strong feeling may
be used to denote the person by whom the feeling is
aroused—my life, my joy, my dread, and so on—and it
certainly would not be a very hazardous stroke to employ
ἔρως in the same manner, though the usual term is ὁ
ἐρώμενος or ὁ ἐραστός. Thus Fritzsche explains Theoc.
ii. 151, αἰὲν ἔρωτος ἀκράτω ἐπεχεῖτο, and, even if this
instance is dubious, phrases like that of Meleager,
Anthol. Pal. v. 166, ἢ νέος ἄλλος ἔρως, νέα παίγνια, or that
of Euripides, *Oed.* frag. 551, Dind., ἑνὸς δ' ἔρωτος ὄντος οὐ
μί᾽ ἡδονή, show how difficult it is to keep the senses
apart. Again, we have the closely allied words ἐρώτυλος
(Theoc. iii. 7), ἐρωτίς (Theoc. iv. 59), and the common

proper names Erotion (Plautus, *Men.* i. 2. 60 ; Martial,
v. 34 ; 37 ; x. 61) and Eros (Martial, x. 80 ; other
instances in Pape and Benseler), all blending in the same
way the ideas of ' love,' ' Cupid,' ' darling ; ' and the latter
at least denoting not sexual passion but the love of parent
for child (cp. Eurip. *Erech.* frag. 360, Dind., ἐρᾶτε μητρός,
παῖδες, ὡς οὐκ ἔστ' ἔρως τοιοῦτος ἄλλος ὅστις ἡδίων ἐρᾶν).
Lastly, in Alciphron, *Epp.* i. 34, we have the very phrase
of which we are in quest, ὁ ἐμὸς ἔρως Εὐθύδημε. If then
there is any violation of usage in the expression of
Ignatius (on the supposition that Origen is right), it is
but slight, and cannot cause surprise in the case of
a writer who treats grammar like a slave.

The Bishop of Durham does not, as I understand him,
deny that Origen's rendering is admissible as a question
of Greek, but maintains that it ' tears the clause out of
the context.' But is this so?

What is Ignatius saying? ' For I that write unto you
am living, but in love with death. My Love is crucified,
and in me there is no earth-fed fire, but living water
speaking in my heart and saying Come hither to the
Father.' Why is he in love with death? Because
Christ, his Beloved, is crucified, and perfect union with
Him will be attained by death, a martyr death like His.
Because, his heart being with Christ, there is no fire of
sin to drown the voice that calls him. If we translate
as proposed by Dr. Zahn and the Bishop of Durham, we
not only do great violence to the word ἔρως, but lose an
impassioned phrase quite in harmony with the general
colour of this highly figurative and enthusiastic passage.

Origen rarely misunderstands, except where some strong prepossession deflects his judgment, and here his mind was biassed rather in the other direction. Notwithstanding the difference of time he was a strong conservative precisely where Ignatius was a bold innovator, but in this one instance he sanctioned the new modes of expression, which, as Lücke pointed out, were brought into vogue largely through the influence of the martyrs, and of Ignatius above all.

It remains only to express my gratitude to those who have helped me on my way; to the authorities of the Bodleian; to Corpus Christi College (my *alma nutrix* to whom I am indebted not merely for the loan of books but for the will and power to profit by them); to the Librarian of Christ Church, whose iron discipline has been relaxed in my behalf; and to many friends whose advice, assistance and sympathy have been of supreme value to me. One there is in particular, of a communion, alas, that is not my own, on whose patience and erudition I have been suffered to make prodigal drafts. To him I could have wished to dedicate this book, *Quicquid hoc libelli Qualecunque*, did I not know too surely that there is much in it of which he cannot approve, and that I should vex the modesty, which veils learning that would grace a professed theologian, by adding his name.

CHARLES BIGG.

OXFORD:
Sept. 18, 1886.

SYNOPSIS OF CONTENTS.

———••———

LECTURE I.

INTRODUCTION. PHILO AND THE GNOSTICS.

LECTURE II.

CLEMENT.

LECTURE III.

CLEMENT.

b

LECTURE IV.

ORIGEN.

LECTURE V.

ORIGEN.

LECTURE VIII.

SUMMARY.

LECTURE I.

In the beginning was the Word, and the Word was with God, and the Word was God.—St. John i. 1.

I PROPOSE to offer in the Lectures, which I am to have the privilege of delivering, a contribution towards the history of Alexandrine Platonism in the Christian Church. It will be my endeavour to sketch the conditions out of which it arose in the teaching of Philo and the Gnostics, to describe its full development in Clement and Origen, to measure its reflex action on Pagan religion and philosophy, and in conclusion to estimate the value of its results, to ascertain, as far as may be, the services it was enabled to render to the Church and to humanity. It is not possible within the limited time at my command to reap the whole harvest of a field so large and so fruitful. But I shall be able at any rate to show what profit is to be looked for. And though we can only follow the main outlines of the subject, we shall succeed perhaps in gaining a just conception of a great crisis in the history of the Church, and of the great men who played a conspicuous part in it.

It was not without reason that the first systematic attempt to harmonise the tradition of faith with the free conclusions of human intellect was made neither at Rome nor at Athens, but in Egypt. Yet it is not to the famous University that we must look for its

B

source [1]. Alexandria still possessed its three great royal foundations, the Museum, the Serapeum, and the Sebastion; its three libraries, its clerical heads, its well-endowed staff of professors and sinecure fellows. Nor did these misuse their advantages. Though the hope of imperial favour drew the more ambitious teachers of philosophy and rhetoric irresistibly towards Rome, letters were still cultivated, and the exact sciences flourished as nowhere else by the banks of the Nile. But the influence of the Pagan University upon Christian thought was distant and indirect. The Greek professor, throned beneath the busts of Homer and Plato, regarded himself as an apostle of Hellenic culture in the midst of an alien and barbarous race; and though a few, like Chaeremon [2], may have bestowed serious attention upon the monuments of the Pharaohs, the impulse would scarcely have passed the limits of a learned curiosity had it acted upon the Greeks alone. It was in the mind of the Jew that Eastern and Western ideas were first blended in fruitful union.

The Jews of Egypt, if we may credit Philo, numbered not less than a million souls. In no city of the Empire were they so wealthy or so powerful as at Alexandria. Of the five regions of the town two were almost entirely given up to them, and they swarmed in the other three.

---

[1] The history of the Alexandrine University may be read in Matter, *Histoire de l'École d'Alexandrie*, 2nd ed., Paris, 1840, or in Parthey's excellent little book, *Das Alexandrinische Museum*, Berlin, 1838. There is some interesting information in Mommsen's fifth volume. The 'sinecure fellows' are the ἀτελεῖς φιλόσοφοι. Hadrian gave one of those places to a successful athlete; see Parthey, p. 94. I infer that the Sebastion or Claudianum had a clerical Head: there is no doubt that it was so in the case of the Museum or the Serapeum; cp. Mommsen, v. 569, 579.

[2] According to Mommsen, v. 579, Chaeremon was an Egyptian. See Müller, *Frag. Hist. Graec.* iii. 495.

Many dwelt in the country districts also, and the convents of their Therapeutae were to be found in every nome [1]. They had their own senate and magistrates, who apportioned the taxation and settled the disputes of the community. They enjoyed the rights of isopolity [2], standing on an equal footing with the Greek burgesses, and possessing immunities denied to the native Copts. It is probable that the great corn-trade offered them facilities which, with the commercial genius of their race, they were not slow in turning to profit. In more than one respect their position offers a striking resemblance to that afterwards enjoyed by their countrymen in Spain.

For our present purpose the first great event in their history is the translation of the Hebrew Scriptures into Greek. In whatever way this most ancient and famous of all Versions came into existence, whether it grew up gradually out of the interpretation of the daily lessons, or was made by the order, and under the patronage of Ptolemy [3], it gave the signal for a remarkable outbreak

---

[1] Philo, *De Vita Cont.* 3.

[2] As to isopolity, see Dähne, i. p. 19. Egypt was governed by the Emperor as a crown colony, and the dignity of all citizens was lower there than in other provinces. But the Jews possessed the same privileges as the Greeks. Burgesses were scourged when necessary by different officers, with a different kind of rod, from the Coptic non-burgesses. Philo complains bitterly that Flaccus had ordered eminent Jews to be flogged like Copts, and not ταῖς ἐλευθεριωτέραις καὶ πολιτικωτέραις μάστιξιν. Tiberius Julius Alexander, a Jew and nephew of Philo, attained to the equestrian dignity and was made governor of Egypt by Nero, though at the cost of apostasy. A vivid picture of the numbers, wealth, privileges, and unpopularity of the Jews in Egypt will be found in Philo, *In Flaccum.* See Siegfried, *Philo,* p. 5; Dähne, *Geschichtliche Darstellung der jüdisch-alexandrinischen Religions-philosophie,* i. 16 sqq. For the magnificence of the Onias Temple at Leontopolis and the great Synagogue at Alexandria, see Delitzsch, *Zur Gesch. der jüdischen Poesie,* pp. 25 sqq.

[3] The story of Aristeas has long been given up. Even that of Aristo-

of literary activity. So far as this was apologetic and propagandist, a branch of that new-born zeal which compassed sea and land to make one proselyte, its history, character, and effect on pagan life and literature, interesting as they are, lie beyond our scope [1]. But side by side with this outward aggressive movement ran another and a different one, the object of which was to appropriate, and to justify the appropriation, of Greek wisdom, to reconcile Judaism with the culture of the Western world. Even before the completion of the Septuagint this tendency was at work. Platonism is discoverable in the Pentateuch, Stoicism in the Apocrypha [2]. It is

bulus appears to be now generally rejected. According to the latter the translation of the Law was made by the order and at the expense of Ptolemy Philadelphus, whose instigator and agent was Demetrius Phalereus; Eus. *Praep. Ev.* xiii. 12. 2. But, as Scaliger first pointed out, Hermippus, a writer of very good note, relates that Demetrius Phalereus was banished by Philadelphus, whose succession to the throne he had endeavoured to prevent. This error discredits the whole statement of Aristobulus, and it is accordingly more than doubtful whether the translation of the Pentateuch was in any way encouraged by Philadelphus, though such a work suits very well with his general character as a magnificent patron of literature. Hence by some the translation is supposed to have grown up gradually out of a custom introduced by Ezra. By the side of the reader of the Law stood an interpreter (Meturgeman) who translated the lesson from Hebrew into the vernacular tongue. See Delitzsch, *Zur Geschichte der jüdischen Poesie,* p. 19; Redepenning, *Origenes,* ii. 158, 217; Siegfried, *Philo,* p. 7. It is certain that the Septuagint Version was made at different times by different hands. The Pentateuch, the oldest portion, dates from the first half of the third century B.C.; the Hagiographa, the most recent portion, was in existence about 150 B.C. Schürer (*Geschichte des jüd. Volkes,* zweit. Theil, 1886, pp. 697 sqq.), says nothing about the Meturgeman, but regards it as clear that the translation was originally a private work, and gradually acquired official recognition. Tischendorf, *Proleg. in Vetus Test.,* leaves the question of Ptolemy's co-operation undecided. Dr. Edersheim, *Life and Times of Jesus the Messiah,* vol. i. p. 26 sq., accepts the account of Aristobulus as substantially correct, and thinks that the whole translation was completed by 221 B.C. at latest.

[1] The student will find full information in Schürer.

[2] The extent to which the translation of the Hebrew books is coloured

probable that every school of Greek philosophy, except
the 'godless Epicurean,' had its representatives among
the Alexandrine Jews. But the favourite was Platonism
as it was then understood, Platonism that is to say
hardened into a system, filled up and rounded off, in its
theology with Peripateticism, in its ethics with Stoicism.
The myths of the poet-philosopher have become dogmas,
and the central point of the whole is the enigmatical
Timaeus. But in yielding thus to the fascinations of Greek
wisdom the Jew stumbled on many difficulties. His own
Scriptures he had been taught to regard as divine and
sufficient. If the doctrines of the Academy were true,
they were true only in so far as they coincided with the
word of God. Thus it became incumbent on the party
of the new learning for the satisfaction of their own
conscience to find Plato in the Law, and for the satisfaction of their more scrupulous countrymen to find the
Law in Plato. These objects, though to some degree
facilitated by the Septuagint translators themselves,
could only be fully secured by violent means. Hence

by Greek philosophy is matter of doubt. Dähne, ii. 11 sqq., and Gfrörer,
Urchristenthum, ii. 8–18, find many traces of adaptation which are disal-
lowed by Frankel, Zeller, and Siegfried. But Siegfried admits that in Gen.
i. 2, ἡ δὲ γῆ ἦν ἀόρατος καὶ ἀκατασκεύαστος, there is an unmistakeable
reference to the κόσμος νοητός. The difficulty of decision arises in part out
of the fact that many ideas were common to the Rabbinical and the Hellen-
istic schools. But the statement in the text that the work of the latter
was facilitated by the LXX translators is amply borne out by the way in
which the latter (i) avoid anthropomorphic phrases—thus the 'repentance
of God,' Gen. vi. 6, disappears; (ii) substitute θεός and κύριος for the
Tetragram; (iii) introduce the later doctrine of Guardian Angels, Deut.
xxxii. 8. This verse in its Septuagint form became in fact the foundation
of the doctrine which, if Rabbinical, is also certainly Platonic. The
influence of Platonism and Stoicism on the Book of Wisdom and Macc. iv.
is unquestioned. See Siegfried, *Philo*, pp. 6 sqq.; Schürer.

the fable of Aristeas, which, transferring to the Greek text the literal inspiration claimed for the Hebrew, rendered possible the application of those modes of interpretation, by which any language could be forced to yield any sense desired. Hence again the fiction of Aristobulus[1], which asserted the existence of a previous and much older translation of the Law. By this means it was possible to argue that Plato was but 'an Attic Moses[2],' and a swarm of treatises on Plagiarism solaced the weaker brethren with ample proof that all the best sayings of all the Greek philosophers were 'stolen' from the Jew, and might lawfully be reclaimed. Thus fortified the Hellenising party moved steadily onward in the development of those ideas, which we now associate with the name of Philo, because he is to us their sole exponent. But in truth even the Logos doctrine, the keystone of the whole structure, was already in place when he took up the work[3].

[1] Eus. *Praep. Ev.* xiii. 12. This positive statement is a pure fiction (see Ewald, *Gesch. des V. I.,* iv. 337, ed. 1864), made for the purpose of supporting his assertion that the peripatetic philosophy was based upon the Law and the Prophets. Clem. *Strom.* v. 14. 97. For the character and influence of Aristobulus, see Valckenär, *Diatribe*; Dähne, ii. 73 sqq.; Ewald; Zeller, iii. 2. 219 sqq. Schürer defends Aristobulus against the charge of forgery, maintaining that he was himself deceived by the adulterated passages which he quotes. Cobet holds the same view; see Preface to Dindorf's edition of Clement, xxv. But there is no ground for it.

[2] The phrase is ascribed to Numenius by Clement, *Strom.* i. 22. 150. Eusebius, *Praep. Ev.* xi. 10. 14, only says that it is with good reason attributed to Numenius. But Clement's language is so clear and positive (Νουμήνιος . . . ἄντικρυς γράφει) that Schürer (p. 830) cannot be right in doubting whether that philosopher was really the author of the phrase.

[3] Siegfried, p. 223: 'Dass er auch hierin Vorgänger hatte, deutet er selbst an. So erwähnt er *de somn.* i. 19 (i. 638) eine ältere Auslegung von Gen. xxviii. 11, welche den τόπος auf den Logos bezog.' Zeller, iii. p. 628, insists upon the remarkable passage in *de Cherubim,* 9 (i. 143) where Philo speaks of both doctrines, that of the Two Powers and that of the Logos, as given to

It is only in a peculiar sense that Philo is to be called a philosopher [1]. His works form a discursive commentary upon the Law, taking up point after point, not in their natural order, but as they spring out of the text before him. And his object is not to investigate but to harmonise. The idealism of Plato is to be discovered in the history of the Patriarchs and the precepts of the Law, and amalgamated with the products of Rabbinical speculation. The religious interest is with Philo the predominant; hence he starts not with the analysis of the act of knowledge, but with the definition of God. On this theme two very divergent views were entertained. Some of the Rabbis, relying upon those passages of the older Scriptures, where the Deity is spoken of as wearing the form and actuated by the feelings of humanity, were Anthropomorphists [2], and expressed this opinion in the simplest and most direct fashion. Others, following the

him by special revelation. Philo, however, may mean only that the conviction of their truth and the sense of their full import were imparted to him in a divine ecstasy, as the knowledge of Christ was given to St. Paul in the same way.

[1] My guides to the understanding of the text of Philo have been Dähne, *Geschichtliche Darstellung der jüdisch-alexandrinischen Religions-philosophie*, Halle, 1834; Grossmann, *Quaestiones Philoneae*; Zeller; and Siegfried, *Philo von Alexandria*, Jena, 1875. The last is excellent and indispensable. All other authorities on the subject will be found in Siegfried or in Schürer, by whom the list of German literature is continued down to the present year. I have seen also the French writers Réville, Soulier, Vacherot, Simon. For the relation between Philo and Rabbinical speculation, a point on which I cannot pretend to form an independent judgment, I have relied implicitly on Siegfried, with some assistance from Gfrörer and Maybaum. I may refer the reader also to Dr. Edersheim's forthcoming article in the Dictionary of Christian Biography, the proof-sheets of which I have been enabled to use by the kindness of the learned author.

Zeller rates him higher than Dähne; iii. p. 594, ed. 1852: 'Was den Philo von seinen Vorgängern unterscheidet ist die Vollständigkeit und Folgerichtigkeit, mit der er ihren Standpunkt zum System ausgeführt hat.'

[2] See Gfrörer, *Das Jahrhundert des Heils*, Stuttgart, 1838, i. p. 276 sqq.

lead of the Prophets, and developing the conception of
the Ineffable Name, refused to think or speak of Jehovah
except as a pure spirit. ' God sees,' said one, ' and is not
seen; so the soul sees and is not seen [1].'
For the Hellenist truth lay wholly in the latter conception, which was maintained by the Peripatetic Aristobulus, and developed by the Platonist Philo. In one
remarkable passage he comments upon the words ' it
repented God that He had made man [2].' To accept such
language in its literal sense is impiety greater than any
that was drowned in the Flood. In truth God is not as
man, is not as the world, is not as heaven. He is above
space, being Himself Space and Place, inasmuch as He
embraces all things and is embraced of none; above time,
for time is but the register of the fluctuations of the
world, and God when He made the world made time
also. His Life is Eternity, the everlasting Now, wherein
is neither past, present, nor future. He is unchanging,
for the Best can change only by becoming worse, which
is inconceivable. Change, again, is the shifting of relations, the flux of attributes, and God has neither relations
nor attributes. Hence He has no name. Man in his
weakness is ever striving to find some title for the
Supreme. But, says Philo, ' names are symbols of
created things, seek them not for Him who is uncreated.'
Even the venerable and scriptural titles of God and Lord
are inadequate, must be understood as metaphors, and
used with reserve. The phrases that Philo himself
prefers to employ are ' the One,' ' He that is,' ' Himself.'

---

[1] Gfrörer, *Das Jahrhundert des Heils,* i. p. 289.

[2] *Quod Deus Immutabilis,* 5 (i. 275) sqq. But I need not give detailed
references for this section. See Siegfried, 199 sqq. ; Dähne, i. 118 sqq.

From all this it follows that God is incomprehensible. We know that He is, to know what He is transcends the powers vouchsafed to man. Thus in the extravagance of his recoil from materialism Philo transformed the good Father and Lord of the Bible into the Eternal Negation of dialectics. But Philo, though he marked out the way for later transcendentalism, does not himself push his argument to its extreme conclusion. He does not mean all that he appears to say[1]. The analytic method is Aristotelian rather than Platonic, and the influences of the *Timaeus*, of Stoicism, of the Bible, all combine as yet to modify its rigour. When Philo tells us that God has no qualities, we are to understand that He is immaterial, and can therefore experience none of those passions that attach to the body[2]. Hence again He cannot be said to possess any of those virtues, that depend upon the regulation of the passions by the reason. But reason itself He possesses in the same sense as man [3]. If He has no relations, this

---

[1] Dähne, i. p. 127 sqq., regards Philo's conception of God as practical Atheism. 'Er philosophirte aber auch gar nicht (wenigstens nicht zuerst) im Interesse des menschlichen Geschlechts, dem er freilich auf diese Weise seinen Gott raubte, sondern lediglich im Interesse dieses Gottes selbst' (p. 136). Siegfried too thinks that he was only able to save religion by a want of philosophic perspicacity, which enabled him to mix up the Stoic doctrine of the Immanence of God with this theory of the Absolute without perceiving that the two were irreconcileable. It is certain that Philo often speaks in Stoic language of God, advancing at times to the very verge of Pantheism; Siegfried, p. 204; Dähne, i. 280 sqq. But he never for a moment ceases to think of God in Platonic fashion as pure Spirit opposed to Matter. Whereas to the Stoic Matter and Spirit were at bottom the same thing; all is ultimately resolved into Matter; Zeller, vol. iii. p. 77, ed. 1852. On the side of theology Philo was no more really Stoic than St. Paul, who also did not hesitate to use the language of Aratus. Those who wish to see what theology becomes in the hands of a Stoic should read the *Homilies*.

[2] See especially *Quod Deus Imm.* 11 (i. 280).

[3] See especially *Quod Deus Imm.* 6 (i. 276). God is changeless, not because

merely means that He wants nothing, and depends on nothing, because He is perfect and the source of all that is[1]. Philo does not intend to exclude the relation of subject and object like Plotinus, who denies that God can be said to think[2]. Again, if God is One, is incomprehensible, so too is the human mind. Of this also, though it is our self, we know only that it is[3]. ' God,' says Philo, ' possesses not intelligence only but reasoning, and using these powers He ever surveys all that He has made, suffering nothing to transgress its appointed order[4].' Neo-Platonism is already in view, but between Plotinus and Philo there are several stages to be passed. One of these is marked by the name of Basilides, another by that of Clement.

It is evident that Philo was not prevented by any metaphysical bar from attributing the work of Providence, or even of Creation, to the Deity. There was however a grave moral difficulty. For the world was

He is a blank, but because He is perfect. ' Since then the soul of man by the soft breezes of science and wisdom calms the surge and seething, roused by the sudden bursting of the fierce blast of vice, and allaying the swelling billows reposes in sunny and windless calm, canst thou doubt that the Incorrupt and Blessed, He who has girded Himself with the might of the virtues and perfection itself and happiness, suffers no change of mind?' He is by no means the Aristotelian Deity who 'thinks Himself.' . . . ' It is clear then that the father must know his children, the artist his works, the steward his charge, and God is in truth Father, Artist, Steward of all that is in heaven or in the world.' Consciousness of the external does not in Philo's view imply change in God, who sees not as man sees in time, but in eternity.

[1] The idea of Relation is defined *De mutatione Nominum*, 4 (i. 583).

[2] *Enn.* iii. 9. 3.

[3] *Legis Alleg.* i. 30 (i. 62) : εἰκότως οὖν ὁ Ἀδάμ, τουτέστιν ὁ νοῦς, τὰ ἄλλα ὀνομάζων καὶ καταλαμβάνων ἑαυτῷ ὄνομα οὐκ ἐπιτίθησιν ὅτι ἑαυτὸν ἀγνοεῖ καὶ τὴν ἰδίαν φύσιν. *De mut. Nom.* 2 (i. 579) : καὶ τί θαυμαστόν, εἰ τὸ ὂν ἀνθρώποις ἀκατάληπτον, ὁπότε καὶ ὁ ἐν ἑκάστῳ νοῦς ἄγνωστος ἡμῖν ἐστι; Τίς ψυχῆς οὐσίαν εἶδεν ;

[4] *Quod Deus Immut.* 7 (i. 277).

created out of pre-existing matter. And matter, though
eternal, was evil—'lifeless, erroneous, divisible, un-
equal[1].' It seemed impossible to bring the Perfect
Being into direct contact with the senseless and corruptible[2]. Hence when Philo speaks of the royal or
fatherly operations of the Deity, he is generally to be
understood as referring not to God Himself but to His
Powers or Ministers. 'Though throned above Creation
He nevertheless fills His world, for by His power, reaching to the utmost verge, He binds together each to each
by the words of harmony.' Here the meaning is so
obscure that it might pass without detection, but the
language that follows is more explicit : 'Though He be
far off, yet is He very near, keeping touch by means of
His creative and regulative Powers, which are close to
all, though He has banished the things that have birth
far away from His essential nature[3].'

What are these Powers? On one side they are the
Angels, on whom a world of curious ingenuity had been
expended in the Jewish schools. On the other they are

[1] *Quis rer. div. haeres.* 32 (i. 495). The idea that Matter is Evil, which exercises so important an influence on the whole system of Philo, rests especially
on his explanation of Gen. i. 31, ' God saw everything that He had made,
and behold it was very good.' But He had not made Matter, and spoke no
praise of this. The belief in the pre-existence of Matter had found acceptance
among the Jews before Philo ; Siegfried, p. 230.

[2] *De vict. offer.* 13 (ii. 261): οὐ γὰρ ἦν θέμις ἀπείρου καὶ πεφυρμένης ὕλης ψαύειν
... θεόν. *De confus. ling.* 34 (i. 431): χρεῖος μὲν γὰρ οὐδενός ἐστιν ὁ τοῦ παντὸς
πατήρ, ὡς δεῖσθαι τῆς ἀφ᾽ ἑτέρων εἰ ἐθέλοι δημιουργῆσαι· τὸ δὲ πρέπον ὁρῶν ἑαυτῷ
τε καὶ τοῖς γινομένοις ταῖς ὑπηκόοις δυνάμεσιν ἔστιν ἃ διαπλάττειν ἐφῆκεν.
Another more tender and certainly more beautiful way of expressing the
same thing is found in passages like *De mundi op.* 6 (i. 5), where it is said
that God's goodness is bounded by the receptivity of His creatures. A
full revelation, an unlimited gift, would undo us. Compare p. 13, below.
Even God's Powers must divest themselves of their ' fire ' before they can
touch our weak and tainted nature without consuming it.

[3] *De post. Caini,* 5 (i. 229).

the Logoi of the Stoic, the Ideas of the Platonist, the thoughts of God, the heavenly models of things upon earth, the types which, imprinted upon matter like a seal upon wax, give to it life, reality, durability[1]. The Ideas, again, could be identified with the discrowned gods of Olympus, the heroes and demons, who in the Platonic religion play a part analogous to that of the angels[2]. In either aspect they are innumerable[3]. But considered as types they may be summed up in two great master-types, considered as Angels they are ruled by two great Archangels, representing one the Goodness, the other the

---

[1] They are ἰδέαι, ἀρχέτυποι ἰδέαι, τύποι, μέτρα, σφραγῖδες. These are Platonic terms denoting the Essence or Form, the principle of reality. Again, λόγοι, λόγοι σπερματικοί, σπέρματα καὶ ῥίζαι καθεθεῖσαι ὑπὸ τοῦ θεοῦ. These are Stoic terms denoting, not the Essence which to the Stoic was matter, but the principle of Life, Force, the particle of divine spirit inherent in things. Again, they are δυνάμεις, ἀσώματοι δυνάμεις, δορυφόροι δυνάμεις, ἄγγελοι, χάριτες. These are Jewish terms. See Grossmann, *Quaest. Phil.* p. 23; Dähne, i. 205 sqq., 253 sqq.

What the student has most to be afraid of is the giving to Philo more consistence and system than he really possesses. In a rapid account it is impossible to avoid this fault. What I have said in the text is I believe in the main correct, but everything is floating and hazy. Thus *De conf. ling.* 34 (i. 431) the Powers are distinct from the Ideas which they create, and apparently from the Angels. They are certainly distinct from the Angels, *De Mon.* ii. 1 (ii. 222). But *De Mon.* i. 6 (ii. 218, 219) they are the Ideas. Nor can I find that the Powers are anywhere expressly identified with the Angels, though Siegfried, p. 211, says that they are.

The Angels and the Logoi are identified, *De Somniis,* i. 19 (i. 638): ἀθανάτοις λόγοις οὓς καλεῖν ἔθος ἀγγέλους. And when we consider the close affinity of λόγος and ἰδέα, and the fact that *the* Logos is the Sum of the Powers, it is very difficult to see how the Angels can be kept apart.

[2] *De gigantibus,* 2 (i. 263); *De somniis,* i. 22 (i. 642): ταύτας δαίμονας μὲν οἱ ἄλλοι φιλόσοφοι, ὁ δὲ ἱερὸς λόγος ἀγγέλους εἴωθε καλεῖν.

[3] As Ideas certainly: see note above. Zeller, p. 619. *De profugis,* 18 (i. 560) Philo counts six powers corresponding in number to the Cities of Refuge. His enumeration is: (1) θεῖος λόγος; (2) ἡ ποιητικὴ δύναμις; (3) ἡ βασιλική; (4) ἡ ἵλεως; (5) ἡ νομοθετική; (6) ὁ κόσμος νοητός. 2 and 4 belong to Goodness, 3 and 5 to Justice, 6 is a mere etcetera = all the Ideas.

Justice of the Eternal[1]. The former, the older and stronger Power, is generally intended in Scripture by the word God, the latter by the word Lord, which Philo apparently did not understand to be used merely as a substitute for the Ineffable Name[2]. If it be asked whether the Powers are persons or not, it is difficult to find a satisfactory reply. In one point of view they are mere abstractions. But in the mind of the Jew these scholastic entities tend inevitably to become things, living beings. The Powers are ideas, but then again they are God's agents, who create the ideas, and stamp them on matter. They are the two Cherubim[3] who keep the gates of Paradise, the two Angels who entered Sodom[4]. Yet Philo never for a moment regards them as existing apart from their source. They are the breath of God's mouth. They are as rays of the sun, which at first are pure, and as incomprehensible as their source, but, as they shoot down through the dim air, lose their fire while retaining their light. Otherwise they would destroy what their mission is to cherish and preserve[5].

---

[1] The names vary. The First, the better and elder, is θεός, ἡ ποιητική, ἀγαθότης, χαριστική, εὐεργέτις; the Second is κύριος, ἡ βασιλική, ἀρχή, ἐξουσία, ἡ νομοθετική, ἡ κολαστική. Siegfried, p. 213; Dähne, i. 231.

[2] Siegfried, p. 203.

[3] *De Cherub.* 9 (i. 144).

[4] *De Abr.* 24. 25 (ii. 19). In Gen. xvii. 1 the words ὤφθη κύριος are explained to mean that the βασιλικὴ δύναμις appeared to Abraham. In Gen. xviii. 2 the three men are ὁ θεὸς δορυφορούμενος ὑπὸ δυεῖν τῶν ἀνωτάτω δυνάμεων, ἀρχῆς τε αὖ καὶ ἀγαθότητος, but the following words again seem to destroy the personality of the Powers, εἷς ὢν ὁ μέσος τριττὰς φαντασίας ἐνειργάζετο τῇ ὁρατικῇ ψυχῇ, *de SS. Abelis et Caini,* 15 (i. 173).

[5] *Leg. Alleg.* i. 13 (i. 51); *Quod Deus Im.* 17 (i. 284); Sieg. p. 216. A point which makes against the personality of the Powers is the way in which they can be broken up and combined; see Dähne, i. p. 242 sqq.;

In all this Philo was following in the track of earlier Jewish speculation[1]. The Rabbis of Palestine had made many efforts to penetrate the mystery of the creatures who in Ezekiel's vision sustain the chariot-throne of the Almighty, and found in them a symbol of the divine justice and goodness. The subject was treated as a profound mystery, and there was a party which discouraged all attempts to pry into it. Only four men, it was said, had penetrated this magic garden, and one only, the great Akiba, had returned in safety. But the Hellenists of Alexandria were more audacious. They had 'eaten too much honey,' and intoxicated by the sweets, of which they had rifled the hives of the Greeks, they dared to speak of the Powers in a way that seemed to impair the unity of God. They had ventured even farther. The duality of Persons did not satisfy their craving for philosophic completeness. Behind this pair of persons, or personifications, there must be one more puissant Being, one more comprehensive generalisation. This was the Logos, a term which Philo found already in use.

Logos[2] is a phrase of the Hellenic schools. It has a

Gfrörer, *Philo*, p. 239. The fact is that Philo wavers between the one mode of conception and the other. This applies to the Logos also. See Zeller, iii. 626.

[1] For this section see Siegfried, p. 211 sq.

[2] An excellent account of those Jewish speculations which paved the way for the Alexandrine Logos theory will be found in Siegfried, pp. 219 sqq. The actual title Logos comes to Philo in a direct line from the Greek Pantheists Heraklitus and the Stoics. The reason why he preferred this title to that of Idea is to be found in the Biblical 'Word of God.' To the Stoic the λόγος κοινός, the λόγος σπερματικός is the Divine Force, the *Anima Mundi* of which Virgil sings—*Aen.* vi. 724: 'Principio caelum ac terras..' Spiritus intus alit, totamque infusa per artus Mens agitat molem et magno se corpore miscet.' It is resolvable ultimately into the Divine Matter. 'Es durfte nur dieser stoischen Logoslehre durch die Unterscheidung des Logos

long history, and had already gathered round itself many associations, that fitted it for the new part it was now to assume. It denotes with equal facility the uttered word, the reasoning mind, or again a plan, scheme, system. It is the Platonic Idea of Good, the Stoic World-Spirit, or Reason of God, immanent in creation which it fosters and sustains. Round this heathen stem clustered a number of ideas that were floating in solution in the schools of the Jews—the Shechinah, the Name of God, the Ten Words of Creation that might perhaps be One, the great Archangel and chief of the Chariot-bearers, Metatron, the Heavenly Man, the High Priest. Philo has gathered together from East and West every thought, every divination, that could help to mould his sublime conception of a Vicegerent of God, a Mediator between the Eternal and the ephemeral. His Logos reflects light from countless facets. It is one of those creative phrases, struck out in the crisis of projection, which mark an epoch in the development of thought.

What the Logos became in the hands of Philo we shall see most clearly by considering him in his fourfold relation—to God—to the Powers—to the World—and to Man.

In his relation to God he is first of all Wisdom [1].

von der Gottheit ihr pantheistisches, durch seine Unterscheidung von dem gebildeten Stoff ihr materialistisches Gepräge abgestreift werden, und der Philonische Logos war fertig' (Zeller, iii. 630). The word is emptied, that is to say, of its true Stoic significance, and becomes partly the Idea, partly the Agent by whom the idea is impressed upon matter.

[1] The precise relation of Wisdom to the Logos is by no means without difficulty, for here as everywhere Philo's language fluctuates. Some have maintained that they are identical. Dähne, i. p. 221, thinks that Sophia is a 'theilkraft' of the Logos; so that Logos may always be used for Sophia, but not the reverse. But Siegfried points out (p. 221, cp. p. 215) that Sophia is sometimes spoken of as the higher principle, the Fountain or

Already, in the Book of Proverbs [1], Wisdom appears
as the eternal Assessor of the Most High—'When He
prepared the heavens I was there.' In the Alexandrine
Book of Wisdom [2], written probably under Stoic influences, this Power assumes new titles and significance.
He is 'the loving Spirit of the Lord that filleth the
earth,' holy, only-begotten, 'the brightness of the everlasting light, the unspotted mirror of the Power of God,
the image of His Goodness.' Philo is but translating
this hymn of praise into scientific terminology, when he
calls the Word the Intelligible World, that is the sum of
the thoughts of God, or again the Idea of Ideas, which
imparts reality to all lower ideas, as they in turn to all
sensible kinds [3]. The Word is the whole mind of God,
considered as travelling outside itself, and expressing
itself in act. Hence he is styled its Impress, its Likeness, its House. This is his abstract Greek side. In his
more realistic Hebrew aspect he is the Schechinah or
glory of God ; or again, as that glory falls upon our sight
only veiled and dimmed, he is the Shadow of God. And

Mother, of the Logos. The differing gender of the two words in Greek,
the one being feminine and the other masculine, was a difficulty. This
Philo endeavoured to solve in the curious allegorism on the name of
Bethuel, *De Prof.* 9 (i. 553). Bethuel signifies 'daughter of God,' that is,
Wisdom. But this virgin daughter is father of Rebecca, that is, Patience.
So all the virtues have feminine names (in Greek), because in relation to
God they are derivative and receptive. But in relation to us they are masculine. Hence we may say that Wisdom, the daughter of God, is a man
and a father, begetting in the soul knowledge, understanding, and all good
and praiseworthy actions. The drift of this passage is no doubt to blend
the Logos with Sophia. The confusion of gender with sex offers a curious
instance of the tendency of Philo's mind to turn abstractions into things.

[1] viii. 27.

[2] i. 6, 7 ; vii. 22 sqq.

[3] *De Mundi Opif.* 6 (i. 5). For the numerous other passages referred to
in this account of the Logos it is sufficient to refer generally to Siegfried
and Grossmann.

growing ever more definite and personal, he is the Son, the Eldest Son, the Firstborn of God. Many of the divine titles are his by right. He too is the Sun, the Darkness, the Monad, God [1], the Second God. In his relation to the other Powers, again, there is the same graduated ascent from the abstract to the real. If the Powers are Ideas, the Word is their Sum. He is the Book of Creation, in which all the subordinate essences are words. But, again, he is their Creator, the King's Architect, in whose brain the plan of the royal city is formed. He stands between them dividing, yet uniting, like the fiery sword between the Cherubim at the gates of Eden. He is their leader, their Captain, their Charioteer, the Archangel of many names.

As regards the world he is on the one side the Archetypal Seal, the great Pattern according to which all is made. He is the Divider, in so far as he differentiates, and makes each thing what it is. He is the Bond, in so far as all existence depends on the permanence of form. Hence in him both worlds, the intelligible and the sensible, form one great whole, a figure of which is the vesture of the High Priest. On the head is the plate of gold with its legend 'Holiness to the Lord;' the blue, the purple, the scarlet of the robe are the rainbow web of Nature; the bells about the feet, whose silver sound is heard when Aaron goeth into the Holy Place, signify the rapt joy of the human spirit when it penetrates into the divine mysteries. The robe is woven of one piece, and may not be rent, because the Word binds all

---

[1] Θεός, but not ὁ Θεός, *De Somn.* 39 (i. 655); the distinction recurs in Origen.

together in life and harmony[1]. So far we are still
breathing Greek air. But then again the Word is the
Instrumental Cause, the Organ of Creation. He is the
Creator, the Helmsman, and Pilot of the universe.
'God with justice and law leads His great flock, the
four elements and all that is shaped thereof, the circlings
of sun and moon, the rhythmic dances of the stars,
having set over them His upright Word, His Firstborn
Son, who will receive the charge of this holy flock as a
Vicegerent of the Great King[2].' Here Philo is thinking,
not of Wisdom, but of the mighty 'God said' of the
Book of Genesis. The word is, not the Spirit only, or
the Mind, but the Will of God[3].

But the crowning interest of these speculations
depends on their relation to human life. What is this
Son of God to us?

The answer is given by the peculiar position of the
Logos, who stands between God and Man partaking of
both natures. For Man, as regards his reason, is the
image of the Logos, as the Logos is the image of God.
Hence the Logos is the Mediator, the Heavenly Man[4],
who represents in the eyes of God the whole family
upon earth. He is not indeed the point of union,
because we may rise above him. The knowledge which

[1] See the beautiful passage in *De migrat. Abr.* 18 (i. 452). Cp. *De Vita Mos.* iii. 14 (ii. 155).

[2] *De Agric.* 12 (i. 308).

[3] Canon Westcott (*Introd. to the Gospel of St. John*, p. xvi) maintains that the Logos of St. John is derived, not from Philo, but from the Palestinian Schools, mainly on the ground that in Philo Logos is Reason and not Will. But to a Platonist like Philo there is no difference between Reason and Will. And the passages referred to in the text are sufficient to show that the Logos of Philo is conceived of as 'a divine Will sensibly manifested in personal action.'

[4] Siegfried, p. 221.

he gives is a lower knowledge, the knowledge of God in
Nature, and our allegiance to him is therefore but
temporary and provisional. But he is necessary as the
door, through which we must pass to direct communion
with his Father.

Here Philo could borrow no light from the Greeks, to
whom the idea of Mediation was foreign ; though, as we
shall see, there were elements in the current Platonism,
which were readily adapted to this end [1].

The Logos then is first the Prophet of the Most
High, the Man whose name is the Dayspring, the
Eternal Law. He is the Giver of the divine Light and
therefore the Saviour, for to the Platonist sin is darkness. But it is not enough that our eyes should be
opened. For the visual ray within us is weakened or
quenched by vice, our rebellions have alienated us from
God. We need therefore an Atonement. Still more
do we need strength and sustenance.

All these requirements are satisfied by the Logos.
For his atoning function Philo found a fitting symbol
ready to hand in the High Priest [2], who since the days
of the Exile, in the abeyance of the throne, had risen in
Jewish eyes to a dignity almost superhuman. His
vesture, as we have seen, was the type of the whole
world, for which he interceded with its Maker. He alone

---

[1] See the doctrine of the Demons in Lecture vii.

[2] See Siegfried, p. 221. The four prayers uttered by the High Priest on
the Day of Atonement, 'most precious fragments of the Liturgy of the Old
Testament Temple worship,' will be found in Delitzsch (*Zur Geschichte
der Jüd. Poesie*, pp. 184 sqq.). The first three, pronounced by the High
Priest with his hand on the head of the sin offering, were (i) for himself
and family ; (ii) for the sons of Aaron ; (iii) for the whole people. The
fourth was uttered immediately on leaving the Holy of Holies. In each
the Ineffable Name was pronounced three times.

might pronounce the Ineffable Name. He alone might enter into the Holy of Holies, behold the glory of God, and yet live. He held this high prerogative, because when he entered into the sanctuary he was, says Philo with an audacious perversion of the text, 'not a man[1].' The true High Priest is sinless; if he needs to make an offering and utter prayer for himself, it is only because he participates in the guilt of the people, whom he represents. Thus the Word is the Supplicator, the Paraclete, the Priest who presents the soul of man 'with head uncovered' before God[2]. He is figured by Aaron, who stands with burning censer between the living and the dead. 'I stand,' Philo makes him say, 'between the Lord and you, I who am neither un-created like God nor created like you, but a mean between the two extremes, a hostage to either side[3].' And as he teaches, as he atones, so he feeds and sus-tains his people, falling upon every soul as the manna fell like dew upon the whole earth. In this sense he is Melchisedech, priest of the Most High God, King of Salem, that is of peace, who met Abraham returning from his victory over the four kings, and refreshed him with the mystic Bread and Wine[4].

---

[1] *De Somn.* ii. 28. (i. 684): ὅταν γάρ, φησίν, εἰσίῃ εἰς τὰ ἅγια τῶν ἁγίων ὁ ἀρχιερεύς, ἄνθρωπος οὐκ ἔσται (Lev. xvi. 17). Τίς οὖν εἰ μὴ ἄνθρωπος; ἆρά γε θεός;

[2] *De Cher.* 5 (i. 141). [3] *Quis Rerum Div. Her.* 42 (i. 502).

[4] Ammon (= Sense) and Moab (= the Intellect divorced from God) refused Israel bread and water. 'But let Melchisedec give wine instead of water, and refresh the soul with pure juice of the grape, that it may be possessed by divine intoxication, more sober than sobriety itself. For he is the Priest Word,' *Leg. Alleg.* iii. 26 (i. 103). *Ibid.* 56 (i. 119) Philo goes on to explain what is this heavenly food of the soul. It is Light, true Education, the knowledge of God, which is given by the Word. The passage is referred to by Clement, *Strom.* iv. 26. 161.

Such a division in the divine nature leads to a corresponding distinction in the moral and spiritual life. To know God in His Powers is one thing, to know Him in Himself is another and a higher. The first is the life of Faith, Hope, Discipline, Effort, the second is that of Wisdom, Vision, Peace. Those who are still struggling upwards in obedience to the Word are servants, whose proper food is milk; those who have emerged into the full light are grown men, the friends of God, the seeing Israel[1].

'How terrible is this place,' cried Jacob awaking from his dream, 'this is none other than the House of God.' So the soul starting up from the sleep of indifference

[1] Philo divides men into two great classes, in each of which there are several subdivisions. I. The godless, the non-moral, the Fool. His guide is the lower intelligence; see *De Migr. Abr.* 12 (i. 446): πορεύεται δὲ ὁ ἄφρων δι' ἀμφοτέρων, θυμοῦ τε καὶ ἐπιθυμίας ἀεί, μηδένα διαλείπων χρόνον, τὸν ἡνίοχον καὶ βραβευτὴν λόγον ἀποβαλών. His highest faculty is lost or debased; he has nothing but the νοῦς γήινος, φιλοσώματος, φιλοπαθής. To this class belong the Sensualist, such as Ham (= θέρμη, Fever); the vain Sophist, such as the 'archer' Ishmael; the Sceptic, such as Cain; the self-seeking politician, such as Joseph. II. The Moral, Spiritual Life. This has two stages—that of the Babe, that of the Perfect. *De Migr. Abr.* 9 (i. 443): ἕτερος νηπίων καὶ ἕτερος τελείων χῶρός ἐστιν, ὁ μὲν ὀνομαζόμενος ἄσκησις, ὁ δὲ καλούμενος σοφία. Their food is νηπία καὶ γαλακτώδης: *ibid.* 6 (i. 440). The Lower Stage has three subdivisions—ἄσκησις, μάθησις, φύσις: *De Som.* i. 27 (i. 646). The consummation—the Higher Stage—whether attained by moral discipline, intellectual training, or natural development, is Wisdom, Perfection.

See Siegfried, pp. 249 sqq.; Dähne, pp. 341 sqq. The two stages are the βίος πρακτικός, the βίος θεωρητικός of the Greek philosophers; the προκοπή and σοφία of the later Stoics; but with this difference, that in Philo both stages are religious. The three avenues to perfection are given by Aristotle, Diog. Laert. v. 18: τριῶν ἔφη δεῖν παιδείαν φύσεως μαθήσεως ἀσκήσεως. But Philo regards them as characteristic of three distinct classes of learners, while the pagan philosopher regarded them as means of improvement which must be employed in combination by every learner. Hence the three classes of Proficients in Seneca, *Epistle* 75, answer to different degrees of progress, not to different lines of progress. This, as will be seen, is nearly Clement's view.

learns with a shock of amazement, that the world is, not a tavern, but a temple. Wherefore it exclaims, 'It is not as I fancied, for the Lord is in this place.' This sensible world is indeed the House of God, the gate of Heaven. For the spiritual world of ideas can be comprehended only by climbing upwards from what we see and feel. 'Those who wish to survey the beauty of a city must enter in at the gate; so those who would contemplate the ideas must be led by the hand by the impressions of the senses [1].' We must know God as He is manifested to us in the experience of life, first by fear of His Justice, then by love of His Goodness, before we can attain to Jerusalem, the Vision of Peace. But the Powers are summed up in the Word. Hence the Interpreter Word is the God of those that are imperfect, but of the wise and perfect the First God is King [2].

The knowledge of the Most High is Vision, the direct personal communion of a soul that no longer reasons but feels and knows. It was reached by Abraham through learning, by 'the wrestler' Jacob through moral effort, by Isaac, 'the laughter of the soul,' through the natural development of a sweet and gracious spirit. It is attainable, if not by all, yet by the purest and keenest sighted, if not in permanence, yet frequently. 'I will not be ashamed to relate,' says Philo, 'what has happened to myself a thousand times. Often when I have come to write out the doctrines of philosophy, though I well knew what I ought to say, I have found my mind

[1] *De Somn.* 32 (i. 649).

[2] *Leg. Alleg.* iii. 73 (i. 128): οὗτος γὰρ ἡμῶν τῶν ἀτελῶν ἂν εἴη θεός, τῶν δὲ σοφῶν καὶ τελείων ὁ πρῶτος. The difference between the knowledge of God in His works and the knowledge of God in Himself (the latter Philo calls the Great Mysteries) is explained in the sublime passage beginning *Leg. Alleg.* iii. 31 (i. 106).

dry and barren, and renounced the task in despair. At
other times, though I came empty, I was suddenly filled
with thoughts showered upon me from above like snow-
flakes or seed, so that in the heat of divine possession
I knew not the place, or the company, or myself, what I
said, or what I wrote [1].'

Here then, but still in a singularly cool and temperate form, we have the second great doctrine of Neo-
Platonism — Ecstasy, the logical correlative of the
Absolute God. As held by Numenius and his followers it is certainly derived from Philo, though here
again there was in Paganism a germ, which only needed
fertilisation. The idea of a personal Revelation comes
to Philo from the Prophetic Vision of the Old Testament. It is already found in Plutarch [2], by whom it is
connected with the frenzy of the Pythoness or the
Corybant. But its later systematic form and scientific
grounding are historically connected with the speculations of the Alexandrine Jew.

Such was the teaching of Philo so far as it falls within
our present scope. We need not dwell upon its relation to historic Judaism. Philo remained to the last
a devout and trusted Jew. Yet he placed a new religion, a Greek philosophic system, above the faith of

---

[1] *De Migr. Abr.* 7 (i. 441). See also the account of the 'divine intoxication' of Samuel's mother, *De Ebrietate*, 36 (i. 380) ; *Quis Rerum Div.
Heres.* 14 (i. 482). *De Vita Contemp.* 2, 3 (ii. 473, 475) actual vision
seems to have been enjoyed by the Therapeutae only in dreams. *De Cher.* 9
(i. 144) Philo says that he had learned the significance of the two Cherubim
and the fiery sword : παρὰ ψυχῆς ἐμῆς εἰωθυίας τὰ πολλὰ θεοληπτεῖσθαι.

[2] See *De Pythiae Orac.* 21, 22 ; *De def. Orac.* 48 ; *Amatorius*, xvi. 4.
Plutarch recognises only the official ecstasy of priest and prophetess. His
attitude is apologetic; he has to explain how it is that the revelation is
sometimes imperfect, deceitful, impure. Enthusiasm is a part of his religion,
but not of his philosophy. See Zeller, vol. iii.

his fathers. He retained the Law as the worship of the Logos; high over this stands the free spiritual worship of the Eternal. The one is but the preparation, and in its ancient national form not even a necessary preparation, for the other. It will be obvious how this facilitated the task of the Christian teacher [1].

But what concerns us at present is his direct influence upon the Church. This falls into two branches, for it is probable that Philonism coloured the New Testament itself, and it is certain that it largely affected the after development of Christian doctrine. The first consequence is no doubt capable of exaggeration. The ideas of the purely Palestinian schools coincided in many points with those of the Alexandrines, of which they formed the basis, and it is perhaps by this fact rather than by any immediate contact that we should explain the resemblances of St. Paul, St. James, and even of the Epistle to the Hebrews, with Philo. But there can be little doubt that St. John acquired from Alexandria that conception of the Word, which first brought Christian theology within the sphere of metaphysics [2].

---

[1] Siegfried, pp. 157 sqq.

[2] Not necessarily from Philo, if, as seems probable, the Logos doctrine is somewhat older than Philo's time. The question turns mainly upon (i) the exact significance and (ii) the date of the Memra of the Targums. May-baum, *Die Anthropomorphien und Anthropathien bei Onkelos*, Breslau, 1870, maintains that in Onkelos 'Word of God' is a mere periphrasis for God, and is never regarded as having a hypostatic existence. Gfrörer, *Jahrhundert des Heils*, i. 310 sqq., maintains the opposite, but regards the idea as unquestionably Alexandrine in origin. With this agrees the view of Dr. Edersheim, *Life and Times of Jesus the Messiah*, vol. i. pp. 46, 56. Siegfried (p. 317) asserts that 'it is universally acknowledged that John borrowed from Philo the name of Logos to express the manifestation of God.' He refers to Ballenstedt, Dähne, Gfrörer, Lücke, de Wette-Brückner, Dorner, Neander, Tholuck, Lutterbeck. Nevertheless his language is too peremptory. Ewald (v. 153 sqq.; vi. 277) holds that the doctrine of the

Philo's influence upon the mind of post-apostolic times was partly helpful, partly detrimental. It was given to the Alexandrine Jew to divine the possibility and the mode of an eternal distinction in the Divine Unity, and in this respect the magnitude of our debt can hardly be overestimated. How large it is we may measure in part by the fact that the doctrine of the Holy Spirit, which has no place in his system, remained for a long time meagre, inarticulate, and uncertain. But the Logos is not Christ, is not the Messiah [1]. Far less is he Jesus, for from the Platonic point of view the Incarnation is an impossibility. Hence though Philo supplied the categories, under which the work of Jesus continued to be regarded, his influence on this side was upon the

Word grew up among the Jews and had become an article of the popular belief as well as a tenet of the schools. And that the book of Enoch shows that before the beginning of the second century B.C. the Word was identified with the Messiah. (Other authorities however regard the Book of Enoch as, in part at any rate, Christian.) Harnack, *Dogmengeschichte*, p. 79, note, says, ' Die Auffassung des Verhältnisses von Gott und Welt im vierten Evangelium ist nicht die Philonische. Daher ist auch die Logoslehre dort im wesentlichen nicht die Philo's.' This is maintained at length by Dr. Westcott, *Introduction to the Gospel of St. John*, pp. xv. sqq., and by Schanz, a recent Roman Catholic editor of the same Gospel. But the difference, while sufficient to show that St. John is applying a partially heathen phrase to a wholly Christian conception, is by no means such as to exclude the possibility of connection, and in any case very little weight can be attached to this line of argument in default of proof that a homegrown Logos doctrine existed in Palestine before the time of St. John.´ Some importance is perhaps to be attached to the fact that in the Pseudo-Clementine *Homilies*, a work which seems to be built upon a Palestinian system, we have God and the Two Powers but not the Logos. Yet the writer was acquainted with St. John, and would surely have given this title to the Son if he had found it current in the Palestinian schools.

[1] The traces of a Messianic hope in Philo are very indistinct. *De Execr.* 9 (ii. 436) the dispersed of Israel shall return from exile : ξεναγούμενοι πρός τινος θειοτέρας ἢ κατὰ φύσιν ἀνθρωπίνης (we should surely read ἀνθρωπίνην) ὄψεως. Siegfried (p. 222) refers this to the Logos. Dähne, p. 437, thinks it not improbable that the Logos is meant.

whole hurtful. To Philo religion is the emancipation
of the intelligence from the dominion of sense. In
such a scheme knowledge is more than Faith[1], Forgiveness has no real place, and Vicarious Suffering no
meaning. Such words as Atonement, Mediator, High
Priest, could not mean to the Platonist what they must
mean to the Christian, and down to the time of Clement
Philo's great name stood between the Church and a
clear understanding of their real signification.

Other parts of his legacy were more questionable
still—his vicious Allegorism, his theory of the Absolute
God. But upon these we shall be compelled to dwell
at some length further on, and therefore need speak no
more in the present place. Let us only add that
Alexandrine intellectualism, though it leads to an over-
estimate of human effort and to a self-centred conception of virtue, has yet the great merit of finding blessedness in the soul itself. The Kingdom of God is within
us, even in this life. Thus it affords the means for
rectifying a tendency very prevalent in the early
Church, that of looking for happiness only in another
world as a compensation for suffering in this. Its

---

[1] Philo speaks of Faith—the most perfect of virtues, the queen of virtues
—in very splendid terms. See especially *De Abrahamo*, 46 (ii. 39); *Quis
Rerum Div. Heres*. 18 (i. 486). But in section 21 of the last-named treatise
it appears to be distinguished from σοφία in the same way as by Clement,
as the cause of obedience, as the characteristic of the lower stage of the
spiritual life. This indeed is a consequence of his system. But Philo
has a clearer view that spiritual health is the one thing desirable, and is
not hampered by the question that pressed heavily on Clement—what
is the minimum condition of salvation? Hence his conception of Faith is
nobler, it may be said more Pauline, than Clement's. So again, not being
troubled by the problem of Responsibility, he uses much stronger and
grander language on the subject of Grace. See Siegfried, p. 307; Denis,
Philosophie d'Origène, p. 222.

reward is holiness, the vision of God; its punishment
is that of being what sinners are. Thus it is directly
opposed in principle, if not always in practice, to the
vulgar paradise of Chiliasm, and even to Asceticism.
For Asceticism, as distinguished from temperance, rests,
not upon the antithesis of spirit and matter, but upon
' other-worldliness,' the delusion that heaven can be
purchased by self-torture in this life.

Our view of the conditions out of which Christian
Platonism sprung would be incomplete without a brief
notice of Gnosticism[1]. It will be needless to enter into
the confused details of the so-called Gnostic systems.
The Aeons of Valentinus and others are but the Ideas
of Plato seen through the fog of an Egyptian or Syrian
mind. They were not understood to affect the unity of
God, and, except as guardian Angels, play no practical
part. Clement and Origen scarcely ever allude to them,
and they have no place at all in the systems of Marcion
and Basilides[2]. For us they have mainly this interest,

---

[1] The standard authorities on the subject of Gnosticism are—Neander,
Church History, vol. 2; Baur, *Die Christliche Gnosis*, Tübingen, 1835;
Matter, *Histoire Critique du Gnosticisme*, 2nd edition, Strasbourg and Paris,
1843; Lipsius, article *Gnosticismus* in Ersch and Gruber, Leipzig, 1860;
Mansel, *Gnostic Heresies*, 1875. All except the last two are anterior in date
to the publication in 1851 of six additional books of the *Philosophumena*
which have given an entirely new view of Basilides. We are concerned
entirely with what Lipsius counts as the second or Alexandrian stage of
Gnosticism. The view taken in the following pages rests mainly on the
Gnostic fragments which will be found collected in Stieren's edition of Irenaeus,
on the *Excerpta ex Theodoto*, and the general impression left on the mind by
the study of Clement, Origen, and the Pseudo-Clementine *Homilies*.

[2] To Valentinus the Aeons were simply the ideas, the thoughts of
God. Tertullian, *Adv. Valentin.* iv: ' Eam postmodum Ptolemaeus
intravit, nominibus et numeris Aeonum distinctis in personales substantias,
sed extra deum determinatas, quas Valentinus in ipsa summa divinitatis ut sensus et affectus motus incluserat.' This is confirmed by a striking
extract from an Epistle of Valentinus given by Clement, *Strom.* ii. 20. 114;

that they complete the work of the Philonic analysis. God is finally separated from His attributes, the Aeons of Reason and Truth, and becomes the Eternal Silence of Valentinus, the Non-existent God of Basilides[1]. It is a mistake to approach the Gnostics on the metaphysical side. There is a certain wild poetical force in Valentinus, but otherwise their world - philosophy is purely grotesque. The ordinary Christian controversialist felt that he had nothing to do but set out at unsparing length their tedious pedigrees, in the wellgrounded confidence that no one would care to peruse them a second time. The interest, the meaning, of Gnosticism rest entirely upon its ethical motive. It was an attempt, a serious attempt, to fathom the dread mystery of sorrow and pain, to answer that spectral doubt, which is mostly crushed down by force—Can the world as we know it have been made by God? ' Cease,' says Basilides, 'from idle and curious variety, and let us rather discuss the opinions, which even barbarians have held, on the subject of good and evil[2].' ' I will say anything, rather than admit that Providence is wicked[3].' Valentinus describes in the strain of an ancient prophet ·the woes that afflict mankind. ' I durst

Stieren, *Irenaeus*, p. 910. But the same thing is probably true of Ptolemy and of Heracleon. The use of the word aeon by the Gnostic writers themselves is obscure. I find it used to denote, (i) God; Heracleon *apud* Origen *in Ioan.* ii. 8 (Lomm, i. 117), τὸν αἰῶνα ἢ τὰ ἐν τῷ αἰῶνι. Hence ὁ ἐν αἰῶνι, *ibid.* xiii. 19 (Lomm, ii. 33), is Jesus: (ii) Aeons = Ideas? = Emanations? *Exc. ex Theod.* 23, *ibid.* 32, ἕκαστος τῶν αἰώνων ἴδιον ἔχει πλήρωμα, τὴν συζυγίαν ; (iii) Angels; *Exc. ex Theod.* 25, the Valentinians λέγουσι τοὺς αἰῶνας ὁμωνύμως τῷ λόγῳ λόγους, Here Aeon = λόγος = Angels = Stars. So in section 7, ἄγνωστος οὖν ὁ πατὴρ ὢν ἠθέλησεν γνωσθῆναι τοῖς αἰῶσιν : cp. St. Paul, Eph. ii. 7. As to the Guardian Angels, see below, p. 33.

[1] *Philos.* vii. 21 : οὕτως οὐκ ὢν θεὸς ἐποίησε κόσμον οὐκ ὄντα ἐξ οὐκ ὄντων.

[2] Stieren's *Irenaeus*, p. 901.

[3] Stieren's *Irenaeus*, p. 903 ; Clem. *Strom.* iv. 12. 82.

not affirm,' he concludes, 'that God is the author of all this[1].' So Tertullian says of Marcion, 'like many men of our time, and especially the heretics, he is bewildered by the question of evil[2].' They approach the problem from a non-Christian point of view, and arrive therefore at a non-Christian solution. Yet the effort is one that must command our respect, and the solution is one that a great writer of our own time thought not untenable[3]. Many of them, especially the later sectaries, accepted the whole Christian Creed[4], but always with reserve. The teaching of the Church thus became in their eyes a popular exoteric confession, beneath their own Gnosis, or Knowledge, which was a Mystery, jealously guarded from all but the chosen few. They have been called the first Christian theologians. We may call them rather the first Freemasons.

There is no better example of the cultivated Gnostic than Plutarch. Perplexed by the nightmare of physical and moral evil this amiable scholar could see no light except in the dualism of Zoroaster[5]. The world was created by Ormuzd, the spirit of Good, but Ahriman, the dark and wicked, had broken in and corrupted all.

---

[1] From the remarkable fragment of the Dissertation on the Origin of Evil, Stieren's *Irenaeus*, p. 912.

[2] *Adv. Marcion.* i. 2.

[3] See J. S. Mill, *Three Essays on Religion*, ed. 1874, pp. 25, 37, 58. Mr. Mill himself rejected the Dualistic solution; *ibid.* p. 185.

[4] Basilides accepted the whole of the Gospel narrative, *Philos.* vii. 27. So did Theodotus. Tertullian, *Adv. Val.* 1 : ' Si subtiliter tentes per ambiguitates bilingues communem fidem adfirmant.' Irenaeus, *Preface*, 2 : οὓς φυλάσσειν παρήγγελκεν ἡμῖν Κύριος ὅμοια μὲν λαλοῦντας, ἀνόμοια δὲ φρονοῦντας. See the accounts of Cerdon, Irenaeus, iii. 4. 3, and Apelles, Eusebius, *H. E.* v. 13 ; Harnack, *Dogmengesch.* p. 186.

[5] *De Iside et Osiride*, 45 sqq.

From Plutarch sprang a succession of purely heathen
Gnostics, against whom, more than a century later,
Plotinus felt it necessary to take up the pen [1]. Between
these and the Gnostics known to Christian controversy
there is no essential difference. Both start from the
same terrible problem, both arrive at the same conclusion, the existence of a second and imperfect God.
They identified this Being with the Creator or Demiurge, and ascribed to him the authorship of the whole,
or the greater part, of the Old Testament. For, though
they allegorised the New Testament, the Gnostics did
not, in any of their voluminous commentaries, apply
this solvent to the Hebrew Scriptures. These they
criticised with a freedom learned from the Essenes [2].
They found there, side by side with the eternal
spiritual law, the code of an imperfect and transient
morality; worse than all, they found there passion,
revenge, and cruelty ascribed to the Most High. It
is not possible to read the remarkable letter of Ptolemy
to Flora, without perceiving that Old Testament exegesis
was the real strength of Gnosticism. It was so powerful because it was so true. On this one point they
retained their advantage to the last. The facts were
in the main as they alleged, and the right explanation
depended on principles equally foreign, at that time, to
Gnostic and to orthodox.

Their views of religion, of salvation, were as various
as their strange and perplexing cosmogonies. We may

[1] Porph. *Vita Plotini,* 16.
[2] Compare the exegesis of the Pseudo-Clementine *Homilies* with that of
Ptolemy's *Epistle to Flora.* The author of the *Homilies* considered that
he was refuting Gnosticism, but there was certainly a historical connection
between his views and those of the Valentinians. See below, p. 34.

leave out of sight the Paulinism of Marcion, and take as
a type the system of Theodotus, a leader of the Eastern
Valentinians, with whose writings Clement had an in-
timate acquaintance[1]. Christ came, he taught, not for
our redemption alone, but to heal the disorders of the
whole universe. For Earth, and Heaven, and even God
Himself, were diseased by the revolt of Wisdom, who in
blind presumption had given birth to she knew not
what. But for man's sake Christ became Man [2], taking

---

[1] It is doubtful what the *Excerpta ex Theodoto* really are. ' Descripta
videntur ex libris Hypotyposeon,' says Valesius on Eus. *H. E.* v. 11. 2.
Zahn, *Forschungen zur Gesch. des N. T. Kanons*, Erlangen, 1884, vol. iii. p.
122, thinks that they are a collection of extracts from the eighth book of
the *Stromateis*. Renan, *Marc-Aurèle*, p. 118, regards them as a collection
of extracts from the writings of the Valentinian Theodotus made by Clement
for his own use, and this seems the best view. It is doubtful again who
Theodotus was. Neander and Dorner think him the same as Theodotus the
money-changer. Zahn inclines, rather fancifully, to identify him with the
Theodas (if that is the right name; the reading is doubtful) of *Strom.* vii.
17. 106, the disciple of Paul and teacher of Valentinus, and thinks that there
may have been a book bearing the name of this supposed pupil of the
Apostle. It should be added that Theodotus is referred to by name only
five times, and that much of the information for which Clement refers vaguely
to 'the Valentinians' may come from some other source. The text is exceedingly obscure and corrupt. Bunsen, *Anal. Ante-Nic.* vol. i, gives the
conjectural emendations and Latin translation of Bernays. The accusations
brought by Photius against the orthodoxy of Clement may rest in part upon a
misunderstanding of this curious and difficult treatise. See also Dr. Westcott's article, *Clement of Alexandria*, in the Dictionary of Christian
Biography.

[2] The Christology of Theodotus differs somewhat from that ascribed to
Valentinus by the author of the *Philosophumena*. (i) The Only-Begotten
God (§ 6; this is I suppose the earliest authority for this reading in John
i. 18), Nous, Aletheia, Logos, Zoe appear to be only different names for
the Spirit of Knowledge, the προβολή, or externalised thought of God.
(ii) Christ is a προβολή of exiled Wisdom who returns to the πλήρωμα to
beg aid for his mother, is detained there, and apparently united to the
Only-Begotten; §§ 23, 39, 44. (iii) Jesus the προβολή of all the Aeons
is sent forth to comfort Wisdom; § 23. (iv) Jesus is never separated from
the Only-Begotten; §§ 7, 43. (v) Jesus descends to the world through the
realm of Space, that is the Demiurge, and takes to himself the Psychic

upon Him our threefold nature, body, soul, and spirit, though His body was spiritual, not gross as ours. Yet He is not the Saviour of all, but of those only who can receive Him, and in so far as they can receive Him[1]. Some there are who cannot know Him, these are they who have flesh but not soul, who perish like the beasts. Some again, the spiritual, are predestined to life eternal[2]. They are akin to the light, knowledge once given leads them on inevitably to perfection, annihilating all their earthly passions. Between these hover 'the psychic,' the feminine souls, to whom faith is granted, but not knowledge. Before the coming of Christ these were creatures of destiny, the sport of evil angels, whom they could not resist[3]. But the Incarnation and Baptism of our Lord broke their bonds, and by faith and discipline they become capable of eternal life[4].

In that future existence the soul needs no body, for

Christ, § 59, the προβολή of the Demiurge, § 47—that is to say, his νοῦς assumes a ψυχή—and weaves for Himself a body ἐκ τῆς ἀφανοῦς ψυχικῆς οὐσίας, § 59. (vi) He was born of the Holy Ghost and the Virgin; § 23. The whole of the Gospel narrative then follows.

[1] § 7: ὁ δὲ αὐτός ἐστι τοιοῦτος ὧν ἑκάστῳ οἷος κεχωρῆσθαι δύναται.

[2] § 56: τὸ μὲν οὖν πνευματικὸν φύσει σωζόμενον, τὸ δὲ ψυχικὸν αὐτεξούσιον ὂν ἐπιτηδειότητα ἔχει πρός τε πίστιν καὶ ἀφθαρσίαν καὶ πρὸς ἀπιστίαν καὶ φθορὰν κατὰ τὴν οἰκείαν αἵρεσιν, τὸ δὲ ὑλικὸν φύσει ἀπόλλυται. The Spiritual, the Elect, are masculine, children of Adam; the Psychic, the Called, are feminine, children of Eve; § 21. This idea is found in the *Homilies.* The Spiritual must be 'shaped' by knowledge; §§ 57, 59: the Psychic must be 'grafted on to the fruitful olive;' § 56, 'changed' from slavery into freedom, from feminine into masculine, §§ 57, 79. Unless they become spiritual they are burnt up in the fire, § 52, body and soul perish in Gehenna (proved by Matt. x. 28), § 51, that is to say before they rise to Paradise the fourth heaven, which earthly flesh may not enter, § 51: this last idea is based upon 2 Cor. xii. 2.

[3] §§ 69–75.

[4] §§ 76–78.

it is itself a body, as the Stoics taught[1]. It is immortal and for ever blessed. But there are degrees of felicity. The spiritual soar up at once through the seven planetary orbits to the Ogdoad, the region of the fixed stars, where is no more labour nor change. There they await the consummation, when Christ, the great High Priest, shall lay aside His soul, and enter through the Cross—that is the upper Firmament—into the Holy of Holies, taking with Him His children, now become pure Words like Himself. The Psychic are cleansed by fire, the sensible and the intellectual fire[2], the pangs of sense, the stings of remorse. Aided and comforted by guardian angels[3], who were 'baptised for them,' while yet they were 'dead in trespasses and

---

[1] § 14, ἀλλὰ καὶ ἡ ψυχὴ σῶμα. For how, the author asks, can the souls who are chastised feel their punishments if they are not bodies? Corporeal also, though in an ever-ascending scale of fineness, are the demons, the angels, archangels and Protoctists, the Only-Begotten, and apparently even the Father; §§ 10, 11.

[2] § 81.

[3] Theodotus appears to distinguish two classes of Angels; those created by the Demiurge, who like all his works are imperfect copies of the existences of the spiritual world, § 47, and the 'male angels,' the creation of the Only-Begotten, § 21. It is by union with these that the 'female soul' becomes masculine and capable of entering the Pleroma. It is these angels that are 'baptised for the dead' (1 Cor. xv. 29). Hence the Valentinian was baptised εἰς λύτρωσιν ἀγγελικήν, in the same Name in which his guardian Angel had previously been baptised; § 22. The male Angels came down with Jesus for our salvation, § 44, and 'pray for our forgiveness that we may enter in with them. For they may be said to have need of us that they may enter in, for without us this is not permitted to them;' § 35. Similar ideas will be found in the religion of Mithra, see below, Lecture vii, and in the *Homilies,* ix. 9 sqq. (though here the union is between the bad man and his demon). So Heracleon says (apud Origen *in Joan.* xiii. 11) that the Samaritan woman's husband is her Pleroma. Cp. also Irenaeus, iii. 15. 2: 'est inflatus iste talis, neque in caelo neque in terra putat se esse, sed intra Pleroma introisse et complexum iam angelum suum.' Also the Valentinian epitaph quoted by Renan, *Marc-Aurèle,* p. 147.

D

sins,' who love them, and yearn for them as their
spiritual brides, they rise, through three 'mansions' or
stages of discipline, to the Ogdoad their final home,
their Rest [1]. Thus spirit, soul, and body, the com-
mingling of which is the cause of all evil and suffering,
are finally separated into their appointed places, and
the healing work of Christ is achieved. It is not difficult to trace here a barbaric Platonism, mingled with
Mazdeism, coloured by the influence of the Ebionites,
and strangely refracted echoes of St. Paul [2]. St. Paul

---

[1] Jesus in his descent puts on the Psychic Christ in τόπος, Space, the
realm of the Demiurge; § 59. It was the Psychic Christ, that is the
Human Nature, that died, § 61, and now sits on the right hand of the
Demiurge, § 62, till the Restitution, 'in order that he may pacify Space
and guarantee a safe passage for the Seed into the Pleroma,' § 38. Then
He lays aside ψυχή and σῶμα and passes through the Veil, § 27, taking
with him His children, His Body, the Church, § 42. Till then the
elect await Him in the Ogdoad, the eighth heaven, the changeless region
of the fixed stars, §§ 26, 63, becoming Words, Intelligent Aeons, λόγοι,
αἰῶνες νοεροί, §§ 27, 64. At the same time the Psychic rise from the
Kingdom of the Demiurge to the Ogdoad, § 63.

[2] The barbaric cast of their Philosophy may be seen in the grotesque
character assumed by the Logoi or Aeons in the popular systems, in
the crude description of the Non-Existent God by Basilides, and generally
in the Gnostic incapacity for abstract ideas. Thus the inner Veil which
divides the Ogdoad from the Pleroma, the world of Ideas, is Heaven.
But one derivation given for the word οὐρανός is ὅρος, a boundary or
division. Horos might mean a pole, such as Greeks employed to mark
the limits of a field. Hence the upper firmament might be called Σταυρός,
the Cross which divides believers from unbelievers ; *Excerpta*, § 42. The
passions were conceived of in Stoic fashion as actual bodies hanging on
to the soul, the προσαρτήματα or προσφυὴς ψυχή. Man thus becomes, says
Clement, a kind of Trojan Horse; *Strom.* ii. 20. 112 sqq. As to the
Mazdeism, there is clear historical proof of the connection of Gnosticism
with the system of Zoroaster ; cp. Lect. vii, the passages referred to above
from Plutarch and Porphyry, Duncker, vol. v. pp. 53 sqq. of the English
translation. As to Ebionitism, I notice the following points of resemblance
between Theodotus and the *Homilies*—Anthropomorphism—the Syzygies—
the antitheses of Male and Female, Fire and Light, Right and Left—the
union of the soul with its Angel—the idea that the Water of Baptism
quenches the fire of sin, suggesting or suggested by the ancient reading in

was held in high esteem by these sectaries, and to their
sinister admiration is largely due the neglect of his
special teaching in the early Church.

This Dualism, this Fatalism, for the three natures are
a modified fatalism, are vain and worse than vain.
They belong to a lower stage of religious life, above
polytheism, yet far below Christianity. From this
semi-barbarism spring all the faults of Gnosticism, its
conceit, its uncertain morality, its chimeras, its peremptory solutions of the insoluble. Like all half-truths it
perished self-convicted, melting away like Spenser's
woman of snow in presence of the living Florimell. It
left a certain mark upon Catholicism, and partly by
shaking the older faiths, partly by preparing men's minds
for a better belief, partly by compelling the leaders
of the Church to ask what they believed and why they
believed it, aided not inconsiderably in the triumph of
the Gospel, and in the development of the Creed[1]. But
in the second century, while it was yet living and
aggressive, it constituted a danger greater than the
Arian controversy, greater than any peril that has ever
menaced the existence of the Faith.

Matt. iii. 15, which tells how a fire shone in the Jordan at the baptism
of Jesus. Lastly, the doctrine of several Incarnations of Jesus is found
in the *Excerpta*, § 19. Zahn is therefore mistaken in saying (p. 123) that
there is no trace of Ebionitism in the Christology of Clement's Theodotus.

[1] The first philosophical statement of the Real Presence is to be found
Excerpta, § 82. To Gnostics is due the importation of the words οὐσία,
ὑπόστασις, ὁμοούσιος into theology. They held the Virgin in high honour ;
Renan, *Marc-Aurèle*, p. 145. They were the first to speculate on the date
of the Nativity, *Strom.* i. 21. 145, and to attempt the portraiture of Christ ;
Iren. i. 25. 6. Beyond this I see nothing but the influence of antagonism.
See however Harnack, *Dogmengeschichte*, pp. 185 sqq.

LECTURE II.

That was the true Light, which lighteth every man that cometh into the world.—St. John i. 9.

ACCORDING to the earliest tradition, that which is preserved in the Pseudo-Clementine Homilies, Christianity was first preached in the streets of Alexandria by Barnabas[1]. But for ages the Egyptians have attributed the foundation of their Church to St. Mark, the interpreter of St. Peter. At a later date the Patriarchs of Alexandria were elected beside the tomb of the Evangelist in the great church of Baucalis, the most ancient ecclesiastical edifice in the city, in close proximity to the wharves and corn-magazines of the crowded harbour.

At the close of the second century the Church of Alexandria was already a wealthy and flourishing community. Its warfare is said to have been comparatively bloodless. Three times within a hundred years Egypt had endured all the horrors of unsuccessful rebellion, and once a sanguinary riot had been occasioned by the dis-

---

[1] *Hom.* i. 8 sqq. The claims of Mark find no support from Clement. But Bishop Lightfoot thinks there is no reason to doubt the tradition ; *Philippians*, p. 223, ed. 1873. See Redepenning, *Origenes,* i. p. 185, note.

The sources employed for this sketch of the history of the Alexandrine Church are *Contextio Gemmarum sive* Eutychii *Patr. Alex. Annales,* Pocock, Oxford, 1656 ; Eutychii *Origines Eccl. Alex.,* Selden, London, 1642 ; Le Quien, *Oriens Christianus* ; Renaudot, *Historia Patriarcharum Alex. Jacobitarum* ; Neale, *Holy Eastern Church.* Some information is to be gathered from the *Oracula Sibyllina,* see Excur. in Alexandre's ed., and much from Clement. Origen's church was that of Palestine. The letter of Hadrian to Servianus in Vopiscus, *Vita Saturnini,* is regarded as a forgery by Mommsen, v. p. 579 note.

covery of the Apis bull[1]. Amid scenes like these the Christians no doubt bore their full share of suffering. But down to the time of Severus there appears to have been no definite persecution of the faith[2]. The execution of Christians was in general a concession to the mob, and it is probable that in Alexandria in ordinary times the populace was held down by a much more severe restraint than elsewhere, the Emperors being always nervously apprehensive of any disturbance by which the supply of corn might be interrupted. Under these favouring circumstances the Church had spread with great rapidity. Already the house-church of the first age had been replaced by buildings specially constructed for the purposes of Christian worship[3], and it would seem therefore that the right of holding land was enjoyed, perhaps under some legal fiction, by the Alexandrine, as it certainly was by the African and Roman communities[4]. In other matters the Egyptian

---

[1] In 115 the Jews of Egypt and Cyrene revolted, and were quelled by Marcius Turbo. The rebellion of Barcochba extended to Egypt, and in the reign of Marcus occurred the insurrection of the Bucoli; see Mommsen, v. 581. The Apis sedition is recorded in Spartian's Life of Hadrian, 12.

[2] Clement says (*Strom.* ii. 20. 125), ἡμῖν δὲ ἄφθονοι μαρτύρων πηγαὶ ἐκάστης ἡμέρας ἐν ὀφθαλμοῖς ἡμῶν θεωρούμεναι παροπτωμένων ἀνασκινδυλευομένων τὰς κεφαλὰς ἀποτεμνομένων. He may be speaking of sufferings in other countries, or Christian blood may have been shed in Alexandria before the official commencement of the persecution of Severus. See Aubé, *Les Chrétiens dans l'Empire Romain*, pp. 117 sqq. Nevertheless persecution was always going on more or less in every province where the governor happened to be weak or hostile. Since the discovery of the Greek text of the Acts of the Scillitan martyrs, this tragedy is known to have occurred in 180, a time otherwise of peace: see Görres, *Jahrb. für Prot. Theol.* 1884, parts ii and iii.

[3] Clement speaks of ' coming from church ' just as we do, *Paed.* ii. 10. 96, μηδὲ ἐξ ἐκκλησίας, φέρε, ἢ ἀγορᾶς ἥκοντα, but does not like Origen refer to the arrangements of the building. See on this subject Probst, *Kirchliche Disciplin*, pp. 181 sqq.

[4] 'Areae Christianorum' are mentioned by Tertullian, *Ad Scapulam*, 3.

Church seems to have moved less rapidly than its neigh-
bours. The traces of a written liturgy in Clement are
scanty and vague[1]. The Eucharist was not yet disjoined
from the Agape. Infant Baptism was not yet the rule.
Discipline was not so severe as elsewhere. The Bishop
was not yet sharply distinguished from the Presbyter,
nor the Presbyter and Deacon from the lay-brother.
The fidelity, with which the Alexandrines adhered to
the ancient democratic model, may be due in part to
the social standing and intelligence of the congregation.
The same reason may account for their immunity from
many of the ecclesiastical storms of the time. Gnosticism indeed was rampant in this focus of East and
West. But of Noetianism, of the Easter controversy,
of Montanism hardly a sound is to be heard[2].

About the same time Callistus was overseer of the cemetery at Rome;
Philos. ix. 12.

[1] Probst (*Liturgie*, p. 9) gives reasons for supposing that the first sketch
of a written Liturgy existed in the middle of the second century, and (*ibid.*
pp. 135 sqq.) finds in Clement traces of a Liturgy resembling in its main outlines that given in the eighth book of the Apostolical Constitutions. It is most
difficult to say what precise facts underlie Clement's allusive phrases. The
only passages, so far as I know, in which written formularies may be referred to are *Strom.* vii. 12. 80, where τὰ ζῷα τὰ δοξόλογα τὰ διὰ Ἡσαίου ἀλ-
ληγορούμενα seem to allude to the Trisagion uttered by the Cherubim and
Seraphim (Renaudot, *Liturgiarum Orient. Collectio*, i. p. 46), and *Protrep.*
xi. 111, where the 'outstretched hands of Christ' may be explained by a
phrase in the ancient Alexandrine Liturgy translated by Ludolfus, from the
Ethiopic (in Bunsen, *Hippolytus*, iv. p. 242), 'ut impleret voluntatem tuam
et populum tibi efficeret expandendo manus suas.' For the Agape and
Infant Baptism, see next Lecture.

[2] Of Noetianism Clement does not speak. He wrote a treatise Περὶ τοῦ
πάσχα, in which he considered the relation of St. John's narrative to that of
the Synoptists; see the Fragments, the best account is that of Zahn, *Forschungen*, iii. p. 32); and the Κανὼν ἐκκλησιαστικὸς ἢ πρὸς τοὺς ἰουδαίζοντας
may have been directed against the Quartodecimans (see Zahn, *ibid.* p. 35).
The Treatises (Sermons, Zahn thinks) on Fasting and the promised but
not written treatise on Prophecy were certainly aimed at the Montanists,
whom he mentions with forbearance, *Strom.* iv. 13. 93; vi. 8. 66. But

Nevertheless wealth and numbers brought dangers of
their own, and Alexandria was driven along the same
road which other Churches were already pursuing. The
lowering of the average tone of piety and morals among
the laity threw into stronger relief the virtues of the
clergy, and enabled them with a good show of justice
and necessity to claim exclusive possession of powers,
which had originally been shared by all male members
of the Church. We can still trace the incidents, by which this momentous change was effected. The most interesting
feature in the Alexandrine Church was its College of
twelve Presbyters, who enjoyed the singular privilege of
electing from among themselves, and of consecrating,
their own Patriarch [1]. They were the rectors of the
twelve city parishes, which included certain districts

---

he does not seem to have been troubled at home by either Montanism or
Judaism.

[1] *Contextio Gemmarum*, p. 331 : ' Constituit autem Evangelista Marcus,
una cum Hanania Patriarcha, duodecim Presbyteros, qui nempe cum Patriarcha
manerent, adeo ut cum vacaret Patriarchatus unum e duodecim Presbyteris
eligerent, cujus capiti reliqui undecim manus imponentes ipsi benedicerent et
Patriarcham crearent ; deinde virum aliquem insignem eligerent quem secum
Presbyterum constituerent loco eius qui factus est Patriarcha, ut ita semper
extarent duodecim. Neque desiit Alexandriae institutum hoc de Presbyteris,
ut scilicet Patriarchas crearent ex Presbyteris duodecim, usque ad tempora
Alexandri Patriarchae Alexandrini qui fuit ex numero illo CCCXVIII. Is
autem vetuit ne deinceps Patriarcham Presbyteri crearent et decrevit ut
mortuo Patriarcha convenirent Episcopi qui Patriarcham ordinarent. . . .
Atque ita evanuit institutum illud antiquius.'   In Selden, p. xxxi.

Cp. Jerome, Ep. 146 (in Migne), *Ad Evangelum :* ' Nam et Alexandriae a
Marco Evangelista usque ad Heraclam et Dionysium Episcopos Presbyteri
semper unum ex se electum in excelsiori gradu collocatum Episcopum
nominabant : quomodo si exercitus Imperatorem faciat.' Eutychius also
tells us that Demetrius was the first to appoint Suffragans. See Bishop
Lightfoot, *Philippians*, Excursus on *the Christian Ministry*. The inference
that there was a prolonged struggle between the two orders is Ritschl's
Entstehung der Altk. Kirche, 2nd ed. p. 432.

outside the walls. Even in the time of Epiphanius they exercised a sort of episcopal jurisdiction [1]. They formed a chapter, of which the Patriarch was President, and to this chapter all provincial letters were addressed. But towards the close of the second century their chief and distinguishing prerogative had been lost. While the Patriarch Julian lay upon his death-bed, he was warned by an angel in a vision, that the man, who next day should bring him a present of grapes, was destined to be his successor. The sign was fulfilled by Demetrius, an unlettered rustic, and, what to later ages seemed even more extraordinary, a married man. In obedience to the divine warning Demetrius was seated almost by force in the throne of St. Mark. He proved a stern and enterprising ruler. He stripped the people of one of their few remaining privileges by the censure, which he pronounced on Origen for preaching while yet a layman, and he broke the power of the Presbyteral College by the appointment of a number of Suffragan Bishops, whom he afterwards persuaded to pass sentence of degradation upon Origen, a sentence which the Presbyters had refused to sanction [2]. From this time the Chapter never succeeded in regaining its prerogative, though the struggle appears to have been protracted till the incumbency of the Patriarch Alexander. Thus was finally abolished this most interesting relic of a time, when there was no essential difference between Bishop and Priest, and of a later but still early time, when the Bishop was chairman or life-president of a

---

[1] Epiph. lxix. 1.

[2] Redepenning, *Origenes*, i. p. 412 ; Huet, *Origeniana*, i. 2. 12 (Lomm. xxii. 44) ; Photius, cod. cxviii.

council of Priests, by whom the affairs of a great city-
churcn were administered in common. A large and rich community, existing in the bosom of
a great University town, could not long submit to exclu-
sion from the paramount interests of the place. Their
most promising young men attended the lectures of the
heathen professors. Some like Ammonius relapsed into
Hellenism, some drifted into Gnosticism like Ambrosius,
some like Heraclas passed safely through the ordeal, and
as Christian priests still wore the pallium, or philosopher's cloak, the doctor's gown we may call it of the
pagan Academy. Learned professors like Celsus, like
Porphyry, began to study the Christian Scriptures with a
cool interest in this latest development of religious
thought, and pointed out with the acumen of trained
critics the scientific difficulties of the Older Testament
and the contradictions of the New. It was necessary to
recognise, and if possible to profit by, the growing connection between the church and the lecture-room.
Hence the catechetical instruction, which in most other
communities continued to be given in an unsystematic
way by Bishop or Priest, had in Alexandria developed
about the middle of the century into a regular institution.

This was the famous Catechetical School[1]. It still
continued to provide instruction for those desirous of
admission into the Church, but with this humble routine
it combined a higher and more ambitious function. It
was partly a propaganda, partly we may regard it as a

---

[1] Schools of a similar description existed at Antioch, Athens, Edessa,
Nisibis; Guerike, *De Schola Alex.* p. 2 ; Harnack, *Dogmengeschichte*, 501
sqq.

denominational college by the side of a secular university. There were no buildings appropriated to the
purpose. The master received his pupils in his own
house, and Origen was often engaged till late at night
in teaching his classes or giving private advice or instruction to those who needed it. The students were
of both sexes, of very different ages. Some were converts preparing for baptism, some idolaters seeking for
light, some Christians reading as we should say for
orders or for the cultivation of their understandings.
There was as yet no rigid system, no definite classifica-
tion of Catechumens, such as that which grew up a
century later. The teacher was left free to deal with
his task, as the circumstances of his pupils or his own
genius led him. But the general course of instruction
pursued in the Alexandrine school we are fortunately
able to discover with great accuracy and fulness of detail.
Those who were not capable of anything more were
taught the facts of the Creed, with such comment and
explanation as seemed desirable. Others, Origen tells us,
were taught dialectically. The meaning of this phrase
is interpreted for us by Gregory Thaumaturgus, one of
the most illustrious and attached of Origen's disciples.
At the outset the student's powers of reasoning and exact
observation were strengthened by a thorough course of
scientific study, embracing geometry, physiology, and
astronomy. After science came philosophy. The writings of all the theological poets, and of all the philosophers except the 'godless Epicureans,' were read and
expounded. The object of the teacher was no doubt in
part controversial. He endeavoured to prove the need of
revelation by dwelling on the contradictions and imper-

fections of all human systems, or he pointed out how the partial light vouchsafed to Plato or Aristotle was but an earnest of the dayspring from on high. But the attitude of Clement or Origen towards Greek thought was not controversial in any petty or ignoble sense. They looked up to the great master-minds of the Hellenic schools with a generous admiration, and infused the same spirit into their disciples. Philosophy culminated in Ethics, and at this point began the dialectic training properly so called. The student was called upon for a definition of one of those words that lie at the root of all morality, Good or Evil, Justice or Law; and his definition became the theme of a close discussion conducted in the form of question and answer. In the course of these eager systematic conversations every prejudice was dragged to light, every confusion unravelled, every error convicted, the shame of ignorance was intensified, the love of truth kindled into a passion. So far the course pursued did not differ essentially from that familiar to the heathen schools. But at this point the characteristic features of the Christian seminary come into view. We find them in the consistency and power, with which virtue was represented as a subject not merely for speculation but for practice —in the sympathy and magnetic personal attraction of the teacher—but above all in the Theology, to which all other subjects of thought were treated as ancillary [1].

It may be doubted whether any nobler scheme of Christian education has ever been projected than this,

[1] The materials for this account will be found in Guerike and the *Panegyric* of Gregory Thaumaturgus (in Lomm. xxv. 339). Gregory is describing the teaching of Origen as he had profited by it in Caesarea. But the description will hold good of his earlier work at Alexandria.

which we find in actual working at Alexandria at the end of the second century after Christ. I have dwelt upon it at some length, partly because of the light it throws upon the speculations of the great Alexandrine divines, partly in view of the charges of ignorance and credulity so often levelled at the early Christians. The truth is, that so far as the Church differed from the rest of society it differed for the better. Whatever treasures of knowledge belonged to the ancient world lay at its command, and were freely employed in its service, and it possessed besides the inestimable advantage of purer morals and a more reasonable creed.

The first master of the Alexandrine school is said to have been the Apologist Athenagoras. But the statement rests upon evidence so insufficient that we may be permitted to disregard it[1]. The teacher, under whom the institution first attains to a place in history, is Pantaenus, a converted Stoic philosopher[2], who in the course of a mission journey to India is said to have discovered a Hebrew version of the Gospel of St. Matthew. He was an author of some eminence, but all that we possess of his writings is a fragment of some half-dozen lines, containing however a sensible and valuable remark on the relations of the Greek and the Hebrew verb. His pupil and successor was the more famous Clement.

Titus Flavius Clemens was a Greek, and probably an Athenian[3]. He was born about the middle of the

[1] The name of Athenagoras is found first in the list of masters of the Alexandrine school given by Philippus Sidetes in a fragment discovered by Dodwell. Guerike inclines to accept the statement. Redepenning, i. 63, regards it as highly doubtful. See also Otto, Proleg. to Athenagoras, p. xxii.

[2] See Guerike, Routh.

[3] Epiph. xxxii. 6 : Κλήμης ὅν φασί τινες ᾿Αλεξανδρέα ἕτεροι δὲ ᾿Αθηναῖον. It

second century, and inherited his name in all likelihood from an ancestor enfranchised by Vespasian or his son. He was the child apparently of heathen parents [1], and Eleusis and the Schools had been to him the vestibule of the Church. Like many another ardent spirit in that restless age he wandered far and wide in quest of truth, till at last in Egypt he 'caught' Pantaenus, 'that true Sicilian bee,' hidden away in modest obscurity, and in his lessons found satisfaction alike for soul and mind. Here at Alexandria he made his home. He received priestly orders [2], and was appointed master of the Catechetical School, at first probably as assistant to Pantaenus. He appears to have fled from the persecution of Severus in 203, and did not return to Egypt. After this date we catch but one uncertain glimpse of him [3], and it would seem that he died about 213.

It is not an eventful biography. Clement was essentially a man of letters, and his genial contemplative

seems a natural inference from the account of his wanderings in *Strom.* i. 1. 11 that he was not a native Alexandrine, and that his starting-point was Hellas. The statement that he was an Athenian is rendered probable by the character of his style, which is deeply tinged with Homeric phrases and bears a strong resemblance to that of Philostratus and the Sophists whom Philostratus describes, and again by his familiarity with Attic usage. See for this last point *Paed.* i. 4. 11 ; 5. 14 ; ii. 11. 117 ; 12. 122. But Dindorf, *Preface*, p. xxvii, tries to make him more Attic than he is. For the special bibliography of Clement the reader may consult Guerike, Dr. Westcott in Dictionary of Christian Biography, Jacobi's article in Herzog, and Dr. Harnack's *Dogmengeschichte*.

[1] Eus. *Praep. Ev.* ii. 2. 64, πάντων μὲν διὰ πείρας ἐλθὼν ἀνήρ, θᾶττόν γε μὴν τῆς πλάνης ἀνανεύσας. We may perhaps infer from the knowledge of the Mysteries displayed in *Protrep.* ii. that he had been initiated. But the teachers to whom he expresses his obligations in *Strom.* i. 1. 11 were all Christians. See the note in Heinichen's Eusebius, *H. E.* v. 11. 3.

[2] *Paed.* i. 6. 37.

[3] Heinichen's Eus. *H. E.* vi. 11. 6. For further information as to the life of Clement see Guerike or Dr. Westcott's article in Dictionary of Christian Biography.

temper rendered him averse to direct controversy and the bustle of practical life. His writings are the faithful mirror of his studies and thoughts, but tell us little of incident. In later times he was considered a marvel of learning. Nor was this estimate ill-grounded, for the range of his acquaintance with Greek literature, ecclesiastical [1], Gnostic, and classical, was varied and extensive. There are indeed deductions to be made. His citations are often taken at second-hand from dubious sources, and he did not sift his acquisitions with the scholar's instinct [2]. He passes many a sharp remark on the rhetori-

---

[1] Clement was acquainted with Barnabas, Hermas, Clemens Romanus, with Melito, Irenaeus (Eus. *H. E.* vi. 13. 9; compare *Strom.* vii. 18. 109 with Irenaeus v. 8, and perhaps *Protr.* xi. 111 with Irenaeus iii. 22. 4; in both Adam is created as a child, and Eve is at first his playmate), possibly with Papias (but the μοναὶ ποικίλαι may come from Irenaeus v. *ad fin.* or elsewhere; see Routh, Papias, frag. 5) and Tatian. With Justin (or the author of the *Cohort. ad Gentiles* and *de Mon.*) and Athenagoras he has certain quotations in common. These however are probably drawn by all three from Hecataeus; cp. *Strom.* v. 14. 113. He has no knowledge of Ignatius or Tertullian. Of other books quoted I may name the Gospels according to the Hebrews and Egyptians, the Revelation of Peter, the Preaching of Peter, the Preaching of Paul (a distinct book), the Acts of Peter (?), the Assumption of Moses (*Adumb.* p. 1008), the Syllogisms of Misael, the Ματθίου παραδόσεις, Doctrina Apostolorum, Duae Viae, Enoch (*Adumb.* 1008), Sophonias (*Strom.* v. 11. 77). Others, the prophecies of Ham, Nicolaus, Parchor, &c., seem to be distinctively Gnostic. References will be found in editions of the Pp. App., Hilgenfeld, Bryennius, &c. I think it probable that he had read the *Homilies*. See Lardner, *Credibility*, vol. 2. A list of quotations from unknown Apocryphal sources will be found in Bishop Kaye.

[2] On the ἀκρισία of Clement see Dindorf, *Preface*, xxii. Even when he quotes κατὰ λέξιν there can be no doubt that hé is generally following some secondary authority, often dishonest Jews, Hecataeus or Aristobulus. Anthologies abounded at Alexandria, and often bore fanciful names, such as λειμών, ἑλικών, κηρίον, πέπλος, παράδεισος (*Strom.* vi. 1. 2). A mere reference to the indices will show that Clement's knowledge of the dramatists is not to be compared with that of Athenaeus. The lengthy passage beginning *Strom.* i. 21, with all its imposing array of authorities, is compiled from Tatian and Casianus. Lastly, though Clement refers to Varro and to Roman

cians [1], but at bottom he is himself a member of their guild, cloudy, turgid, and verbose. But Theology had not yet driven out the Muses. His love of letters is sincere, and the great classics of Greece are his friends and counsellors. Even the comic poets are often by his side. If we look at his swelling periods, at his benignity and liberality and the limitations of his liberality, at his quaint and multifarious learning, at his rare blending of gentle piety and racy humour, we shall find in him a striking counterpart to our own author of the Liberty of Prophesying.

Clement is not a great preacher, for he has neither acted nor witnessed such a soul's tragedy as that disclosed by Augustine in his Confessions. He is no such comforter for the doubting and perplexed as the fearless Origen. Still less is he one of those dialecticians who solace the logical mind with the neatness and precision of their statements. He is above all things a Missionary. For one thus minded the path of success lies in the skill, with which he can avail himself of the good, that lies ready to his hand. He must graft the fruitful olive on to the wild stem, and aim at producing, not a new character, but a richer development of the old.

This is his guiding principle. The Gospel in his view is not a fresh departure, but the meeting-point of two customs and history in four or five places, he seems to have been almost wholly ignorant of the West.

[1] They are ' a river of words, a drop of sense,' or like old boots of which all but the tongue is worn out (*Strom.* i. 3. 22), full of quibbles and disputes about shadows (*Strom.* vi. 18. 182 ; *Strom.* i. 5. 29). Clement says of those who give themselves up to Rhetoric, 'as most do,' that they have fallen in love with the handmaid and neglect the mistress. This last figure is from Philo, *De Congr. Erud. Grat.* 27 : the handmaid is Hagar, secular knowledge ; the mistress Sarah, divine philosophy. He disparages style, *Strom.* i. 10. 48 ; ii. 1. 3.

converging lines of progress, of Hellenism and Judaism. To him all history is one, because all truth is one. 'There is one river of Truth,' he says, 'but many streams fall into it on this side and on that[1].' Among Christian writers none till very recent times, not even Origen, has so clear and grand a conception of the development of spiritual life. The civilisation of the old world had indeed led to idolatry. But idolatry, shameful and abominable as it was, must be regarded as a fall, a corruption[2]. The fruits of Reason are to be judged not in the ignorant and sensual, but in Heraclitus, in Sophocles, in Plato. For such as these Science had been a covenant of God[3], it had justified them as the Law justified the Jew[4]. He still repeats the old

---

[1] *Strom.* i. 5. 29. So a drachma is one and the same, but if you give it to a ship-captain it is called ' fare,' if to a revenue officer ' tax,' if to a landlord ' rent,' if to a schoolmaster ' fee,' if to a shopkeeper ' price ;' *Strom.* i. 20. 97, 98. Truth is like the body of Pentheus, torn asunder by fanatics, each seizes a limb and thinks he has the whole ; *Strom.* i. 13. 57. This last famous simile is borrowed from Numenius, Eus. *Praep. Ev.* xiv. 5. 7.

[2] It was a corruption of Star-worship which God gave to the Gentiles as a stepping-stone to a purer religion ; *Strom.* vi. 14. 110 sq. This idea, which is also found in Origen (Redepenning, ii. 27), is based partly on a misinterpretation of Deut. iv. 19 (see Potter's Note), partly on the history of Abraham as told by Philo. The origin of Mythology Clement has analysed with considerable skill ; *Protrep.* ii. 26. But in general he hovers between the two views prevalent in the early Church. Sometimes he speaks of the gods, with Euemerus, as ' dead men,' sometimes as ' demons.' Athenagoras, Tertullian, Minucius Felix combine these two beliefs and represent the gods as dead men whose temples, images, and tombs were haunted by the demons for the sake of the steam and blood of the sacrifices.

[3] *Strom.* vi. 8. 67.

[4] *Strom.* i. 5. 28 ; vi. 5. 42 sqq. Philosophy is an imperfect gift bestowed οὐ προηγουμένως ἀλλὰ κατ' ἐπακολούθημα, *i. e.* not by special revelation but as a natural consequence of the possession of reason. Hence its righteousness is imperfect and preparatory, and cannot avail those who deliberately reject the Gospel ; *Strom.* i. 7. 38. It justified the Philosopher when it led him to renounce idolatry, vi. 6. 44, and carry his principles into practice, vi. 7. 55. But δίκαιος δικαίου καθὸ δίκαιός ἐστιν οὐ διαφέρει, vi. 6. 47.

delusion that the Greek philosopher had 'stolen' his
best ideas from the books of Moses [1]. But his real belief
is seen in the many passages where he maintains that
Philosophy is a gift not of devils [2] but of God through
the Logos, whose light ever beams upon his earthly
image, the intelligence of man. 'Like the burning
glass, its power of kindling is borrowed from the sun [3].'

It was not only a wise but a courageous view. The
Apologists had not as a rule been hostile to secular
learning, but they made little use of it. Pleading for
toleration, for life, to educated men they laboured to
prove that the Christian doctrines of God, the Word,
Virtue, Immortality, are those of all true philosophy,
that Revelation is the perfection of Common Sense [4].
But they did not go beyond this; their object was not to
set out the whole of Christian teaching, still less to
coordinate it. The Gnostics alone had attempted this.
But the Gnostics endeavoured to combine the Evangelical theory with wholly alien beliefs. Hence, rejecting
the Old Testament, they denied what all Christians

Christ preached in Hades not only to Jews but to Greeks; it would be 'very
unfair,' πλεονεξίας οὐ τῆς τυχούσης ἔργον, that the latter should be condemned
for ignorance of what they could not know. See for other quotations,
Guerike, Redepenning, *Origenes*, i. 139 sqq.

[1] Clement refers to the Greek Philosophers the words of our Lord, John x. 8.
Yet all their knowledge was not 'stolen;' *Strom.* i. 17. 87. But he maintains
the hypothesis of 'theft' at great length, v. 14. 89 sqq.

[2] Here too Clement vacillates. *Strom.* v. 1. 10 he adopts the doctrine of
the *Homilies* (or Enoch?) that the fallen angels betrayed the secrets of
heaven to their earthly wives. Elsewhere philosophy is a fruit of the indwelling of the divine spirit, the ἐμφύσημα, *Protr.* vi. 68; *Strom.* v. 13. 87.
Its doctrines are ἐναύσματά τινα τοῦ λόγου, *Protr.* vii. 74. Or it is given
by the good Angels, *Strom.* vi. 17. 156 sqq.

[3] *Strom.* vi. 17. 149. *Strom.* i. 5. 37 it is finely compared to God's rain
which falls upon all kinds of soil and causes all kinds of plants to grow.

[4] See Harnack, *Dogmengeschichte*, pp. 379 sqq.

regarded as the principal evidence of the Divinity of Christ, their Docetism reduced Redemption to a purely moral and intellectual process, their Dualism cut away the testimony of Scripture and of experience to the existence and character of God[1]. There arose a violent reaction. Irenaeus maintains that God has given to us two infallible criteria, our own senses and Scripture, and that all beyond is superfluous and fallacious. Tatian inveighs against the Schools with fierce derision. Hermias and Tertullian[2] assert with the Book of Enoch that Greek Science is the invention of devils, the bridal gift of the fallen Angels to the daughters of men. This opinion was strongly represented at Alexandria, which was indeed the hotbed of Gnosticism. The ruling party there was that of the Orthodoxasts, whose watchword was 'Only believe,' who took their stand upon the Creed and refused to move one step beyond[3].

Even in that age and place Clement saw and dared to proclaim, that the cure of error is not less knowledge but more. Hence he strenuously asserted not only the merits of Philosophy in the past but its continuous necessity in the Church[4]. Not merely does learning

---

[1] This argument against Dualism is nowhere so forcibly expressed as by the ingenious editor of the *Recognitions,* ii. 52 : 'Aperi nobis ... quomodo tu ex lege didiceris deum quem lex ipsa nescit.' *Ibid.* 60: 'Da ergo nobis ... sensum aliquem novum per quem novum quem dicis deum possimus agnoscere; isti enim quinque sensus, quos nobis dedit creator deus, creatori suo fidem servant.' Simon Magus replies that the sixth sense required is Ecstasy, and Peter in answer finely exposes the vanity of such a source of knowledge.

[2] See Irenaeus, ii. 26, 27; Tert. *Apol.* 35; *De Idol.* 9; Hermias, *ad init.* (cp. Otto's *Prolegomena,* pp. xliii. sqq.); Tatian, 25 sqq.

[3] The ὀρθοδοξασταί, *Strom.* i. 9. 45. He calls them also φιλεγκλήμονες, ψοφοδεεῖς. They demand ψιλὴν τὴν πίστιν, i. 1. 18; 9. 43. For a lively but malicious picture of this party by the hand of a clever unbeliever, see Origen, *Contra Celsum,* iii. 44–78.

[4] *Strom.* i. 5. 28.

grace the preacher, not merely does it impart clearness,
security, elevation to the convictions, but it is essential
to conduct. For Christianity is a reasonable service.
The virtue of Justice in particular is impossible without
intelligence. Science is the correlative of Duty. And
though Scripture is the all-sufficient guide, even here
the Christian must borrow assistance from the Schools.
For Philosophy is necessary to Exegesis. 'Even in the
Scriptures the distinction of names and things breeds
great light in the soul[1].'

Thus, however much the field of enquiry is limited by
Authority, learning is still indispensable as the art of
expression, as logic, as ethics, as sociology, as philology.
But the Alexandrines went further. They professed
and exhibited the most entire loyalty to the Creed.
But outside the circle of Apostolical dogma they held
themselves free. They agreed with the Orthodoxasts
that Scripture was inspired. But their great Platonic
maxim, that 'nothing is to be believed which is unworthy of God,' makes reason the judge of Revelation[2].
They held that this maxim was a part of the Apostolical tradition, and accordingly they put the letter of the
Bible in effect on one side, wherever, as in the account of
Creation or of the Fall, it appeared to conflict with the
teaching of Science. But though there is in them a

[1] *Strom.* i. 2. 19, 20; 20. 99, 100; vi. 6 sqq., 10 sqq. The Lord answered Satan with a play upon the word 'bread,' i. 9. 44, 'and I fail to see
how Satan, if he were, as some consider, the inventor of philosophy and
dialectics, could be baffled by the well-known figure of amphiboly.' For
the relation of Science to Duty see especially *Strom.* i. 9. 43; 10. 46; for
its service to Exegesis, i. 9. 44 sq.; vi. 10. 82.

[2] This maxim is enunciated by Clement, *Strom.* vi. 15. 124; vii. 16. 196,
and lies at the root of Allegorism. It is the guiding principle also of the
Homilies (ii. 40, πᾶν λεχθὲν ἢ γραφὲν κατὰ τοῦ θεοῦ ψεῦδός ἐστιν), and of
the Gnostics.

strong vein of Common Sense or Rationalism, they
were not less sensible of the mystic supernatural side
of the religious life than Irenaeus. The difference is,
that with them the mystical grows out of the rational,
that they think always less of the historical fact than of
the idea, less of the outward sign than of the inner
truth. Their object is to show, not that Common Sense
is enough for salvation, but that neither Faith without
Reason nor Reason without Faith can bring forth its
noblest fruits, that full communion with God, the
highest aim of human effort, can be attained only by
those who in Christ have grown to the stature of the
perfect man, in whom the saint and the thinker are
blended together in the unity of the Divine Love.
Hence they represent on one side the revolt of Pro-
testantism against Catholicism, on the other that of
Mysticism against Gnosticism. And their great service
to the Church is, that they endeavoured faithfully to
combine the two great factors of the spiritual life.

The Canon of Scripture had already assumed very
nearly its permanent form [1]. Gradually, with infinite
care and discussion, those documents, which could be

---

[1] See Dr. Westcott, *On the Canon*, pp. 354 sqq., ed. 1881 : 'Clement it
appears recognised as Canonical all the books of the New Testament
except the Epistle of St. James, the second Epistle of St. Peter, and the
third Epistle of St. John. And his silence as to these can prove no more
than that he was not acquainted with them.' Most of the references to
James given in the Index are doubtful. But in *Strom.* vi. 18. 164 there
seems to be a clear allusion to the 'royal law' of love. And the mention
of James with Peter, John, and Paul as the founders of Christian Gnosis,
Strom. i. 1. 11 ; vi. 9. 68, would be very remarkable unless James were
known to Clement as a Canonical writer. Again, Eusebius (*H. E.* vi. 14) and
Cassiodorius both testify that James was commented upon in the *Hypotyposes*. On the authority attributed by Clement to Barnabas and the
Revelation of Peter (both were included in the *Hypotyposes*), see Dr. Westcott, App. B.

regarded as possessed of Apostolical authority, had been
set apart to form the New Testament. And as the
circle was drawn closer, as the living voice of Prophecy
died away, so the reverence for the canonical books grew
higher, till they were regarded as inspired in the same
sense as the older Scriptures. But, as soon as men began
to read the New Testament as a divinely given whole,
they could not fail to be struck by the violent contrast
between the teaching of St. Paul and the whole system
of the existing Church. Down to this time no trace of
'Paulinism' is to be found, except among the Gnostics.
Even Clement apologises for treating 'the noble Apostle[1],'
as he calls him, with the same deference as the Twelve.
But he does so without hesitation, and the working of
the new leaven is seen at once in his view of Knowledge,
of the Resurrection, of Retribution. Indeed, we may
characterise this period as the first of those Pauline
reactions, which mark the critical epochs of theology.
It is the age of Irenaeus and the Alexandrines. But
while the leading motive of the former is the Incarnation, the mystical saving work of Christ, the guiding
principles of the latter are the goodness of God and
the freedom of Man. Hence Paulinism assumed very

---

[1] Ὁ ἀπόστολος, ὁ καλός, θεσπέσιος, γενναῖος ἀπόστολος. The passage
referred to is *Strom.* iv. 21. 134, Ἰστέον μέντοι ὅτι, εἰ καὶ ὁ Παῦλος τοῖς
χρόνοις νεάζει εὐθὺς μετὰ τὴν τοῦ κυρίου ἀνάληψιν ἀκμάσας, ἀλλὰ οὖν ἡ γραφὴ
αὐτῷ ἐκ τῆς παλαιᾶς ἤρτηται διαθήκης ἐκεῖθεν ἀναπνέουσα καὶ λαλοῦσα.

Clement maintains against the Ebionites that St. Paul is in complete
accordance with the Jewish Scriptures. At the same time he regards him,
like Origen, as one of the chief authorities for the use of Allegorism. On
the terms 'Judaism,' 'Jewish Christian,' 'Paulinism,' see Dr. Harnack's
excellent remarks (*Dogmengeschichte*, pp. 215 sqq.). Dr. Harnack also sets
the Simon Magus myth in a true historical light (*ibid.* p. 179). It is
cheering to notice the dying away of the wilful Tübingen theories, on
which so much erudition and ingenuity have been wasted.

different shapes in the Western and the Eastern doctors[1].
In the former the antithesis of the First and the Second
Adam is already pointing the way to the Augustinian
doctrine of Grace, in the latter the vision of the great
day, when' Christ shall deliver up the kingdom to His
Father, leads on to Universalism.

The second great question arising out of the completion of the Canon was that of the Unity of Scripture.
This the Catholic strenuously asserted, the Gnostic denied
or admitted only with large reservations.

What is the relation of the Old Testament to the
New? What is that Law which Jesus came not to
destroy but to fulfil? The Ebionites replied that it was
the Spiritual Law, that is to say the Moral Law, with
the addition of certain positive precepts—circumcision,
the sabbath, abstention from blood[2]. The general body

---

[1] Harnack, *Dogmengeschichte*, pp. 424 sqq.

[2] I refer to the *Homilies*. Circumcision is there regarded as of eternal
obligation; thus in the *Epistle of Peter* and *The Contestation* it is ordered that
the sacred books of the sect shall be entrusted to none but a circumcised
believer. In' the body of the work this condition is not insisted upon. But
Clement had become a Jew at Rome; iv. 22. The observation of the
Sabbath, again, is not insisted upon, but it underlies the ἐβδομάδος μυστήριον
of xvii. 10. The precepts of the Spiritual Law are given in vii. 4. Abstention
from blood was the law of the whole Church (see *Or. Sibyllina*, ii. 96; viii.
402; Eusebius, *H. E.* v. 1. 26; Tert. *Apol.* 9; Clement, *Paed.* ii. 1. 17;
Origen, *In Rom.* ii. 13, Lom. vi. 128). It was falling into desuetude in the
time of Augustine; see note in Heinichen on Euseb. *H. E.* v. 1. 26. The
Sabbath was kept as a holy day; see Bingham, xiii. 9. 3. It was still
necessary to argue the higher sanctity of the Lord's Day, the eighth day.
Hence the earnest iteration with which Clement dwells on the 'Ογδοάδος
μυστήριον, *Strom.* iv. 17. 109; v. 6. 36; 14. 106; vi. 14. 108; 16. 138.
In the last passage he argues that Light was created on the first day, then
follow six days of creative work, then the eighth a repetition of the first.
I may notice here that in one passage (*Strom.* v. 11. 74) Clement speaks of
the Law as actually forbidding Sacrifice. This is the view of the *Homilies*,
of Barnabas, ii. 9, of the *Epistle to Diognetus*, iii. iv, and of the *Praedicatio
Petri* apud *Strom.* vi. 5. 41. It is a good instance of Clement's erudite
uncertainty.

of the Church differed from this definition only in so far
as they rejected the rite of circumcision. But the Ebionites went on to declare, that the whole of the Old Testament, so far as it was not in strict agreement with this
standard, is a forgery of the Evil Spirit. They involved
in one sweeping condemnation the Temple ritual, the
history of the wars, and the Monarchy, and a large part
of the prophetic writings[1]. This was in substance the
view of the Gnostics also. These maintained that the
Author of the Old Testament is described sometimes
as evil, sometimes as imperfect, commanding fierce wars
of extermination, caring for sacrifice, governing by payment and punishment. He is Just, they said, at best,
but surely not Good.

Clement, whose intellect is penetrating but not systematic, did not grasp the whole range of the problem
before him. He leaves for Origen the task of dealing
with those passages, in which, as the Gnostics affirmed,
the Scriptures attribute direct immorality to Jehovah,
and confines himself to the proposition that goodness is
not inconsistent with severity, that He who teaches must
also threaten, and He who saves correct. Justice, he
insists, is the reverse side of Love. ' He, who is Good
for His own sake, is Just for ours, and Just because He
is Good[2].' The moral Law then, though inferior to the
Gospel Law, because it works by fear and not by love,
and reveals God as Lord but not as Father, is yet one

---

[1] Not all the prophets; see the references in Lagarde's edition of the
Homilies. In particular, Is. vii. 6, ix. 6 are applied to Christ, *Hom.* xvi. 14,
from which it would seem that the first chapter of Matthew was not omitted
by the Ebionites. This was quite consistent with a denial of Christ's
Divinity, as in the case of Theodotus of Byzantium ; *Philos.* vii. 35.

[2] *Paed.* i. 10. 88 ; the theme is dwelt upon at great length in this book
from chap. 8 onwards. Cp. *Strom.* i. 27. 171 ; ii. 7. 32 sqq. ; iv. 3. 9.

with it in the way of development, as a needful preparatory discipline, as a step in the divine education of the
world, or of the individual[1]. The rest of the Old Testament, though in one sense transient, has yet an eternal
significance as the shadow of good things to come, as
revealing Christ throughout, though but in riddles and
symbols. It has therefore a high doctrinal value for
those who can read it aright. Already the Sacrificial
Law was looked upon as the charter of the Christian
hierarchy[2]. But this opinion, so pregnant of consequences in later times, Clement deliberately rejects. In
this point he differs from Origen, by whom the Priest
and Levite are regarded as types of the Christian
Presbyter and Deacon, though even he does not carry
the parallel so far as was afterwards done.

The method by which this inner harmony is discoverable, the key to the riddles of the Old Testament, is Allegorism. What this singular system effected in the hands
of the Alexandrine Jew, we have already seen. By the
Christian it was adapted to fresh purposes—the explanation of Prophecy and of the New Testament itself. It
was in universal use, and was regarded by all as one
of the articles of the Ecclesiastical Canon or Tradition[3].

---

[1] For the unity of Inspiration, and so of all Scripture, see *Strom.*
ii. 6. 29; iii. 11. 76; iv. 21. 132; iv. 22. 135; vi. 13. 106; vi. 15. 125; vii.
16. 95; vii. 18. 107. The Law is inferior to the Gospel as teaching only
abstinence from evil, yet this is the way to the Gospel and to well-doing;
iv. 21. 130. The Law and Prophets taught in riddles what the Gospel
teaches clearly; vi. 7. 58; 15. 123. The Law governs by fear, ii. 6. 30,
and reveals God as Lord, i. 27. 173, a very Philonic passage.

[2] In the Testament of the Twelve Patriarchs. See Lightfoot, *Philippians,*
pp. 252 sqq.

[3] Origen, *De Princ.*, Preface, 8. Clement appears to distinguish between
two traditions, the Ecclesiastical and the Gnostic, the κανὼν τῆς ἐκκλησίας,
Strom. i. 1. 15; 19. 96; vii. 15. 90; 16. 95, 104, and the γνωστικὴ παράδοσις,

We shall be compelled to revert to this topic at a later period, and it will be sufficient here to notice, that the Alexandrines differed from their contemporaries in three important points. They regarded Allegorism as having been handed down from Christ and a few chosen Apostles, through a succession, not of Bishops, but of Teachers[1]. They employed it boldly, as Philo had done before them, for the reconciliation of Greek culture with the Hebrew Scriptures. And lastly they applied it to the New Testament, not merely for the purpose of fanciful edification, but with the serious object of correcting the literal, mechanical, hierarchical tendencies of the day[2]. This is in truth the noblest side of Allegorism, for here it deals with cases, where the antithesis of letter and spirit is most real and

Strom. i. 1. 15, or γνῶσις, iv. 15. 97. The latter was communicated by Christ to James, Peter, John, Paul, and the other Apostles, vi. 8. 68, but only to the Four, i. 1. 11 ; cp. iv. 15. 97. The former is the Little, the latter the Great Mysteries. The former gives the facts of the Creed, and Faith and Obedience, being 'watered' by Greek philosophy, lead up to the spiritual interpretation of the facts. See the opening of *Strom.* i. generally. The Gnostic tradition is secret in so far as all Christians do not as a matter of fact understand it, yet not secret in so far as all ought to understand it. Hence Clement, *Pæd.* i. 6. 33, denies that the Church has διδαχὰς ἄλλας ἀπορρήτους, while he yet speaks of τὸ τῆς γνώμης ἀπόρρητον, *Quis Dives Salvus*, 5 ; *Strom.* i. 1. 13. The difference between this teaching and Origen's is merely verbal.

[1] See *Strom.* i. 1. 11 ; vi. 9. 68.

[2] I may notice here that Clement speaks of Four Senses of Scripture. The MS. reading τετραχῶς in *Strom.* i. 28. 179 is quite right, in spite of the doubts of Bishop Potter and Sylburg. Compare § 176, ἡ μὲν οὖν κατὰ Μωυσέα φιλοσοφία τετραχῆ τέμνεται, that is to say into History, Legislation (= Ethics), Sacrifice (= Physics), and Theology or Epopteia (= Dialectic or Metaphysics). Here the three higher divisions answer to the branches of Philosophy as taught in the Greek schools. In § 179 Clement repeats this : ' We must interpret the law in four ways as giving a type, or a moral command or a prophecy.' The literal sense is omitted. The identification of Sacrificial Typology with Physics is very arbitrary. Theodotus, *Excerpta*, § 66, speaks of Three Senses, the Literal, the Parabolic, and the Mystical, just like Origen, but finds them only in the New Testament.

vital. Yet it was this crowning merit of the Alexandrines
that led to one of their most serious errors. On many
points—the explanation of those much-contested words,
Priest, Altar, Sacrifice, the Body and Blood of Christ,
the Power of the Keys, Eternal Life, Eternal Death—
they were at variance with the spirit of the age. Hence
they were driven to what is known as Reserve. The
belief of the enlightened Christian becomes a mystery,
that may not be revealed to the simpler brother, for
whom the letter is enough. They strove to justify themselves in this by texts of Scripture, but their Reserve is
in fact the 'medicinal lie¹' of Plato, the freemasonry of
the Gnostics, and their best defence is that in practice it
is little more than a figure of speech.

From the Unity of Truth flows the necessity of Revelation. For all knowledge must rest ultimately on the
same small group of Axioms, which cannot be proved, as
the Greek understood proof². There is then no third term
between a self-communication of the Divine and absolute
scepticism.

The ultimate and therefore, strictly speaking, only indemonstrable axiom of religious philosophy is that, which
concerns the Being and the Nature of God. By the
grace of the Logos He has been known though imperfectly in all ages and climes to those, who diligently
sought Him. But to us He is revealed in the New
Testament as a Triad³—Father, Son, and Holy Ghost.

¹ *Strom.* vii. 9. 53, of the Gnostic: ἀληθῆ τε γὰρ φρονεῖ ἅμα καὶ ἀληθεύει,
πλὴν εἰ μή ποτε ἐν θεραπείας μέρει, καθάπερ ἰατρὸς πρὸς νοσοῦντας ἐπὶ σωτηρίᾳ
τῶν καμνόντων ψεύσεται ἢ ψεῦδος ἐρεῖ κατὰ τοὺς σοφιστάς.

² *Strom.* ii. 4. 13; vi. 7. 57 sq.

³ *Strom.* v. 14. 103. The word is used by Theophilus, *Ad Autol.* ii. 15.
But it is doubtful whether Theophilus was the first to employ it. Cp.
Excerpta ex Theod. § 80, where it is said that the believer διὰ τριῶν ὀνομάτων

What is the exact signification of these titles? What is the precise relation to one another and to us of the Entities they denote? The answer to these questions was the first and most difficult task of Christian Theology.

From the very outset all Christian sects baptised and pronounced the benediction in the Triple Name. Even those, who could not understand, did not venture to abjure this authoritative formula, and the problems agitated, serious as they undoubtedly were, turned solely upon the manner of its explanation. Some like the author of the *Homilies*, and the Gnostics generally, tried to fit it on, by the most violent methods, to opinions derived from external sources[1]. Others endeavoured to reconcile the One with the Three, by what is known as Emanationism. The Son, the Holy Spirit, were occasional expansions of the Divine Nature, shooting forth like rays from a torch, and again absorbed into the parent flame[2]. Others, again, regarded the Three Names as three phases, or manifestations, of the One Divine Activity [3]. But the main body of the Church asserted

πάσης τῆς ἐν φθορᾷ τριάδος ἀπηλλάγη. The form of the antithesis seems to imply that the Three Names were already spoken of as a Trias.

[1] The *Homilies* afford perhaps the most striking of all external proofs of the authenticity of the Baptismal Formula. The Son, one of the two powers of God, is emphatically 'not God.' The Holy Spirit is a mere occasional emanation, 'a hand put forth' for the purpose of creation and then 'drawn back again,' xvi. 12; 15; xx. 8. Yet the sect which adhered to this Jewish ante-Philonic system baptised in the Triple Name, ix. 19, and used the doxology, iii. 72. The point is urged by Dorner, vol. i. p. 168 of the English translation. A widely different view is maintained by Harnack, *Dogmengeschichte*, p. 56; Scholten, *Die Taufformel*.

[2] The Son, Justin, *Trypho*, 128 (p. 458 in Otto's ed.). This passage is wrongly referred to by Bishop Potter, and apparently by Siegfried, p. 334, as giving Justin's own opinion. The Holy Spirit, Athenagoras, p. 48 of Otto's ed.

[3] Perhaps the Alogi, see Dorner; but Dr. Schaff (*Dict of Christian Biog.*, Alogians) doubts this. The Monarchians, Neander, ii. p. 295 of the English

the Deity and Personality of the Son, and, though with less unanimity, those also of the Holy Ghost, and spoke of the Three as united in Power or in Spirit.

The Christian doctrine differed from that of Philo in many important features. In the latter, as we have seen, a certain doubt hangs over the number and even the existence of the Powers. They are a divination, a poet's vision of what may be, of what must be, but hardly more. And, because they form an indefinite series, the Powers are essentially inferior to their source. The Divine Energy is degraded as it approaches the sphere of material existence, the Logos has the light but not the fire of God. It is because he is inferior that he is the Demiurge, the Eternal Himself may not be brought into contact with evil. But the Christian held that God made the world out of nothing, and made it good. Hence the concrete is no longer polluted, and creation is a mark rather of the exaltation than of the inferiority of its Agent. 'In Him was Life.' Thus there remains no other difference between the Father and the Logos than that between the One and the Many, an eternal antithesis, which in Clement's view implies the mutual necessity of the two terms, in that of Origen, who lays more stress upon the idea of causation, a distinction of dignity but not of nature. This mode of thought was immensely strengthened by the Incarnation, by which

translation. Monarchianism was especially strong in Rome, Eus. *H. E.* v. 28; *Philos.* ix; Tert. *Adv. Prax.* It is to be regarded neither as the prevailing view of the Roman Church, nor as a heresy introduced at a late date, but as an ancient opinion which had always existed side by side with the belief in a Personal Trinity. The incompatibility of the two modes of conception was not distinctly realised till towards the end of the second century. The chronology and details of the history of Monarchianism are very obscure. See Harnack, 564 sqq.

humanity is taken up into the bosom of the Divine, and
the deepest humiliation becomes a gauge of the Love
and Wisdom that prompted it.   Again in Philo there is
scarcely a trace of any Messianic hope, while, in the belief
of the Christian, Christ is at once the Giver, the Sum, and
the Accomplisher of all Revelation.   Other functions,
that especially enhance the distinction between the two
points of view, are those of Pardon and of Judgment.

On the other hand, in one remarkable point the ideal
of Christianity was in danger of falling below that of
Philo.   For there was a tendency in less philosophical
minds to distinguish between the unspoken and the
spoken Word, to conceive of the Son, the Divine Reason
or Logos, as at first immanent in the mind of the Father
and assuming hypostasis for the purpose of Creation[1].

It is at this point that Clement takes up the thread.
But it must be observed, that he is never controversial
nor even historical in his method.   His horizon is limited
by the Eastern world.   He never glances at Monarchianism, which was already perhaps the subject of fierce
debate in Rome.   Hence it is difficult to trace the exact
relation of his ideas to those of his predecessors or
contemporaries.

The knowledge of God is necessarily the starting-point
of the religious philosopher.   But how is God to be
known?   Philo dwells upon the lessons to be learned
from the order and beauty of Creation.   These give a
true though inadequate picture of Jehovah, and form the

---

[1] Philo does not apply to the Divine Logos the distinction of ἐνδιάθετος
and προφορικός.   It is employed by Theophilus, *Ad Aut.* ii. 10. 22, by
Tertullian, *Adv. Prax.* 5, and the author of the *Philos.* x. 33. Irenaeus rejects
these terms as Gnostic, ii. 28. 6.   See Baur, *Dreieinigkeit*, pp. 163 sqq. ;
Lehrb. der Chr. Dogmengesch. p. 105.

creed of the lower life, of those who have not risen above
the guidance of the Logos. But Clement knows the
world only through books, and hardly touches upon this
fruitful and persuasive theme[1]. For him the channels of
revelation are only Scripture and abstract reason. He
ought on his own principle to have regarded the second
as merely ancillary to the first. This however is far
from being his real view. Scripture gives us such an idea
of God, as is sufficient to start and guide us in our efforts
to attain moral purity. But purity is only a negative
state, valuable chiefly as the condition of insight. He who
has been purified in Baptism and then initiated into the
Little Mysteries, has acquired that is to say the habits
of self-control and reflection, becomes ripe for the Greater
Mysteries[2], for Epopteia or Gnosis, the scientific knowledge of God. From this point he is led on by the

[1] He touches upon it, *Protrep.* i. 5; iv. 63. But we should notice that
the *Protrepticus* is addressed to the unconverted heathen.

[2] The three stages are represented loosely by the three surviving treatises
of Clement. The *Protrepticus* is an exhortation to the heathen world to
turn to the Word, the Light, and leads up to Baptism. The *Paedagogus*
shows how the baptised Christian is further purified by discipline which
eradicates passion = τὰ καθάρσια, τὰ μικρὰ μυστήρια. The *Stromateis* as we
have them are a rambling account of the moral side of Gnosis. They
describe Book i the relation of Faith to Education; Book ii the definition
of Faith and its relation to Knowledge; Book iii the Gnostic virtue of
Temperance; Book iv Courage and Love; Book v Relation of Faith to
Symbolism; Book vi Knowledge, Apathy, the use of Philosophy; Book vii
description of the Gnostic life. The last two books conclude what he calls
the ἠθικὸς τόπος, and were to be followed by an investigation of the ἀρχαί,
the Gnosis proper. This he never wrote. The logical treatise which
forms Book viii may have been intended as an introduction to the Christian
metaphysics. Thus Clement never really reached the μεγάλα μυστήρια or
ἐποπτεία. See *Strom.* i. 1. 15; v. 11. 71; vi. 1. 1; vii. 4. 27; *Protrep.* xii.
118 sqq.; *Paed.* i. 1. For a fuller analysis of his writings, see Westcott,
Clement of Alexandria, in Dict. of Ch. Biog.; Overbeck, *Theol. Lit. Ztg.*,
1879, No. 20; and *Hist. Ztschr.*, N. F., Bd. xii. pp. 455-472; Zahn,
Forschungen. Other information in Fabricius, Dähne, *De γνώσει.*

method of Analysis or Elimination[1]. 'Stripping from concrete existence all physical attributes, taking away from it in the next place the three dimensions of space, we arrive at the conception of a point having position.' There is yet a further step, for perfect simplicity has not yet been gained. Reject the idea of position, and we have reached the last attainable abstraction, the pure Monad.

This is God. We know not what He is, only what He is not. He has absolutely no predicates, no genus, no differentia, no species. He is neither unit nor number, He has neither accident nor substance. Names denote either qualities or relations. God has neither. 'He is formless and nameless, though we sometimes give Him titles, which are not to be taken in their proper sense, the One, the Good, Intelligence, or Existence, or Father, or God, or Creator, or Lord.' These are but honourable phrases, which we use, not because they really describe the Eternal, but that our understanding may have something to lean upon[2].

The next step must obviously be to find some means of restoring to the Supreme Being the actuality, of which He has been deprived in this appalling definition. This Clement effects through the doctrine of the Son. 'The God then, being indemonstrable, is not the object

---

[1] ἀνάλυσις, *Strom.* v. 11. 71, or κατὰ ἀφαίρεσιν, Alcinous, chap. 10. The same method is applied by Maximus Tyrius, xvii. 5 sqq. See Lecture V *ad in.*

[2] The leading passages are *Strom.* v. 11. 71; 12. 81 sq.; vi. 18. 166; cp. also ii. 2. 6. God is ἐπέκεινα τοῦ ἑνὸς καὶ ὑπὲρ αὐτὴν μονάδα, *Paed.* i. 8. 71. But though this really means the same as ἐπέκεινα τῆς οὐσίας, Clement avoids the use of this Platonic phrase. God is or has οὐσία, *Strom.* ii. 2. 5; iv. 26. 162; v. 10. 66; Fragment of περὶ προνοίας, Dindorf, iii. 497; Zahn, iii. 40. Clement departs from Plato again in applying the term Infinite to God.

of knowledge, but the Son is Wisdom, and Knowledge, and Truth, and whatever else is akin to these, and so is capable of demonstration and definition. All the powers of the Divine Nature gathered into one complete the idea of the Son, but He is infinite as regards each of His powers. He is then not absolutely One as Unity, nor Many as divisible, but One as All is One. Hence He is All. For He is a circle, all the powers being orbed and united in Him.'

The Son in this Pythagorean mode of statement is the circle, of which the Father is the central point. He is the ideal Many, the Mind, of which the Father is the principle of identity. He is in fact the consciousness of God [1].

We are here brought into contact with one of the most pregnant thoughts of the second century. Clement it will be seen, though Philo is before his eyes, has taken the leap from which Philo recoiled. He has distinguished between the thinker and the thought, between Mind and its unknown foundation, and in so doing has given birth to Neo-Platonism [2].

[1] *Strom.* iv. 25. 156. If Zahn is right (*Forsch.* iii. 77) in ascribing to the *Hypotyposes* the fragment preserved by Maximus Confessor, Clement expressly denied to God any consciousness of the external world. He sees the object only as mirrored in the Son. This will then be the signification of the words ὡς ἴδια θελήματα ὁ θεὸς τὰ ὄντα γινώσκει. Routh (vol. i. p. 378) with better reason attributes the fragment to Pantaenus. But in any case Clement's meaning seems to be clear.

[2] The doctrine of the Absolute God Clement may have drawn through Basilides or Valentinus from Aristotle. The conception of the Son as the Father's complement, the νόησις which the Father νοεῖ, is not, so far as I am aware, to be found in any Gnostic writer. Contrast with Clement's language *Excerpta*, § 7. The doctrine of Numenius, as I shall endeavour to show in Lecture vii, is quite different. Nor can Clement have been indebted to Ammonius Saccas. For Ammonius would be only about thirty years of age in 290 A. D. Philosophers rarely began to teach before

It is essentially a heathen conception, and can be developed consistently only on heathen principles. Clement has gone astray from the first by his mode of approaching the subject. The question as he has posed it is, not what is Spirit? or what is the Idea of Good? but a very different one, what is the simplest thing conceivable? And he assumes that this is, and that it is the cause of all that exists. Nothing that is part of the effect can belong to the Cause. Hence, instead of seeking for the Perfect Being, he has fallen upon this futile method of Analysis, which deals with words not with things, and asks, not what is divisible in reality, but what is divisible in logic. The result is a chimera, a bare Force, which neither is nor is not, neither thinks nor thinks not, a Cause divided by an impassable gulf from all its effects. Nor has Clement been at any pains to surround his doctrine with the needful explanations and safeguards. This work he left entirely to Plotinus.

Some indeed of the consequences Clement foresaw. Thus he tells us that man may become by virtue like the Son, but not like God [1]. Others he does not appear to have felt at all. The transcendental God, who is not the object of knowledge, can be approached only by a faculty other than reason, by direct Vision or Ecstasy,

that age, and Ammonius, who is said to have been originally a porter, probably did not attain any eminence till even a later period of life. This renegade Christian was most likely himself indebted to Clement. On the relation of Clement to Plotinus, see especially A. Richter, *Neu-Platonische Studien*, Halle, 1867. Also Dähne, *De γνώσει*: Vacherot, *Histoire de l'École d'Alexandrie.*

[1] *Strom.* vi. 14. 114, it is impious to suppose (as the Stoics did) that the virtue of God and that of man are the same. 'Some Christians,' however, maintained that man by virtue becomes like God, *Strom.* ii. 22. 131. See Irenaeus, v. 6; Tert. *De Bapt.* 5; *Recognitions*, v. 23; Dähne, *De γνώσει*, p. 103 note.

F

but Clement does not teach this[1]. He believed in the
revelation of God by His Son. But what gospel has
revealed this Monad, how could He be revealed, what
good would the revelation do us if given, or how could
we test the revelation? The true conclusion from
Clement's premisses is the moral paradox, which has
been maintained with consummate ability from this
very place[2], that, as we can know nothing of God, we
must accept without question whatever we are told.
But he was far from thinking this, and his whole argument against Gnosticism proceeds upon the assumption,
that the Goodness and Justice of God are the same in
kind as our own. It is true that he sometimes draws a
distinction between having virtue and being virtue, from
which we might suppose that, like Philo, he regarded
the difference between human and divine morality as
lying in the mode of its possession. But this merely
proves, that in practice he denies, what in theory he
asserts, because to the Christian conscience God is, and
must be, not the Everlasting No, but the Everlasting Yea[3].

Clement's mode of statement is such as to involve
necessarily the Unity, Equality, and Eternity of the
First and Second Persons[4]. It has been asserted, that

[1] *Strom.* v. 11. 74. Direct Vision is granted only in heaven ; the instrument of knowledge in this life is Dialectic. See next Lecture.

[2] The allusion is to Dean Mansel's *Limits of Religious Thought*, the
Bampton Lectures for 1858. The reader who is interested in the discussion
of the point should refer also to the controversy between Dean Mansel and
Mr. Goldwin Smith, and to F. D. Maurice's *What is Revelation?* Cambridge,
1859 ; and *Sequel to the Inquiry what is of Revelation*, Cambridge, 1860,
with the Reply of Dean Mansel.

[3] The distinction between having virtue and being virtue is applied, not to
God but to the Gnostic, *Strom.* iv. 6. 40 ; vii. 7. 38. God is νοῦς ; *Protrep.* x. 98 ; *Strom.* iv. 25. 155 ; vi. 9. 72 : is good, just, beneficent, omniscient ;
v. 14. 141 ; vi. 15. 141 ; 17. 155.

[4] See passages in Bull, ii. 6.

he hardly leaves sufficient room for a true distinction of Hypostasis [1]. But, though he possesses no technical name either for Substance or Person [2], there is no doubt that the latter conception was clearly present to his mind. 'O mystic wonder,' he exclaims, ' One is the Father of All, One also the Word of All, and the Holy Ghost is One and the same everywhere [3].' His method of developing this proposition is determined partly by language inherited from his predecessors, partly by veins of thought afterwards seized and expanded by Origen. But he differs in a marked degree both from his pupils and his teachers.

Many of the phrases which he applies to the Son— the Name, the Face, the House of God, and so on—are borrowed from Philo [4]. From Christian writers he had learned to speak of Christ as 'begotten of the Will of

[1] Dorner, vol. i. p. 288 ; Cognat, *Clément d'Alexandrie*, p. 448.

[2] Substance is τὸ ἄρρητον, πνεῦμα, φύσις. But the word οὐσία is already emerging into use as the distinctive expression. See note above, p. 63. *Strom.* vi. 16. 138. Person is φύσις, *Strom.* vii. 2. 5 ; τὸ ἕν, *Paed.* i. 6. 42 ; and even ὑπόστασις, *Strom.* ii. 18. 96 : τῆς τρίτης ἤδη μονῆς (so we should read, not μόνης, as Potter, Klotz, Dind.) συναπτούσης ἐπὶ τὴν τοῦ κυρίου τετάρτην ὑπόστασιν. The third 'mansion' is Charity, which joining on to the Person of the Lord makes up the τετράς of Virtues. Potter is quite mistaken in explaining this obscure passage so as to make τετάρτη ὑπόστασις signify ' humanam Christi naturam quae cum tribus divinis personis numerata quaternionem quodammodo efficit.'

[3] *Paed.* i. 6. 42 ; iii. 12. 101 ; *Strom.* vi. 7. 58.

[4] Name of God, *Strom.* v. 6. 38 : Face, *Paed.* i. 7. 57 ; *Strom.* v. 6. 34 : Image, ἄνθρωπος ἀπαθής, Heavenly Man, *Paed.* i. 12. 98 ; *Strom.* v. 14. 94 : High Priest, *Strom.* v. 6. 32 : Charioteer, *Paed.* iii. 12. 101 : Pilot (perhaps directly from Numenius), *Strom.* vii. 2. 5 : Idea or Sum of Ideas, *Strom.* v. 3. 16 : Sum of the Powers, *Paed.* i. 8. 74 ; *Strom.* iv. 25. 156 : House of God, *Paed.* i. 9. 81 : Melchisedech, *Strom.* iv. 25. 161 : The Mystic Angel, *Paed.* i. 7. 56 sqq. Ebionite is the identification of Christ with ' the Beginning,' *Strom.* v. 6. 38 ; vi. 7. 58. Valentinian probably is the Angel of the Great Council, *Paed.* i. 5. 24, cp. *Excerpta*, § 43 and the representation of Christ as chief of the Seven Protoctists, *Strom.* v. 6. 32, 35 ; vii. 6. 143.

the Father,' as 'coming forth for the sake of creation[1].'
But to Clement such words could only mean, that the
difference of Persons is first manifested in their external
relations.   He rejects the distinction between the
Spoken and the Unspoken Word[2].   There was no
doubt in his mind as to the timeless Personality of the
Logos. 'If God is Father,' he says, 'He is at the same
time Father of a Son[3].' Again God is Just from all
eternity because the Son is in, yet distinct from, the
Father, so that the 'equipoise' of knowledge and love
between the Two is the first idea of justice[4].

He does not indeed shrink from giving expression to
the ministerial capacity implied in the very name of
Son.   In a famous passage of the *Stromateis*[5] all
rational existence is figured as a vast and graduated
hierarchy, like a chain of iron rings, each sustaining and
sustained, each saving and saved, held together by the
magnetic force of the Holy Spirit, which is Faith.   It is
the belief in the solidarity of all that thinks and feels,
which was afterwards the master-thought of Origen.
Father, Son, and Holy Spirit are succeeded by the
orders of Angels, and these in their turn by men.   If
we look upwards, the Son is 'next to the Almighty,' 'a
kind of Energy of the Father.' If we look downwards,
He is the Great High Priest, in whom all are reconciled

[1] *Strom.* v. 3. 16. Similar language is used by Tatian, *Ad Graecos*, 5;
Theophilus, *Ad Aut.* ii. 22; Tertullian, *Adv. Prax.* 5.

[2] *Strom.* v. 1. 6; Nitzsch, *Dogmengesch.* i. 203; Redepenning, *Origenes*,
i. 112. But Zahn, *Forsch.* iii. 145 note; Harnack, *Dogmengesch.* 531 note,
explain the passage differently. In *Strom.* vii. 2. 5, the words οὐκ ἀπο-
τεμνόμενος imply a rejection of the word προβολή by which the Generation
of the Son was sometimes described.

[3] *Strom.* v. 1. 1.

[4] See the three remarkable passages, *Paed.* i. 8. 71, 74; 10. 88.

[5] vii. 2. 9.

to God. But the idea of subordination is strictly secondary in Clement. The text 'none is good save One' does not mean to him, what it meant to his scholar[1]. Always he recurs to the essential Unity of the Father and the Son. He has no scruple about prayer to the latter[2]. 'Let us pray to the Word—Be propitious, O Teacher of thy children, Father, Charioteer of Israel, Son and Father, Lord who art Both.' So complete is the union, that he does not hesitate to transfer to the Son the peculiar titles of the Father. If the one is 'beyond all intelligible,' so also is the other, if the one is Almighty, so also is the other, and, following the example of Philo and Justin, Clement applies to the Son passages of the Old Testament, where Lord is employed as the substitute for Jehovah[3].

[1] *Paed.* i. 8. 74.

[2] *Paed.* iii. 12. 101 ; *Strom.* vii. 12. 72. See also the first Hymn to the Saviour Christ appended to the Pedagogue. It is probably genuine; Redepenning, i. 121.

[3] The Son is ἐπέκεινα τοῦ νοητοῦ, *Strom.* v. 6. 38. He is παντοκράτωρ, *Paed.* i. 5. 24; iii. 7. 39 ; *Protrep.* viii. 81 ; *Strom.* iv. 3. 148 : κύριος, *Paed.* i. 7. 56, 57 : the Father alone is perfect, for in Him is the Son, and in the Son the Father, *Paed.* i. 7. 53. The passages usually quoted as showing Clement's tendency to Subordinationism are *Strom.* vii. 1. 2, πρεσβύτερον ἐν γενέσει ; vii. 2. 5, the Father is ὁ μόνος παντοκράτωρ ; *Strom.* v. 1. 6, the Son is a δύναμις, vii. 2. 8 an ἐνέργεια, *Paed.* iii. 1. 2 a διάκονος of the Father; *Protrep.* x. 110 He is made equal to the Father ; *Paed.* iii. 12. 98 He is the ἀγαθὸν βούλημα of the Father ; *Strom.* vi. 7. 59 Creation runs up to the Father, Redemption to the Son. Rufinus, *Epil. in Apol. Pamphili,* Clement sometimes ' filium Dei creaturam dicit.' This must refer to the word κτίζειν used of Wisdom (Prov. viii. 22), *Strom.* v. 14. 89. Even ποιεῖν might be used, *Strom.* vi. 7. 58 (in a quotation from the Πέτρου κήρ.), ὃς ἀρχὴν τῶν ἁπάντων ἐποίησεν. Cp. *Adumb. in* 1 *Joan.* p. 1009, ' hae namque primitivae virtutes ac primo creatae ' of the Son and Holy Spirit. On the interpretation of this passage of the Book of Proverbs, see Huet, *Origeniana,* ii. 2. 21 (Lomm. xxii. 176); Rosenmüller, *Hist. Interp.* iii. 216, 229 ; Baur, *Dreieinigkeit.* Bull and Dorner do not regard Clement as a Subordinationist. Huet maintains the opposite view. Redepenning occupies an intermediate position. The statement of Photius that Clement spoke of two

Down to this point the expansion of Christian doctrine had been facilitated by the speculations of Philo. But here the light of philosophy fails. Philo had no Trinity, unless the World be counted as the third term. Hence perhaps it resulted, that a certain doubt hangs over the Personality of the Holy Spirit in Hermas, in Athenagoras, and even in Hippolytus[1], not to speak of later times.

Clement proposed to enter at length upon the subject in a separate treatise, perhaps with a special view to Montanism[2]. But the plan was never carried out. Hence, though there is no doubt that he regarded the Spirit as a distinct hypostasis[3], we cannot state with precision how he considered the Third Person to be related to the First and Second. It is the Holy Spirit, equally with the Logos, who speaks by the Prophets[4]. It is He, as we have seen, who binds together the Church Visible and Invisible[5]. It is He whose 'dew' washes away our sins, and sanctifies both soul and body[6]. Out of this last office of sanctification arises the only point, that Clement has deemed it needful to define. The Third Person of the Platonic Trinity is the World Spirit, of which the soul of man is a part or effluence. Clement is jealous of the slightest approach to Pantheism, and takes occasion more than once to warn his readers, that the Holy Spirit, though

Logi must rest upon a blunder ; see Dr. Westcott, *Clement of Alexandria*, in Dict. Christ. Biog.; Zahn, *Forsch.* iii. 144 ; and Lect. viii.

[1] See the commentators on Hermas, *Sim.* v. 6 ; Athenag. *Supplicatio*, 10 ; Hippolytus, *Contra Noetum*, 14. p. 52, ed. Lagarde. The author of the *Philosophumena* in the sketch of vital Christian doctrine with which he concludes his work omits all mention of the Holy Spirit.

[2] *Strom.* v. 13. 88.

[3] *Paed.* i. 6. 42 ; iii. 12. 101 ; *Strom.* v. 14. 103 ; vii. 2. 9 ; Redepenning, i. 122 ; Guerike, ii. 134.

[4] *Protrep.* i. 8 ; viii. 79.   [5] *Strom.* vii. 2. 9.

[6] *Quis D. Salvus*, 34 ; *Strom.* iv. 26. 163.

said to be breathed into the believer, is present in the
soul not as a part of God, not in essence, but in power.
What he means he explains by a quotation from the
Apostolic Barnabas. 'Wherefore in us as in a temple
God truly dwells. But how? By the word of His faith,
by the calling of His promise, by the wisdom of His
statutes, by the precepts of His doctrine[1].'

We have yet to speak of the Incarnation and the
redeeming work of Jesus.

The Word, the whole Word, took flesh of the Virgin
Mary, and became Man. Jesus alone is both God and
Man[2]. He who is God became Man, that we might
become gods[3]. It has been doubted whether Clement
ascribed to the Lord a human soul, but without reason,
for it is the soul of Jesus that was our Ransom[4]. But
His Flesh was not wholly like ours, inasmuch as it was
exempt from all carnal desires and emotions, even the
most necessary and innocent[5]. And as his Platonic dis-

---

[1] *Strom.* vii. 14. 87 ; vi. 16. 138 ; ii. 20. 117 ; v. 13. 88.

[2] See esp. *Strom.* iii. 17. 102 ; *Protrep.* i. 7 ; x. 106 ; *Quis D. Salvus*,
37. In the last very striking passage the words τὸ ἄρρητον αὐτοῦ πατήρ, τὸ
δὲ ἡμῖν συμπαθὲς γέγονε μήτηρ refer to the Eternal Generation, from which
Clement passes on to the Incarnation.

[3] *Protr.* i. 8 ; cp. *Strom.* iv. 23. 152 ; vii. 3. 13; 10. 56 ; 13. 82, referring
to John x. 34. The same strong phrase is used by the author of the *Philos.*
x. 34, γέγονας γὰρ θεός . . . οὐ γὰρ πτωχεύει θεὸς καὶ σὲ θεὸν ποιήσας εἰς
δόξαν αὐτοῦ. It is a favourite with Origen also.

[4] Redepenning, i. 401 : 'Clemens nur von einer Verbindung des Logos mit
einem menschlichen Körper ohne Seele weiss.' But *Paed.* i. 2. 4, He is
ἀπαθὴς τὴν ψυχήν ; cp. *ibid.* i. 9. 85, ὁ τὸ μέγιστον ὑπὲρ ἡμῶν τὴν ψυχὴν
αὐτοῦ ἐπιδιδούς, and *Q. D. S.* 37. Clement probably held with Origen that
the Ransom was specially the Soul and not the Body of Christ.

[5] *Strom.* vi. 9. 71, He was ἀπαξαπλῶς ἀπαθής, and ate and drank only to
forestall Docetism. *Strom.* iii. 7. 59 the opinion of Valentinus is quoted,
apparently with approval. Indeed the view of Clement differs but little
from that of Valentinus and Apelles, who held that the Saviour's body was
propriae qualitatis, Tert. *de Res. Carnis*, 2 ; *Adv. Marc.* iii. 11 ; *Philos.* vii.

like of the body has led Clement here, though no
Docetist, perilously near to the confines of Docetism,
so another Platonic theory, that all suffering is corrective,
has induced him to speak of the Passion of Jesus as
undesigned by God. 'We must say then that God did
not prevent it, for this alone saves both the providence
and the goodness of God.' But in truth Clement has
saved neither. What he has done is to introduce dis-
sension into the counsels of the Most High [1].

Clement's Christology is often spoken of as meagre
and unsatisfactory. In one aspect this is unjust. For
Clement's idea of the Saviour is larger and nobler—may
we say less conventional?—than that of any other doctor
of the Church. Christ is the Light that broods over all
history, and lighteth every man that cometh into the
world. All that there is upon earth of beauty, truth,
goodness, all that distinguishes the civilised man from
the savage, the savage from the beasts, is His gift. No
later writer has so serene and hopeful a view of human
nature as Clement, and though this may seem to depress
his estimate of the Redeemer, it surely exalts in the
same measure his belief in the fostering bounty of the
Eternal Word. Especially is the goodness of Christ
manifested towards His Church, to whom He has given
a life, and promised a future, which He alone can bestow.

But if we ask why the Birth, the Passion, the Cross?
why Jesus redeemed us in this way, and no other?
Clement has no answer. It may be urged that all

38. This was also the teaching of Theodotus, see above, p. 32. The curious
tradition recorded *Adumb. in Epist. Joan.* i. p. 1009 refers apparently to
the flesh of Jesus after the Resurrection, but it is doubtful whether this passage is not an interpolation. See Dr. Zahn's note.

[1] *Strom.* iv. 12. 86.

answers are but formal. Or that Clement speaks the
language of the whole sub-apostolic age. But this is
only partially true. The spirit of Hellenism lies heavier
on Clement than on others, and led him to draw a line
between the Cross and the Ascension, between the
'death unto sin' and the 'new life unto righteousness,'
which though it has connections with Scripture, is yet
not Scriptural. We shall see farther on how he regards
the Passion of our Lord, Redemption, as the source of
Fear and Hope, but most strangely not of Love.

By His death Christ Ransoms us from the powers of
evil[1], and bestows upon us Forgiveness, relieving us
thereby not merely from the punishment, or guilt, but
from the ignorance, which is the power of sin.   Forgiveness was undoubtedly a most difficult idea to the Alexandrines, who believed firmly in the changelessness of
God, and carried their faith in the wholesome necessity
of correction so far, that they admitted a quantitative
relation between the offence and its chastisement. They
held that Pardon can be freely bestowed only in Baptism,
and that the Christian should be taught to look, not upon
the Crucified, but upon the Risen Lord, the fountain not
of pardon, but of life[2].   Jesus again reconciles us to God.

---

[1] For the λύτρον, see *Q. D. S.* 37 ; 42 ; *Paed.* i. 5. 23, and elsewhere.
Clement does not say expressly to whom the ransom is paid ; see however
Protrep. xi. 111. Distinguish from ἀπολύτρωσις, complete emancipation
from sin, perfected only in the other life, *Strom.* vii. 10. 56.

[2] The free pardon purchased for us by Christ is expressly limited to actual
sin committed before Baptism, *Q. D. S.* 40, τῶν μὲν οὖν προγεγενημένων θεὸς
δίδωσιν ἄφεσιν τῶν δὲ ἐπιόντων αὐτὸς ἕκαστος ἑαυτῷ. Cp. *Strom.* ii. 14. 58 ;
iv. 24. 153; 25. 154. Christ, as God, forgives sins, and then disciplines the
believer as Man, *Paed.* i. 3. 7. It should be observed that forgiveness in
Clement's mind signifies not merely the cancelling of a penalty, but the
cure of that ignorance which is the cause and strength of sin. Sin done
before Baptism, in darkness, does not necessarily imply badness of heart,

He is our Propitiation, but this word, which, if more than a figure of speech, is so supremely difficult, Clement leaves unexplained[1]. Notwithstanding his Allegorism Clement quotes few Messianic prophecies, and, in respect of typology, does not venture beyond the track marked out by Philo and Barnabas, except when authorised by the New Testament. Hence the only sacrificial title, which he distinctly applies to our Lord, is that of the Lamb of God[2].

To the Christian pilgrim, in the lower life, Christ manifests Himself as Physician, Shepherd, Tutor, Lawgiver, calming the fever of passion by gentle words of admonition or bitter roots of fear. This He does as Man, by virtue of His humiliation and perfect obedience

hence for this no remedy is necessary except light. In all other cases the penalty is itself the earnest of forgiveness.

[1] He rarely touches upon this aspect of Redemption. *Paed.* iii. 12. 98, καὶ αὐτὸς ἱλασμός ἐστι περὶ τῶν ἁμαρτιῶν ἡμῶν, ὥς φησιν ὁ Ἰωάννης (i. 2. 2), ὁ ἰώμενος ἡμῶν καὶ σῶμα καὶ ψυχήν. *Protrept.* i. 6, υἱοὺς ἀπειθεῖς διαλλάξαι πατρί : x. 110, ὁ καθάρσιος καὶ σωτήριος καὶ μειλίχιος . . . ὁ σπονδοφόρος καὶ διαλλάκτης καὶ σωτὴρ ἡμῶν λόγος. *Paed.* iii. 1. 2, μεσίτης γὰρ ὁ λόγος. Everywhere the barrier is not God's wrath, but man's impurity.

[2] *Paed.* i. 5. 24, Christ is ἀμνὸς τοῦ θεοῦ in respect of His innocence : *Strom.* v. 6. 32, He is the Lamb with seven eyes of Rev. v. 6 : *Strom.* v. 11. 70 ; vii. 3. 14, He is ὁλοκάρπωμα, in the latter passage ὑπὲρ ἡμῶν ἱερευθέντα : *Paed.* i. 5. 23, Isaac is ἱερεῖον ὡς ὁ κύριος : *Paed.* i. 6. 47, the blood of Abel is a type : *Paed.* i. 8. 61, Joshua : *Paed.* i. 11. 97, Christ is our ἱερεῖον : *Protr.* xi. 111, the outstretched hands of Moses are a type : *Paed.* ii. 8. 75, the burning bush foreshadows the crown of thorns: *Paed.* ii. 9. 81, Lot the Just : *Paed.* iii. 12. 85, ἐλυτρώθημεν . . . τιμίῳ αἵματι ὡς ἀμνοῦ ἀμώμου καὶ ἀσπίλου Χριστοῦ (Peter i. 1. 19) : *Strom.* v. 11. 72, the Tree of Life : v. i. 8, Abraham, the Elect Father of Sound, is the Logos (from Philo) : *Strom.* vi. 11. 84, the 318 servants of Abraham signify Christ (from Barnabas ; this is the only passage where Clement appears to imply literal inspiration ; 318, in Greek writing ΤΙΗ, denotes the Cross and the name ΙΗΣΟΥΣ) : iii. 12. 86, Land of Jacob (from Barnabas ; another very forced allegory) : v. 6. 32, the High Priest's Mitre signifies Christ the Head of the Church (adapted from Philo) : vi. 11. 88, David's lyre is a type : iv. 25. 161, Melchisedech (from Philo).

unto death[1]. Gradually He makes Himself known to us in the higher life as God, feeding us in the Eucharist, or Agape, with His Body and Blood, the sacred food of Gnosis, becoming our Light, our Truth, our Life, bestowing upon us the Adoption of Sons, binding us in closest unity with the Spirit, leading us on to the holy mountain, the better Cithaeron, the spiritual Church[2]. Clement speaks of Jesus as our High Priest, but only in the Philonic sense, as our Representative and Intercessor[3]. The idea of the 'Recapitulation' of all men in Christ as the second Adam, so fruitful in the brooding soul of Irenaeus, is strange to him. He looks upon Redemption. not as the restitution of that which was lost at the Fall, but as the crown and consummation of the destiny of Man, leading to a righteousness such as Adam never knew, and to heights of glory and power as yet unscaled and undreamed. 'The Word of God became Man, in order that thou also mayest learn from Man, how man becomes Gôd[4].'

---

[1] *Protrept.* i. 7, τὸ εὖ ζῆν ἐδίδαξεν ἐπιφανεὶς ὡς διδάσκαλος, ἵνα τὸ ἀεὶ ζῆν ὕστερον ὡς θεὸς χορηγήσῃ : *Paed.* i. 3. 7, τὰ μὲν ἁμαρτήματα ὡς θεὸς ἀφιείς, εἰς δὲ τὸ μὴ ἐξαμαρτάνειν παιδαγωγῶν ὡς ἄνθρωπος.

[2] See especially the fine outburst at the close of the *Protrepticus*, and the opening of the *Paedagogus.*

[3] *Protrept.* xii. 120 ; *Strom.* vii. 2. 9.   But *Strom.* v. 11. 70, though Ἀρχιερεύς is not used, Christ offers Himself to the Father as a θῦμα ἄπυρον, a phrase borrowed from Euripides, 'the scenic philosopher.' In v. 10. 66 He is the ἄπορον θῦμα of Plato, *Rep.* ii. p. 378 A. So closely are Clement's reminiscences of the Classics intertwined with his theology.

[4] *Protrept.* i. 8.   The reader will find it instructive to compare with this sketch of the Christology of Clement, Dr. Harnack's account of the teaching of Irenaeus, *Dogmengeschichte*, p. 478 sqq.

LECTURE III.

And now abideth faith, hope, charity, these three: but the greatest of these is charity.—1 COR. xiii. 13.

CLEMENT did not admit the pre-existence of the soul or the eternity of Matter [1], but in other respects followed closely the Philonic view of Creation. God of His goodness and love created the world of Ideas, the invisible heaven and earth, and in accordance with this divine model the Word gave shape and substance to the material universe [2]. The six days are not to be understood literally. They express in an allegory the differing dignity of the things recorded to have been created on each in succession [3]. The pre-eminence of Man is further shown by the fact, that he was not called into existence by a mere command, but moulded, if we may so speak, by the very hands of God [4], who breathed into his nostrils the 'spirit,' or 'intellect,' the 'sovereign faculty' of the tripartite soul [5]. Thus Man received at

---

[1] The eternity of matter is denied, *Strom.* v. 14. 89. The pre-existence of the soul is rejected, *Strom.* iii. 13. 93; iv. 26. 167; *Eclogae Proph.* § 17. Yet it appears to be implied, *Q. D. S.* 33, 36; *Strom.* vii. 2. 9.

[2] *Strom.* v. 6. 39; 14. 93 sq.

[3] *Strom.* vi. 16. 142.

[4] *Paed.* i. 3. 7.

[5] Clement analyses the ψυχή, *a.* philosophically into ἐπιθυμία, θυμός and λογισμός from the ethical point of view, *Strom.* iii. 10. 68, and into the τρία μέτρα or κριτήρια, αἴσθησις, λόγος, νοῦς from the logical, *Strom.* ii. 11. 50 (the latter is from Philo, see Potter's note); *b.* theologically, *Strom.* vi. 16. 134 sqq., into ten parts, corresponding mystically to the Decalogue. From the point of view of the New Testament these ten faculties may be summed up in two, the δισσὰ πνεύματα. The first σάρξ, σαρκικὸν πνεῦμα, τὸ ὑποκείμενον, the animal and emotional nature, is actually materialised

birth the 'image,' and may acquire by a virtuous life the 'likeness,' of God, or rather of the Son. The 'image,' the Reason, may be blurred and defaced, but can never be wholly destroyed. It is the 'love-charm,' which makes Man dear to God for his own sake [1]. It is the fountain of that natural yearning, which makes the child always unhappy, when banished from his Father's home. It is by this that he receives, understands, recognises his Father's voice.

But here there arises a difficulty, which had never before been felt in all its force. If God made all things out of nothing, what is the cause of Evil? According to the heathen Platonist, and even in the eyes of Philo, it was Matter. God's purpose was limited and frustrated by the nature of the substance, on which He was compelled to work. The Gnostics carried this view so far as to maintain, that creation was the act of a rebellious spirit, who mingled together things that ought to have been kept apart. But the Christian believed that Matter, as well as Form, was created by God. How then were the imperfections of the universe, pain, sin, waste, inequality, to be accounted for? They can be no

by sin and is cast off in heaven, *Strom.* v. 6. 52 ; the second is the πνεῦμα proper, the νοῦς or λόγος in Platonic, the ἡγεμονικόν in Stoic, the ἐμφύσημα in Philonic language. In the latter consists the likeness to God, or rather to the Son; *Protrept.* x. 98 ; *Paed.* i. 3. 7 ; *Strom.* ii. 19. 102 ; v. 13. 87 ; vi. 9. 72. It is to be distinguished from the Holy Spirit which is said προσεπιπνεῖσθαι, *Strom.* v. 13. 88. M. Denis is quite mistaken in ascribing the error of Tatian to Clement, *Philosophie d'Origène,* p. 225.

[1] *Paed.* i. 3. 7, the ἐμφύσημα is a φίλτρον which makes man dear to God for his own sake. See also *Protrept.* x. 100, πέφυκε γὰρ ἄλλως ὁ ἄνθρωπος οἰκείως ἔχειν πρὸς θεόν : *Strom.* v. 13. 87, man has an ἔμφασις θεοῦ φυσική. But on the other hand, *Strom.* ii. 16. 74, God has no φυσικὴ σχέσις with man. Man's spirit is not a part of God as on the Pantheistic theory. Otherwise He would be partaker in our sins.

part of the intention of Him, who gave all things being because He is Good.

Here again Clement does not grasp the whole range of the problem. He is not affected by the disorder of external Nature, as was the troubled and far-glancing spirit of Origen. To the former all that seems to demand explanation is the existence of Sin, and for this he found an adequate reason in the Freedom of the Human Will.

This conception is as new as the difficulty out of which it sprang. It is to be found in the Apologists, but the Alexandrines were the first to define it and make it the foundation of a system.

St. Paul speaks of Freedom from conflicting motives, but never of Freedom of the Will. There are those who being servants of sin are free from righteousness, those again who being free from sin are servants to God. Between these stand a third class, who are in bondage yet longing to break their fetters—'to will is present with me, but how to perform that which is good I find not.' This is in fact the doctrine of the Platonist, who held that the soul has two instinctive and antagonistic movements, that of Reason towards the Ideal and that of Sense towards Gratification, and that the man is then only truly free, when his sovereign faculty soars freely towards the Good unimpeded by the clamour of Desire. In what sense Will itself is free the Greeks did not attempt to decide. Generally speaking they regarded it as the expression of character, and did not or could not clear up the previous question, how character itself is formed [1].

---

[1] The difficulty was felt but not removed by Aristotle. See especially

Yet precisely at this point, where Plato and St. Paul are in substantial agreement, the Alexandrines broke loose from their allegiance. There were strong reasons for this revolt. They had to account for the Fall of the First Man. This was no mere academical thesis, it was pressed upon them by an active, subtle, and formidable antagonist. If Adam was created perfect, said the Gnostic, he could not have fallen. He was then created imperfect, and in that case the Creator was the cause of his imperfection, and must therefore be imperfect Himself[1]. Closely connected with this argument is the Gnostic Dualism and their peculiar doctrine of predestination. At a later period, when Gnosticism was practically vanquished, Augustine did not hesitate to maintain that, though God predestines, He is yet not the author of evil. But to the Alexandrines this did not seem possible. Determinism in any shape appeared to them to impugn both the divine goodness and the divine right to punish sin, and though they held that in truth God does not punish, they would not acknowledge this in set terms. Hence they were driven to make Will an independent faculty, knowing both good and evil and choosing between them, selecting and in fact creating its own motive. The actual phrase Free Will, *Liberum Arbitrium,* is due to Tertullian, but it expresses with

---

Eth. Nic. iii. 5. 17, εἰ δέ τις λέγοι ὅτι πάντες ἐφίενται τοῦ φαινομένου ἀγαθοῦ, τῆς δὲ φαντασίας οὐ κύριοι, ἀλλ' ὁποῖός ποθ' ἕκαστός ἐστι τοιοῦτο καὶ τὸ τέλος φαίνεται αὐτῷ, κ.τ.λ.

[1] The Gnostics went so far as to assert that ὁ μὴ κωλύσας αἴτιος, he who did not prevent evil is the cause of the evil. The argument is retorted upon them with nnanswerable force in the *Recognitions,* ii. The Demiurge is evil because he tolerates evil. Why then does God tolerate the Demiurge? The difficulty was strongly felt by Clement, whom it drove to the assertion that Christ's Passion was not ordained by the Father, *Strom.* iv. 12. 86 sq.

Latin precision what Clement and Origen really mean.

No wise man will attempt to find a precise solution for the eternal antinomy of Freedom and Necessity. It is enough to point out what the Alexandrines did. In their recoil from Gnosticism they abolished Necessity altogether, and gave Freedom a new meaning. We can only judge of their action by its results. It has become possible to ask whether God can do wrong, and almost a heresy to speak of Christ as begotten by the Will of the Father. And already the door is opened for all the barren disputes, that troubled the Church and the Schools from the days of Augustine to those of Pascal[1].

Evil then in Clement's view is, not a Power, but an Act. It is not the Platonic 'lie in the soul,' nor the Pauline 'law of sin,' not a vicious motive nor a false belief, because these have no constraining force. Vice consists in acting the lie, and we need not act it unless we choose. Clement could not then believe in any inherited depravity of human nature. This follows indeed already from his opinion, that the Reason comes in each case fresh from the hands of its Maker. Adam

---

[1] Origen has formally explained the Alexandrine doctrine of Freedom in the third book of the *De Principiis*. Neither he nor Clement clearly saw what Jeremy Taylor insists upon, that 'in moral things liberty is a direct imperfection, a state of weakness, and supposes weakness of reason and weakness of love.' But practically they admit, as we shall see, that at a certain point in the upward progress Grace absorbs the Will, and that at a certain point in the downward progress evil becomes second nature. Thus the demons have sinned so deeply ' ut revocari nolint magis quam non possint,' *De Princ.* i. 8. 4. But this point of irremediable depravity, of complete ἀκολασία, they refused to fix. This seems to be the essential difference between the Alexandrines on the one hand and the Gnostics and Augustine on the other. Mehlhorn, *Die Lehre von der menschlichen Freiheit nach Or.*, Zeitsch. für Kirch. Gesch. 2 Band, p. 234, is referred to by Dr. Harnack, but I have not seen the article.

was created perfect, yet not perfect ; perfect inasmuch as
every faculty was sound and apt for virtue, not perfect
inasmuch as virtue was not yet actualised by obedience.
He fell by lust, and so we all fall[1]. There is no entailed
necessity between his sin and ours. But though Free
Will and Reason, both gifts of God, are enough for
guidance in this world, they cannot tell, us fully what
God is, they cannot bring us into living communion
with Him. 'Each of us justifies himself.' 'The true
Gnostic creates himself.' Men may 'choose to believe
or to disbelieve[2].' Yet Faith itself is a grace[3]; 'the
ball-player cannot catch the ball unless it is thrown to
him.' We are created capable of wisdom, goodness,

---

[1] The soul does not come from the parent, *Strom.* vi. 16. 135. For
the original estate of Adam see *Strom.* iv. 23. 150; vi. 12. 96. The
Serpent was pleasure, *Protrept.* xi. 111, and the precise sin may have been
that the first parents anticipated the time fixed by God for their marriage,
Strom. iii. 17. 103. Compare Philo, *De Mundi Op.* 55 (i. 37) sqq. 'Ita
vix alia Adamum primo vixisse conditione noster censet quam posterorum
infantes,' Guerike, i. p. 143. Clement does not admit any hereditary guilt.
For (i) God punishes only voluntary sins, *Strom.* ii. 14. 60 ; and again,
those sins which are not imputed are those which are μὴ κατὰ προαίρεσιν,
Strom. ii. 15. 66. (ii) The sins forgiven in Baptism are always spoken
of as actual sins. (iii) Infant Baptism, a practice which is very closely
connected with the tenet of Original Sin, is never certainly mentioned by
Clement. Mr. Marriott (article *Baptism* in *Dict. Christian Antiquities*)
cites *Paed.* iii. 11. 59, τῶν ἐξ ὕδατος ἀνασπωμένων παιδίων, but in this treatise
παιδίον is used of ' babes in Christ ' without any reference to age. (iv) In
Strom. iii. 16. 100 Clement replies to the Encratites, who forbade marriage
on the ground that the children are accursed, λεγέτωσαν ἡμῖν ποῦ ἐπόρνευσεν
τὸ γεννηθὲν παιδίον, ἢ πῶς ὑπὸ τὴν τοῦ Ἀδὰμ ὑποπέπτωκεν ἀρὰν τὸ μηδὲν
ἐνεργῆσαν. (v) The causes of sin are ὕλης ἀσθένεια and ἄγνοια, *Strom.* vii.
3. 16. Yet Adam is the type, though not the source, of sin, *Protrept.*
xi. 111. So also *Adumb. in Ep. Judae,* p. 1008, ' Sic etiam peccato Adae
subjacemus secundum peccati similitudinem,' where the negative is omitted,
as by Origen, in the well-known verse, Rom. v. 14. But I doubt very much
whether this passage, which goes on to lay down the doctrine of Reprobation
is from the hand of Clement.

[2] *Strom.* iii. 9. 65 : vii. 3. 13 : iv. 25. 157.

[3] *Strom.* ii. 4. 14 : iii. 7. 57.

G

felicity, which yet we can only attain by grasping the
Divine Hand outstretched to lift us up. 'Not without
special grace does the soul put forth its wings [1].'

The secrets of this diviner life cannot be expressed in
rules and formulas. But there is a point where grace
and nature meet, which is the proper field of discipline.
Knowledge must be gradually assimilated. Love must
creep before it can fly. Christ has revealed to us all
truth, but truth is precept before it is conviction. It is
by obedience to Authority, that the carpenter and the
pilot acquire their skill. So the Christian life begins in
Faith [2], that is belief in the desirability of the End, and
willing submission to the Means in their regular pro-

---

[1] The ball-player, *Strom.* ii. 6. 25. So in *Paed.* i. 6. 28 regeneration
is compared to waking or the removal of a cataract ; we open our eyes
and the light streams in. The words 'no man can come to Me except
my Father draw him,' Clement explains differently at different times,
Strom. iv. 22. 138 ; v. 13. 83. In the latter passage he quotes with approval
the saying of Plato in the *Meno*, that virtue comes to those to whom
it comes, θείᾳ μοίρᾳ. Compare also v. 1. 7 ; vi. 6. 45 ; *Q. D. S.* 10, 21.

[2] See especially *Strom.* ii. 2, 3, 4. Clement was very anxious to connect
Faith, the Christian watchword, with philosophy. Plato, who refers it
(*Rep.* vi. *ad finem*) to the τμῆμα τοῦ αἰσθητοῦ and regards it as unintelligent
belief in material objects, gave him no assistance, and perhaps helped to
mislead him. He found better definitions in Aristotle, *Topics*, iv. 126 B.
18, ἡ πίστις ὑπόληψις σφοδρά, in the προαίρεσις of the *Ethics*, in the Epicurean
πρόληψις, in the Stoic συγκατάθεσις. It is the faculty by which we grasp
the ἀρχαί. These to Clement are not, as to the Stoic and Epicurean, the
facts of sense alone, but the *a priori* data of deduction identified with
the articles of the Creed. Hence Faith in *Strom.* ii. 4. 13, 14 is an act
of νοῦς conditioned by αἴσθησις. That is to say, experience brings home
to us and ratifies the dicta of Revelation. Hence Knowledge and Faith
may be spoken of as in substance identical ; *Strom.* iv. 16. 100 ; v. 1. 2 ;
vi. 17. 155 ; vii. 2. 5. But generally speaking ψιλὴ πίστις is sharply
distinguished from Gnosis. It is the μία καθολικὴ σωτηρία, *Paed.* i. 6. 30,
or rather the πρώτη πρὸς σωτηρίαν νεῦσις, *Strom.* ii. 6. 31. But 'honour'
is more than salvation, vi. 13. 109. Faith is in fact the minimum condition
of admittance into the Kingdom of Heaven. But it is not full spiritual
life, *Paed.* i. 1. 3, ἴσαι δ᾽ οὐκ ἐστὸν ὑγίεια καὶ γνῶσις.

gression. But we can learn only within the school, and we must first be cleansed. Hence the gate of the Church is the Baptism of Regeneration. Herein we receive Forgiveness, the only free forgiveness, of all past sins, which leaves the mind like a sheet of blank paper, not good yet 'not bad,' we are brought within the circle of light, within reach of all wholesome sacraments and aids. We have started fairly in the race for the eternal crown [1].

Beyond this point stretches out the Christian Life, and here begins the most distinctive portion of Clement's teaching. We shall fail to do him justice unless we bear steadily in view the two influences that determined his path—on the one hand the love of St. Paul, on the other the dread of Gnosticism, a dread which did not prevent him from seeing that this peculiar form of error answered to a real and pressing need of the human mind. Gnosticism was in one aspect distorted Paulinism. The cure lay in a full and true presentation of the Apostle's teaching. But Clement only half understood

---

[1] The *locus classicus* on Baptism is *Paed.* i. 6. It carries with it a double grace, Forgiveness and Light. For the first see § 30, πάντα μὲν οὖν ἀπολουόμεθα τὰ ἀμαρτήματα οὐκέτι δέ ἐσμεν παρὰ πόδας κακοί. Light in a sense has been given before, for πίστις and κατήχησις precede Baptism. But πίστις ἅμα βαπτίσματι ἁγίῳ παιδεύεται πνεύματι. The gift is perfect, because it is the gift of the perfect God. That is to say, it is objectively perfect; our subjective perfection, τὸ τέλος, the Promise, Rest, is attained only in the Resurrection. It is a perfect gift at first imperfectly grasped. Clement gives no details about κατήχησις. *Strom.* i. 19. 96 he speaks of the οὐκ οἰκεῖον καὶ γνήσιον ὕδωρ of heretical baptism. The only ritual usage he mentions is that of giving milk and honey to the newly baptised at their first communion, *Paed.* i. 6. 35. See Tertullian, *De Cor. Mil.* iii; Bingham, xii. 4. 6; Probst, *Kirchliche Disciplin*, p. 321. Probst finds allusions to Confirmation and to a week of instruction and daily communion succeeding Baptism, *Sakramente*, pp. 159 sqq., 193 sqq., but they are very dubious. Infant Baptism appears to have been not the rule at Alexandria, see above, p. 81.

St. Paul, and in his desire to win back the sectaries he draped Christianity in a Gnostic garb.

He saw around him a system little better than the liberal form of Judaism out of which it sprang. The new wine was fermenting in old bottles, the Christian still trembled beneath the handwriting of ordinances. If we read the *Doctrine of the Apostles*, we find there a law which differs from the Mosaic mainly in being more searching and elaborate. The circumstances of the time were such as to confirm and even justify this legalism. Crowds were pressing into the Church, mostly ignorant and undisciplined, some rich and wilful. They brought with them the moral taint, the ingrained prejudices of their old life. We learn from many sources that the same incongruous blending of the Gospel with pagan superstitions, which recurred during the conversion of the Northern Barbarians, existed in some degree in the second and third centuries [1]. Discipline, teaching, supervision, direction, were absolutely necessary to the purity and maintenance of the Faith, and no wise man would attempt to weaken the growing authority of the Priest.

Yet there were those again for whom this atmosphere was not the best, devout souls whose life was hidden with Christ in God, men and women of cultivated thoughtful minds, who fretted under a system of routine and dictation administered, we may suppose, not unfrequently, by ignorant and fanatical officers. Social and

---

[1] See Münter, *Primordia Ecclesiae Africanae*, pp. 6, 68, 95. The curses on tombstones by which the grave was secured against violation were often copied with slight alterations from the formulas in use among Pagans. See Mr. Ramsay's article, *Cities and Bishoprics of Phrygia*, Journal of Hellenic Studies, Oct. 1883, p. 400.

personal distinctions were perhaps greater in those days
than they have ever been since, and in times of intense
religious excitement these distinctions shape themselves
into forms of character, which, though held together by
the most powerful of all bands, are yet as different as it
is possible for children of the same family to be.   Nowhere do we see this more clearly than in the history of
the Martyrs.   There were those who died, as Polycarp,
Perpetua, Blandina, Christlike blessing their persecutors;
there were those who brought their fate on their own
heads by wild defiance, and went to meet it like Pristinus drugged to insensibility by the fumes of wine;
there were others again, like Peregrinus, who found
suffering for the Name an easy road to profit, and if the
worst happened to notoriety [1].   It was out of this diver-
gence of type that the Gnostic made his gain.   What
was the Christian teacher to do?   How was he to deal
with the spirit of discontent and disillusion which he
knew to be at work?   It was impossible to alter the
existing framework of the community.   But there might
be a life within a life, a Church within a Church, a quiet
haven for the spiritually free.

Had Clement written a few years later he would have
taken refuge in the distinction between nominal and real
Christianity, between the Visible and the Invisible
Church.   But he lived in a time of transition.   As yet
the ancient view that all the brethren were in process of

---

[1] For Pristinus see Tertullian, *De Jej.* 12; Münter, *Prim. Eccl. Afr.* p.
183.   The history of Peregrinus will be found in Lucian.   He was actually
a confessor, and it was not his own fault that he was not a martyr.   That
these were not isolated instances is clear from the earnestness with which
Clement maintains against Heracleon that even those who had denied Christ
in their lives washed away their sins by martyrdom; *Strom.* iv. 9. 72 sqq.

salvation, though shaken, was not abandoned.　Hence he
falls back upon his philosophy, and finds the solution in
the Two Lives of Philo, the practical and contemplative
Life of Plato and Aristotle, still more exactly in the
Stoic distinction between Proficiency and Wisdom [1].　He
thought he found the same idea in certain antitheses of
St. Paul's — the milk and the solid food — faith and
knowledge or mysteries—the spirit of bondage and the
spirit of adoption—faith and hope which are less than
charity.　There were indications in the Roman Clement,
in Hermas, in Barnabas [2], that pointed in the same
direction.　Other cherished ideas appeared to fit in—the
opposition between the servant and the son of God, between God the Lord and God the Father, between the
letter and the spirit, between the Human and the Divine
Natures of Christ.　Gathering all these hints into one,
Clement proclaims that the life of the ordinary believer,
that is to say of the great body of the Church, is a
lower life.　Its marks are Faith, Fear and Hope [3]—unquestioning obedience to the letter of Authority, a
selfish motive, a morality of abstinence from wrong.
It is the sphere of discipline, of repression, of painful
effort.　Its crown is Holiness [4], the negative virtue of

---

[1] See the description of the Stoic προκοπή or Proficiency in Seneca,
Ep. 75.

[2] Clem. Rom. i. 1. 2 ; 7. 4 ; 36. 2 ; 40. 1 ; 41. 4 ; 48. 5 ; Hermas, *Vis.* i.
2. 1 ; Barnabas, 1. 5 ; ii. 2. 3 ; v. 4 ; vi. 9 ; ix. 8 ; x. 10 ; xiii. 7.　In
Hermas and Barnabas the connection of Gnosis with Allegorism is clearly
asserted.

[3] *Strom.* ii. 12. 55 ; iv. 7. 53.　Sometimes he drops Fear, and speaks of
the ἁγία τριάς, Faith, Hope and Charity, corresponding to the three mansions in the Father's House.

[4] *Strom.* iv. 22. 135, ἡ ἀποχὴ τῶν κακῶν, ἐπιβάθρα γὰρ αὕτη προκοπῆς
μεγίστης : vi. 7. 60, ἡ ἀποχὴ τῶν κακῶν ἥν τινες τελείωσιν ἡγοῦνται καὶ ἔστιν
ἁπλῶς τοῦ κοινοῦ πιστοῦ Ἰουδαίου τε καὶ Ἕλληνος ἡ τελείωσις αὕτη.

Self-Control. It is a state of salvation, but not of peace
or joy. Above it stands the Higher Life, that of the true
Gnostic, the life of Love, Righteousness, Knowledge,
of serene and reasonable convictions, of glad and spon-
taneous moral activity, in which the spirit of man is so
closely wedded to the spirit of his Lord that there is no
more recalcitrance, and freedom is merged in the *beata
necessitas non peccandi.*

Thus Clement insisted as against the Gnostic that
purity is the condition of insight, as against the Ortho-
doxast that law is meant to issue in freedom. On these
two piers he built his *Via Media* the Christian Gnosis.
It is a compromise between the Church and the world,
but the later history of Catholicism is enough to prove
how inevitable is such a concession to a body that will
govern and yet purify society.

As against the Gnostic, again, Clement protests that
the Two Lives are not divided by any law of nature.
The one must and should grow out of the other, the one
is incomplete without the other. All men, all women are
called, as he says, 'to philosophise [1],' to strive upwards
to the highest ideal. Yet the distinction in itself is evil,
and Clement has expressed it in such a way as to make
not a distinction but a real difference, a breach of principle and continuity. The spiritual life is one because
Love, its root, is one. But this Faith, which in the
Lower Life leads through Fear and Hope to Love, is
itself not Love, but imperfect intellectual apprehension ;

[1] *Paed.* i. 4; 6. 33 : *Strom.* iv. 8. 59, 68; 19. 118–124.   In this last
passage he refers to Judith, Esther, Susanna, Miriam, and a host of women
famous in Greek story, but to none of those mentioned in the New Testament, and quotes from Euripides the character of a good wife as a pattern
for the Christian matron.

not personal trust in the Saviour, but a half-persuasion of the desirableness of what the Saviour promises[1]. The belief, the morality, the reward are all external. Fear and Hope are the life, not the outer husk which shields and protects the life till it is strong enough to act by itself. Clement has attempted to seize the Pauline doctrine of Grace without the Pauline doctrine of Faith[2]. He has superposed the Gospel freedom upon the Aristotelian theory of Habit, upon 'reasonable self-love,' upon the legal Christianity of his time, without seeing that between these two an entirely new element must come into play.

This element he has endeavoured to supply by banishing Fear and Hope from the Higher Life. 'Perfect Love casteth out Fear,' which indeed is not a motive but a check. But disinterestedness, which is what Clement wants, does not depend upon the presence or absence of Hope, but on the nature of the thing hoped for. That which was mercenary in its original conception does not become less mercenary because Hope is swallowed up in fruition. In Clement's view the supreme End of all is

---

[1] Clement partly realised all this. To the Platonist the νοῦς has an ἔρως for the νοητά. The spark of knowledge contains the spark of desire, and this is kindled to a flame by better knowledge gained through practice, *Strom.* vi. 17. 150 sqq.

[2] How little Clement understood what St. Paul means by Faith will be seen from the following quotations. *Strom.* vi. 13. 108, 'thy faith hath saved thee' was said not to Gentiles, but to Jews who already abounded in good works. vi. 12. 98, Faith is not good in itself, but as leading to Fear and Hope. vi. 13. 111, every act of the Gnostic is a κατόρθωμα, every act of the simple believer a μέση πρᾶξις. He constantly uses these Stoic phrases. vi. 12. 103, 'Faith was accounted to Abraham for righteousness when he had advanced to that which is greater and more perfect than faith. For he who merely abstains from wrong is not righteous unless he adds well-doing and knowledge of the reason why he ought to do some things and not do others.' iv. 18. 113, Love is the motive of the Gnostic, Fear that of Faith.

not Love but Knowledge, and this misplacement of the
Ideal involves an egotism which he vainly struggles to
escape.   He succeeds in placing felicity within the soul,
in the fulness of spiritual life, but he has not really
advanced beyond the point of view of Philo.

But Fear he has handled in a truly Christian spirit.
It is not the fear of the slave who hates his master, it is
the reverence of a child for its father, of a citizen for the
good magistrate.   Tertullian, an African and a lawyer,
dwells with fierce satisfaction on terrible visions of torment.   The cultivated Greek shrinks not only from the
gross materialism of such a picture, but from the idea of
retribution which it implies.   He is never tired of repeating that Justice is but another name for Mercy.
Chastisement is not to be dreaded, but to be embraced.
' The mirror is not evil to the ugly face because it shows
it as it is, the physician is not evil to the sick man
because he tells him of his fever.   For the physician is
not the cause of the fever.'   Still more evidently true is
this of Jesus.   ' The Lord who died for us is not our
enemy.'   Here or hereafter God's desire is not vengeance but correction.   In truth it is not He that
punishes, but we that draw chastisement on our own
heads [1].

The life of Faith, as he has described it in the later
books of the Pedagogue, is in beautiful accordance with
these maxims [2].   It is a life, like that of the Puritans in

---

[1] *Paed.* i. 8. 62, ἐκλαθόμενοι δὲ τὸ μέγιστον αὐτοῦ τῆς φιλανθρωπίας ὅτι
δι᾽ ἡμᾶς ἄνθρωπος ἐγένετο: *ibid.* 67, ὡς ἀληθῶς ἀγαθὰ πάσχουσιν οἱ δίκην
διδόντες: *ibid.* 69, αἱρεῖται δὲ ἕκαστος ἡμῶν τὰς τιμωρίας αὐτὸς ἑκὼν ἁμαρ-
τάνων, αἰτία δὲ ἑλομένου θεὸς ἀναίτιος.   For the mirror see *Paed.* i. 9. 88.
The same simile is found in Epictetus, ii. 14. 21.   It was probably a Stoic
commonplace.

[2] Clement's doctrine on the subject of Pleasure is to be found in *Paed.* ii,

Milton's youth, of severe self-restraint, but built on broad principles, not captious and not gloomy. It should be as the Stoics taught, 'according to Nature,' hence all artificial desires are evil. But Clement condemns on the one hand the self-torture in which some of the Gnostics emulated the Hindoo Fakirs, on the other the Stoic paradox that things external are things indifferent. Here again he is Aristotelian. Innocent pleasure is the salt of life. Wealth rightly used is a blessing. The first requisite is the beauty of virtue, the second the beauty of health ; Christ Himself was not beautiful in person [1]. Many thoughts are suggested by this charming

---

iii; *Strom.* iii. iv. His general aim is to moderate the antique rigour in favour of the wealthier classes. His leading principle is the ζῆν κατὰ φύσιν of the Stoics, but he rejects the older Stoic doctrine of the ἀδιάφορα, *Strom.* iv. 5. 19, and adopts the more modern distinction of external circumstances into προηγμένα and ἀποπροηγμένα, which comes to the same thing as the threefold division of Good characteristic of Peripateticism, *Strom.* iv. 26. 164, 166. His chief axioms are that pleasure as such is not to be desired by the Christian, and that to be 'according to nature' it must be strictly limited to the end which God intended it to promote. Hence the rule of marital continence, the prohibition of the use of the 'bones of dead animals,' ivory and tortoiseshell, of dyes, and artificial hair. No ring is allowed but a signet. There is a natural and an unnatural use of flowers. 'For in spring-time to walk abroad in meadows dewy and soft and springing fresh with jewelled flowers delights us with a natural and wholesome fragrance, and we suck their sweetness as do the bees. But it is not meet for grave men to carry about in the house a plaited chaplet from meads untrodden.' The stern prohibition of the use of cut flowers is one of the most singular features of primitive Christian discipline. It is hardly necessary to refer to the *De Cor. Mil.* of Tertullian. Art he disparages, but the signet may bear a simple Christian emblem, a dove, a fish, a ship in full sail, a lyre, an anchor, a fisherman. But he was quoted on this account in the Iconoclastic controversy as a favourer of Christian imagery, Photius, *Cod.* 110. Generally speaking, he gives innocent pleasure a liberal scope. 'Wine,' he says, quoting Plato, 'makes a man good-tempered, agreeable to his company, more lenient to his slaves, more complaisant to his friends.' He is much less austere than Origen.

[1] *Strom.* iii. 17. 103 ; vi. 17. 151.

and authentic picture of daily Christian life. We see the vulgarity and thinly-veneered barbarism of Roman luxury giving way to true courtesy and refinement. We see the Church, no longer oppressed by instant expectation of the Last Day, settling quietly down to her task of civilising the world. Already her victory is assured.

Those who have been trained in the school of Jesus the Pedagogue are fitted for, are imperatively summoned to a better service. Clement delights to speak of the Higher Life in terms borrowed from Eleusis. It is the Greater Mysteries, of which Christ is the Hierophant and Torchbearer. Such language is partly conventional and common to all the Platonists of the time [1]. Again it is intended to conciliate the Gnostics and the religious heathen, who had all been initiated, as probably Clement himself had been in his youth. But it is also connected with, and tends to strengthen, the unfortunate doctrine of Reserve.

In the Higher Life Faith gives way to Knowledge, Fear and Hope to Love, while Holiness is merged in Righteousness.

Knowledge, Gnosis, Clement has defined in words taken partly from Philo, partly from the Stoics. From the first he learned that it is the intuitive communion of the intelligence with the Ideas, from the latter that being science it is indefectible [2]. To the Christian doctor

---

[1] It is to be found in Plato himself and Aristotle (see Lobeck, *Aglaophamus*, p. 128), in Philo, and in Plutarch.

[2] It is ἕξις, διάθεσις, κατάληψίς τις βεβαία καὶ ἀμετάπτωτος, ἐπιστήμη ἀναπόβλητος. Clement uses the strongest language to express the union of the Gnostic with his knowledge; it is ἑνότης, οἰκείωσις, ἀνάκρασις, the ἀίδιος θεωρία becomes his οὐσία, his ζῶσα ὑπόστασις. He no longer has goodness, he is goodness, *Strom.* iv. 22. 136; 25. 157; vi. 9. 71; vii. 12. 79. This

Christ is not only the Sum of the Ideas, but the co-equal Son of God, and Gnosis therefore is the ' apprehensive contemplation' of God in the Logos, and not, as in Philo, of God above the Logos[1]. Yet there is a progress in the object of Knowledge, measured by the varying aspect of Christ, who in the Lower Life is manifested chiefly on the human side as Physician, Tutor, and so on, in the Higher chiefly on the divine as Light, Truth, Life. Holiness is the indispensable preliminary of knowledge, which is partly Theology, but still more the experimental knowledge of Christ. The Gnostic is the ' pure in heart' who 'sees God.' ' He that would enter the fragrant shrine,' says Clement, quoting the inscription over the temple gate of Epidaurus, ' must be pure, and purity is to think holy things[2].' He is the ' approved money-changer,' whose ' practised senses' are the touchstone of truth. His Faith has become Conviction, Authority is superseded by the inner light. To him the deep things of Scripture are revealed. He reads the spirit beneath the letter. In Christ he understands past, present, and future, the theory of Creation, the symbolism of the Law, the inner meaning of the Gospel, the mysteries of the Resurrection[3]. He sees the vital harmony of dogma with dogma, of all dogmas with Reason[4]. In a word, he is an Allegorist. Moral purity and assiduous study of Scripture are the only training

language is important as bearing on his doctrine of Grace. We have here the *beata necessitas non peccandi.* Again it entirely excludes Ecstasy.

[1] Gnosis is always *in* Christ; *Strom.* iv. 25. 155; v. 3. 16; vi. 9. 78. Nay, the Saviour *is* our knowledge and spiritual paradise ; vi. 1. 2.

[2] *Strom.* v. 1. 13. Another favourite quotation is from Plato's *Phaedo,* p. 67, οὐ καθαρῷ γὰρ καθαροῦ ἐφάπτεσθαι μὴ οὐ θεμιτὸν ᾖ.

[3] *Strom.* vi. 7. 54.

[4] The συναφὴ τῶν δογμάτων, *Strom.* i. 2. 20.

that is absolutely necessary[1]. But Clement well knew the importance of mental cultivation. His Gnostic still reads Plato in his leisure moments. 'He is not like the common run of people who fear Greek philosophy as children fear a goblin lest it should run away with them[2].'

Of Knowledge Love is at once the life-element and the instrument. For 'the more a man loves the more deeply does he penetrate into God[3].' But here again, most unhappily, Stoicism comes in, and casts the chill shadow of Apathy over the sweetest and simplest of Christian motives. Platonism also helped to mislead. For though the Alexandrines held that Matter is the work of God, they could not wholly divest their minds of the old scholastic dislike of the brute mass and the emotions connected with it. The first thought suggested by the Incarnation is Fear. Love is not of Jesus, but of the Logos, the Ideal. Clement could not bear to think that the rose of Sharon could blossom on common soil[4]. This was the price he paid for his Transcendental Theology.

Love makes man like the beloved. But Christ, like God, was absolutely passionless. So too were the Apostles after their Master's Resurrection. So too must the Gnostic be. Self-control, Holiness, has made

---

[1] The majority of the Christians had not received a regular education and some did not know their letters, *Strom.* i. 20. 99. Erudition is sometimes hurtful to the understanding, as Anaxarchus said, πολυμαθίη κάρτα μὲν ὠφελέει κάρτα δὲ βλάπτει τὸν ἔχοντα, *Strom.* i. 5. 35.

[2] *Strom.* vi. 10. 80; 18. 162.

[3] *Q. D. S.* 27.

[4] The most singular instance of Clement's disparagement of human love is to be found in *Strom.* vii. 12. 70, where married life is regarded as superior to celibacy because it offers so many more temptations to surmount.

the reason absolute master of the brute in the centaur man.   He will feel those desires which, like hunger or thirst, are necessary for self-preservation, but not joy nor sorrow nor courage nor indignation nor hatred.   He lives in the closest union with the Beloved, so absorbed in the Divine Love that he can no longer be said to love his fellow-creatures in the ordinary sense of the word [1].

There were many in Clement's own time who shrank from this too ethereal ideal, which, to use his own phrase, 'touches earth with but one foot.'   If we take away hope and joy, they urged, will not the Christian be swallowed up by the sorrows of life?   And if all union with the Beautiful is preceded by aspiration, how can he be passionless who aspires to the Beautiful [2]?   How can we rise without desire, and how can we desire the extinction of desire?   It is the argument afterwards pressed with irresistible force by Bossuet and Bourdaloue against Fénelon.   Clement replies, 'Love is no more desire but a contented self-appropriation, which restores the Gnostic into oneness with Christ by faith, so that he needs neither time nor place.   For by Love he is already in that scene where he will one day dwell.   And having anticipated his hope by Gnosis he desires nothing, for he holds in closest possession the very object of desire.'   It is the Love which we mortals feel 'in our diviner moments, when Love is satisfied in the completeness of the beloved object.'   So absolute is its content, that if it were possible to separate eternal salvation from the knowledge of God, and a choice were given to the

---

[1] The leading passages on the subject of Apathy and disinterested Love are *Strom.* iv. 6. 30; 18. 111; 22. 135–146; vi. 9. 71; 12. 100; 16. 138.

[2] *Strom.* vi. 9. 73.

Gnostic, he would without hesitation choose the latter. It is the paradox of Mysticism :—

> Be not angry; I resign
> Henceforth all my will to thine:
> I consent that thou depart,
> Though thine absence breaks my heart;
> Go then, and for ever too;
> All is right that thou wilt do[1].

Of this Ideal (for it is perhaps no more[2]) enough has been said. Clement no doubt overshot the mark. It remains to be seen whether by so doing he encouraged presumption, or led weakness astray. The answer is to be found in the rigour with which he insists upon Holiness as the indispensable condition, on Righteousness as the indispensable fruit of Love.

Like all the early Fathers he attached a very real sense to the word Righteousness. 'Ye were justified by the name of the Lord, ye were made just as He is, and joined in the closest possible union with the Holy Spirit[3].' It is not mere abstention from evil, which

---

[1] It was insisted upon by the Quietists. It is a paradox because the separation is impossible. The Kingdom of Heaven is within you. Milton makes Satan complain, 'Which way I go is hell, myself am hell;' and the converse is true also. But Clement knew this well; cp. *Strom.* v. 10. 63, τὸ δὲ ἀγνοεῖν τὸν πατέρα θάνατός ἐστιν, ὡς τὸ γνῶναι ζωὴ αἰώνιος. Nor did the Quietists think otherwise. Bossuet did not venture directly to deny the mystic paradox, which is in fact admitted in the Articles of Issy. But I must refer my readers to Mr. Vaughan's charming *Hours with the Mystics*, vol. ii. pp. 170, 217, 380, ed. 1856.

[2] Clement ascribes Apathy to Christ and to the Apostles after the Resurrection, *Strom.* vi. 9. 71. As regards men he uses sometimes very strong language. The Gnostic becomes a god upon earth, iv. 23. 149; vii. 3. 13; 10. 56: he is ἰσάγγελος ἐνταῦθα φωτεινὸς δὲ ἤδη, vi. 13. 105. On the other hand, *Paed.* i. 2. 4; *Strom.* iv. 21. 130; *Q. D. S.* 40, more sober language is employed; Christ is the only perfect man, passion cannot be wholly eradicated in this life, the wise man touches no known sin. It is the *posse non peccare*, not the *non posse peccare*. But Clement is less introspective than Origen. The mere frailty of human nature does not distress him so long as he feels that his heart is safe in Christ.

[3] *Strom.* vii. 14. 87. On Righteousness, see especially the fine passage,

is Holiness, the virtue of the Lower Life, but the free active joyous service of those who are sanctified. It is life which needs no rule. The Gnostic, says Clement in language very like that of Madame de Guyon, has no virtue, because he is virtue. Nature is absorbed by Grace. It is easier to do good than to leave it undone, hence 'good works follow Gnosis as shadow follows substance[1].' Contemplation is the Gnostic's chief delight, the next is active beneficence, the third is instruction, the work of making others like himself. God gives him an exceeding great reward, the salvation of other men[2].

Thus Apathy, Detachment, make the sanctified believer not less but more useful to his kind. It is important to add, in view of the objections afterwards urged against the Quietists, that Clement lays great stress upon the observance of the existing Church disci-

---

Strom. vi. 12. 102. Origen distinguishes two modes of Righteousness, Innocence, the effect of Baptismal Forgiveness, and the active virtue of Justice. Clement speaks only of the latter. The just man is faithful, but the faithful man is not necessarily just. Faith is salvation, but not righteousness; it gives the will, but not immediately the power to do right. Faith is life, righteousness is health (ὑγίεια). It would seem then that we might be 'saved' without good works, but Clement never expressly deals with/this question. He seems to assert the opposite, *Strom.* v. 1. 7, χάριτι γὰρ σωζόμεθα οὐκ ἄνευ μέντοι τῶν καλῶν ἔργων, but here perhaps σωτηρία is used in the sense of ὑγίεια. On the necessity, the 'merit' of good works, see *Strom.* v. 13. 86; vii. 12. 72; 14. 108.

[1] *Strom.* vii. 13. 82.

[2] *Strom.* iv. 22. 136. In ii. 11. 46 the three characteristics of Gnosis are θεωρία—ἡ τῶν ἐντολῶν ἐπιτέλεσις—ἀνδρῶν ἀγαθῶν κατασκευή : vi. 17. 160 the Gnostic is compared to a παιδοτρίβης who teaches in three ways, κατὰ παρακολούθησιν, putting the pupil in the requisite posture and making him do the thing required ; καθ᾽ ὁμοίωσιν, by example and emulation ; κατὰ πρόσταξιν, when the pupil has mastered all his exercises and simply requires to be told which he is to perform : the last may refer to spiritual direction : vii. 1. 3 the life of the Gnostic is a constant θεραπεία of two kinds, βελτιωτική, in which he resembles the presbyter, ὑπηρετική, in which he resembles the deacon. See Baur, *Christliche Gnosis*, p. 507.

pline, the regular use of all the ordinary means of Grace. I will not here dwell upon what he says about Public Worship, the reading of Scripture, the Eucharist, Almsgiving, Fasting [1]. It will be sufficient to state his views on the subject of Prayer [2], the point on which the Quietists departed most widely from the lines he laid down. The Gnostic prays without ceasing. He would rather forego the grace of God than enjoy it without prayer. But indeed this is impossible. For our holiness must cooperate with the providence of God, if the blessing is to be perfect. Holiness is a correlative of Providence [3]. For God Himself is a voluntary agent. He does not 'warm like fire' as Plutarch thought, nor can we receive His best gifts involuntarily, even if they be given before we ask.

But God reads the heart, and therefore few words are needed or none. 'Ask,' He says, 'and I will do, think, and I will give [4].' Good is the prayer which Christians utter in the church, with head and hands uplifted, and foot raised at the Amen, as if to soar above earth.

---

[1] Public Worship in the morning, *Paed.* ii. 10. 96: Fasting on Wednesday and Friday, *Strom.* vii. 12, 75. The Scripture says (Tobit xii. 8), ἀγαθὸν νηστεία μετὰ προσευχῆς, νηστεῖαι δὲ ἀποχὰς κακῶν μηνύουσιν ἀπαξαπλῶς: observance of the Lord's Day, *Strom.* vii. 12. 76: Reading of Scripture, *Paed.* ii. 10. 96; *Strom.* vii. 7. 49; Almsgiving, *Q. D. S.* 33; *Strom.* ii. 15. 96, ἐλεημοσύναις οὖν καὶ πίστεσι ἀποκαθαίρονται αἱ ἁμαρτίαι: on the Eucharist see below.

[2] See generally *Strom.* iv. 23. 148; viii. 7. 35 sqq.

[3] ἀντεπιστροφή, ἀντίστροφος, *Strom.* vii. 7. 42. The reference to Plutarch (an author whom Clement several times quotes) is *non posse suaviter vivi sec. Epic.* xxii, οὔτε γὰρ θερμοῦ τὸ ψύχειν ἀλλὰ τὸ θερμαίνειν ὥσπερ οὐδ' ἀγαθοῦ τὸ βλάπτειν. This will further illustrate what was said in Lecture I on Plutarch's connection with Gnosticism.

[4] αἴτησαι καὶ ποιήσω· ἐννοήθητι καὶ δώσω, a favourite quotation (see *Strom.* vi. 9. 78; 12. 101; vii. 7. 40; 12. 73) from some apocryphal book.

H

Good is prayer at the three hours[1], with face turned towards the East, as even pagans use. But better still is the inner colloquy of unspoken supplication for which no place or time is set apart, the praise of him who ploughs, of him who sails upon the sea. The Gnostic's prayer is chiefly Thanksgiving and Intercession, as was that of our Saviour. Beyond this he will ask only for the continuance of the blessings he enjoys, for he desires nothing that he has not, and the Father's Will is enough for him.

The prayer of the Gnostic, even when speechless, is still conscious and active. It is far removed from the blank vacuity of the soul which, as Molinos says, 'lies dead and buried, asleep in Nothingness[2]' — thinking without thought of the Unconditioned. The Silent Prayer of the Quietist is in fact Ecstasy, of which there is not a trace in Clement.

For Clement shrank from his own conclusions. Though the father of all the Mystics he is no Mystic himself. He did not enter the 'enchanted garden' which he opened for others. If he talks of 'flaying the sacrifice,' of leaving sense behind, of Vision, of Epopteia, this is but the parlance of his school. The instrument to which he looks for growth in knowledge is not trance, but the disciplined reason. Hence Gnosis when once attained is indefectible, not like the rapture which Plotinus enjoyed but four times during his acquaintance with Porphyry, which in the experience of Theresa

---

[1] *Strom.* vii. 7. 40 ; the Gnostic rose also at intervals during the night to pray, *Paed.* ii. 9. 79 ; *Strom.* vii. 7. 49.

[2] 'Endormie dans le néant,' Molinos, *Guide Spirituelle*, iii. 20. 201. I owe the reference to La Bruyère, *Dialogues sur le Quiétisme*, vol. ii. ed. Servois.

never lasted more than half-an-hour[1]. The Gnostic is no Visionary, no Theurgist, no Antinomian.

These dangers were not far away in the age of Montanus and the Neo-Platonists. The Alexandrines have perhaps too much 'dry light,' but their faith was too closely wedded to reason and the written word to be seduced by these forbidden joys. Mysticism is as yet a Pagan solace. The time for a purely Christian mysticism, which Gerson evolves not from the reason but from the emotions, had not yet arrived. Yet Clement laid the fuel ready for kindling. The spark that was needed was the allegorical interpretation of the Song of Songs. This was supplied, strange to say, by Origen, the least mystical of all divines.

Every baptised Christian, who has not been 'cut off' like a diseased limb by solemn judicial process, is a member of the Church upon earth, is therefore within the pale of salvation. The Church[2] is the Platonic City of God, 'a lovely body and assemblage of men governed by the Word,' 'the company of the Elect.' She is the Bride of Christ, the Virgin Mother, stainless as a Virgin, loving as a Mother. She is One, she is Catholic, be-

---

[1] Porphyry, *Vita Plotini*, 23, p. 116, ed. Firmin-Didot. For St. Theresa see Barthélemy Saint-Hilaire, *L'École d'Alexandrie*, pp. xlv, lxxix; for Gerson, *ibid.* lxii, xcviii. Vacherot in his third volume traces the connection of the Alexandrines with mediaeval mysticism. Dähne, *De Γνώσει*, p. 112, insists that Clement himself was a mystic. It depends upon the meaning which we attach to the word. In one sense all believers in the unseen are Mystics; in another, all believers in whom the emotional element predominates largely over the intellectual. I have taken Mysticism as co-extensive with Ecstasy. Of this again there are several degrees, ranging from the inarticulate communion of the Quietists to pictorial visions. Such visions were regarded with suspicion by Mystics of the higher class, such as St. John of the Cross. See Vaughan, *Hours with the Mystics.*

[2] *Strom.* iv. 26. 172; vii. 5. 29; iii. 6. 49; 11. 74; *Paed.* i. 6. 42; *Strom.* vii. 17. 107 (one, true, ancient, catholic), 108 (apostolic).

cause the doctrine and tradition of the Apostles is one; the heretic who has forsaken her fold has 'an assembly devised by man,' 'a school,' but not a Church [1]. One in belief, but not in mechanism. Peter is the first of the Apostles [2], but the See of Peter is never named. The West is as unknown to Clement as it was to his favourite Homer. Yet in this One Church there is a distinction. There are those who within her fold live as do the Gentiles, these are the flesh of Christ's Mystical Body; there are those who cleave to the Lord and become one spirit with Him, the Sons of God, the Gnostics; these are the Holy Church, the Spiritual Church; these, and they who are in process to become as these, are the rings which have not dropped from the magnetic chain, but in spiritual union with saints and angels 'wait for the Rest of God [3].'

The *Stromateis* were written during the Patriarchate of Demetrius amid the bustle and excitement of a revolution. But no echo of the strife penetrated the tranquil

---

[1] διατριβή, *Strom.* vii, 15. 92 : ἀνθρώπιναι συνηλύσεις, vii. 17. 106. The notes of heresy are contempt of apostolical tradition, vii. 16. 95, ὁ ἀναλακτίσας τὴν ἐκκλησιαστικὴν παράδοσιν, and defiance of Scripture, which the Gnostics reject in part, vii. 16. 97, παρεπέμψαντο τὰς γραφάς, or interpret by vicious methods out of φιλαυτία. Those who use only water in the Eucharist are heretics, i. 19. 96 ; and there is also a heretical baptism, *ibid.* On the asceticism and in some cases lax morality of the Gnostics, see *Strom.* iii. The 'Phrygians' are not called heretics, iv. 3. 93.

[2] *Q. D. S.* 21, ὁ μακάριος πέτρος ὁ ἐκλεκτὸς ὁ ἐξαίρετος ὁ πρῶτος τῶν μαθητῶν ὑπὲρ οὗ μόνου καὶ ἑαυτοῦ τὸν φόρον ὁ σωτὴρ ἐκτελεῖ.

[3] *Strom.* vii. 11. 68 : in vii. 14. 87 the Gnostics are the Holy Church, the Spiritual Body of which those who only bear the name of Christian and do not live according to reason are the flesh. Had this point of view been habitual to him Clement must have written very differently about the Lower Life. The Invisible Spiritual Church, the Communion of Saints, is compared to a chain of rings upheld by a magnet, vii. 2. 9. It is the Church of the First Born, *Protrept.* ix. 82.

seclusion in which Clement lectured and composed. He reflects with calm fidelity the image of the antique times in which he had himself been reared. His heart is with the Republic; he is the Samuel of the new monarchy.

One of the chief pillars of the aggressive theory of Church polity was the claim of the Christian ministry to be regarded as lineal successors of the sacrificial hierarchy of the Jews. But to Clement the true anti-type of Levite or Hiereus is the Gnostic, the son or daughter of God, who has been anointed like King, Prophet, or High Priest of the Law, but with the spiritual unction of the Holy Ghost [1]. The Gnostic sacrifice is that of praise, of a contrite spirit, of a soul delivered from carnal lusts; the incense is holy prayer; the altar is the just soul, or the congregation of believers [2]. Beyond this there is no sacrifice except the ‘costly,’ the ‘fireless’ Victim once offered upon the Cross [3]. Clement quotes the famous verse of Malachi, but the ‘pure offering’ is the knowledge of God as Creator derived by the heathen from the light of the universal Word [4]. The much disputed text about the power of the keys he never cites at all, and in the Penance controversy, which was already agitating men's minds, he follows Hermas, allowing but one Absolution for mortal sin after Baptism, a view highly unfavourable

---

[1] ἱερεῖς, *Strom.* iv. 25. 157 sq.; vii. 7. 36. In *Strom.* vi. 13. 106 the Gnostic is a true Presbyter, though he be not honoured πρωτοκαθεδρίᾳ.

[2] The sacrifice, *Paed.* iii. 12. 90; *Strom.* ii. 18. 79, 96; v. 11. 67 (imme-diately after an allusion to the Eucharist); vii. 3. 14; 6. 31, 32. The last cited passage explains the terms altar, incense.

[3] *Strom.* v. 11. 66, 70. See also passages quoted in Lecture II.

[4] *Strom.* v. 14. 136. The verse had already been applied to the Eucharist in the *Doctrine of the Apostles*, Irenaeus and Justin.

to the growing authority of the Bishop[1]. He rarely
mentions the three orders of Clergy[2], and never in connection with the Sacraments. The rich man should
have a domestic chaplain or spiritual director, who is to
be 'a man of God[3].' The unlearned brother is not to
trust his private judgment, but the interpreter of Scripture is no doubt the Gnostic. The one office assigned
to the Presbyter is that of 'making men better,' and this
is also the special function of the Gnostic.

It seems most probable that at this time, in the
Church of Alexandria, the Eucharist was not yet distinguished in time, ritual, or motive from the primitive

---

[1] *Strom.* ii. 13. 56. Clement follows Hermas, *Mand.* iv. 3, almost
verbally, though without naming his authority. He supports this view
by Heb. x. 26, 27. Clement nowhere expressly draws a distinction between
mortal and venial sins, but it is implied here and in *Strom.* vi. 12. 97, where
he speaks of μετάνοια δισσή, the first being conversion, the second repentance
for minor daily sins. It is the first, repentance of mortal sin, that could
only be repeated once after baptism. It is singular that in *Q. D. S.* he does
not enter upon the question. (I observe that in § 39 the right reading is undoubtedly ὡς μὴ ὑπενηνέχθαι τέλεον, οὗτος οὐ κατεψήφισται.) For further
information see Lecture vi.

[2] *Strom.* vi. 13. 107. Bishop, Priest, and Deacon symbolise the 'three
Mansions,' the thrée degrees of the Angelic Hierarchy: iii. 12. 90, Priest
and Deacon distinguished from λαικός: vii. 1. 3, Priests exeŗcise the
βελτιωτική, Deacons the ὑπηρετική θεραπεία: vi. 13. 106, Priests have
πρωτοκαθεδρία, sitting probably in a semicircle with the Bishop in their
centre round the east end of the church: *Paed.* i. 6. 37, ποιμένες ἐσμὲν οἱ
τῶν ἐκκλησιῶν προηγούμενοι.

[3] *Q. D. S.* 41. Probst, *Sakramente*, p. 261, unhesitatingly identifies the
Man of God with the Priest. It is just possible that we have here the same
admonition as in Origen, *Sel. in Psalmos,* Hom. ii. 6 (Lom. xii. p. 267),
'tantummodo circumspice diligentius, cui debeas confiteri peccatum tuum.
Proba prius medicum.' He may mean that the chaplain is to be a priest, but
a worthy priest. But were there more than twelve priests in Alexandria,
and in any case can there have been enough to supply domestic chaplains to
all the rich men who needed them? I do not doubt that the chaplain is to
be a Gnostic who is a judge in spiritual matters, *Strom.* vii. 7. 45. Rufinus,
before his ordination, seems to have held such a post in the household of
Melania. Compare note above, p. 96. Probst, I may add, endeavours to

Supper of the Lord[1]. Of this, the Agape, the Love-
Feast, or Banquet, there were two forms, the public and
the private, the first celebrated at a full gathering of the
brethren on fixed evenings in the church, the second in
private houses[2].

prove that the Gnostic is the Priest by combining what Clement says of the
Gnostic, of Moses, of the Law, and of Christ the Shepherd.

[1] This statement, that the Eucharist at Alexandria was not yet separated
from the Agape and that both were celebrated together in the evening, may
seem doubtful, and indeed I make it with some hesitation. It may be argued,
on the other side, (i) That the separation was already made in the West, as
we see from Justin and Tertullian, and is found immediately after Clement's
time in Palestine, *teste* Origen. (ii) That the word Eucharist is employed
by Clement for the Elements, *Strom.* i. 1. 5, and for the rite, *Paed.* ii. 2. 20;
Strom. iv. 25. 161. (iii) That there was a morning service at Alexandria,
though we are not told that it included the Eucharist, *Paed.* ii. 10. 96. On
the other hand, (i) the Liturgy, so far as we can judge, is not nearly so
developed in Clement's church as in that of Origen ; (ii) the Agape in both
its forms is distinctly mentioned, the Eucharist as a separate office is
not ; (iii) the word Eucharist is employed of the Agape, *Paed.* ii. 10.
96. (iv) The Agape is mentioned in the Sibylline Oracles—*Or.* viii. 402, 497,
temp. Trajan or Hadrian ; *Or.* v. 265, *temp.* Antoninus Pius—while the
Eucharist is not : see Alexandre, ii. 547. It is true that both these authorities are anterior in date to Clement. (v) Dionysius of Alexandria still uses of
the rite of Communion the same word, ἑστίασις, which in Clement means the
Agape, Eus. *H. E.* vi. 42. 5, καὶ προσευχῶν αὐτοῖς καὶ ἑστιάσεων ἐκοινώνησαν.
(vi) Lastly, I do not know of any passage in an Oriental writer before
Clement's time in which the Eucharist appears as a distinct and substantive office. In the *Doctrine of the Apostles* Hilgenfeld observes upon the
word ἐμπλησθῆναι in chap. 10, ' eucharistia vere coena communis nondum
separata ab Agape.' And from Socrates, v. 22, it appears that the Agape
lingered on in the churches of Upper Egypt longer than elsewhere. We
may infer from this perhaps that Alexandria also had clung to the primitive
usage after it had been abandoned by others.

[2] The public Agape is the δημώδης ἑστίασις of *Paed.* ii. 1. 12. But we
read of τὸν κεκληκότα, *ibid.* § 10. This is the δοχή. Yet further the ' Feast'
is universal and daily, *Paed.* ii. 10. 96, ἑσπέρας δὲ ἀναπαύσασθαι καθήκει
μετὰ τὴν ἑστίασιν καὶ μετὰ τὴν ἐπὶ ταῖς ἀπολαύσεσιν εὐχαριστίαν. Here
Clement obviously means the ordinary house supper. So again, *Strom.* vii.
7. 49, αἱ πρὸ τῆς ἑστιάσεως ἐντεύξεις τῶν γραφῶν, ψαλμοὶ δὲ καὶ ὕμνοι παρὰ τὴν
ἑστίασιν πρό γε τῆς κοίτης. No priest can have been present in the vast
majority of cases; the devotional exercises of the family and the ' thanksgiving' constituted the meal an Eucharist. The phrase in *Q. D. S.* 23, πόμα
καθ' ἡμέραν ἐνδιδοὺς ἀθανασίας, may perhaps thus be explained. The private

The first was still disfigured by those excesses and disorders, which St. Paul sharply rebuked, but a century of discipline had not eradicated. It was preceded by reading of the Scriptures, psalms and hymns. After this the Bread and Wine were blessed, and then distributed by the deacons [1]. Viands of every kind, often costly and richly dressed, were provided by the liberality of the wealthier brethren. Clement does not attempt to lay any puritanical restrictions upon social enjoyment. He enforces the rule prohibiting the taste of blood or of meat offered to idols, he explains the code of good manners, and insists upon moderation. The Christian must eat to live, not live to eat. He must not abuse the Father's gifts. He must show by precept and example that the heavenly banquet is not the meat that perisheth, but love, that the believer's true food is Christ [2].

All that Clement says upon this subject is of the highest value to those who wish to recast for themselves a faithful image of the Church life of the end of the

Agape is the ordinary evening meal also in Cyprian, *Ep.* 63. § 16. p. 714, ed. Hartel. In a somewhat later time the clergy appear to have been generally but not always present at the δοχή, which has become a charity dinner, to which especially poor old women were invited, *Const. Ap.* ii. 28. The Council of Laodicea prohibited the Agape in churches, can. 28, and in private houses, can. 58. Mansi, iii. 563. Hefele. 'Hoc modo in totum eucharistia ab agapis distincta et separata fuit,' Böhmer, *Dissertationes Juris Eccles.* Lipsiae, 1711, diss. iv. The consecration of the Eucharist by laymen was not unknown in Tertullian's church, *Exhort. Cast.* vii.

[1] Supper followed the Eucharist, see *Paed.* ii. 1. 11, μετὰ τὴν ἐν λόγῳ τρυφήν. The deacons carried round the supper as well as the consecrated bread and wine; see the following words, συμμεταφερομένης αὐτῶν, ὡς εἰπεῖν, τῆς ἀκρασίας πρὸς τῶν διακόνων.

[2] The description of the Agape will be found at the opening of *Paed.* ii. For a similar and equally graphic account of the coarse vulgarity of Alexandrine luxury, see Philo, *De Vita Cont.* 5 (ii. 477). The contrast between the heathen man of the world and the Christian gentleman as drawn by Clement is most instructive.

second century. But of all his phrases the most important are those which assure us, that the ordinary evening meal of a Christian household was in a real sense an Agape. It was preceded by the same acts of worship; it was blessed by thanksgiving; it was a true Eucharist. The house father is the house priest. The highest act of Christian devotion is at the same time the simplest and most natural. Husband, wife and child, the house slave, and the invited guest gathered round the domestic board to enjoy with thankfulness the good gifts of God, uplifting their hearts in filial devotion, expanding them in brotherly bounty and kindness. To us the word Eucharist has become a term of ritual, whose proper meaning is all but obsolete. To the Greek it was still a word of common life—thanksgiving, the grateful sense of benefits received, of good gifts showered by the good Father on mind and heart and body. ' He that eateth eateth unto the Lord and keepeth Eucharist to God . . . so that a religious meal is an Eucharist [1].'

All these good gifts sum themselves up in one, the gift of the Son. In the Eucharist, in its narrower sense, we eat the flesh and drink the blood of Christ, 'hallowed food,' of which the bread and wine given by Melchisedech to Abraham was a type [2]. It is 'a mystery passing strange [3].' ' I will, I will impart to you this grace also, the full and perfect bounty of incorruption. I give

---

[1] *Paed.* ii. 1. 10, ὡς εἶναι τὴν δικαίαν τροφὴν εὐχαριστίαν.

[2] *Strom.* iv. 26. 161. The figure is from Philo, and must be interpreted by Philo's light.

[3] μυστήριον παράδοξον, *Paed.* i. 6. 43: the following quotation is from *Protrept.* xii. 120. The chief passages on the subject of the Eucharist are, besides these two, *Paed.* ii. 2. 19 sq.; *Strom.* v. 10. 66. Other notices in *Paed.* i. 5. 15; 6. 38; *Strom.* i. 10. 46; 19. 96; v. 11. 70; vi. 14. 113; *Q. D. S.* 23.

to you the knowledge of God. I give to you my perfect
Self.' Christ's own Sacrifice, the charter of His High
Priesthood, is the condition of His sacramental agency.
But what is the special boon that He conveys in that
supreme moment, when His sacrifice co-operates with
ours, when 'in faith' we partake[1] of the nourishment
which He bestows? Not forgiveness—that gift is bestowed in the laver of Regeneration, and if lost must be
regained by the stern sacrament of Penance—but incorruption, immortality[2]. The Bread, the Wine mingled
with Water, are an allegory. 'The Blood of the Lord
is twofold. One is fleshly, whereby we have been ran-
somed from corruption'—in Baptism—'one is spiritual,
with this we have been anointed'—in the Eucharist.
The Body is Faith, the Blood is Hope, which is as it
were the lifeblood of Faith. 'This is the Flesh and
Blood of the Lord, the apprehension of the Divine
power and essence.' 'The Blood of His Son cleanseth
from all sin. For the doctrine of the Lord which is
very strong is called His Blood[3].'

The elements are 'hallowed food'; 'the meat of
babes, that is to say the Lord Jesus, that is to say the
Word of God, is spirit made flesh, hallowed flesh from
heaven[4].' These phrases have been interpreted in very

[1] *Paed.* ii. 2. 20, ἧς οἱ κατὰ πίστιν μεταλαμβάνοντες.
[2] *Paed.* ii. 2. 19; iii. 1. 2.
[3] For these four quotations see *Paed.* ii. 2. 19; i. 6. 38; *Strom.* v. 10.
66; *Adumb. in Ep. Joan. I.* p. 1009. I quote the last book always with
hesitation.
[4] *Strom.* iv. 26. 161; *Paed.* i. 6. 43. The two opposing views are
maintained by Döllinger, *Die Eucharistie in den drei ersten Jahrb.*, Mainz,
1826, and Probst, *Liturgie*, on the one hand, and by Höfling, *Die Lehre
der ältesten Kirche vom Opfer im Leben und Cultus*, Erlangen, 1851.
Upon the whole Höfling's view appears to me to be correct. But I must
in fairness add, what I do not remember to have seen mentioned, that the

different senses. One writer sees in them the doctrine of Transubstantiation, another the doctrine of Zwinglius.

Those who read Clement as a whole, who reflect upon his strong antithesis of the letter, the flesh, to the spirit, who take into due account his language on the subject of Priest and Sacrifice, and his emphatic declaration that 'knowledge is our reasonable food [1],' will be inclined to think that the latter view is far nearer to the truth. Christ is present in the Eucharist as Gnosis, 'in the heart, not in the hand.' The Elements are a symbol, an allegory [2], perhaps a vehicle, an instrument, inasmuch as they are ordained by Christ Himself, and to substitute

doctrine of the Real Presence is stated, *Excerpta*, 82, ὁ ἄρτος καὶ τὸ ἔλαιον ἁγιάζεται τῇ δυνάμει τοῦ ὀνόματος οὐ τὰ αὐτὰ ὄντα κατὰ τὸ φαινόμενον οἷα ἐλήφθη, ἀλλὰ δυνάμει εἰς δύναμιν πνευματικὴν μεταβέβληται. And the precise idea of transubstantiation was familiar to Clement, *Paed.* i. 6. 40, πάσχει δὲ τὴν μεταβολὴν κατὰ ποιότητα οὐ κατ' οὐσίαν. He is speaking of the change of the mother's blood into milk, and his point is that the Faith of the Lower Life is the same in substance as the Gnosis of the Higher. It is barely possible that there may be also some allusion to the Elements, but I do not think there is.

[1] *Strom.* v. 11. 70, λογικὸν ἡμῖν βρῶμα ἡ γνῶσις : i. 10. 46, ἵνα δὴ φάγωμεν λογικῶς : v. 10. 66, βρῶσις γὰρ καὶ πόσις τοῦ θείου λόγου ἡ γνῶσίς ἐστι τῆς θείας οὐσίας : *Adumb. in Ep. Joan. I.* p. 1011, sanguis quod est cognitio. There is a remarkable departure from the ordinary symbolism in the very obscure passage, *Paed.* ii. 2. 19, 20. Clement's drift is that those are to be praised who abstain from wine altogether, and he illustrates this by the mixed chalice. The Wine is the Blood, the symbol of Redemption, Baptism, Faith, and Discipline ; the Water is the Spirit, the better gift.

[2] *Paed.* ii. 2. 32, αἷμα τῆς ἀμπέλου, τὸν λόγον τὸν περὶ πολλῶν ἐκχεόμενον εἰς ἄφεσιν ἁμαρτιῶν εὐφροσύνης ἅγιον ἀλληγορεῖ νᾶμα : i. 6. 47, ἣ γὰρ καὶ οὐχὶ οἶνος ἀλληγορεῖται. Much depends on the meaning of the word Allegory and the purpose of the Alexandrine *Disciplina Arcani.* On this I shall speak in Lecture iv. It may be noticed here that Clement mentions the kiss of peace, *Paed.* iii. 11. 81 ; the practice of anointing the eyes with a drop of the wine from the lips (a bare allusion), *Paed.* ii. 12. 129 ; and tells us, *Strom.* i. 1. 5, that some clergymen made the communicant take his piece of bread instead of giving it to him, lest they should become partakers in the sin of the unworthy recipient ; see Probst, *Liturgie,* pp. 135 sqq.

any other figure for the one so ordained is heresy. But the veil, though a holy thing because it belongs to the sanctuary, is not the mystery that it shrouds, the allegory is not the truth that it bodies forth.

The chief article of the Christian Gnosis was that of the Future Life. It was as interesting to Pagans as to Christians. ' What will become of the soul after death?' asks Plotinus, as he enters upon this universally fascinating theme. The immortality of the soul was positively denied by none but the 'godless Epicureans.' But the doctrine of the Resurrection was peculiar to the Church, and, while it strengthened her hold upon the masses, was a great stumbling-block in the way of the educated. The Platonist looked upon the body as the ' dungeon of the soul,' and could not understand how any pious man should expect a good God to renew and perpetuate that degrading bondage.

Within the Church itself there was some variety and much confusion of thought. Tertullian and many others held that the soul itself was material [1]. From this followed the terrible belief of Tatian, that it dies with the body, and is raised again with the body, by an act of Divine power, for an eternity of suffering or joy. Others, especially Arabian Christians, held that after dissolution the soul sleeps unconscious, till awakened to life by the restoration of its organism. But the majority believed in an intermediate yet conscious state of existence in Hades or Paradise, extending to the Day of Judgment,

[1] A Montanist sister in one of her visions saw a soul ' tenera et lucida et aerii coloris et forma per omnia humana,' *De Anima*, 9. Tatian's doctrine in *Oratio ad Graecos*, 13. For the Arabians, Eus. *H. E.* vi. 37 ; Redepenning, *Origenes*, ii. 105 sqq. The ψυχοπαννυχία may perhaps be found also in Athenagoras, *De Res.* 16, though Otto thinks not.

when the soul is reunited to the body, from which it has been for a time divorced.

The Resurrection itself they interpreted in the most literal sense. It would be a resurrection of 'this flesh,' of the identical body which had been dissolved by death. The 'change,' spoken of by St. Paul, was strictly limited to the accession of the new attribute of incorruption [1]. Closely allied to this view was the widespread opinion of the Chiliasts, who, resting upon the prophecies of Isaiah and the Apocalypse, believed that after the first Resurrection the saints should reign in the flesh upon earth for a thousand years under the sceptre of Christ. Chiliasm, which in vulgar minds was capable of the most unhappy degradation, was in turn strengthened by the urgent expectation of the End of the World. In the lower strata of Christian society prophecies on this subject were rife. At this very time a calculation, based on the numerical value of the letters composing the word Rome, fixed the downfall of the Empire and the coming of Christ for judgment for the year 195 A.D.[2] The Montanists held that the appointed sign was the appearance of the New Jerusalem in heaven; and this sign was given during the expedition of Severus against the Parthians, when for forty consecutive mornings the vision of a battlemented city hanging in the clouds was beheld by the whole army[3].

[1] See Irenaeus, v. 13; Athenagoras, *De Res.*

[2] The four letters composing the word Ρωμη = 948, hence it was supposed the empire would last that number of years, *Or. Sib.* viii. 148. When this expectation was frustrated by the course of events, the authors of the last four Sibylline books struck off 105 years from the Roman Fasti and fixed upon the year 305 in the reign of Diocletian. See much curious information upon similar speculations which recurred again and again from the persecution of Nero downwards, Alexandre, ii. pp. 485 sqq.

[3] Tertullian, *Adv. Marc.* iii. 24; Münter, *Primordia Eccl. Afr.* p. 141.

There were differences of opinion again as to the
nature, object, duration, of the sufferings that await the
wicked in the life to come, especially among the outlying
sects. The Valentinians, as we have seen, taught 'conditional immortality,' and regarded the future life as a
state of education, of progress through an ascending
series of seven heavens. The Clementine *Homilies*, a
work composed under strong Judaic influences, expresses
different views in different places. In one the sinner is
warned that eternal torments await him in the life to
come. In another St. Peter proclaims that those who
repent, however grievous their offences, will be chastised
but for a time, that those who repent not will be tortured
for a season and then annihilated [1]. The Church at large
believed in an eternity of bliss or of woe. Yet among
the Montanists prayers and oblations were offered up on
behalf of the departed, and it was thought that these
sacrifices could in certain cases quicken the compassion
of God towards those who had died in sin. The widow
prayed that her lost husband's pangs might be alleviated,
and that she might share with him in the First Resurrection. Perpetua, the matron lily of martyrs, in that jail
which seemed to be a palace while her baby was at her
breast, cried for mercy upon the soul of her little brother,
who had died unbaptised [2].

---

[1] Eternal torments in i. 7; xi. 11 : the other view in iii. 6.

[2] Tertullian, *De Monogamia*, 10, the widow prays for her husband's soul;
'enimvero et pro anima eius orat, et refrigerium interim adpostulat ei et in
prima resurrectione consortium, et off rt annuis diebus dormitionis eius:' *De
Cor. Mil.* 3, 'oblationes pro defunctis, pro natalitiis, annua die facimus'
(here he rests the usage on tradition, and not on Scripture : but he may mean
only that the oblation is not scriptural as the use of prayer is sanctioned by
2 Tim. i. 18): see also *De Exhort. Cast.* 11. All these treatises are Montanist according to Münter. Montanist also in the opinion of Valesius are

Clement never composed his promised treatise on the Resurrection, and it is not always easy to attach a definite meaning to his allusive style.   But the general outline of his teaching is sufficiently clear.   He rejects with scornful brevity the fancies of Chiliasm[1].   The Resurrection body is not ' this flesh,' but, as St. Paul taught, a glorified frame, related to that which we now possess as the grain of corn to the new ear, devoid in particular of the distinctions of sex[2].   The change is wrought by fire.   Even Christ rose 'through fire.'   Fire is here the agent not of chastisement, but of that mysterious sublimation by which our organism is fitted for existence in a new sphere.

For the sinner the fire burns with a fiercer intensity, because it has a harsher office.   It is the pang of unsatisfied lusts that gnaw the soul itself for want of food, the sting of repentance and shame, the sense of loss.   It

the Acta of St. Perpetua.   As to the latter it should be observed that the little brother Dinocrates for whom Perpetua intercedes had certainly died unbaptised.   For his father was a Pagan—Perpetua herself was baptised in the prison—and the effect of her prayer is that Dinocrates is admitted to the benefits of baptism.   ' I saw Dinocrates coming forth from a dark place very hot and thirsty, squalid of face and pallid of hue ... And hard by where he stood was a tank full of water, the margin whereof was higher than the stature of the child, and he stood on tiptoe as if he would drink.'   Again, 'on the day on which we lay in the stocks,' she prays, and sees Dinocrates cleansed, dressed, and cool, drinking eagerly of the water. ' Then I knew that he was released from pain.'   Further, the privilege of intercession is granted to Perpetua by revelation as a special mark of favour. So Clement appears to restrict it to the Gnostic.   The practice of prayer for the dead was certainly uncommon at the end of the second century.   It is not found in Origen, for *in Rom.* ix. 12 is confessedly from the hand of Rufinus.

[1] *Strom.* vii. 12. 74, the Gnostic, τῶν κοσμικῶν καίτοι θείων ὄντων ἐπαγγελιῶν κατεμεγαλοφρόνησεν.   Guerike considers that these words refer. to Chiliasm, ii. p. 163.

[2] *Paed.* i. 4. 10 ; 6. 46.   In this last passage it is said that Christ rose 'through fire,' which changes the natural into the spiritual body, as earthly fire changes wheat into bread.   But the resurrection body may still be called flesh, *Paed.* ii. 10. 100 ; iii. 1. 2.

is ministered not by fiends but by good angels[1], it is
alleviated by the prayers of the saints on earth[2].

There can I think be no doubt (though it has been
doubted) that Clement allowed the possibility of repentance and amendment till the Last Day. At that final
Assize there will be found those who, like Aridaeus[3], are
incurable, who will still reject, as man always can reject,
the proffered grace. But he nowhere expressly limits
probation to this brief life. All his theory of punishment[4], which is strictly Platonic, for he hardly ever
quotes Scripture in this connection[5], points the same
way. And many passages might be adduced which
prove how his maxims are to be applied. 'Let them
be chastised,' he says of the 'deaf serpents' who refuse
to hear the voice of the charmer, 'by God, enduring His
paternal correction before the Judgment, till they be
ashamed and repent[6].' In that fiery trial even Sodom

[1] *Strom.* v. 14. 90 ; vii. 2. 12.

[2] The Gnostic, οἰκτείρει τοὺς μετὰ θάνατον παιδευομένους διὰ τῆς κολάσεως
ἀκουσίως ἐξομολογουμένους, *Strom.* vii. 12. 78. Yet Clement does not expressly say that he prays for them.

[3] *Strom.* v. 14. 90 : in iv. 24. 154 the 'faithless' are as the chaff which
the wind driveth away.

[4] The object of κόλασις is threefold—amendment, example, and protection
of the weak, *Strom.* i. 26. 168 ; iv. 24. 154 ; vi. 12. 99. The distinction
between κόλασις and τιμωρία, *Strom.* iv. 14. 153 ; *Paed.* i. 8. 70, the latter
is the rendering of evil for evil, and this is not the desire of God. Both
κόλασις and τιμωρία are spoken of in *Strom.* v. 14. 90, but this is not to be
pressed, for in *Strom.* vi. 14. 109 the distinction between the words is
dropped and both signify purgatorial chastisement.

[5] Isaiah iv. 4 is quoted, *Paed.* iii. 9. 48, and Cor. i. 3. 10–13, *Strom.*
v. 4. 26.

[6] *Strom.* vii. 16. 102. Repentance is attributed to the dead again in
Strom. vi. 14. 109. If it be asked *which* repentance Clement speaks of
here (see note above, p. 102), the instance of Sodom and Gomorrha, *Adumb.
in Ep. Judae,* p. 1008, is very strong. It rests upon Ezekiel xvi. 33, 55, and
is employed by Origen in the same way. Even stronger is the language of
Strom. vii. 2. 12, παιδεύσεις ... τοὺς ἐπὶ πλέον ἀπηλγηκότας ἐκβιάζονται

and Gomorrha cried unto God and were forgiven.   There is no difference between his teaching and that of Origen, except that he generally seems to be thinking of the doom of Christians, that he regards probation as ceasing at the Day of Judgment[1], and that he does not contemplate the possibility of a fall from grace in the after-life.

Even the just must be purged by the ' wise fire[2],' before they are fit for the presence of the Most Holy God.   Not at once can they see face to face, or enter into possession of those good things which 'eye hath not seen nor ear heard.'   When the burden of sin has been laid down, when the angels have taken their appointed ' toll[3],' the spirit must still grow in knowledge, rising in due course through the seven heavens of the Valentinian, through the three ' mansions ' or ' folds ' prefigured by the triple hierarchy of the Church[4].   Some—those who have

μετανοεῖν.   The question of the orthodoxy or heterodoxy of the Alexandrines in this part of their teaching turns entirely upon the word 'repentance,' to which we shall recur in Lecture VIII.

[1] See *Strom.* vii. 2. 12.   It should be observed that the word προκρίσεις here may refer to 'previous judgments' in this life; that is to say, to the Sacrament of Penance : compare *Adumb. in Ep. Petri.* i. p. 1007.

[2] *Strom.* vii. 6. 34, πῦρ οὐ τὸ παμφάγον καὶ βάναυσον ἀλλὰ τὸ φρόνιμον λέγοντες, τὸ διικνούμενον διὰ ψυχῆς τῆς διερχομένης τὸ πῦρ.   Cp. *Eclogae Proph.* 25. p. 995, and Minucius Felix, xxxv, illic sapiens ignis membra urit et reficit ; carpit et nutrit.   There is an allusion to Isaiah iv. 4, but the actual phrase 'wise fire' comes from Heraclitus and the Stoics.

[3] The Angels who guard the road up to the highest heaven 'take toll' of the passer-by, *Strom.* iv. 18. 117.

[4] Clement may have taken the seven heavens from Valentinus or from the Revelation of Sophonias, *Strom.* v. 11. 77.   He found allusions to them in Plato's *Timaeus*, p. 31 ; in Clemens Romanus, i. 20 (of the 'lands' beyond the ocean); in St. Paul, and elsewhere.   The same idea is found in the book of Baruch (Origen, *De Princ.* ii. 3. 6), and in Aristo, Fragment iv. in Otto, *Corp. App.* vol. ix. p. 363.   See also Hermas, *Vis.* iii. 4, and note there in the ed. of Gebhardt and Harnack.   The seven days of purification are a type, *Strom.* iv. 25. 158.   The μοναὶ ποικίλαι are from Papias (Fragm. v. in Routh).   They answer to the three stages of Fear, Hope, and Love,

I

brought forth thirty, or sixty, or a hundredfold, yet have fallen short of what they might have been—mount no higher than this[1]. But the Gnostic, scaling from glory up to glory, will attain at last to the stature of the perfect man, and find rest upon the holy mountain of God, the Church that is above all.   There in the changeless Ogdoad, a name borrowed from the Valentinian by the Catholic, as indeed is the greater part of this description, he shall dwell for ever with Christ, the God and Guardian of his faith and love, beholding the Father no longer ' in a glass darkly,' but with the direct unclouded vision of a pure heart, in light that never fades[2].

Clement speaks of this final consummation as Rest. But it is the rest of God, ' who ceases not from doing good[3].'   There is no absorption, no confusion of subject and object.   It is the rest not of unity but of perfect similarity, perfect reciprocity, the polar rest of a soul energising in unimpeded knowledge and love.   Farther than this Clement does not dare to pry into the sanctuary of Light.   ' I say no more glorifying the Lord[4].'

to the three divisions of the Temple, to the three kinds of seed, *Strom.* vi. 14. 114, to the three grades of the hierarchy, vi. 13. 107.

[1] This seems to be clearly meant in *Strom.* iv. 18. 114 ; vi. 14. 108, 114; cp. also *Ecl. Proph.* 56.   But if so, the *poena damni* never wholly ceases, *Strom.* vi. 14. 109.

[2] *Strom.* iv. 25. 158 ; vi. 14. 108 ; vii. 10. 56, 57.

[3] *Strom.* vi. 12. 104.

[4] *Strom.* vii. 3. 13.

LECTURE IV.

Again the kingdom of heaven is like unto treasure hid in a field; the which when a man hath found he hideth, and for joy thereof goeth and selleth all that he hath, and buyeth that field.—St. Matt. xiii. 44.

CLEMENT as we have seen is a philosopher of a desultory and eclectic type and so far as the needs of his tranquil spirit led him on. Egypt is his world, Gnosticism his one trouble. Origen had travelled to Rome in the West and Bostra in the East, and had found everywhere the clash of arms. But apart from this he was not one of those who discover the rifts in their harness only on the morning of the battle. His sceptical intelligence pries unbidden into every defect, and anticipates the hostile thrust. He stands to his arms for life or death, like a Dominican theologian of the thirteenth century, or an English divine of the nineteenth. The range of his activity is amazing. He is the first great scholar, the first great preacher, the first great devotional writer, the first great commentator, the first great dogmatist. But he is nothing else. Already we have entered upon the joyless age of erudition. The beauties of Hellenism, in which Clement still delighted, are a withered flower, and Christian art is as yet unborn.

The life of Origen extended from 185 A.D. to 254 A.D., from the reign of Commodus to that of Valerian and Gallienus. During this long and eventful period his activity was constant, varied and distinguished, and friends and enemies, both equally ardent, have left us large materials for his biography. It is impossible here to deal exhaustively with a subject so wide. We must content ourselves with touching upon the most characteristic features [1].

He was 'by race an Egyptian,' a Copt, one of the children of the soil, despised by the Greek colonists for their animal-worship and their petulant turbulence, and treated even by the upright Roman law on the footing of slaves. Son as he was of Christian parents he yet bore the name of one of his country's deities, Origenes, child of Hor, the god of Light [2]. From his blood he drew that fiery ardour which long tribulation softened but could not quench. He was a martyr by race, but a stern schooling was needed before he learned to drink the cup as God had mixed it for him. When his father

[1] For fuller information about the biography of Origen the reader should consult Thomasius, Redepenning, or Huet. Denis, *Philosophie d'Origène*, is a most valuable aid to the study of his system of doctrine. Dr. Harnack's *Dogmengeschichte* is also very useful. Redepenning, ii. 472, gives a list of editions. The special literature will be found in Möller's article in Herzog, in Nitzsch, *Dogmengeschichte*, or in Ueberweg, *Grundriss der Gesch. der Philosophie*. All my references are to the edition of Lommatzsch, the volume and page have been noted where it seemed desirable.

[2] G. J. Voss was the first who gave the right derivation of the name of Origen ; Redepenning, i. 421. Suidas, Erasmus, Halloix, Cave were satisfied with the impossible etymology, 'born in the mountains.' Origen is commonly spoken of by the by-name Adamantius, which, according to Photius, Cod. 118, means the same as Doctor Irrefragabilis, ὅτι ἀδαμαντίνοις δεσμοῖς ἐῴκεσαν οὓς ἂν δήσειε λόγους, according to Jerome denotes his indefatigable capacity for labour (hence Jerome also calls him χαλκέντερος), according to Huet the firmness with which he stood like a rock against Heretics. For the heathen philosopher of the same name see Porphyry, *Vita Plotini*, 20 ; Eunapius, *Vita Porphyrii*, p. 457 ; Ruhnken, *Diss. philologica de vita et scriptis Longini*, in his ed. of Longinus, Oxford, 1806. Epiphanius endeavoured to save the reputation of Origen by inventing a second author of the same name, to whom he ascribed the more heterodox articles of Origenism, *Haer.* lxiii. 1 ; lxiv. 3. The Praedestinati auctor, *Haer.* 42, calls this phantom heresiarch Syrus scelera issimus, and adds a third Origen, who denied the Resurrection. See Huet, *Origeniana*, i. 1. 7.

Leonidas fell a victim to the persecution of Severus, nothing but the womanly sense of his mother prevented Origen, then a boy of seventeen, from drawing destruction on his own head by open defiance of the authorities. The destitute orphan found shelter in the house of a wealthy Alexandrine lady, but neither gratitude nor the sense of a common misfortune could induce him to behave with civility to her Gnostic chaplain. Shortly afterwards, at the age of eighteen, he found independence in the mastership of the Catechetical School, left vacant by the flight of Clement. He breathed his own spirit into his pupils, of whom six at least perished. Nor was it Origen's fault that he did not share their fate. He visited them in prison, he acted as their advocate, and gave them the brotherly kiss in open court. We are not surprised to hear that he narrowly escaped stoning in the streets, or that he was hunted from house to house by the gendarmery. What is remarkable is that he escaped, and even contrived throughout the reign of terror to keep his school together. It is probable that the edict of Severus, which was directed against converts only, did not touch him, and that so long as he abstained from formal defiance he was personally safe [1]. And he had already learned that formal defiance was suicide.

The second path that allures the wilful martyr is that of self-torture. Like Buddha, like Marcus Aurelius, like Wesley, like many another enthusiast in every age and clime and church, Origen flung himself into asceticism only to learn the truth of the old Greek adage, 'He who starts in the race before the signal is given is whipped.'

---

[1] An excellent account of the persecution of Severus will be found in Aubé, *Les Chrétiens dans l'Empire Romain.* See also Münter, *Primordia Eccl. Afr.*

He sold the manuscripts of the Greek classics, which he had written out with loving care, for a trifling pension, in order that he might be able to teach without a fee, and subjected himself for some years to the severest discipline by night and day. This was the time of his bondage to the letter. He would carry out with severest fidelity the precept of the Saviour, 'provide neither gold nor silver . . . neither two coats, neither shoes.' He went, as is well known, even farther than this, and did what was condemned at once by the wholesome severity of the Roman law, and the conscience, if not the actual ordinance of the Church. This error too he learned to renounce, but not wholly nor frankly, for to the last he looked with a sombre eye on the affections of the flesh.

Rebellion is the third temptation of undisciplined zeal, and this charge also may be laid to Origen's account. Here unhappily our materials are too scanty for a clear and dispassionate judgment. The bare facts are that in the year 215 Origen, being then at Caesarea, accepted the invitation of Alexander, Bishop of Jerusalem, and Theoctistus, Bishop of Caesarea, to expound the Scriptures before the assembly of the Church, though as yet a layman, and that in 228 he was ordained at the same place by the same Bishops. We cannot tell how far these acts were in violation of the existing discipline. Both were lawful in Palestine, both were regarded by Demetrius as unlawful. If the rule was more stringent at Alexandria, it was possibly a recent innovation. We do not know how far the dispute was complicated by the character of the Patriarch, by the teaching and conduct of Origen, or by the peculiar position of the Alexandrine Presbytery. But it is significant that the

extreme penalty of degradation was carried only by the
voices of the newly created suffragan bishops, against
the inclination of the priests. These latter could not but
sympathise with a victim of the same usurpation that
lay so heavy on themselves.

For our present purpose the importance of the incident
is that it marks the final renunciation by Origen of that
narrow legal spirit, which leads by many paths to the
one goal of servitude. He was learning in strange and
unexpected ways the true meaning of the Christian
sacrifice. He had been willing and eager to 'give his
body to be burned,' he had 'given all his goods to feed
the poor,' and his reward had been not the martyr
crown but the martyr spirit, 'love which beareth all
things.' Now, when he had found his true career in
indefatigable labour for the Word of God, and sought to
sanctify his toil and enlarge his influence by the name
and authority of a priest, what he sought was given to
him, but at the cost of banishment and obloquy. Such
discipline was needed before this high impatient spirit
could obey with docility the bridle of God.

Many years before this it had become manifest in
what direction Providence was leading him. As a child
he had received by his father's care not only a minute
knowledge of Scripture, a great part of which he learned
by heart, but a thorough training in what was called the
encyclic discipline—the grammar, rhetoric and science
which formed the ordinary education of a youth of good
family. Hebrew, a rare accomplishment, and philosophy[1], he acquired while so absorbed in school work

---

[1] Origen does not name the professor whose lectures he attended. The
belief that it was Ammonius Saccas rests upon the statement of Porphyry.

that he could find time for study only by curtailing the hours of sleep. His literary activity began in 223, when he would be thirty-eight years old, and continued incessantly to the end of his life. Like many other men of studious habits he found the labour of composition irksome, but Ambrosius, a wealthy and intelligent man whom Origen had reclaimed from Gnosticism, continually spurred him on, and overcame the physical difficulty by providing him with a number of shorthand writers and copyists. From this time his labours were unremitting. 'The work of correction,' he says in one of his letters, 'leaves us no time for supper, or after supper for exercise and repose. Even at these times we are compelled to debate questions of interpretation and to emend MSS. Even the night cannot be given up altogether to the needful refreshment of sleep, for our discussions extend far into the evening. I say nothing about our morning labour continued from dawn to the ninth or tenth hour. For all earnest students devote this time to study of the Scriptures and reading [1].'

Such was his life during the progress of the *Hexapla*, and indeed at all times. The volume of writing thus produced was enormous. But it is evident that no man can accomplish the best work of which he is capable under these conditions, harassed by the demands of

Porphyry, who was an excellent man, no doubt spoke in good faith, but he has confused the heathen Origen whom he once knew with the Christian Origen whom he can never have known, and therefore no weight at all can be attached to what he says. The teacher may well have been Ammonius, but it is by no means certain. For even if that distinguished man was already in the chair, it appears from the opening of the *Eunuchus* ascribed to Lucian, that at a great school there were two professors of each of the four sects of philosophy. Their stipend was 10,000 drachmas per annum. See notes in Heinichen on Eusebius, *H. E.* vi. 19.

[1] From the *Epistle to a Friend about Ambrosius*, in Lomm. xvii. p. 5.

pupils, toiling with feverish anxiety to master the ever-growing mountain of minute facts, and in hardly won intervals pouring out the eager flow of extemporaneous thought to nimble-fingered stenographers[1]. The marvel is not that Origen composed so much, but that he composed so well.

And to these professional labours must be added a far-reaching personal influence, with all its responsibilities and engagements. Origen was essentially a man of the student type, but he wielded that powerful charm which attaches to high intellectual gifts when combined with an ardent and sympathetic nature. His pupil Gregory Thaumaturgus speaks of his 'sweet grace and persuasion mingled with a certain constraining force[2],' and uses towards him that strong Greek word by which Plato describes the love of the soul for its ideal. Such a charm is a practical power, and works with more freedom and pungency in a private station of life. It

---

[1] Ambrosius, whom Origen calls his ἐργοδιώκτης, taskmaster, provided him with seven stenographers, and the same number of calligraphists. We may compare them with the staff of a modern lexicographer. But Origen used them for his commentaries and other composition. Thus *In Joan.* vi. 1 (Lom. i. p. 176) he complains that his work has been at a standstill because the συνήθεις ταχυγράφοι were not with him. After the year 246 his extemporaneous Homilies were taken down by shorthand writers.

[2] From the *Panegyric* of Gregory Thaumaturgus, 6 (in Lom. xxv). The student of Origen should certainly begin with this graphic and loving though too rhetorical sketch of the great master. Gregory was on his way to the Roman law school at Berytus, where he was to study for the bar. But by a series of accidents, which he regarded afterwards as divinely ordered, he fell in with Origen at Caesarea, and could not tear himself away. 'It was as if a spark fell into my soul and caught fire and blazed up, such was my love for the Holy Word and for this man its friend and advocate. Stung by this desire I forgot all that seemed to touch me most nearly, my studies, even my beloved jurisprudence, my country, my relatives, my present mission, the object of my travels.' Gregory stayed with Origen for five years, became a bishop, and was famed for his miracles.

constituted Origen the unofficial representative, arbiter, peacemaker of the Eastern Church. A provincial governor consults him on affairs of the soul, the Christian or half-Christian Emperor Philip corresponds with him, the Empress Mother Mammaea summons him to Antioch and provides him with a guard of honour [1]. The Churches of Achaea and Arabia make him their umpire, and peace follows his award. In the furnace of affliction he has grown to be one of those magnetic natures that test the capacity for love and veneration in every one that comes within their sphere.

Origen had long learned to acquiesce in the prevalent view of the Easterns that martyrdom involves a high responsibility, that the Christian has no right either to fling away his life or to fix the guilt of blood upon 'the powers ordained of God.' The Church would gladly have restricted this Olympian contest to her chosen athletes. Hence he quitted Alexandria during the Fury of Caracalla, which though not specially directed against Christians, no doubt involved them. Once again he fled from the persecution of Maximin to Caesarea of Cappadocia, where in the house of Juliana he whiled away the stormy days in labour upon the *Hexapla*. What thoughts solaced him during this dry and gigantic task we know from the treatise on Martyrdom, composed at this time for the benefit of his friend Ambrosius, who had been thrown into prison, 'a golden book' it has been called

---

[1] The date of the interview with Mammaea is doubtful. Baronius, Tillemont and De la Rue (see Huet) place it in 218. Redepenning, i. 372, in 223; this is Huet's own opinion. Aubé, pp. 306 sqq. throws it forward to 232, on the ground that it was after the ordination of Origen, but I am not aware what reason he has for this statement. On the vexed question of the relation of Philip to Christianity see Huet and Aubé, pp. 470 sqq.

with truth, for it touches not a single false note. At last his own summons came. He was incarcerated in the persecution of Decius, and treated with a severity which shattered his frame already enfeebled by labour and old age.

He was buried in Tyre, where for centuries his tomb, in the wall behind the high altar, formed the chief ornament of the magnificent cathedral of the Holy Sepulchre. Tyre was wasted by the Saracens, but even to this day, it is said, the poor fishermen, whose hovels occupy the site of that city of palaces, point to a shattered vault beneath which lie the bones of 'Oriunus[1].'

We may consider his voluminous and many-sided works under three heads—Textual Criticism, Exegesis, and Religious Philosophy. The first of these does not properly fall within the scope of our enquiry, but a brief notice may be permitted for the sake of the side-light which it throws upon the character of our author.

He devoted much time and labour to the text of the New Testament, which was already disfigured by corruptions, 'some arising from the carelessness of scribes, some from the evil licence of emendation, some from arbitrary omissions or interpolations[2].' Already the records were perverted in numberless passages, not only by Gnostic audacity, but by those minor variations which constitute what are known as the Western and Alexandrine families. Between errors of the latter class and the genuine reading he had no means of deciding except the perilous canon of intrinsic probability, which

---

[1] I owe this fact to Dr. Westcott's article, *Origen and the beginnings of Christian Philosophy*, in the Contemporary Review for May, 1879.

[2] *In Matth.* xv. 14 (Lom. iii. 357).

he applies with much acuteness, but at the same time with severe caution[1]. All that he could hope was to purify his own MS. or MSS.[2] (for he used more than one, and those of different families) from manifest faults of transcription and from recent and obvious depravations. This he effected with care and ability. The *Exęmplaria Adamantii* acquired the authority of a standard, and derived additional importance from the fact that a copy was presented by Eusebius to the Emperor Constantine. But Origen's fame as a critic rests chiefly upon the *Hexapla.* In controversy with the Jews the Christian disputant was constantly baffled by the retort, that the passages on which he relied were not found, or were otherwise expressed, in the Hebrew. Several new translations or recensions of the whole or part of the LXX had been produced, in which the discrepancies of the Alexandrine Version from the original were brought into strong relief. Origen saw clearly the whole of the difficulties involved, and with

---

[1] See the *Diss. critica de Cod. IV Evang. Origenis* in Griesbach, *Opuscula Academica,* vol. i. Origen sometimes makes conjectures in his Commentaries, but never admitted them into his text. Thus he thought the words ' thou shalt love thy neighbour as thyself' spurious in Matt. xix. 19 (see *In Matth.* xv. 14), but he does not venture to expunge them. He supports the reading Γεργεσήνων in Matt. viii. 28 and the parallel passages, but it is doubtful whether he actually inserted it in his MS. ; see *In Joan.* vi. 24 ; Redepenning, ii. 184 note ; and Tischendorf. Bethabara he found in some copies. In Rom. v. 14 the majority of his MSS. omitted the μή, *In Rom.* v. 1 (Lom. vi. 344). There were bolder critics in his time. Some wished to set aside the story of Dives and Lazarus, *In Joan.* xxxii. 13 (Lom. ii. 447) ; the words ' to-day thou shalt be with me in Paradise,' *In Joan.* xxxii. 19 (Lom. ii. 481) ; and the advice given to slaves, 1 Cor. vii. 21, *In Rom.* i. 1 (Lom. vi. 12).

[2] Redepenning, ii. 182 sqq.; Griesbach, p. 240. The latter scholar pointed out that the text of Mark used by Origen for *In Matth.* was Western, while that quoted in the *In Joan.* is Alexandrine. See Gregory, *Prolegomena* to Tischendorf, p. 189 ; Westcott and Hort, p. 113.

characteristic grandeur and fearlessness determined upon producing an edition of the Old Testament that should exhibit in parallel columns the Hebrew text and the rival versions, thus bringing before the eye of the enquirer in one view the whole of the evidence attainable[1]. At the same time he corrected and supplemented the LXX from the other versions, chiefly those of Theodotion and Aquila. This gigantic and costly scheme was rendered feasible by the munificence, and facilitated by the active cooperation, of Ambrosius.

The *Hexapla*, the first great achievement of Christian erudition, is impressive in many ways, not least as a proof of the intelligence and sincerity of the community to which it was addressed. But with all his devotion and learning Origen was not a consummate master in the higher functions of criticism. His equipment was insufficient. His knowledge of Hebrew was respectable, and for his age remarkable, but not profound. He had a fair acquaintance with the grammar and dictionary, but had not penetrated into the genius of the language[2].

[1] Field, in his magnificent work, *Origenis Hexapla*, xlviii. does not think that Origen had a distinctly controversial purpose in view. But see Redepenning, i. 234. 375 ; ii. 170. The *locus classicus* is *In Matth.* xv. 14. Partly owing to the plan followed by Origen, partly to the haste and inaccuracy of transcribers, the *Hexapla* caused very serious changes in the text of the LXX. Jerome, *Praefatio in Librum Paral.*, Migne, vol. xxviii. p. 1323 ; Schürer, p. 701.

[2] Redepenning, i. 367 ; ii. 166. 198 ; Ernesti, *Opuscula Philologica et Critica*. There is however some reason for lowering this estimate. *In Num.*, Hom. xiv. 1, Aiunt ergo qui hebraicas literas legunt, in hoc loco Deus non sub signo tetragrammati esse positum, de quo qui potest requirat (Redepenning thinks these words may have been inserted by the translator); *Contra Celsum*, i. 34, ἡ μὲν λέξις ἡ ᾿Ααλμά, ἣν οἱ μὲν ἑβδομήκοντα μετειλήφασι πρὸς τὴν παρθένον, ἄλλοι δὲ εἰς τὴν νεᾶνιν, κεῖται, ὥς φασι, καὶ ἐν τῷ Δευτερονομίῳ ἐπὶ παρθένου. Origen does not speak of his own knowledge on this important and much debated point, and the authorities on whom he relied misled him, for the word *almah* is not found in the passage to which

Again he was hampered by prejudice. He regarded the LXX as an independent and inspired authority, and, like Justin, accounted for its variation from the Hebrew by supposing that the latter had been deliberately falsified by the Jews[1]. In this way he explained the absence from the Canon of the Apocryphal Books. On one occasion he had employed in a public debate doctrinal proofs taken from the History of Susanna. This drew upon him an epistle from Julius Africanus, in which it was shown with great force and ingenuity that this addition to the Book of Daniel could not have been composed in Hebrew[2]. Origen with much learning and some little warmth refused to be convinced, but the honour of arms remained with Africanus, whose letter indeed is a signal refutation of the epithets 'credulous' and 'uncritical' so often applied to the age in which, and the men by whom, the Canon of the New Testament was settled.

Of the stately *Hexapla* time has spared us nothing but a gleaning of scattered fragments. The original MS. perished probably when the library of Caesarea was destroyed by the Arabs in the middle of the seventh century, and its immense size—it consisted of not less than fifty great rolls of parchment—must have prevented its ever being copied as a whole, though the revised LXX

he refers, Deut. xxii. 23–26. It is evident from the *Ep. ad Afric.* that Origen could not walk alone in Hebrew. Hence Boherellus inferred ' Origenem hebraice plane nescivisse.' See Rosenmüller, iii. 63. 23. 153.

[1] Justin, *Trypho*, 71 ; Otto, p. 256.

[2] The chief point urged by Africanus is the play of words σχῖνος σχίσις, πρῖνος πρίσις. Origen struggles against this cogent argument in the *Ep. ad Afric.* But in a Fragment from *Strom.* x. (Lom. xvii. p. 74) he admits that *if* the paronomasia does not exist in Hebrew the objection is fatal. The *if* is not critical but theological. See Schürer, p. 717.

was circulated separately, and indeed still exists in a
Syriac translation[1]. But of the exegetic work of Origen
a very considerable mass is still extant, partly in the
authentic Greek, partly in Latin translations. The
surviving remains cover a large part both of the Old
and of the New Testaments, and afford ample material
for judging the method and substance of his teaching.
Yet they are but a portion of what he accomplished.
In the form of Scholia, Homilies or Commentaries he
expounded nearly every book in the Bible, and many
books were treated in all three ways.

The Scholia[2] were brief annotations, such as are commonly found on the margin of ancient MSS. The
Homilies and Commentaries require a fuller notice.

Already the old prophesyings and speaking with
tongues, except among the Montanist sectaries, have
disappeared before the growing reverence for Scripture
and the increasing stringency of discipline. Their place

---

[1] The Syro-Hexaplar text is probably nearly all in existence, though till
all the Fragments have been published it cannot be known what deficiencies
may exist. See the articles *Versions* in Dict. of Bible by Tregelles and
Syrische Bibelübersetzungen by Nestle in Herzog ; Field ; Ceriani, *Codex
Syro-hexaplaris Ambrosianus*, Milan, 1874 ; Lagarde, *V. T. ab Origene
recensiti frag. apud Syros servata quinque*, Göttingen, 1880 ; Dr. T. Skat
Roerdam, *Libri Judicum et Ruth*, Hauniae, 1861 ; the last-named authority
gives full and elaborate prolegomena.

[2] Jerome, Preface to his translation of the *Homilies on Ezekiel*, 'Scias
Origenis opuscula in omnem Scripturam esse triplicia. Primum eius
Excerpta, quae Graece σχόλια nuncupantur, in quibus ea quae sibi videbantur
obscura atque habere aliquid difficultatis summatim breviterque perstrinxit.'
In the Preface to his Comm. on Matthew, Jerome calls them 'commaticum
interpretandi genus.' The word σημείωσις, which also occurs, appears to be
used in the general sense of 'notes,' which were sometimes perhaps σχόλια,
sometimes extracts from the Commentaries or Homilies, *Origeniana*, iii. 1. 4,
but see Redepenning, ii. 376 ; Ernesti, *Opuscula Philologica*. Such are the
fragmentary extracts, chiefly from Catenas and of somewhat doubtful
authenticity, published as Selecta. See the *monita* in De la Rue. Gallandi,
vol. xiv., *App.*, has collected many fragments that are not given in Lommatzsch.

was supplied by the Homily[1] or Discourse, a name
derived from the philosophic schools, expressive of the
character of Christian eloquence, which was didactic and
not rhetorical. In the days of Origen, and in Palestine,
(for his priestly activity belongs wholly to the time after
his exile from Egypt) public worship was held no longer
in the large room of some wealthy brother's house, but in
buildings definitely appropriated for the purpose, in which
the Bishop and his clergy were seated in a semicircle
round the decorated Altar[2]. The service was divided
into two portions, corresponding to what were afterwards
known as the Mass of the Catechumens and the Mass of
the Faithful. To the first, which was held daily, belonged
the reading of Scripture, the Sermon, and apparently
certain prayers[3]; to the second, celebrated on Sundays
and festivals, the prayers properly so called and the
Eucharist. At the first catechumens, even heathen, were
allowed to be present; from the second all, save the
baptised, were rigidly excluded.

The Lessons were often of considerable length, com-
prising as much as three or four of our modern chapters,
and went on in regular order, and the preacher expounded the whole or a portion of each according to
the direction of the presiding bishop[4]. It is probable

---

[1] Redepenning, ii. 212 sqq. The terms κήρυγμα and διάλεξις were also in use.

[2] *In Jesu Nave,* Hom. x. 3 (Lom. xi. 104); *In Judices,* Hom. iii. 2 (Lom. xi. 237); Probst, *Kirchliche Disciplin,* p. 212.

[3] Many of the Homilies end with the admonition to stand up and pray, e.g. *In Luc.* xxxix. Catechumens were addressed *In Luc.,* Hom. vii. Heathen were sometimes present, *In Jerem.,* Hom. ix. 4 (Lom. xv. 210).

[4] The Lesson read before the Sermon on the Witch of Endor included 1 Sam. xxv. xxvi. xxvii. xxviii. Origen, standing in the pulpit, asks which of the four περικοπαί he is to take for his subject, ὅ τι ποτε βούλεται ὁ ἐπίσκοπος προτεινάτω τῶν τεσσάρων, ἵνα περὶ τοῦτο ἀσχοληθῶμεν, and the Bishop replies, 'the Witch of Endor.' There was as yet only one lesson, taken sometimes from the Old, sometimes from the New Testament. At

that the friendly prelate of Caesarea suffered Origen to follow his own plan; hence his Homilies form a continuous exposition of the several books. They were delivered before a mixed, shifting, and not always orderly congregation. The services were daily and long. Some of the brethren would attend only on feast-days, and not always then. Some left the church before the sermon began, or if they remained, gathered in knots in the farther end of the building, the place of the heathen and unbaptised, 'turning their backs on the Word of God and busying themselves with secular gossip.' There were broad differences again in knowledge and morality. Some thought it not inconsistent with their Christian profession to haunt the circus or the amphitheatre; some fluctuated between Gnosticism and the Church.; some were still tainted with heathen superstitions; some, sincere but ignorant, interpreted the promises of the Gospel in the most gross and carnal sense, or 'believed of God what would not be believed of the cruelest of mankind.' Hence the duty of Reserve, which Origen everywhere professes, weighs upon him with especial urgency in the Homilies[1].

The Homilies are rather what we should call Lectures than Sermons. His object in the pulpit, Origen tells us, is not the explanation of the letter so much as the

a somewhat later period there were four, divided into two pairs, the first pair from the Old, the second from the New Test., and between the two readings a psalm was sung, *Const. App.* ii. 57, but no trace of this usage is found in Origen, Redepenning, ii. 221 sqq.; Probst, *Liturgie*, 152. Many of Origen's Homilies must have taken an hour and a half in the delivery.

[1] The behaviour of the women was especially troublesome, 'quae tantum garriunt, quae tantum fabulis obstrepunt, ut non sinant esse silentium. Iam quid de mente earum, quid de corde discutiam, si de infantibus suis aut de lana cogitent aut de necessariis domus,' *In Exod.* Hom. xiii. 3: cp. *In Num.* Hom. v. 1; *In Lev.* Hom. ix. 5. 7. 9; *In Gen.* Hom. x. 1; *Philocalia,* i. 8 *ad fin.*; Redepenning, ii. 229.

edification of the Church; hence he dwells here almost entirely upon the moral and spiritual sense[1]. There is abundance of allegory but little exhortation, still less unction or pathos. Origen does not wind himself into the heart. He has not the blithe geniality of Clement, whose cloistered life seems never to have felt a storm. In Origen there is a subdued fire that reveals the tale of mental suffering and exhausting toil. Hence that austere solemnity, that absolute sincerity, that breadth and dignity of mind, which still grasp and detain the reader with the same spell that was cast upon Gregory. Origen is emphatically 'a man of God,' strong and subtle yet infinitely humble and gentle, a true *Ductor Dubitantium*, because he knew there was much that he did not know and yet was not afraid. His style is almost everywhere loose and prolix, owing to his habit of extemporaneous speech or dictation. This applies to the Commentaries as well as to the Homilies. Where he used the pen it is terser and more collected. But it is always simple and direct, flowing straight from the heart, devoid of every ornament, and owing its force entirely to that glowing fusion of thought and feeling by which it is informed.

[1] *In Lev.* Hom. i. 1; *In Num.* Hom. xiv. 1. The reader may acquire a just idea of Origen as a preacher by perusing *In Gen.* viii; *In Lev.* vii; *In Luc.* xiv. The Homilies on *Judges* we know to have been written, though extempore passages were added in the delivery, see Hom. i. 3: 'Sed et illud quod dicentibus nobis occurrit,' &c. Beyond this passage I am not aware of the existence of any positive evidence as to which of his works were written with his own hand, though some, e.g. the *In Joan.*, we know were not. But I cannot think that the *De Principiis*, the *De Oratione*, or the *De Martyrio* belonged to the latter class. Eustathius complains of Origen's ἄμετρος φλυαρία; Theophilus called him 'Seminarium loquacitatis;' Erasmus on the other hand praises his brevity, Huet, *Orig.* iii. 1. 1; Redepenning, ii. 252. Some interesting remarks will be found in Rothe, *Geschichte der Predigt*, Bremen, 1881.

The plan which he laid down for himself in the Commentaries [1] was to give first the literal, then the moral, then the spiritual sense of each verse in regular succession. The text is but the threshing-floor on which he pours out all the harvest of his knowledge, his meditations, his hopes. Any word may open up a train of thought extending throughout all Scripture and all time. Hence there is much repetition and confusion. Even here the object is not so much instruction as the deepening of the Christian life. We lose in perspicuity, but we never miss the inspiriting sense of immediate contact with a great character.

To us, though not to himself nor to the men of his time, Origen's merit as an expositor rests mainly upon the skill and patience with which he evolved the real and natural sense of the Bible [2]. He himself saw clearly that

---

[1] I may recommend to the reader the allegory on the Treasury *In Joan.* xix. 2 ; the passage on the Death of Christ, *ibid.* xxviii. 14 ; on Faith, *ibid.* xxxii. 9 ; the allegory on the Mercy Seat, *In Rom.* iii. 8, and the Exposition of the Parables in St. Matthew. The latter Commentary is generally superior to that on St. John. But those who wish to see Origen at his best will seek him where he is least allegorical, in the *Contra Celsum*, or the treatises on *Prayer* and on *Martyrdom.*

[2] Perhaps the best instance of Origen's merits and defects in dealing with the literal sense is to be found in his comments on the opening words of St. John's Gospel *In Joan.* i. 16 onwards. In the New Testament he is always excellent, but we must compare him with the ancient commentators on Homer, not, as Rosenmüller practically does, with the best modern divines. I have adhered to Origen's own distinction of the literal from the mystic sense. But it must be remembered that many of the most important passages in the N. T. are figurative, and that it is precisely in the explanation of these that the merit of Origen is to be found. Perhaps his supreme excellence lies in his clearness and courage in pointing out difficulties, the moral anomalies which beset the Gnostic and the ignorant Christian, the apparent non-fulfilment of the Messianic hope which rebuffed the Jew (see for all this the opening of the *Philocalia*) ; the contradictions of the Evangelists, *In Joan.* x. 3. sqq. ; the chronological difficulty involved in the 'four months before harvest,' *In Joan.* xiii. 39 ; the historical difficulty in the title βασιλικός, *In Joan.* xiii. 57. If he often creates perplexities out of insigni-

this is the foundation of everything. If we measure
him by the best modern commentators, we may be
struck by his deficiencies. But in relation to his own
age his services are extraordinary. He need not fear
comparison with the great pagan grammarians. He
took great pains as we have seen to ascertain the text;
he insists on the necessity of fixing the precise meaning
of the words, and for this purpose will hunt a phrase
through the whole Bible with a fertility of quotation
truly prodigious, when we remember that it rests upon
unaided memory. He never slurs a difficulty, raising
and discussing every doubt that can by any possibility
suggest itself. Hebrew he knew but imperfectly, and
this is a fatal defect in dealing with the LXX. But in
the New Testament he displays an accurate and intelligent appreciation of Greek grammar. Where he fails it is
from preconceived ideas, from the hairsplitting and over-
subtlety which are the Nemesis of Allegorism, or from
deficiency of that sense of humour which corrects the
extravagances of Clement. He cannot understand irony,
and the simpler a thing is the more difficult he makes
it [1]. Such scientific knowledge as the times could supply
is at his call [2], and he had travelled in Palestine with a

ficant verbal distinctions, this is still a fault on the right side. For details
see Redepenning, ii. 200 sqq. ; Rosenmüller. Ernesti, *Opuscula Philologica et
Critica*, rates him very high as the founder of textual criticism and scientific
inductive exegesis.

[1] A good instance of this is this treatment of the gift of Caleb to his
daughter Achsa (Joshua xv. 19), 'Et accepit Gonetlam superiorem et
Gonetlam inferiorem . . . Videtis quia vere auxilio Dei opus est ut haec
explanari queant,' *In Jesu Nave*, Hom. xx. 4.

[2] It did not amount to much. See the account of the different kinds of
pearls *In Matt.* x. 7. Origen thought that the popular beliefs that serpents
spring from the spinal marrow of dead men, bees from oxen, wasps from
horses, beetles from asses, that serpents have a knowledge of antidotes, that
the eagle uses the ἀετίτης λίθος as an amulet for the protection of its young

keen eye for the geography of the Gospels. Philosophy
too was at his command, though he does not rate it so
high as Clement [1]. 'Few,' he says, 'are those who have
taken the spoils of the Egyptians and made of them the
furniture of the tabernacle.' Learning is useful, he tells
his pupil Gregory, but the Scriptures are their own best
key. 'Be diligent in reading the divine Scriptures, yes,
be diligent ... Knock and the doorkeeper will open unto
thee ... And be not content to knock and to enquire,
for the most necessary aid to spiritual truth is prayer.
Hence our Saviour said not only " knock and it shall be
opened," and " seek and ye shall find," but "ask and it
shall be given you [2]." '

were possibly true, *Contra Celsum*, iv. 57. 86. But he is no worse than
Celsus himself or Pliny. Similar absurdities are to be found in Clement.
For Origen's other accomplishments, see *Origeniana*, ii. 1 ; Redepenning,
i. 219. M. Denis, p. 14, rates them very low. Indeed absorbed as Origen
was in the drudgery of tuition from his eighteenth year, it is impossible
that he can have gone profoundly into any line of knowledge not immediately connected with his special studies.

[1] For the use that he made of philosophy, see the *Panegyric* of Gregory,
and the account of his method of teaching in Lecture II. M. Denis, *Philosophie d'Origène*, p. 30, says : 'Il ne conservait de l'esprit philosophique que
l'insatiable curiosité,' and complains, in the chapter on *Anthropologie*, of his
neglect of ethics, psychology and politics. The duties of citizens would not
have been a safe theme for a Christian writer under the heathen Empire.
Psychology again is for another reason an exceedingly difficult subject for a
Christian, because he cannot isolate it, because he has to regard above all
things the point of junction with metaphysics, and with the metaphysics of
Revelation. Clement and Origen were the first to attempt the problem from
this point of view. The same difficulty attaches to the theory of Ethics.
The practice of Ethics is undervalued both by Clement and Origen, though
not so markedly by the latter. Hence it is a just criticism, ' Qu'il y a bien
plus à apprendre sur l'observation intérieure non seulement dans Saint
Augustin ou dans Saint Jérome, mais encore dans Tertullien.' The remarks
of M. Denis are brilliant and in the main accurate, but the plan of his work
compels him to approach Origen obliquely, and view him in a false light.
Origen is before all things a theologian, but a philosophical theologian. The
reader may consult with advantage Harnack, *Dogmengeschichte*, pp. 514 sqq.

[2] From the *Epistola ad Gregorium*. The difference between the attitude of

But it is when the sense is ascertained, or as he calls it 'cleansed,' that the supreme task of the Commentator first comes into view. By all the means that science can bring to our aid we can do no more than attain to the 'letter that killeth,' that bald first sense of Scripture which fluctuates between Atheism and Superstition. We must believe only what is worthy of God. Where then are we to find the true divine message? Origen like Clement held firmly to the unity and inspiration of all Scripture, and therefore like Clement he was driven to find the answer to this question in Allegorism. There is however considerable difference in detail between the two teachers.

Clement is content to accept Allegorism as a fact, as a part of Tradition. It was sanctioned by the practice of Philo and Barnabas, and appeared to derive authority from certain passages of Scripture. This is not enough for Origen, whose reason works always with a broad poetic sweep, and never rests till it has brought the particular affirmation under the scope of some all-embracing law. To him Allegorism is only one manifestation of the sacramental mystery of Nature. There are two heavens, two earths—the visible is but a blurred copy of the invisible. The divine wisdom and goodness, which are the cause of both, are in this world of ours distorted by refraction arising from the density of the medium. Yet they may be discerned by those that have eyes to see. Allegorism, Teleology, the argument from Analogy are all different aspects of one great truth. God made man in His own image and likeness,

Clement and Origen towards philosophy is well described by M. Denis, *Introduction.*

and so perhaps He made other creatures in the image
and likeness of other heavenly things.   Hence the grain
of mustard, which, though it is the least of all seeds,
when grown is the greatest among herbs, and becometh
a tree, may be a parable of the kingdom of heaven . . .
What is true of seeds is true also of trees, of animals.
Again in the grain of mustard lurks more than one
analogy to eternal verities, for it is a symbol also of
faith.   'If a man have faith as a grain of mustard seed
he may say unto this mountain, Be thou removed!' There
are then in this one seed many virtues serving as symbols
of heavenly things, and of these virtues the last and
lowest is that whereby it ministers to our bodily needs.
So with all else that God made—it is good for the use
of man, but it bears also the imprint of celestial things,
whereby the soul may be taught, and elevated to the
contemplation of the invisible and eternal.   Nor is it
possible for man, while he lives in the flesh, to know anything that transcends his sensible experience, except by
seizing and deciphering this imprint.   For God has so
ordered His creation, has so linked the lower to the
higher by subtle signatures and affinities, that the world
we see is, as it were, a great staircase, by which the mind
of man must climb upwards to spiritual intelligence [1].

From this Law of Correspondence springs incidentally
the profound observation that suggested the *Analogy.*
' He, who believes the Scripture to have proceeded from
Him who is the Author of Nature, may well expect to
find the same sort of difficulties in it as are found in the

---

[1] The passage quoted is from *In Cant. Canticorum,* iii. (Lom. xv. 48).
Consult also *In Lev.* Hom. v. 1 (Greek text in *Philoc.* chap. i. *ad fin.*) and
De Princ. iv.

constitution of Nature.' But the antagonists whom Origen had in view were not so much the Platonic Deists as the Jew and especially the Gnostic. Hence the turn which he gives to the argument is in the main different from that of Bishop Butler.

Scripture has in general three senses—the literal, the moral, and the spiritual[1]. Not that every passage is susceptible of all three modes of interpretation. Many texts have no literal sense at all. Some, like the Decalogue, have a moral signification, of such a kind that it is needless to seek farther. The distinction between the two higher senses is not always very clearly drawn, as there are regions where the one shades off into the other by very fine gradations. But there is an abundance of passages where they are so sharply defined as to show us exactly what Origen meant. Thus the grain of mustard is first the actual seed, then faith, then the Kingdom of Heaven. So again the 'little foxes' of the Song of Songs are typical, in the second sense of sins affecting the individual, in the third of heresies distracting the Church[2]. The moral embraces all that touches the single soul in this life, in its relation to the law of right, or to God ; the spiritual includes all ' mysteries,' all

---

[1] Redepenning, i. 299 sqq. ; *Origeniana*, ii. 2. 13 (Lom. xxiii. 254). For the spiritual sense Origen uses more than a score of different terms, Red. p. 305. Some have thought that he made a triple division of the spiritual into allegoric, tropologic, and anagogic, or a double into allegoric and anagogic, but without sufficient reason. That there were neither more nor less than three senses was proved by Prov. xxii. 20, καὶ σὺ δὲ ἀπόγραψαι αὐτὰ σεαυτῷ τρισσῶς εἰς βουλὴν καὶ γνῶσιν ἐπὶ τὸ πλάτος τῆς καρδίας σου. They answer to body, soul, and spirit, and are alluded to in the waterpots holding ' two or three firkins apiece,' and in the *Shepherd* of Hermas, a book, 'qui a nonnullis contemni videtur,' where Grapte, Clement, and Hermas represent the three classes of believers. *De Princ.* iv. 11.

[2] *In Cant. Cantic.* iv. (Lom. xv. p. 83 sqq.).

the moments in the history of the community, the Church, in time and still more in eternity.

To interpret and set forth these mysteries, these moral enigmas, is the task of Allegorism. But we must now notice that this Biblical alchemy is capable of application to two distinct purposes. One is negative and apologetic, the other is positive and didactic. Origen employed it in both directions with singular freedom and address. But it is his use of the negative side that is the more characteristic.

He held that innumerable passages in both Testaments have no sense at all except as Allegories[1]. Neither Clement nor Philo expressly affirmed this, though the idea certainly lurked within their minds[2]. But Origen was not the man to disguise from himself or from others the exact nature of what he was doing. Many passages of Scripture, he says, are excluded from belief by physical impossibility. Such are those which speak of morning and evening before the creation of the Sun, the story of the Fall, and the carrying up of our Lord into an exceeding high mountain by Satan in the Temptation. Others again imply moral impossibilities. Such are those which speak of the child as punished for the sin of the parent, the law that on the Sabbath no Jew should take up a burden or move from his place, the precepts of the Saviour not to possess two coats, to pluck out the offending eye, to turn the right cheek to him that has smitten the left. Yet another class are rejected by the enlightened conscience. Such are the

---

[1] *De Princ.* iv. 15 sqq.

[2] Philo comes very near denying the literal sense in *De Ebriet.* 36 (i. 379), Σαμουὴλ δὲ γέγονε μὲν ἴσως ἄνθρωπος, παρείληπται δὲ οὐχ ὡς σύνθετον ζῷον ἀλλ᾿ ὡς νοῦς λατρείᾳ καὶ θεραπείᾳ θεοῦ μόνον χαίρων.

adventures of Lot, the cruelties of the Jewish wars, the execrations of the Psalms. All these antinomies of Scripture were forced upon him on one side by the Ebionite and Gnostic, on the other by the Greek philosopher, who was beginning to study the Bible in a spirit of not wholly unfriendly curiosity, and was violently repelled by these proofs, as he thought them, of Jewish barbarism. Origen felt the embarrassment most acutely, and his fearless logic saw but one way of escape. These passages, he admitted, in their literal sense are not true. Why then, urged the adversary, are they found in what you Christians call the Word of God? To this he replied that, though in one sense untrue, they are in another the highest, the only valuable truth. They are permitted for an object. These impossibilities, trivialities, ineptitudes are wires stretched across our path by the Holy Spirit, to warn us that we are not in the right way. We must not leap over them; we must go beneath, piercing down to the smooth broad road of the spiritual intelligence. They are the rough outer husk, which repels the ignorant and unfit reader, but stimulates the true child of God to increased exertion. The letter is the external garb, often sordid and torn, but 'the king's daughter is all glorious within.' It is as if the sunlight streamed in through the crannies of a ruinous wall; the wall is ruinous in order that the sunlight may stream in [1].

Origen could not rest content with an easy optimism like that of Clement, who stopped short at the assertion of the unity of Divine Justice and Goodness. For there

---

[1] The foundations of this section will be found in *De Princ.* iv. and the *Philocalia.*

was that in Scripture which appeared to him irreconcileable with both. These passages were in fact the key
of the Gnostic position. What the Gnostic asserted was
not merely that Justice and Goodness are different
things, but that God as He is depicted in the Old Testament is certainly not good, though He may be called
just in the sense in which that epithet is applied to
earthly rulers, who, though harsh and vindictive, do not
punish without a reason. The difficulty is certainly
there, and Origen with his far-sighted intrepidity fixes
and grapples with it. It is a serious effort to solve a
serious and, if left unsolved, fatal objection.

We may notice also in passing the biographical interest of his mature teaching on this point. If we compare
what he says in the *De Principiis*, where he treats the
command about the two coats as purely figurative,
with the passionate asceticism of his youth, we shall
see how the letter had been to him in very truth at
once a stumbling-block and a cranny in the wall. It
was by bruising himself in the fiery endeavour to obey,
that he learned what obedience really means.

On its negative side Allegorism then is apologetic, on
its positive it is the instrument for the discovery of
Mysteries[1]. What these are we have seen already in

[1] The word Mystery is used in two senses. First of the Christian worship
or ritual, the modern Sacraments. Of these, though their general nature
could not be kept secret, all minute knowledge was reserved for those who
had the right to be present at their enactment. In this respect they resembled the Mysteries of Samothrace or Eleusis, hence the name. So Ignatius,
Ad Eph. 12, speaks of Christians as συμμύσται : cp. *Ad Trall.* ii. 3 : see
also *Ep. ad Diognetum*, 1 ; Tertullian, *Apol.* 7. In this sense that of natural
reserve, of reluctance to lay bare the whole organism of the Church to un-
sympathetic hearers, the *Disciplina Arcani* is no doubt very ancient, though
its growth can be traced. It cannot have been viewed as a rule of conscience by St. Paul who on the ship ' took bread and gave thanks to God

the case of Clement, and shall see more clearly still as we advance. In both respects it must be handled with a certain reserve. The rule of Economy was directed partly against the mocking heathen ; that which is sacred must not be given to dogs. But it had also another and even more serious application as a law of forbearance towards the weaker brethren. From these too 'it is good to hide the mystery of the King [1].' Origen does not distinguish between the higher and lower Life quite in the same way as Clement, who regards all Christians as members of the true Church, though ranked in an

before them all.' Second, of what we may call Theology the doctrine of the Trinity, of Angels, of the Resurrection, the explanation and idealisation of rites, the hidden meaning of the Law. In this sense the word Mystery is found in the New Testament. Ignatius hints at mysteries concerning the unseen world which he is not at liberty to divulge, *Ad Smyrn.* vi. 1 ; *Trall.* v. 2. The word might be used of the visions of the Montanists. But in the Alexandrines it means almost always intellectual interpretation, in fact theology. See Probst, *Kirchliche Disciplin*, 303 sqq. ; Bingham, x. 5, and Mr. Haddan's article *Disciplina Arcani* in Dict. of Christ. Ant.

[1] Tobit xii. 7 quoted *Contra Celsum*, v. 19. Many passages were thought to inculcate the duty of Reserve. Clement, *Strom.* v. 10. 63, cites μυστήριον ἐμὸν ἐμοὶ καὶ τοῖς υἱοῖς τοῦ οἴκου μου, Theodotion's version of Isaiah xxiv. 16 (but he quotes it from a Gospel, probably the Gospel according to the Egyptians ; Hilgenfeld, *Novum Test. extra Can. Rec.* iii. p. 46. The verse is used in the same way in the *Homilies*, xix. 20. See note in Field), and *Strom.* ii. 2. 8, Proverbs v. 16, μὴ ὑπερεκχείσθω σοι ὕδατα ἐκ τῆς σῆς πηγῆς, where the negative is not found in the Hebrew. In the New Testament it was based mainly upon Matt. vii. 6 ; Mark iv. 34. In Clement and Origen it is almost always spoken of as intended for the protection of the weaker brethren. Thus the main reason why Scripture speaks in allegories is to stimulate enquiry, and one principal difference between the simple believer and the Gnostic is that all allegories are withheld from the former. See especially *Paed.* ii. 8. 73, where Clement breaks off his explanation of the mysteries involved in the Crown of Thorns with the words, ἀλλ' ἐξέβην γὰρ τοῦ παιδαγωγικοῦ τύπου τὸ διδασκαλικὸν εἶδος παρεισάγων. Origen professes his inability to say all that might be said on the mysteries of the Trinity and Eternal Punishment in an exoteric treatise, *Contra Celsum*, vi. 18. 26, yet it is not the doctrines but the allegories involved that he finds it impossible to explain to unbelievers. See also the passages referred to above, p. 129.

ascending scale of faith and knowledge. He takes a much severer view of the insufficiency of nominal Christianity, and on the other hand accentuates the distinction between theology and acquiescence. Hence the difference between the Two Lives has a marked tendency to pass over, on the side of knowledge into that between professional and unprofessional, between cleric and lay, on the side of conduct into that between the Visible and Invisible Church[1].

'The holy Apostles,' he says, 'in preaching the faith of Christ declared with the utmost clearness whatever they thought necessary to salvation, even to those who are slothful in the investigation of divine science, leaving the reason of their assertions to be sought out by those who should deserve the excellent gifts of the Spirit, and especially the graces of utterance, wisdom and knowledge. But as to other things they affirmed indeed that they are, but why or whence they did not explain[2].' He

---

[1] Origen speaks of the three degrees of Christian perfection, distinguished by Faith, Hope, and Charity, *In Rom.* iv. 6 (Lom. vi. 271) and elsewhere. The distinction between the Two Lives is laid down *In Joan.* xx. 26 sqq. as by Clement, the ἁπλούστερον πιστεύοντες who do not understand the word which they obey, the slaves whose motive is Fear, are opposed to the sons, οἱ διορατικώτερον κατανοοῦντες (the Seeing Israel). Even Paul was by nature a child of wrath, so are we all; we become adopted sons by using the light and power given to us, especially by loving our enemies. Compare *In Joan.* xx. 15; *Prol. in Cant. Cantic.*, where again the stress is laid upon Love. Elsewhere more value is assigned to Knowledge, and so the distinction at times seems to coincide very nearly with that between Clergy and People, *Contra Celsum*, i. 9; *In Jesu Nave*, Hom. xvii. But even among the Clergy there were those who could speak only of the literal and moral senses, and so belonged to the lower class, *In Lev.* Hom. xiii. 1. 3. The difference between the Visible and Invisible Church in the sense of nominal and real Christianity is very forcibly expressed *In Matt.* xii. 12. See further in Lecture VI.

[2] *De Princ.* i. 3. The following passage is from *In Num.* Hom. v. 1. It will be observed that though the son of Kohath is a communicant, the rule of

found a symbol of this distinction of believers in the arrangements for carrying the Tabernacle on the march. Aaron and his sons were to wrap the sanctuary and all the vessels of the sanctuary in the appointed covering of badgers' skins or cloths of blue and scarlet, 'after that the sons of Kohath shall come to bear them, but they shall not touch any holy thing lest they die . . . they shall not go in to see when the holy things are covered lest they die.' So in our ecclesiastical observances there are some things that all must do, but that all cannot understand. Why for instance we should kneel in prayer, or why we should turn our faces to the East, could not I think be made clear to everybody. Who again could easily expound the manner of celebration of the Eucharist, or of its reception, or the words and actions, the questions and replies of Baptism? And yet all these things we carry veiled and covered upon our shoulders, when we so fulfil them as they have been handed down to us by the Great High Priest and his Sons.' Only the son of Aaron, the man of spiritual intelligence, might gaze upon the holy things naked and unveiled. To the son of Kohath belonged unquestioning obedience; he carried the burden, but was forbidden to demand the reason. Nor might the son of Aaron declare it. To uncover the mystery, to explain that which the bearer was not able to comprehend, was spiritual homicide.

The nature and scope of the Alexandrine *Disciplina*

Reserve, 'nolite mittere sanctum canibus,' applies to him, *In Lev.* Hom. vi. 6; xii. 7. *In Num.* Hom. iv. 3, ' Aut si res poscit proferre et inferioribus, id est imperitioribus, tradere, ne nuda proferat, ne aperta ostendat et penitus patentia ; alioquin homicidium facit et exterminat plebem.'

Arcani[1] are sufficiently clear from these extracts, which
might be indefinitely multiplied. The Reserve or
Economy of Clement and Origen was directed mainly
against Christians of the simpler sort, and its object was
to save them from waters too deep for them, to guard
them from discussions involving doubts that would certainly perplex, and might altogether mislead, a faith
earnest and correct, though supported by slender intellectual gifts. In plain words the faith of the son of
Kohath is Catholicism, and that of the son of Aaron
is Idealism, and the Allegorism of Clement and Origen
is a plea for the utmost freedom of thought, on condition that it keeps within the teaching of Christ and
His Apostles, and is couched in a learned language.

Only by perverse ingenuity can it be twisted into an
argument in defence of the very mode of conception
against which it is especially directed[2]. The Eucharist

[1] Probst would restrict this phrase (first used by Meier, a professor of
Helmstädt in 1677) to the rule forbidding the revelation of the Christian
rites to heathen and distinguish it from the pedagogic Economy, which may
be expressed in the words of the Council of Trent: 'Apud rudem vero
plebem difficiliores ac subtiliores quaestiones quaeque ad aedificationem
non faciunt, et ex quibus plerumque nulla fit pietatis accessio, a popularibus
concionibus secludantur. Incerta item vel quae specie falsi laborant evul-
gari ac tractari non permittunt,' *Kirchliche Disciplin*, pp. 303 sqq. Perhaps
the distinction is not ill grounded, for Origen is certainly reticent as to the
ritual of the Eucharist, *In Lev.* Hom. ix. 10. It may be noticed here that
he uses the phrase ' sancta sanctorum ' to express not the secrecy but the
spiritual nature of the Eucharist, the difference between worthy and unworthy
recipients, *In Lev.*, Hom. xiii. 6 ; *Prol. in Cant. Cantic.* (Lom. xiv. 314).
As regards theology there is really no secret at all. So far as Clement and
Origen had explicit views they declared them in one place or another. M.
Denis says of the latter, ' Nul parmi les docteurs de l'Église n'use moins de
la méthode de parler par l'économie quoiqu'il en reconnaisse l'utilité et la
sagesse.'
[2] As by Bellarmine and his followers, see Bingham, x. 5. The argument
from the *Disciplina Arcani*, in its strict logical form, proceeds on the axiom

is doubtless one of the mysteries, to be spoken of with
guarded reserve in the presence not only of heathen, but
of simple or careless believers. But it is a mystery
in precisely the same sense as any other, and precisely
the same solvent must be applied, before we can obtain
the spiritual truth hidden beneath the rough ore of the
words. 'Even in the New Testament there is a letter
which killeth him who does not spiritually consider
what is said. If according to the letter you follow the
very words of Christ . . . unless ye eat my Flesh and
drink my Blood, this letter killeth[1].' Nor was it the
greatest of the mysteries. There was doubtless a party
in the Church who attached a very literal sense to these
words of the Saviour, and bitterly resented any attempt
to idealise them. But the danger of wounding the
simple faith and suggesting doubts that might weaken
the sanctions of morality lay in a different direction—in
speculations upon foreknowledge, predestination and
birth-sin, in attempts to penetrate the secrets of the
Eternal Gospel, the doctrine of angels and demons, and
the history of the soul after death. Of these it is said
they are ' mysteries which may not be entrusted even
to paper[2].'

It is possible to defend the practice of Reserve, if it

that complete silence is absolute proof, and that, failing this, the less the
evidence the more certain the conclusion. This is obviously absurd. Hence
the *Disciplina Arcani*, as a controversial weapon, has been superseded by
the doctrine of Development, though it is still employed to eke out insufficient evidence.

[1] *In Lev.* Hom. vii. 5 (Lom. ix. 306).

[2] *In Rom.* ii. 4, of the mode in which the souls of good men operate
after dissolution as good angels, those of the wicked as bad angels, it is
said that these things are 'ne chartulae quidem committenda mysteria.'
Compare the *Prol. in Cant. Cantic.* (Lom. xiv. 320).

be taken to represent the method of a skilful teacher, who will not confuse the learner with principles beyond his comprehension[1]. This however is by no means what the Alexandrines intended. With them it is the screen of an esoteric belief. They held that the mass of men will necessarily accept the symbol for the idea, will, that is, be more or less superstitious. It is enough if their superstition is such as to lead them in the right direction. This is a necessary corollary of the new compromise between the Church and the world, a taint inherited from the Greek schools in which Truth was not a cardinal virtue. Freedom remains, but it is a freedom of the *élite*, which may be tolerated so long as it does not cry aloud in the streets. But let us remember the Alexandrines were pleading for the freedom, not for the restriction. It was not altogether their fault, if they were driven to approximate on this point to the dreaded Gnostics.

Origen differs from Clement in regarding Allegorism rather as a personal gift than as an inherited tradition[2]. He differs from him still more in the volume, ingenuity, beauty of his applications of the method. All Scripture becomes transparent beneath his touch; the 'crannies

---

[1] It is so defended by J. H. Newman, *Arians*, i. 3. pp. 40 sqq. 3rd ed.; see also the *Apologia pro Vita Sua ;* and by Origen himself, *Contra Celsum*, iii. 52 sqq.

[2] Clement's few Allegorisms are almost without exception borrowed. We may say that he regarded not only the sanction but the substance of this mode of interpretation as given by Tradition. Origen feels that he has a personal illumination : *In Levit.* Hom. viii. 1, 'putas possumus veteris instrumenti formas novi testamenti gestis et sermonibus coaptare? Possumus, si nos ipsum Dei Verbum et juvare et inspirare dignatur.' In this respect he is more of a Mystic than Clement, but Rosenmüller, iii. p. 146, is harsh in comparing him to the fanatics of the Inner Light.

in the wall' multiply and widen, till the wall itself disappears. The dangers of such a mode of procedure are obvious, and there were not wanting those who urged them, though they directed their protest mainly against its application to the New Testament[1]. Many probably were offended by precisely those features of Origen's teaching which were of the deepest and most permanent value. But there are objections which may be pressed without suspicion of narrowness or prejudice.

The Alexandrine method as applied by Origen is undoubtedly unsound. He appeals to the examples of Christ and St. Paul[2], and to a certain limited extent with justice. But his rules of procedure, his playing with words and numbers and proper names, his boundless extravagance are learned not from the New Testament, but through Philo from the puerile Rabbinical schools[3]. Yet we must distinguish. On its apologetic side Allegorism is seen at its worst. When the Stoics assure us that the heathen deities are but symbols of the forces of Nature, and turn the hideous myths of Zeus or Dionysus into a manual of physical science; when Philo makes Tamar represent the soul widowed from sensual delights; when Clement turns the unclean meats

---

[1] *In Lev.* Hom. xvi. 4, ' dicet fortassis auditor quid iterum hic euresilogus agit:' *In Gen.* Hom. xiii. Here the objection is to Allegorism in general. But in application to the Old Testament it was in universal use among orthodox Christians.

[2] *In Num.* Hom. i. 3, Apostolo nobis Paulo spiritualis intelligentiae semina respergente; *In Num.* Hom. iii. 3, Non possum illuc adscendere nisi praecedat me Paulus. He is referring to the Epistle to the Hebrews, which he certainly regarded as the work of St. Paul, *De Principiis*, preface, 1; though he thought that the actual wording of the Epistle was due not to the Apostle himself but to one of his disciples, Eus. *H. E.* vi. 25. 11.

[3] For the relation of Origen's allegorism to that of Philo, see Siegfried, pp. 351 sqq.

into vices that are to be shunned, we rebel. This is
not the meaning. Such paltering with the text is not
honest, and in this respect there was reason in the reproach of Celsus that Jews and Christians alike were
ashamed of their Bible. Yet let us not be harsh. To
us it is not difficult to allow that the Old Testament is
the history of a people and not merely of a religion, that
God's revelation is progressive, that He speaks by human
messengers, that something has been permitted because
of the hardness of men's hearts. But to the Alexandrines,
bound as they were by their Jewish theory of inspiration
and beset by eager foes, it was not easy to admit all
this. Concessions are not readily made by men struggling
for all that they hold dear. Nor indeed was the notion
of historical development familiar to their times. Perhaps we may say that its first fruitful germ is found in
the Church, in the qualified admission of the inferiority
of the Old Testament to the New. The Alexandrines
went so far as to explain certain passages—those which
attribute human figure and emotions to God—by the
principle of accommodation or condescension, and Origen
even admitted the existence of degrees of inspiration [1].
Through these observations lay the way to a clear
solution of the difficulty. But though the key was
actually in the lock, Origen did not turn it. The time
had not yet come.

---

[1] See especially *In Joann.* i. 4 onwards. The Law is inferior to the
Gospel; in the New Testament the Epistles stand below the Gospels, and
of the Gospels the ἀπαρχή is that of John, 'whose sense none can grasp
unless he has fallen upon the breast of Jesus and received from Jesus Mary
to become his mother.' Compare also *Contra Celsum*, iv. 8, where again he
hints at the subject, but declines to pursue it because it is a Mystery : ἔχει δέ
τι ὁ περὶ τούτων λόγος μυστικώτερον καὶ βαθύτερον καὶ μὴ πάνυ τι φθάνειν
δυνάμενον ἐπὶ τὴν δημωδεστέραν ἀκοήν.

Again, of the positive use of Allegorism it is not possible to speak without qualification. What is the value of the mysteries which it aims at discovering? Does it really discover mysteries at all? One critic regards it as wholly futile, 'an excellent means of finding what you already possess.' To another it is *fecunda mater errorum, superstitionum, fanaticarum-que opinionum.* Yet a third considers it to have been the bulwark of orthodoxy against the sceptical literal method of the school of Antioch [1]. The truth is that it means very different things in relation to the Law and to the Gospel, and within the sphere of the latter in relation to the Church of the Present and to the Church of the Future.

As regards the Old Testament, it is a dangerous and in its actual use a delusive method, delusive because it proceeds upon the exaggeration of a truth. If we think of that long Revelation, unfolding itself gradually through centuries, and growing ever fuller and clearer as it proceeds, we cannot deny that its earlier stages contained the germ of the later, that much was anticipatory and preparative, that God granted to chosen spirits a vision more or less distinct of the long-hoped-for consummation. The Priest, the King, the Prophet foreboded with increasing clearness the Lamb of God, the Son of David, the Man of Sorrows. There were shadows of good things to come; there were vaticinations; there were types. But it does not follow that all was type; it does not follow that the type is a perfect and elaborate figure of the

---

[1] The first reference is to M. Denis, who has many clever epigrams on this subject; the second to Rosenmüller; the third to Cardinal Newman, *Development of Christian Doctrine,* p. 343, ed. 1878.

antitype. The Alexandrines erred in both ways. They found symbols where there was no symbol; they treated symbols not as indications, as harbingers, but as proofs. Thus they undertook to demonstrate Christian doctrine by passages which in the belief of the Jew were not Messianic at all, or, if Messianic, had not been fulfilled. They neglected the difference between before and after. As we look back, we see many things in the Old Testament which find their explanation only in the New. We see how the providence of God was leading his people up to precisely this issue and no other. Like the minister of Queen Candace, we recognise under Philip's guidance that Isaiah prophesied not of himself but of Jesus. So the old in a thousand points illustrates, prognosticates, confirms the new. But the shadow is not a demonstration, for the very reason that it is a shadow. The road by which we are guided is the right road, but until we reach the goal we cannot be certain whither it will lead us. The early Christians forgot this, forgot the doubts and perplexities through which they had themselves attained their bourne. Hence their angry amazement at the blindness and obstinacy of the Jew.

The Alexandrines are open to this animadversion. They found in the Old Testament what they already possessed, what they could not have found unless they had possessed it. But at any rate they found nothing more. They avoided the worst excesses. They are always intelligent and reasonable, and their extravagance is that of the poet-philosopher, not that of the dogmatist. And they did not invert their Allegorism. They found the New Testament in the Old, but they had far too clear a sense of the spirituality of true religion to

attempt to carry the Old over into the New. They
evaporated the letter ; they did not stereotype the spirit.

What Allegorism signified as applied to the Church
of the Present and to the Church of the Future has been
partly explained, and we shall have to recur to the point
again.   Let us only notice here that it is to speculations
on the latter subject, on Eschatology, that the charge of
presumption applies.   Here too there is a truth.   All
language that we use, that even Christ could use, of the
world behind the veil, is necessarily mythical, figurative.
But in this case we have not yet reached the bourne, and
therefore the key to the hieroglyph is wanting.   This
Irenaeus saw; this Origen refused to see.   There were
questions to which he felt some answer must be found.
There were questions on which he obtained real though
limited and uncertain light.   Indeed it was not his
nature to rest content.   He held with Philo, that even if
truth be unattainable the happiness of man lies in the
ceaseless pursuit of this ideal, that ever flies as he
advances.   'If we see some admirable work of human
art,' he says, 'we are at once eager to investigate the
nature, the manner, the end of its production; and the
contemplation of the works of God stirs us with an
incomparably greater longing to learn the principles, the
method, the purpose of creation.'   'This desire, this
passion,' he continues, 'has without doubt been implanted in us by God.   And as the eye seeks light, as
our body craves food, so our mind is impressed with the
characteristic and natural desire of knowing the truth of
God and the causes of what we observe[1].'

---

[1] *De Princ.* ii. 11. 4.   In the translation of this passage I have borrowed
the language of Dr. Westcott, *Cont. Review*, May, 1879, p. 335.

This is noble language, and the modest devotion with which he strove to fulfil it is equally noble. If we are less aspiring, let us not say presumptuous, it is because we have learned from him, because we dare not gaze upon the darkness of excessive light that even 'the eagle eye of Origen [1]' failed to pierce.

[1] The phrase is from Cardinal Newman's lines on the Greek Fathers, *Verses on Various Occasions*, 1868, p. 83.

LECTURE V.

Believe Me that I am in the Father, and the Father in Me.—St. John xiv. 11.

Why callest thou me good? there is none good but One, that is, God.— St. Matthew xix. 17.

WE have already seen what Origen regarded as the proper task of the Christian philosopher. Tradition, embodying the teaching of the Apostles, has handed down certain facts, certain usages, which are to be received without dispute, but does not attempt to explain the why or the whence. It is the office of the sanctified reason to define, to articulate, to co-ordinate, even to expand, and generally to adapt to human needs the faith once delivered to the Church.

What then is the utterance of Tradition? It tells us that there is One God who created all things out of nothing, who is Just and Good, the Author of the Old as of the New Testament, the Father of our Lord Jesus Christ: that Jesus Christ was begotten of the Father before every creature, that through Him all things were made, that He is God and Man, born of the Holy Spirit and the Virgin Mary, that He did truly suffer, rise again, and ascend into heaven: that the Holy Ghost is associated in honour and dignity with the Father and the Son, that it is He who inspired the saints both of the Old and of the New Dispensation: that there will be a Resurrection of the dead, when the body which is sown in corruption will rise in incorruption, and that in

the world to come the souls of men will inherit eternal
life or suffer eternal punishment according to their
works : that every reasonable soul is a free agent,
plotted against by evil spirits, comforted by good angels,
but in no way constrained : that the Scriptures were
written by the agency of the Spirit of God, that they
have two senses, the plain and the hidden, whereof the
latter can be known only to those to whom is given the
grace of the Holy Spirit in the word of wisdom and
knowledge [1].

Here then we have the pith and substance of that
doctrine which, in Alexandria at any rate, was taught to
all Christians in the time of Origen. It differs from the
Nicene Creed in that it does not use the terms ' Very
God' or ' Homoousian' of the Son, in that it asserts the
moral attributes of God, the creation of the world out of
nothing, the spiritual nature of the Resurrection Body,
the connection of punishments and rewards with conduct,
the eternity of punishment, the existence of Angels, the
freedom of the Will, the double sense of Scripture. It
is rather a *Regula Fidei* [2] than a Creed in the strict
sense of the word. But the language is already so

[1] *De Principiis*, preface, 4 onwards. Origen, like Clement, had the
strongest persuasion that all his speculations lay within this norm. ' Servetur
vero ecclesiastica praedicatio per successionis ordinem ab apostolis tradita,
et usque ad praesens in ecclesiis permanens : illa sola credenda est veritas
quae in nullo ab ecclesiastica et apostolica discordat traditione.' Yet there
is a sense in which the perfect Christian rises above Tradition, *In Joann.* xiii.
16. This thought also is shared by Clement. In both Knowledge is more
than Faith, and Ordinances, though always obligatory, cease to be
necessary.

[2] The κανὼν ἐκκλησιαστικός, κανὼν τῆς ἐκκλησίας, or τῆς παραδόσεως, or τοῦ
εὐαγγελίου, or again, ἡ ἀποστολικὴ καὶ ἐκκλησιαστικὴ ὀρθοτομία τῶν δογμάτων
of Clement. The latter has nowhere set out his creed in the same systematic
way as Origen, but there is a complete agreement between the two.

framed as definitely to exclude the Gnostics, the Noetians, possibly the Chiliasts, and certainly all those who
doubted the Personality of the Holy Spirit.

Within these limits all is open ground. Even the
definition of the terms, especially of the word 'eternal,' is
subject to reverent but free discussion. And Origen has
availed himself of this liberty to the fullest extent.
One of his earliest works is the *De Principiis*, ' On First
Principles,' that is to say on the *data* of the Creed, in
which he maps out the field of investigation, and expresses with fearless candour all his doubts, beliefs,
suggestions, divinations about each article in turn. He
was already of mature age when he composed this
treatise, and his voluminous later writings are little more
than an expansion of the ideas there set down. Much
might be said of the *De Principiis*, the most remarkable
production of ante-Nicene times, but it has three merits
at least that must not be omitted. Origen never slurs
a difficulty, never dogmatises, never consciously departs
from the teaching of Scripture. It is in this last point
that he differs most, in point of method, from Clement,
who not unfrequently leaves us in doubt as to the precise
Scriptural basis of his ideas. Sometimes Origen's interpretations are wrong; sometimes again he attaches
undue weight to particular expressions. Certain texts
seem to dominate him and colour all his views[1]. But
his most daring flights always start from some point in
the written Word. The connection with the particular
passage under discussion may be of the most fanciful
kind, but the opinion itself is never arbitrary.

We shall obtain the clearest view of Origen's teaching

---

[1] Denis, p. 56.

by following in the main the plan traced in the *De Principiis,* and proceeding from those high problems that touch upon the nature of God to the consideration of His Economy, His dealings with the Church and the soul of man.

The heathen Celsus lays down three methods [1] by which men may attain to a certain, though limited, knowledge of God. They are Analysis, Synthesis, and Analogy. The nature and results of the first we have seen in the case of Clement. Synthesis is the inductive mode, by which we gather from the constitution of the world an idea of Him by whom the world was made. Analogy is the poet's faculty bodying forth in a myth, a simile, that which language is inadequate to express. Thus Plato in the *Republic* compares the Idea of Good to the Sun. Origen insists on the contrary that the Christian knows God in a way better than any of these, as revealed in the Incarnate Christ. Yet to some extent he admits the use of Synthesis. For the world was made by God through Christ, and still bears the legible imprint of its Author.

Accordingly he takes his point of departure from the words of our Saviour ' God is a Spirit,' from the words of St. John ' God is Light [2].' ' It must not be supposed then that God is a body, or in a body, but a simple

---

[1] *Contra Celsum,* vii. 42. 44.   They are defined also by Alcinous, chap. 10. Compare Maximus Tyrius, xvii. 8.   The three methods of Celsus appear to answer to his three classes of religious teachers, σοφοί, φιλόσοφοι, and ἔνθεοι ποιηταί. M. Denis complains, p. 85, that the passage in Celsus is ' très brouillé.' But the text as given in Lomm. is quite clear. M. Vacherot, *École d'Alexandrie,* iii. p. 220, has a chapter on the Method of the Alexandrines, but the references given above will suffice to show that he is entirely wrong in his assertion that ' la pensée qui la domine et l'inspire est étrangère aux écoles grecques.'

[2] *De Principiis,* i. 1.

intellectual nature, admitting of no addition at all. There
is in Him no greater or less, no higher or lower, for He
is the Monad, the Unit, Mind, the Fountain of all
mind.' From this first conception flow the negative
attributes of the Divine Nature, and here Origen is
compelled in spite of his disclaimer to make a certain
use of the method of Analysis. Being Mind God is
incorporeal [1]. This point, owing perhaps to the influence of Stoicism, had as yet been very imperfectly
apprehended in the Church, and it is not the least of
Origen's merits that he seizes upon it with insight and
decision, proving the immateriality, that is in fact the
existence of the soul, and so of God, by an argument
resembling the famous *Cogito ergo sum* [2]. Being incorporeal God is independent of the laws of Space
and Time, omniscient, omnipresent, unchanging, incomprehensible. His dwelling-place is the thick darkness.
'How unsearchable are His judgments, and His ways
past finding out.' He has in a sense no titles, and His
fittest name is He That Is.

Thus far Origen is in agreement with his predecessors,
though rather with Philo than with Clement. But here
he strikes off into a wholly different train of thought.
Our knowledge of the Divine spreads out on all sides

---

[1] In the view of the *Homilies*, the Valentinians, Melito (see Routh, and
Heinichen's note on Eus. *H. E.* iv. 26. 2), Tertullian, *Adv. Praxeam*, 7,
God is corporeal. Even Irenaeus finds the image of God in the body of man,
v. 6. 1, and not as the Alexandrines in the νοῦς. Anthropomorphism lingered
on long in the East. It is one of the chief merits of the Alexandrines that
they treated this point with no less emphasis and distinctness than Philo.
Two great difficulties were the facts that the term ἀσώματος is not Scriptural,
though found in the *Doctrina Petri*, where the words 'Non sum daemonium
incorporeum' were attributed to the Saviour after the Resurrection, and that
πνεῦμα does not in itself connote immateriality. See *De Princ.*, praefatio, 8 ;
In Joann. xiii. 24 ; *De Oratione*, 23, 24.

[2] *De Princ.* i. 1. 7 ; ii. 11. 4 ; iv. 36 ; Denis, p. 310.

into the inconceivable, but it is rooted in the positive. Before we can know what He is not, we must know what He is ; the titles Good, Wise, Just, which we apply to Him, are inadequate but not untrue. God is incomprehensible. But the cause of the incomprehensibility is in us, not in Him. His dwelling is the thick darkness, but He Himself is Light ; and the more nearly we approach Him the more completely will the darkness melt away into light. There will come a time when, becoming one spirit with the Word, we shall see Him face to face, and know even as we are known. Even now we are not left without some understanding of Him which, imperfect as it may be, is yet true as far as it goes. We see Him dimly revealed in Creation. The order, the beauty of Nature are scintillations of the Divine goodness, as far inferior to their source as the sunbeams that stream through a keyhole to the Sun itself; yet authentic, homogeneous. Still more veritably we see Him in the Word, for ‘he who hath seen the Son hath seen the Father,’ seen Him in the express Image of His Person, though only in such degree as the divine grace has enabled him [1].

Again, God being unchanging, eternal, must needs be passionless. Scripture attributes to Him wrath, hatred, repentance, but only in condescension to our infirmities. He is righteous and good, and desireth not the death of a sinner. Punishment is not His work, but the necessary consequence of sin [2]. There will come a time in the restitution of all things when it will no longer

[1] *De Princ.* i. 1.
[2] The justice and goodness of God are maintained, *De Princ.* ii. 5, with great force and subtlety.

be possible to speak of the wrath of God. But though
Origen cannot think of the Deity as agitated by passions
in the narrower sense of the word, by mental disturbance
or unreason of any kind, it follows from the language
already cited that he was far from regarding Him as
devoid of attributes. 'The Father Himself and God
of all,' he says, 'is longsuffering, merciful and pitiful.
Has He not then in a sense passions? The Father
Himself is not impassible. He has the passion of
Love [1].'

Hence when Celsus, in true Platonic fashion, using
almost the very words of Philo or Clement, asserts that
God has no name, because He has no passions in the
sense of attributes that can be denoted by a name,
Origen replies with a distinction. It is true, he admits,
in a sense, that no name can express the exact nature
of the properties of God, just as no single word will
express the difference between the sweetness of a date
and the sweetness of a fig. Yet both are sweet; we
know what the term means in each case, and the dis-
parity of the meanings is not so great but that they

[1] *In Ezech.* Hom. vi. 6. See also the exceedingly beautiful passage, *In
Num.* Hom. xxiii. 2, where he dwells on the same subject at length. But
he concludes with a retractation, as if he felt that he had been carried too far :
' Haec autem omnia, in quibus vel lugere vel gaudere vel odisse vel laetari
dicitur Deus, tropice et humano more accipienda sunt ab Scripturis dici.
Aliena porro est divina natura ab omni passionis et permutationis affectu, in
illo semper beatitudinis apice immobilis et inconcussa perdurans.' Yet
Origen had experienced that state of consciousness, exemplified for us by all
exalted Christian spirits, in which joy and sorrow cease to be passions and
are no longer contraries. He did not clearly see that what is true of Goodness and Justice is true of Love and Sympathy. They differ not in themselves,
but in their objects. Or again, we may say he did not clearly see that self-
sacrifice is divine, and that the Incarnation is only the most striking instance
of an universal law. Yet in the passages quoted he has given expression to
this truth, though with timidity.

are in substance identical[1]. The same reasoning will
apply to those epithets which are common to virtuous
men and to God. We cannot comprehend God, we
cannot explain Him, for He is infinitely better than all
we can think about Him. But if we argue from the
justice of man to the justice of God, we are proceeding
like the geometer from the imperfect to the perfect, not
like the alchemist from the known to the unknowable.
It will be seen that the God of Origen is no longer
the Unconditioned. He is not Absolute but Perfect,
and perfection is itself a condition. He is perfectly wise,
perfectly just, perfectly mighty, but the perfection of
these attributes consists precisely in the fact that they
are limited by one another[2]. From this consideration
flow Origen's peculiar views as to Creation. Nature
is not infinite; God created all things by number and
measure because perfect wisdom cannot comprehend
an unlimited object. Nature again is eternal. The existence of the universe can in a sense be measured by
time, for time and the world began together, time is

---

[1] *Contra Celsum*, vi. 65.

[2] See *De Princ.* ii. 9. 1 : 'Non enim, ut quidam volunt, finem putandum
est non habere creaturas ; quia ubi finis non est nec comprehensio ulla nec
circumscriptio esse potest.' So the Wisdom of Solomon says, xi. 20, that
God created all things 'in numero et mensura ;' *De Princ.* iv. 35 (Greek,
text), μηδεὶς δὲ προσκοπτέτω τῷ λόγῳ εἰ μέτρα ἐπιτίθεμεν καὶ τῇ τοῦ θεοῦ
δυνάμει, ἄπειρα γὰρ περιλαβεῖν τῇ φύσει ἀδύνατον τυγχάνει. Other passages
in Redepenning, ii. 290. Like the English Platonist Henry More, Origen
finds the idea of God in that of the Perfect Being. His point of view is
moral, not like that of Clement pseudo-metaphysical. Hence all the so-
called negative attributes sink at once into a secondary place. The more
the reader reflects upon this the more important I feel persuaded he will see
it to be. What an absurd yet mischievous word is 'infinite,' purely material
in all its associations, and as unmeaning when applied to spirit as 'colour-
less' or 'imponderable' would be. Yet it is habitually used as if it were the
highest term of reverence. To a Platonist 'infinite' means almost the same
as 'evil.' Limitation is of the essence of truth and of beauty.

the register of the world's life. But in another sense creation is timeless. Creator and Creation are correlative notions; the one cannot be thought of without the other. God must indeed precede logically, as the cause is in conception prior to the effect, but His inner perfection implies external realisation. From the first He was King, He was righteous, because there was something not Himself that He could rule in righteousness. Otherwise we must suppose a change in Him, a development, a passage from the potential to the actual. But this it would be impious to think of God, who from the first is Act, is Perfect. Readers of Lucretius will recollect the Epicurean argument against Creation which Origen appears to have here in view. And it is evident how little he would have been embarrassed by modern geology [1].

From the same mode of thought flows a qualified Optimism similar to that of Leibnitz or Butler. Origen does not shut his eyes to the manifold traces of disorder and inequality in Nature. Nevertheless, despite the existence of 'hideous monsters and vermin,' of physical

---

[1] *De Princ.* i. 2. 10 : 'Quemadmodum pater non potest esse quis, si filius non sit, neque dominus quis esse potest sine possessione sine servo, ita ne omnipotens quidem Deus dici potest, si non sint in quos exerceat potentatum ; et ideo ut omnipotens ostendatur Deus omnia subsistere necesse est.' See the whole section. Origen is of course speaking of the first heaven and earth, not of that world in which fallen men live, the ' mundus hic qui ex certo tempore coepit' of *De Princ.* iii. 5. 1. The Epicurean argument against creation was based upon the impossibility of God beginning to do anything. Cicero, *De Nat. Deorum*, i. 9 : 'Quid autem erat, quod concupisceret Deus mundum et signis et luminibus, tamquam aedilis, ornare ? Si ut ipse melius habitaret ; antea videlicet tempore infinito in tenebris tamquam in gurgustio habitaverat :' Lucretius, v. 165 sqq. The same argument in Origen's mind proved the Eternal Generation of the Son and the eternity of Creation. Later theologians regarded it as admirable in the first case and abominable in the second.

and moral wrong, he held that the world is good because it answers to the plan of a wise Creator[1]. Nay it is the best of all possible worlds. For if there could have been a better, we must suppose either that the Divine Power was insufficient to realise it, or that the Divine Wisdom failed to conceive it. Such an optimism was peculiarly easy to the Platonist, who regarded the world as a scene not of probation only but of correction, and linked the imperfections of man's environment with the sin of a previous life. But this tenet does not affect the main position, which is in fact that of Bishop Butler, ' that we are not competent judges of this scheme from the small parts of it that come within our view in the present life.'

But Origen went farther than this, and drew or appeared to draw the startling conclusion that God cannot do anything that He has not done. This was actually maintained by Abelard, ' though,' as he adds, ' this opinion of ours has few or no supporters, and differs widely from the utterances of the Saints, and somewhat from reason itself[2].' It is not indeed certain that Origen formally inferred this consequence, though it was laid to his account by enemies who accused him of teaching that God is All-Ruler but not Almighty. But the inference does not seem to involve any distortion of the facts. For Origen regarded the Divine Goodness, Wisdom, Power as working in perfect harmony and co-extension, so as to be in fact different aspects of the same energy. If God's Power is limited, it is limited not by the resistance of matter, for God created matter and made

---

[1] *In Joann.* xiii. 42.
[2] I owe the quotation to Huet, *Origeniana,* ii. 1. 1.

M

it what it is, but by His own reason and His own beneficence. That He can do nothing that is evil is admitted by all. Origen possibly, Abelard certainly, advanced a step farther, and declared that He can leave undone nothing that is good. For otherwise in our desire to get rid of one restriction we are compelled to admit another of a far more dangerous kind, because impeaching either the Wisdom or the Goodness of Him who, if any gradation of His virtues is conceivable, is Good and Wise even before He is Mighty.

The Christian Deity is One in Three. But in what sense One, in what sense Three? These questions were already the subject of fierce debate, especially at Rome, where the fire that had long been smouldering had been kindled into a blaze by the action of two Popes. Victor had excommunicated Theodotus, who denied in some sense the Divinity of Jesus [1]. Callistus had expelled from the

---

[1] Eus. *H. E.* v. 28. 6 : Βίκτωρ Θεόδοτον τὸν σκυτέα, τὸν ἀρχηγὸν καὶ πατέρα ταύτης τῆς ἀρνησιθέου ἀποστασίας, ἀπεκήρυξε τῆς κοινωνίας, πρῶτον εἰπόντα ψιλὸν ἄνθρωπον τὸν Χριστόν. See notes in Heinichen. But the anonymous writer quoted here is by no means accurate in his statements. Theodotus, if he is the same as Theodotus of Byzantium, did not assert that 'Christ was a mere man,' nor was he the inventor of his doctrine. He belonged to the Ebionite school, and taught that 'Jesus was a man born of the Virgin, according to the will of the Father, who having lived the life of other men but in perfect piety, afterwards at his baptism in Jordan received the Christ, who came down from above in likeness of a dove. Hence the miraculous powers did not work in Him till the Spirit which Theodotus calls Christ came down and was manifest in Him;' *Philos.* vii. 35. The passage continues : θεὸν δὲ οὐδέποτε τοῦτον γεγονέναι οὗτοι θέλουσιν ἐπὶ τῇ καθόδῳ τοῦ πνεύματος, ἕτεροι δὲ μετὰ τὴν ἐκ νεκρῶν ἀνάστασιν. There must be some error in the text here, as οὐδέποτε cannot be reconciled with ἐπὶ τῇ καθόδῳ τοῦ πνεύματος. Probably the words οὗτοι . . . ἀνάστασιν are a gloss. What Theodotus taught was that the preexistent Christ was not God ; cp. x. 23. He held doubtless with the *Homilies* that he was the Eldest Power but yet not God in the strict sense of the word. I observe that the party violence of this anonymous author has turned what is an argument in favour of the doctrine of the Trinity into an argument against it. See Lecture ii. p. 59.

Church the Noetians, who denied the Personality of the Son and the Holy Ghost[1]. Origen had visited Rome during the papacy of Zephyrinus[2], and was keenly alive to the perils of the crisis. Hence his views and language exhibit a marked advance upon those of his predecessor. The terminology indeed is still fluctuating and uncertain, but the later usage is already all but established. The word for Person in Origen is commonly *Hypostasis*, that for the Divine Nature is less determinate but is frequently *Ousia*[3]. The two expressions were current

Harnack, *Dogmengeschichte*, p. 573 sqq., gives the latest authorities on the subject.

[1] Harnack,*Dogmengeschichte*, pp. 601 sqq.; *Philos.* ix. 11 sqq. Noetianism, Monarchianism, Patripassianism, Modalism.Unitarianism should be regarded in one sense as an ancient, in another as a recent opinion. Doubtless in some form or another it had existed before the debate reached the acute stage. But the sentiment which prevails is the sentiment of the majority.

[2] Eus. *H. E.* vi. 14. 10: ὁ μέντοι Ἀδαμάντιος, καὶ τοῦτο γὰρ ἦν τῷ Ὠριγένει ὄνομα, Ζεφυρίνου κατὰ τούσδε τοὺς χρόνους τῆς Ῥωμαίων ἐκκλησίας ἡγουμένου ἐπιδημῆσαι τῇ Ῥώμῃ καὶ αὐτός που γράφει λέγων ' εὐξάμενος τὴν ἀρχαιοτάτην Ῥωμαίων ἐκκλησίαν ἰδεῖν.'

[3] For Person we have ὑπόστασις, *In Joann.* ii. 6, ἡμεῖς μέντοι γε τρεῖς ὑποστάσεις πειθόμενοι τυγχάνειν : οὐσία ἰδία, *ibid.*, δογματίζων μηδὲ οὐσίαν τινὰ ἰδίαν ὑφεστάναι τοῦ ἁγίου πνεύματος : ἰδιότης and οὐσία κατὰ περιγραφήν, *In Joann.* ii. 2: οὐσία alone, *In Joann.* i. 30 *ad fin.*, ii. 18 : ὑποκείμενον, *In Jerem.* Hom. viii. 2 : the two combined, *De Orat.* 15, ἕτερος κατ' οὐσίαν καὶ ὑποκείμενόν (so English ed. and de la Rue, al. ὑποκείμενός) ἐστιν ὁ υἱὸς τοῦ πατρός. For Substance, οὐσία is used, *In Joann.* x. 21 (Lom. i. p. 350), οἴονται ἐκ τούτων παρίστασθαι μὴ διαφέρειν τῷ ἀριθμῷ τὸν υἱὸν τοῦ πατρός, ἀλλ' ἐν οὐ μόνον οὐσίᾳ ἀλλὰ καὶ ὑποκειμένῳ τυγχάνοντας ἀμφοτέρους κατά τινας ἐπινοίας διαφόρους οὐ κατὰ ὑπόστασιν λέγεσθαι πατέρα καὶ υἱόν : *De Orat.* 23 (Lom. xvii. p. 183), οἱονεὶ ἀφιστὰς τὴν οὐσίαν τοῦ θεοῦ ἀπὸ πάντων τῶν γεννητῶν : *In Matth.* xvii. 14 (Lom. iv. 116) we have τὸ ἐν ὑποκειμένῳ : *Cels.* viii. 12, ὄντα δύο τῇ ὑποστάσει πράγματα ἐν δὲ τῇ ὁμονοίᾳ καὶ τῇ συμφωνίᾳ καὶ ταὐτότητι τοῦ βουλήματος. I have not noted other instances of the use of οὐσία, but in the Latin translations *substantia* occurs frequently ; *In Num.* Hom. xii. 1 ; *In Rom.* vii. 13 ; viii. 5 ; *De Princ.* i. 2. 5 ; *In Levit.* Hom. xiii. 4 ; *In Cant. Cantic.* iii. (Lom. xv. 56), qui ibi Trinitas propter distinctionem personarum, hic unus Deus intelligitur pro unitate substantiae. But here we may trace the hand of Rufinus.

M 2

in the philosophy of the time, and mean precisely the
same thing. The difference between them appears to
be merely this, that *Ousia* is properly Platonic, while
Hypostasis, a comparatively modern and rare word, is
properly Stoic. To the Platonist *Ousia* denoted the
Idea, by participation in which the thing is what it is,
which is prior to and above the thing. To the Stoic both
words signified the thing itself, the essential substratum
which, having no qualities, is yet the vehicle of all
qualities [1]. *Hypostasis* bears also the meaning of an

---

[1] The definition of οὐσία is given at length by Origen, *De Orat.* 27 (Lom.
xvii. 210): ἡ μέντοι κυρίως οὐσία τοῖς μὲν προηγουμένην τὴν τῶν ἀσωμάτων
ὑπόστασιν εἶναι φάσκουσι (that is by the Platonist) νενόμισται κατὰ τὰ
ἀσώματα τὸ εἶναι βεβαίως ἔχοντα .... τοῖς δὲ ἐπακολουθητικὴν αὐτὴν εἶναι
νομίζουσι προηγουμένην δὲ τὴν τῶν σωμάτων (that is to the Stoics) ὅροι αὐτῆς
οὗτοί εἰσι· οὐσία ἐστὶν ἡ πρώτη τῶν ὄντων ὕλη .... ἢ τὸ πρῶτον ὑπόστατον
ἄποιον. In this latter sense it is identical with ὑποκείμενον, which already in
Aristotle means the substantia materialis, ὕλη quae determinatur per formam,
or οὐσία cui inhaerent πάθη συμβεβηκότα. See the *Index* of Bonitz. This
was the view of the Stoics; see Ritter and Preller, *Hist. Phil. Gr. et Rom.*
§ 403. In this sense the οὐσία was said ὑφίστασθαι or ὑφεστάναι, and from
this verb is formed ὑπόστασις. The latter in the precise sense of substance
is exceedingly rare, and as far as I can gather distinctively Stoic. It became
naturalised in Latin as *Substantia* in the time of Seneca and Quintilian.
Cicero attempted to represent οὐσία by *Essentia*—Seneca, *Ep.* 58 *ad in.*,
cupio, si fieri potest, propitiis auribus tuis, *essentiam* dicere. Si minus
dicam et iratis. Ciceronem auctorem huius verbi habeo, puto locu-
pletem—but this harsh form did not live in classic Latin. There is a
remarkable passage in Socrates, *H. E.* iii. 7, where we are informed
that Irenaeus, a grammarian, in his *Atticistes* calls the word *Hypostasis*
barbarous because the ancients did not use it or gave it a wholly
different sense. But he continues, ἰστέον μέντοι ὅτι, εἰ καὶ οἱ παλαιοὶ
φιλόσοφοι τὴν λέξιν παρέλιπον, ἀλλ᾽ ὅμως οἱ νεώτεροι τῶν φιλοσόφων συνεχῶς
ἀντὶ τῆς οὐσίας τῇ λέξει τῆς ὑποστάσεως ἀπεχρήσαντο. The συνεχῶς
is a great exaggeration. The reader will find οὐσία fifty times when he
finds ὑπόστασις once. Lastly, these scientific terms were introduced into
theology by the Gnostics: οὐσία, ὑπόστασις, ὑποκείμενον, ὁμοούσιος all occur
in Irenaeus, i. 5. 1. Yet it should be added that ὑπόστασις is used by Tatian
(Otto, pp. 22, 28); οὐσία and ὑπόστασις by Athenagoras, *De Res.* 1. Suppl.
24 (Otto, pp. 130, 188); ὑπόστασις in the *Ep. ad Diog.* 2; and οὐσία by

actually subsisting entity, the manifestation of the essence in the phenomenon. But this sense belongs to *Ousia* also, so that the theological distinction between the two terms is purely arbitrary. In the West *Persona* and *Substantia* are already familiar to Tertullian[1]. Of these terms, *Persona*, a singularly material word, belongs not to the schools but to the Latin law courts, and means 'a party,' 'an individual,' with all his legal duties and rights. *Substantia* is a translation of *Hypostasis*. Thus it came about that the same word, which in the metaphysical East signified Person, was employed by the prosaic and law-loving West for Substance; an unhappy confusion which gave rise to much acrimonious debate[2].

Melito, *De Incar. Christi* (Routh, i. p. 121), τὰς δύο αὐτοῦ οὐσίας, of the two natures in Christ.

[1] *Adv. Prax.* 2. Gregory Nazianzen, *Orat.* xxi. 46, regards *Persona* as a translation of πρόσωπον. It is true that πρόσωπον, under Hebrew influences, had imbibed the notion of individuality. But we may venture to think that Gregory has inverted the actual course of things. The reason why the Westerns adopted the word *Hypostasis* for Substance is no doubt that *Substantia* existed in Latin, while *Essentia* did not. In this sense in Latin theology *Hypostasis* is a translation of *Substantia*. The same is true I believe of the word πρόσωπον, which is first found in Hippolytus, *Contra Noetum*, 14, ed. Lagarde, p. 52, and the *Philos.* ix. 12. These authors (or this author, for Dr. Döllinger appears to have demonstrated that the *Philos.* is the work of Hippolytus) write in Greek but think in Latin. Their style is steeped in Latin idioms. And besides, it is highly unlikely that they would have selected a Greek phrase to emphasise the point of a dispute which was being eagerly debated on all sides in colloquial Latin. For the legal use of *Persona* compare Cic. *pro Milone*, 12, itaque illud Cassianum *cui bono fuerit* in his personis valeat. For other information on these famous words see Baur, *Dreieinigkeit*, i. 446, note ; Liddon, *Bampton Lectures*, ed. 10, p. 33, note ; Huet, *Origeniana*, ii. 2. 3 ; Bull, *Defence of the Nicene Creed*, vol. i. pp. 188, 236, English translation of 1851.

[2] See the account of the Council of Alexandria in 362, Mansi, iii. p. 350. Jerome, *Ep.* xv. *ad Damasum* (in Migne, vol. xxii. p. 355), complains that he is looked upon as a heretic in the East because he would not use the

The controversy of the times turned mainly upon what was called by Western divines 'the mystery of the Economy¹,' the right mode that is to say of apprehending the personal difference, especially as regards the relation of the Father to the Son. The problem of the Unity was of course involved in this, but it was not the immediate point at issue; hence the phraseology on this side was less guarded and precise. For Origen and the men of his time the great object was to establish the true Personality of Christ, to show that though God He yet was not the Father. Their reasoning applies also to the Holy Spirit, but not so pointedly; and as regards the Third Person, there is still some degree of hesitation and obscurity which the Alexandrines, and in particular Origen, did much to dissipate.

phrase 'tres hypostases.' He objects that the formula is not Apostolical, but this applies equally to his own mode of statement.

¹ Tertullian, *Adv. Praxeam*, 2 : Quasi non sic quoque unus sit omnia, dum ex uno omnia, per substantiae scilicet unitatem, et nihilominus custodiatur οἰκονομίας sacramentum, quae unitatem in trinitatem disponit. *Ibid.* 3 : Sed monarchiam sonare student Latini, οἰκονομίαν intelligere nolunt etiam Graeci.   Hippolytus, *Contra Noetum*, 14 (ed. Lagarde, p. 52), δύο μὲν οὐκ ἐρῶ θεοὺς ἀλλ᾽ ἢ ἕνα, πρόσωπα δὲ δύο, οἰκονομίᾳ δὲ τρίτην τὴν χάριν τοῦ ἁγίου πνεύματος, πατὴρ μὲν γὰρ εἷς πρόσωπα δὲ δύο ὅτι καὶ ὁ υἱός, τὸ δὲ τρίτον τὸ ἅγιον πνεῦμα. πατὴρ ἐντέλλεται, λόγος ἀποτελεῖ, υἱὸς δὲ δείκνυται, δι᾽ οὗ πατὴρ πιστεύεται, οἰκονομίας συμφωνίᾳ (this is surely the right reading ; Lagarde has οἰκονομίᾳ συμφωνίᾳ) συνάγεται εἰς ἕνα θεόν. *Ibid.* 4 (p. 46, Lagarde), μυστήριον οἰκονομίας.   A little lower down the word appears to bear even in this usage its ordinary sense of 'dispensation.' *Ibid.* 14 (p. 53, Lagarde), γινώσκων οὖν ὁ πατρῷος λόγος τὴν οἰκονομίαν καὶ τὸ θέλημα τοῦ πατρός, ὅτι οὐκ ἄλλως βούλεται δοξάζεσθαι ἢ οὕτως.   But it has evidently acquired a technical sense.   Baur, *Dreieinigkeit*, ed. 1841, p. 178, ' Es liegt in ihm der Begriff einer durch eine Vielheit sich vermittelnden Einheit.'   Tatian, *Ad Graecos*, 5 (p. 24 of Otto's ed.), γέγονε δὲ (ὁ λόγος) κατὰ μερισμόν, οὐ κατὰ ἀποκοπήν· τὸ γὰρ ἀποτμηθὲν τοῦ πρώτου κεχώρισται, τὸ δὲ μερισθὲν οἰκονομίας τὴν αἵρεσιν προσλαβὸν οὐκ ἐνδεᾶ τὸν ὅθεν εἴληπται πεποίηκεν.   If he were asked how the Son could be distinguished from the Father without impairing the perfections of the Father, Tatian replies, ' this is the mystery of the Divine Will.'   But see the note in Otto.

The definition of the Father is already contained in its main outlines in what has been said about the Deity. The specific attributes of the First Person will be best ascertained by considering His relation to the Second and the Third. The Son then is a Hypostasis, Living Wisdom, or, as He is entitled in the Acts of Paul, in the first rude attempt at definition, 'a living animal[1].' He is verily and substantially God, and therefore of necessity co-eternal and coequal with the Father. On the first point there is no shadow of doubt as to Origen's meaning. 'There never can have been a time when He was not. For when was that God, whom John calls the Light, destitute of the radiance of His proper glory, so that a man may dare to ascribe a beginning of existence to the Son ... Let a man, who ventures to say there was a time when the Son was not, consider that this is all one with saying there was a time when Wisdom was not, the Word was not, the Life was not[2].' Nor, if

---

[1] *De Principiis*, i. 2. 3 : Unde et recte mihi dictus videtur sermo ille, qui in Actibus Pauli scriptus est, quia 'hic est verbum animal vivens.'

[2] *De Princ.* iv. 28. Nothing can be stronger than Origen's language on the co-eternity of the Son : ' Qui autem initium dat Verbo Dei, vel Sapientiae Dei, intuere ne magis in ipsum ingenitum Patrem impietatem suam iactet, cum eum neget semper Patrem fuisse, et genuisse Verbum, et habuisse Sapientiam in omnibus anterioribus vel temporibus vel saeculis vel si quid illud est quod nominari potest.' Origen is the inventor of the phrase οὐκ ἔστιν ὅτε οὐκ ἦν, famous afterwards as the watchword of the Catholics against the Arians, *De Princ.* i. 2.9 ; iv. 28 ; *In Rom.* i. 5. Nor can we suspect here the hand of Rufinus, for the phrase is guaranteed not only by Pamphilus in his *Apology*, but by Athanasius, *De Decr. Syn. Nic.* chap. 27, ed. Migne. Further, as if this were not enough, Origen warns his reader that when we say the Son ' never ' had a beginning we are speaking not of Time but of Eternity : Nam et haec ipsa nomina temporalis vocabuli significantiam gerunt, id est *quando* vel *nunquam* ; supra omne autem tempus, et supra omnia saecula, et supra omnem aeternitatem intelligenda sunt ea, quae de Patre et Filio et Spiritu Sancto dicuntur ; *De Princ.* iv. 28. Father, if we may so speak, is the most ancient title of God : *De Princ.* i. 2. 10, non

we keep in view his most deliberate and emphatic utterances, can there be any doubt about the second. The proof is taken from the Epistle to the Hebrews, where the Son is called 'the express image of the Hypostasis of God;' from the Book of Wisdom, where He is 'the unspotted mirror of the power of God.' For the property of a mirror is to reflect every feature, every act of him that looks therein, without the slightest change. Hence the Saviour Himself says, 'All mine are thine and thine are mine,' 'What things soever the Father doeth these also doeth the Son likewise;' and St. John in the Apocalypse applies to Christ the Ineffable Name, 'Thus saith the Lord God, who is, and who was, and who is to come[1].'

But Scripture carries us beyond this, giving to the Son a number of titles to denote His *Epinoiai*, His economic functions, His relations to the world[2]. In this sense the Father is One and Simple, while the Son is Many. He is, firstly, Wisdom, the perfect image of the mind and will of God, which He expresses in crea-

potest antiquior esse in Deo Omnipotentis appellatio quam Patris: per Filium enim omnipotens est Pater. On this point of the Coeternity there cannot be any doubt as to Origen's meaning. See the Excursus of Maranus in Lomm. vol. xxii. p. 351.

[1] *De Princ.* i. 2.

[2] *In Cant. Cant.* iii. (Lom. xv. p. 29): Et ne mireris, si idem ipse et arbor vitae et diversa alia dicatur, cum idem et panis verus, et vitis vera, et agnus Dei, et multa alia nominetur. Omnia namque haec Verbum Dei unicuique efficitur, prout mensura vel desiderium participantis exposcit: secundum quod et manna, qui cum esset unus cibus, unicuique tamen desiderio (desiderii ?) sui reddebat saporem. The peculiarity of Origen's view is that he endeavours to arrange these titles of Christ in an ascending scale, and regards them as denoting successive stages of the believer's progress and receptivity. This was a Valentinian idea. *Excerpta ex Theodoto*, 7, ὁ δὲ αὐτός ἐστι τοιοῦτος ὢν ἑκάστῳ οἷος κεχωρῆσθαι δύναται, and a similar view gave their name to the Docetae (see the Dict. of Christ. Biog.). But the graduation of the titles is necessarily difficult, obscure, and fluctuating.

tion. Secondly, He is the Word, 'because He is as it were
the interpreter of the secrets of the divine intelligence,'
the channel of Revelation [1]. Hence He is also the Life
and the Truth, the giver and sustainer of physical being
and spiritual well-being. These are properties of His
Deity which can never change. Others He has as the
God-Man, Propitiation, Physician, Shepherd, Redemption, the True Bread, the True Vine, the Lamb of God.
These are accidental, for had man never fallen into sin
they would have been needless [2]. Origen compares these

[1] Wisdom is the first and highest of the Epinoiai : *In Joann.* ii. 6, προεπι-
νοουμένης τοῦ λόγου σοφίας. In this sense Christ is the Mind of God,
continens in semet ipsa universae creaturae vel initia vel formas vel species,
De Princ. i. 2. 2. All things were created according to the ideas which God
had previously brought to consciousness (προτρανωθέντας) in Wisdom, as
a house, a ship is built according to the plan or scheme existing in the mind
of the builder ; *In Joann.* i. 22. Here we have the King's Architect of Philo.
In this sense He may be the κόσμος νοητός, *In Joann.* xix. 5 ; cp. *Contra
Celsum,* v. 22, 39 ; vi. 64. In the *De Princ.* ii. 3. 6 Origen does not reject
the doctrine of Ideas, but merely denies the independent existence of the
κόσμος νοητός : utique a nostris alienum est mundum incorporeum dicere, in
sola mentis phantasia vel cogitationum lubrico consistentem. As Wisdom
Christ is Creator ; *In Joann.* i. 22, δημιουργὸς δὲ ὁ Χριστὸς ὡς ἀρχή, καθὸ σοφία
ἐστί. The Epinoia of the Word comes after that of Wisdom, *De Princ.* i. 2. 3 ;
In Joann. i. 22. It is the outer aspect, if we may so say, of the Son's Divinity,
the side on which He communicates with the world, the first link in the chain
between God and man. See Denis, *Philosophie d'Origène,* pp. 89 sqq.

[2] Origen distinguishes, *In Joann.* i. 22, between the Epinoiai which belong
to Christ as properties of His eternal Nature and those which are accretions,
assumed for the purpose of Redemption. It is in respect of the latter that
the Son is Many, while the Father is One. To the latter class belong Firstborn from the Dead, ἱλαστήριον, Light, Shepherd; to the former, Wisdom,
Word, Life, Truth. Τάχα γὰρ σοφία ἔμενε μόνον, ἢ καὶ λόγος, ἢ καὶ ζωή,
πάντως δὲ καὶ ἀλήθεια· οὐ μὴν δὲ καὶ τὰ ἄλλα ὅσα δι' ἡμᾶς προσείληφε. *In
Joann.* i. 30, the latter are the αἰσθητά, the former the νοητά, and here comes
in the distinction between the Two Lives as in Clement. Those who know
Christ only as αἰσθητός are ruled by Him as Man ; those who have risen to a
perception of the νοητά are βασιλευόμενοι ὑπὸ τῆς προηγουμένης φύσεως τοῦ
μονογενοῦς, governed by Christ as God. The reader will observe how
closely this is connected with the teaching of Philo, though the Christian
could not admit that the Word is God only of the imperfect.

Epinoiai to the steps of the Temple leading up to the Holy of Holies. The lower flight is the Humanity, the upper the Divinity, the whole make up our knowledge of the Saviour [1]. We have already seen the same idea in Clement, though not so clearly developed.

'Let no one think,' says Origen, 'that we are introducing a distinction into the essence of the Son [2].' But the mode of expression has given rise to misunderstanding. It is not meant that Christ will ever put off His Humanity [3] or that we shall ever cease to need Him, for even at the climax of all things He will still be the Life and the Truth. We shall see the Father face to face, but only because we shall be 'one spirit with the Lord.' In this sense only Origen believed that the work of Redemption and Mediation will have an end. We shall see the Father no longer in the Son, but as the Son sees Him, in the day when God shall be all in all [4]. But to

---

[1] *In Joann.* xix. 1 (Lom. ii. 149). In this passage in ὥσπερ τῶν ἀναβαθμῶν ὁ μονογενής ἐστι πρῶτος ἐπὶ τὰ κάτω read ὁ μέν ἐστι πρῶτος. *In Joann.* xxxii. 19 there are Epinoiai of the believer corresponding to those of Christ. He is first the slave, then the disciple, the little child, the child, the brother of Jesus, the son of God.

[2] *In Joann.* i. 30 *ad fin.* Huet charges Origen with asserting that the title Word belongs to the Son only accidentally, like those of Light and Shepherd, but he is entirely wrong. The reader of the *Origeniana* must be on his guard throughout. Huet's timidity leads him into frequent errors, in spite of his learning and his sincere desire to do justice. Maranus and de la Rue are not only more generous but safer guides.

[3] See the end of this Lecture.

[4] *In Joann.* xx. 7. The reader may consult M. Denis, p. 379. There is, however, an important distinction. We shall no longer see the Father in the Son, but we, being in the Son, shall see the Father face to face. And in this sense the work of Mediation does not cease. See *De Princ.* iii. 5. 6 sq., Cum ipsis et in ipsis Ipse quoque subiectus dicitur Patri. *De Princ.* iii. 6. 1 Origen quotes John xvii. 21, 24, 'Pater, volo ut ubi ego sum et isti sint mecum, et sicut ego et tu unum sumus ita et isti in nobis unum sint.' This is one of his favourite texts. The same idea is developed, *In Levit.* Hom. vii. 2. Here again the reference is to 1 Cor. xv. 28. Why

Origen, as to Clement, the belief in Jesus as Redeemer is the note of the lower life. We must rise above the sensible to the intelligible, from obedience to love and knowledge, from Jesus to the Word. Redemption is forgiveness and healing discipline, and the true Christian has ceased to need these. Hence the startling phrase that ' to know Christ crucified is the knowledge of babes [1].' Or again, ' Blessed are those who want the Saviour no longer as Physician, Shepherd, Redemption [2].' But Origen's outlook is darker than that of Clement. He throws the higher life farther and farther back, and exhibits a growing intensity of devotion towards the Son of Man.

The heathen Platonists have attained, says Origen, by the light of Nature to a knowledge of the Father and even of the Son; but the belief in the Holy Ghost is the distinguishing prerogative of Christianity [3]. The statement marks his sense of the importance of this article of the Creed, which he did much to strengthen and expand. He has indeed no technical word to denote the relation of the Third to the other Persons,

does the Apostle say ' then shall the Son Himself be subject to the Father?' Not that He needs subjection to the Father, but on my account, in whom He has not yet perfected His work, He is said to be as yet not subject. But when He shall have finished His office and brought all His creatures to the top of perfection, then He Himself shall be called subject in those whom He hath put under the Father, and in whom He has perfected the work that the Father gave Him to do, that God may be all in all. Then and not till then Christ's joy shall be full.

[1] *In Joann.* i. 20, φύσει μὲν αὐτοῦ ἀρχὴ ἡ θεότης, πρὸς ἡμᾶς δέ, μὴ ἀπὸ τοῦ μεγέθους αὐτοῦ δυναμένους ἄρξασθαι τῆς περὶ αὐτοῦ ἀληθείας, ἡ ἀνθρωπότης αὐτοῦ, καθὸ τοῖς νηπίοις καταγγέλλεται Ἰησοῦς Χριστός, καὶ οὗτος ἐσταυρωμένος. So also *Ibid.* xix. 3.

[2] *In Joann.* i. 22.

[3] The leading passages on the subject of the Holy Spirit are *De Princ.* i. 3; ii. 7; *In Joann.* ii. 6.

nor does he ever definitely bestow upon Him the title
of God¹. But the idea, if not the word, is clearly there.

¹ In *De Princ.* ii. 7. 1 he appears even to deny it: 'Nam ut concedamus
Marcioni vel Valentino posse differentias deitatis (of Father and Son) in-
ducere . . . quid inveniet ut differentiam Spiritus Sancti introducat.' But he
certainly spoke of the divinity of the Holy Spirit ; *Ibid.* § 3, the Montanists ' minora quam dignum est de ejus divinitate sentientes erroribus se ac
deceptionibus tradiderunt.' Basil (*De Spir. Sancto,* vol. ii. p. 358, ed. Paris,
1638), who considers that the doctrine of Origen was not sound on all
points, quotes from the *In Rom.*, αἱ ἱεραὶ δυνάμεις χωρητικαὶ τοῦ μονογενοῦς
καὶ τῆς τοῦ ἁγίου πνεύματος θεότητος, and adds, οὕτως οἶμαι τὸ τῆς παραδόσεως
ἰσχυρὸν ἐνῆγε πολλάκις τοὺς ἄνδρας καὶ τοῖς οἰκείοις αὐτῶν δόγμασιν ἀντιλέγειν.
The latter remark is unjust. Tradition was certainly on the side of Origen
as against Basil ; for the title Deus is first expressly bestowed upon the
Holy Spirit by Tertullian in his Montanist treatise *Adv. Praxeam,* 3. 13 ;
cp. Baur, *Dreieinigkeit,* ed. 1841, p. 177 note. In the Preface to the
De Principiis, § 4, it is affirmed that the praedicatio apostolica does
not decide of the Spirit utrum natus an innatus. Jerome has utrum
factus an infectus. Apparently Rufinus read γεννητὸς ἢ ἀγέννητος,
Jerome γενητὸς ἢ ἀγένητος. The words are constantly interchanged in
MSS. *In Joann.* ii. 6 Origen starts several questions—whether the Spirit
has a hypostatic existence; whether He is one of the all things which
were made (ἐγένετο) through the Son; whether He is less or greater
than the Son. The first he answers by affirming the Three Hypostases.
The reply to the second is very hesitating and tortuous. It is perhaps the
worst instance of the evil of his extemporaneous method of composition. At
first (p. 110 Lom.) he regards it as the more pious and true conclusion that the
Spirit is not included in the ' all things ' that were made by the Son. But
τοῦ υἱοῦ χρῄζειν ἔοικε τὸ ἅγιον πνεῦμα, διακονοῦντος αὐτοῦ τῇ ὑποστάσει οὐ
μόνον εἰς τὸ εἶναι ἀλλὰ καὶ σοφὸν εἶναι καὶ λογικὸν καὶ δίκαιον, καὶ πᾶν
ὅτιποτοῦν χρὴ αὐτὸ νοεῖν τυγχάνειν κατὰ μετοχὴν τῶν προειρημένων ἡμῖν
Χριστοῦ ἐπινοιῶν. And three pages further on (p. 113 Lom.) he slides into
the affirmative, ταῦτα δὲ ἐπιπολὺ ἐξήτασται σαφέστερον ἰδεῖν βουλομένοις πῶς,
εἰ πάντα διὰ τοῦ λόγου ἐγένετο, καὶ τὸ πνεῦμα διὰ τοῦ λόγου ἐγένετο ἓν τῶν
πάντων τυγχάνον. Thus the relation of the Spirit to the Son appears to be
analogous to that of the Son to the Father. Perhaps this need not be understood as directly contradicting *De Princ.* i. 3. 4, neque enim putandum
est quod etiam Spiritus Filio revelante cognoscit. Si enim revelante Filio
cognoscit Patrem Spiritus Sanctus, ergo ex ignorantia ad scientiam venit.
De Princ. ii. 2. 1 we read, Sicut ingenitum Filium generat Pater et Spiritum
Sanctum *profert*; *In Rom.* vii. 1, Qui vere ex ipso Deo *procedit*; *De
Princ.* i. 2. 13, In eo fonte de quo vel natus est Filius vel *procedit* Spiritus
Sanctus. But in these passages Rufinus is hardly trustworthy. To the
third question he replies finally that the Spirit is ὑποδεέστερον τοῦ δι' οὗ

The full divinity of the Holy Spirit lay enfolded in the
Baptismal formula, and is the logical consequence of the
assertion of His hypostasis. His eternity Origen teaches
as distinctly as that of the Son; His equality is virtually
though not so clearly contained in many passages.
Thus He is 'associated in honour and dignity with the
Father and the Son.' He is one of the adorable Trinity
which is wholly present in each of the Persons. And
Origen himself invokes the Holy Spirit in prayer [1].
It is He that in the beginning moved upon the face of
the waters [2]; He that is to be understood both in Old and

ἐγένετο. Γίγνεσθαι, γενητός, were not in themselves incorrect words to use
either of the Son or of the Holy Spirit; see *Orig.* ii. 2. 23 (Lom. xxii.
p. 184), with the note of Maranus, and Exc. v. at end of volume. But the
Bishop of Durham, *Apost. Fathers*, part ii. vol. 2. sect. 1. p. 90, inclines to
doubt this. How cautious Origen is may be seen, *De Princ.* i. 3. 3:
Verumtamen usque ad praesens nullum sermonem in scriptis sanctis
invenire potuimus per quem Spiritus Sanctus factura esse vel creatura
diceretur, ne eo quidem modo, quo de Sapientia referre Salomonem supra
edocuimus. He found κτίζειν used of Wisdom but not of the Holy Spirit.
The idea suggested, *In Joann.* ii. 6, that the work of redemption was properly
the function of the Holy Spirit, but that He, being unable to sustain the
task, delivered it over to the Son, is, as Maranus pointed out, a mere
scholastic ἀπορία illustrating only the freedom with which Origen moved.
    [1] See *De Princ.* i. 3 throughout; *In Joann.* vi. 17 (Lom. i. 227), τῷ
ἐμπαρέχοντι ἑαυτὸν τῇ θειότητι τῆς δυνάμεως τῶν τῆς προσκυνητῆς τριάδος
ἐπικλήσεων, quoted by Basil, *De Spir. Sancto*, 29; *De Princ.*, Preface, 4,
Honore ac dignitate Patri ac Filio sociatum tradiderunt Spiritum Sanctum;
In Levit. Hom. i. 1, Ipse igitur nobis Dominus, ipse Sanctus Spiritus
deprecandus est, ut omnem nebulam omnemque caliginem, quae peccatorum
sordibus concreta visum nostri cordis obscurat, auferre dignetur; *In Isai.*
Hom. i. 4, Denique ut unitatem Deitatis in Trinitate cognoscas solus
Christus in praesenti lectione nunc peccata dimittit, et tamen certum est a
Trinitate peccata dimitti; *Ibid.* iv. 1, Non iis sufficit semel clamare
'Sanctus,' neque bis, sed perfectum numerum Trinitatis assumunt, ut multi-
tudinem sanctitatis manifestent Dei, quae est trinae sanctitatis repetita com-
munitas, sanctitas Patris, sanctitas unigeniti Filii et Spiritus Sancti. See
Denis, pp. 117 sqq.
    [2] *De Princ.* i. 3. 3. Participation in the work of Creation is again assigned
to the Holy Spirit, *De Princ.* iv. 30, on the authority of Psalm xxxiii. 6,
Verbo Domini coeli firmati sunt, et spiritu oris eius omnis virtus eorum.

New Testament by the words Spirit or Holy Spirit. But His special work is that of sanctification. The Father gives being to all that exists; the Son imparts reason, Logos, to all that is capable of it; the Holy Ghost works life in those that believe. Hence though all men may be said to participate in the First and Second Persons, not all men share in the Third. It is He that creates in man the capacity to receive Christ, first as Justice, then as Wisdom, and so on in ever-deepening affinity, till at last the gift of being becomes worthy of the Giver. Man is made what God meant him to be, good and permanently good, by the ceaseless ministrations of the Holy Spirit. Thus it may be said that the Son and the Holy Spirit are the cause of the knowledge of God, that the Holy Spirit is the substance of the graces of the Father[1].

Thus far the Alexandrines cleared and defined the notion of the Divine Persons. But a not less difficult task remained behind. Granting the triple Personality, where then is the Unity, or as it was called the Monarchy? The question was involved in Noetianism, it was pressed upon the Church from without by Celsus, the champion of reformed Heathenism. It involved the very essence and existence of the faith. If Christianity was Monotheism in the sense of Noetus, where was the reality of the work of Jesus? if it were not Monotheism in the sense

This is important, as showing that in *De Princ.* i. 3. 5 the words ' ut operationem specialem Spiritus Sancti et specialem Patris ac Filii describamus' are not inserted by Rufinus. This is a sufficient answer to the strictures of Theophilus, Jerome and Justinian, for which see the *Origeniana.*

[1] *De Princ.* i. 3. 5; *Prol. in Cant. Cant.* (Lom. xiv. 307) ; *In Joann.* ii. 6; *In Jerem.* Hom. viii. 1. Substance of the graces, ὕλη τῶν χαρισμάτων. As the Son is ἔμψυχος σοφία, so the Holy Spirit is ἔμψυχος χάρις, though this phrase is not actually used.

of Celsus, in what was it better than the religion of Mithra, and what became of its exclusive claims? We enter here upon one of the most fiercely decried portions of Origen's teaching[1]. Let it be observed by way of caution that he had no paper money, no accepted phrases to pass current instead of thought; that speaking of the most awful mystery that can exercise the mind of man, he expresses himself by no means with neatness and precision, but with becoming hesitation, as of one who hears only 'fragments of the mighty voice,' and faithfully endeavours to render the whole of what he hears. Hence his language is partly that of later times, partly not; most startling when most Biblical. Rufinus, the translator of the *De Principiis*, has doubtless tampered with his text. But we have abundant means of checking his divagations. There is no important point on which we cannot produce the exact meaning of Origen[2].

---

[1] The chief among the ancient assailants of Origen and Origenism were Methodius, *De Resurrectione*, fragments only are extant, but there is an abstract of the work in Photius, Cod. 234; Eustathius, *De Engastrimytho*, in Migne, vol. xvii. 614; Epiphanius, *Haereses*, lxiv; *Ep. ad Joann. Ep. Hieros.*, Latin translation in Jerome's *Epistles*, 51, Migne, vol. xxii; Theophilus, *Paschal Letters*, i. 2. 3, Greek fragments in Migne, vol. lxv. 54, Latin translations in Jerome's *Epistles*, 96, 98, 100, Migne, vol. xxii; Jerome, *Epp.* 84, *Ad Pammachium et Oceanum*, 124 *Ad Avitum*, Migne, vol. xxii; *Apologia adv. libros Rufini*; Justinian, *Adv. Origenem* or *Ad Menam*, Mansi, ix. 487; Migne, lxxxvi. 946; Labbe, v. 635.

[2] The life and works of Rufinus (whose cognomen is variously given as Toranus, Turranius, or Tyrannius) will be found in Migne, vol. xxi. See also *Origeniana*, ii. 4. 10; Redepenning, ii. 61, 68, 254; Neander, iv. 447 (Eng. Trans.); Gieseler, *Lehrbuch der Kirchengeschichte*, 1824, part i. p. 284 sqq. Rufinus, a monk of Aquileia, in 372 accompanied a pious and wealthy lady Melania to the East as a kind of domestic chaplain, though not yet ordained. In Palestine, where he remained till 397, living for a part of the time with the hermits on the Mount of Olives, he had a serious quarrel with Jerome, arising out of the dispute between Epiphanius and

Let us begin with passages representing the line of thought that was afterwards predominant. Origen insists that both terms of the antinomy, the One and the Many, must be equally kept in view. Thus in the Homily on the Shew Bread, one of his most remarkable allegories, the bread, he says, is made of two-tenths of flour. It is significant then of the two Persons, for ten, the perfect number, is emblematic of Deity. The loaves are laid one upon another to show that they are one mass, one

John of Jerusalem. The latter was accused of Origenism and Rufinus took his part. On his return to Italy he began to translate Greek theological works into Latin at the request of friends, in particular the *De Principiis*. This led to a renewal of hostilities with Jerome, and drew upon Rufinus the censure of Pope Anastasius, though he does not appear to have been formally condemned. He died in Sicily, whither he had fled for shelter during the invasion of Alaric. Here in sight of the blazing villages of Calabria, in the midst of horrors that might seem to denote the approaching end of all things, he found comfort in the mystical commentary on the Song of Songs. Besides the *De Principiis* he gave to Latin the pseudo-Clementine *Recognitions*. The Westerns appear to have been at this time profoundly ignorant of Greek speculations, and Rufinus was much in the position of the scholars who first introduced modern German theology into England. To him we owe the Latin version of the *Homilies* on Genesis, Exodus, Leviticus, Numbers, Joshua, Judges, 1 Samuel (the last probably, Red. ii. 255), Psalms 36–38, the *Commentaries* on the Song of Songs, and Romans, and the *De Principiis*, with the *Apology* of Pamphilus. The translation of the *Homilies* on the Song of Songs, Isaiah, Jeremiah, Ezekiel, Luke, is by Jerome. The author of the version of the latter part of the Commentary on Matthew is unknown. We have also some fragments of the translation of the *De Princ.* by Jerome, and of a Homily on Job by Hilarius Pictaviensis. Rufinus has described his mode of translation very candidly (see his Prefaces to Numbers, Joshua, Psalms, *De Princ.* i. and iii, and the peroratio to *In Rom.*). He dealt with great freedom, expanding, condensing, combining, expurgating, and amending. The gist of Jerome's attack upon the translation of the *De Princ.* is not that Rufinus had softened or omitted unorthodox expressions on the subject of the Trinity (for he had done the same thing himself in his version of the Homilies on Isaiah), but that he had supported and strengthened Origen's views on the subject of the Fall, Restitution, &c. The worst that can be said of Rufinus is that his judgment and temper were not perfect. Huet treats him very harshly in order to relieve Jerome.

Bread. 'For I cannot separate the Son from the Father, the Father from the Son.' Yet again, the loaves are placed in two layers to denote the Personal distinction. 'We call Him Father who is not Son, Him Son who is not Father[1].' Again, elsewhere the Persons are numerically distinct[2]. But this is not to be taken to imply local division. 'For to ascribe division to an incorporeal substance is the act not only of extreme impiety but of the dullest folly[3].' Hence the Generation of the Son is to be regarded as a continuous process. 'The Father did not beget His Son and let Him go from Himself, but always begets Him[4].' For this reason he rejects the phrases which earlier writers had employed,—that of

[1] *In Levit.* Hom. xiii. 4.
[2] The Noetians hold μὴ διαφέρειν τῷ ἀριθμῷ τὸν υἱὸν τοῦ πατρός, *In Joann.* x. 21. So Justin, *Apol.* i. 22, the Son ἕτερός ἐστι τοῦ θεοῦ ἀριθμῷ ἀλλ' οὐ γνώμῃ. Again, *Trypho*, 56 (Otto, p. 192).
[3] *De Princ.* i. 2. 6 : Observandum namque est ne quis incurrat in absurdas fabulas eorum qui prolationes quasdam sibi ipsis depingunt, ut divinam naturam in partes vocent, et Deum patrem quantum in se est dividant, cum hoc de incorporea natura vel leviter suspicari non solum extremae impietatis sit verum ultimae insipientiae.
[4] *In Jerem.* Hom. ix. 4, *ad fin.* : οὐχὶ ἐγέννησεν ὁ πατὴρ τὸν υἱὸν καὶ ἀπέλυσεν αὐτὸν ὁ πατὴρ ἀπὸ τῆς γενέσεως αὐτοῦ ἀλλ' ἀεὶ γεννᾷ αὐτόν. Origen goes on to illustrate his meaning by the simile of the Torch and the Ray. Huet regards with suspicion this figure, which was indeed used by unorthodox writers to give the idea of an occasional emanation, emitted from and again absorbed into the parent flame. See above, p. 59, note. But de la Rue defends it with perfect success, though the language of *De Princ.* i. 2. 7, 11 hardly needs defence. Cp. also *In Joann.* xxxii. 18 (Lom. ii. 470), ὅλης μὲν οὖν οἶμαι τῆς δόξης τοῦ θεοῦ αὐτοῦ ἀπαύγασμα εἶναι τὸν υἱόν. The idea of occasional emanation attaches also to the phrase Prophoric Logos, that is Spoken Word, which Origen rejects, *In Joann.* i. 23 (Lom. i. 50): καὶ μάλιστα, ἐπεὶ συνεχῶς χρῶνται τῷ ἐξηρεύξατο ἡ καρδία μου λόγον ἀγαθόν, οἰόμενοι προφορὰν πατρικὴν οἱονεὶ ἐν συλλαβαῖς κειμένην εἶναι τὸν υἱὸν τοῦ θεοῦ καὶ κατὰ τοῦτο ὑπόστασιν αὐτῷ, εἰ ἀκριβῶς αὐτῶν πυνθανοίμεθα, οὐ διδόασιν. *De Princ.* i. 2. 4 Origen rejects also the Adoption theory. *Ibid.* i. 2. 6 the Son's existence depends upon the Will of the Father and the Divine Generation is illustrated by the relation of volition to intelligence.

N

Projection, that of the Prophoric Logos,—and prefers
the beautiful simile of the Torch and the Ray. So far
his view is that known as Circumincession, the idea of
perfect mutual interpenetration. He has addressed himself mainly to the relation between Father and Son. But
what is true of them is true of the whole Trinity.
But still it may be asked in what precisely does the
unity consist? In this particular form the question had
as yet hardly been posed, and it would have been better
had it never been stated. The most we can do is to
agree upon a word, and at such altitudes words lose their
vitality. But it was not Origen's nature to gloss over a
difficulty, and in those days of Polytheism it would not
perhaps have been safe to do so. He will give then
what answer he can, though he well knows what the
answer is worth. At one time in reply to Celsus he
places the unity in perfect moral harmony. 'We worship
the Father of Truth, and the Son who is Truth, Two in
Person, but One in agreement and concert and identity
of will.' It is a union like that of the Church, 'the multitude of them that believed were of one heart and one
soul [1].' At another time he uses the expression One in

---

[1] *Contra Celsum*,viii. 12. After quoting John xiv. 11, 'I am in the Father
and the Father in Me,' Origen proceeds, εἰ δέ τις ἐκ τούτων περισπασθήσεται
μή πη αὐτομολοῦμεν πρὸς τοὺς ἀναιροῦντας δύο εἶναι ὑποστάσεις πατέρα καὶ
υἱόν, ἐπιστησάτω τῷ ἦν δὲ πάντων τῶν πιστευσάντων ἡ καρδία καὶ ἡ ψυχὴ μία,
ἵνα θεωρήσῃ τὸ ἐγὼ καὶ ὁ πατὴρ ἕν ἐσμεν. Ἕνα οὖν θεόν, ὡς ἀποδεδώκαμεν,
τὸν πατέρα καὶ τὸν υἱὸν θεραπεύομεν . . . . ὄντα δύο τῇ ὑποστάσει πράγματα,
ἕν δὲ τῇ ὁμονοίᾳ καὶ τῇ συμφωνίᾳ καὶ τῇ ταυτότητι τοῦ βουλήματος. The
same definition supported by the same illustration was censured in the case
of Abbot Joachim by the Fourth Lateran Council in 1215; see Mansi, xxii.
981 sqq., or Denzinger, *Enchiridion*, § 358. Abbot Joachim preached also
'the Eternal Gospel,' though he gave to the phrase a political significance
and used it to express the social and religious reformation yearned for by
the enthusiasts of his time. M. Denis, pp. 576 sqq., appears to me to
underrate the connection between Origen and Joachim.

Substance, and Pamphilus even ascribes to him the famous *Homoousion* of the Nicene Fathers [1]. This however could not be his definite opinion, partly because the word *Ousia* or Essence still means at times Person or Hypostasis; partly because from either point of view, the Stoic or the Platonic, it was by no means clear whether God could be spoken of as having *Ousia* at all, because He is rather ' above all *Ousia* [2]; ' partly again because the term belongs

[1] Frag. 3 from commentary *In Hebr.* quoted by Pamphilus in his *Apology*, Quae utraeque similitudines (vapor virtutis Dei and aporrhoea gloriae Omnipotentis purissima) manifestissime ostendunt communionem substantiae esse Filio cum Patre. Aporrhoea enim ὁμοούσιος videtur, id est unius substantiae cum illo corpore ex quo est vel aporrhoea vel vapor (Lom. xxiv. 359). The word ὁμοούσιος is used by Heracleon to denote the natural affinity which he in common with the other Valentinians conceived to exist between the Pneumatic and God and between the Hylic and the Devil, *In Joann.* xiii. 25 ; xx. 18 (Lom. ii. 43, 241). This idea is rejected both by Clement, *Strom.* ii. 16. 74 ; iv. 13. 91, and by Origen. In this usage the word means made of the same stuff, of the same genus, governed by the same laws, but does not imply equality. In this sense it is applied to the Son by the author of the *Homilies*, xx. 7. The Son is ὁμοούσιος τῷ θεῷ ἰσοδύναμος δὲ οὔ. As a term of theology the word appears to have been first employed in these ways by Gnostics and Ebionites. In the passage quoted above from Origen it appears for the first time in its later Nicene sense, for I cannot regard the passage in the *Adumbrationes*, p. 1009, as Clement's, though Zahn, *Forschungen*, p. 138, thinks otherwise. The word was not regarded as orthodox by the Antiochene Fathers, see Routh, iii. p. 314. Like many other words it acquired a technical meaning which at first undoubtedly it did not possess. Bull, book ii. chapter 1, may still be read with advantage, though he endeavoured to prove too much. Ὁμοούσιος is certainly not ' a word of which the precision and exactness precluded all attempt at equivocation.' See also Harnack, *Dogmengeschichte*, pp. 531 sqq.

[2] See *Contra Celsum*, vi. 64. Celsus says, οὐδ' οὐσίας μετέχει ὁ θεός. No, replies Origen, μετέχεται γὰρ μᾶλλον ἢ μετέχει. So the Saviour, οὐ μετέχει μὲν δικαιοσύνης· δικαιοσύνη δὲ ὢν μετεχέται ὑπὸ τῶν δικαίων. . . Πολὺς δὲ ὁ περὶ τῆς οὐσίας λόγος καὶ δυσθεώρητος . . . . πότερον ἐπέκεινα οὐσίας ἐστὶ πρεσβείᾳ καὶ δυνάμει ὁ θεὸς μεταδιδοὺς οὐσίας . . ἢ καὶ αὐτός ἐστιν οὐσία. . . . Ζητητέον δὲ καὶ εἰ οὐσίαν μὲν οὐσιῶν λεκτέον καὶ ἰδέαν ἰδεῶν καὶ ἀρχὴν τὸν μονογενῆ καὶ πρωτότοκον πάσης κτίσεως, ἐπέκεινα δὲ πάντων τούτων τὸν πατέρα αὐτοῦ καὶ θεόν. *In Joann.* xix. 1 (Lom. ii. p. 149), ἵν' οὕτως ἔλθῃ ἐπὶ τὸ ἐνιδεῖν τῇ οὐσίᾳ ἢ τῇ ὑπερέκεινα τῆς οὐσίας δυνάμει καὶ φύσει τοῦ

to the vocabulary of science and not of Scripture, and even in science denotes not knowledge but the absence of knowledge. For the *Ousia* is precisely that about a thing of which we are wholly ignorant. Hence again, taking his stand upon the words of our Saviour 'that they may know Thee the only true God,' upon the words of St. Paul 'to us there is but One God the Father,' he seeks for the ground of unity in the derivation of the Second Person from the First, of the Third from the Second and First. The Father is 'the God,' 'the only true God.' The Son is 'God' without addition, because His Deity is derived [1].

The Son, as we have seen, possesses all the attributes of God, His Goodness, His Wisdom, His Power. He possesses them in full and perfect measure, not accidentally but substantially and unchangeably, not precariously but by virtue, if we may so speak, of a law of the Divine Nature. He is begotten, not created. The Son is in the Father, the Father in the Son, and no schism is conceivable between them. Yet the Word is the Splendour of the Divine Glory, the Image of the Father's Person; in a word He is the Son. The Father is the 'Fountain' from whom His Divinity is 'drawn [2].'

Θεοῦ. If οὐσία be taken in its Platonic sense as signifying Idea it is prior to the Thing, and thus the Idea of God would be above God; again, the Ideas are sometimes spoken of as created by God. If the word be taken in its Stoic sense, we arrive at a distinction between the πρώτη ὕλη and the πάθη of the Deity. Words like these, which represent or are supposed to represent the teaching of sensible experience, explain without explaining that which 'eye hath not seen.'

[1] *In Joann.* ii. 2, 3, 18 ; xiii. 25 ; xxxii. 18 ; *Contra Celsum*, viii. 14, 15.

[2] *In Joann.* ii. 2, σπάσας τῆς θεότητος εἰς ἑαυτόν. 'Hoc est portionem divinitatis non divinitatem' remarks Huet, with whom agrees M. Denis, p. 110. This is laying far too much stress upon a word. Besides, had Origen written τὴν θεότητα, he would have meant that the Son had deprived the Father of Deity.

It is the difference between Cause and Effect, and in this
aspect it sometimes seems to Origen immense[1].	Yet if
we look downwards, if we compare the God Son with
the highest of created things, with principalities and
archangels, there is a gulf more enormous still, because
of another kind.

We shall however wrong Origen, if we attempt to
derive his Subordinationism from metaphysical con-
siderations.	It is purely Scriptural, and rests wholly
and entirely upon the words of Jesus, 'My Father is
greater than I,' 'that they may know Thee the only true
God,' 'None is Good save One.'	The dominant text in
Origen's mind was the last.	Hence he limits the rela-
tivity to the attribute to which it is limited by Christ
Himself.	The Son is Very Wisdom, Very Righteous-
ness, Very Truth, perhaps even Very King, but not Very
Goodness.	Perfect Image of the Father's Goodness, but
not the Absolute Good, though in regard to us He is the
Absolute Good[2].	There are indeed passages where

---

[1] *In Joann.* xiii. 25, πάντων μὲν τῶν γενητῶν ὑπερέχειν οὐ συγκρίσει ἀλλ'
ὑπερβαλλούσῃ ὑπεροχῇ φαμεν τὸν Σωτῆρα καὶ τὸ πνεῦμα τὸ ἅγιον ὑπερεχό-
μενον τοσοῦτον ἢ καὶ πλέον ἀπὸ τοῦ πατρός, ὅσῳ ὑπερέχει αὐτὸς καὶ τὸ ἅγιον
πνεῦμα τῶν λοιπῶν.	Observe the words οὐ συγκρίσει, the Son and Holy
Spirit are not to be compared with created things.	With this passage
should be contrasted *In Matth.* xv. 10, πλείων γὰρ ἡ ὑπεροχὴ πρὸς τὰ
ὑποδεέστερα ἀγαθὰ ἐν τῷ Σωτῆρι, καθό ἐστιν εἰκὼν τῆς ἀγαθότητος αὐτοῦ τοῦ
θεοῦ, ἤπερ ἡ ὑπεροχὴ τοῦ θεοῦ ὄντος ἀγαθοῦ πρὸς τὸν εἰπόντα Σωτῆρα ὁ πατήρ,
ὁ πέμψας με, μείζων μου ἐστίν· ὄντα πρὸς ἑτέρους καὶ εἰκόνα τῆς ἀγαθότητος
τοῦ θεοῦ.

[2] The boldness with which Rufinus corrected his text is nowhere more
evident than in *De Princ.* i. 2. 13.	The most important passage of the
original Greek is given in Justinian, *Ad Menam* : οὕτω τοίνυν ἡγοῦμαι καὶ ἐπὶ
τοῦ σωτῆρος καλῶς ἂν λεχθήσεσθαι ὅτι εἰκὼν ἀγαθότητος τοῦ θεοῦ ἐστιν, ἀλλ'
οὐκ αὐτοαγαθόν.	Καὶ τάχα καὶ υἱὸς ἀγαθός, ἀλλ' οὐχ ὡς ἁπλῶς ἀγαθός.	Καὶ
ὥσπερ εἰκών ἐστι τοῦ θεοῦ τοῦ ἀοράτου καὶ κατὰ τοῦτο θεός, ἀλλ' οὐ περὶ οὗ
λέγει αὐτὸς ὁ Χριστός, ἵνα γινώσκωσί σε τὸν μόνον ἀληθινὸν θεόν· οὕτως εἰκὼν

Origen hesitatingly suggests the question whether there
may not be in the Father abysses of knowledge, glory,
power beyond all that is given to the Son[1]. These
however must not be insisted upon. Where he pro-
nounces his real thought, the difference between the
Persons is conceived not as quantitative nor as quali-
tative, but as modal simply. The Son *qua* Son is
inferior to the Father *qua* Father.
' Speculate not,' says Gregory Nazianzen, ' upon the
Divine Generation, for it is not safe . . . let the doctrine
be honoured silently . . . It is a great thing for thee to
know the fact; the mode we cannot admit that even

ἀγαθότητος ἀλλ' οὐχ ὡς ὁ πατὴρ ἀπαραλλάκτως ἀγαθός. The best comment
on this passage is afforded by *In Matth.* xiv. 7, αὐτὸς γάρ ἐστιν ὁ Βασιλεὺς
τῶν οὐρανῶν, καὶ ὥσπερ αὐτός ἐστιν ἡ αὐτοσοφία καὶ ἡ αὐτοδικαιοσύνη καὶ ἡ
αὐτοαλήθεια, οὕτω μήποτε καὶ ἡ αὐτοβασιλεία. But here again it will be
observed not τὸ αὐτοαγαθόν. Now as the whole existence of the Son is
derived from the Father, and He is therefore strictly speaking no more
αὐτοσοφία than αὐτοαγαθόν, it will be evident that Origen is here struggling
against his own principles and endeavouring to reduce the doctrine of
Derivation and Subordination, which he had inherited from his predecessors,
to the narrowest limits consistent with the direct teaching of Scripture.
There is a sense even in which the Son may be called the Absolute Good,
if not in respect of God yet in respect of man : ὡς μὲν πρὸς τὸν πατέρα εἰκών
ἐστιν ἀγαθότητος, ὡς δὲ πρὸς τὰ λοιπὰ ὅπερ ἢ τοῦ πατρὸς ἀγαθότης πρὸς αὐτόν,
In Matth. xv. 10. What struck later ages as the novelty and audacity of
Origen's doctrine was in truth its archaism and conservatism. 'La vérité,
c'est que la pensée d'Origène se meut dans deux directions tout opposées.
Lorsqu'il ne suit que la logique et les idées où sa fervente piété l'inclinait,
il va à l'égalité des personnes divines. Lorsqu'il s'en tient à la tradition . . .
il recule devant les conséquences de sa piété et de la logique, et se jette à
l'extrémité opposée ;' Denis, p. 111.

[1] *De Princ.* iv. 35, ὥστε καὶ ἐν τῷ νοεῖν ὁ πατὴρ μειζόνως καὶ τρανοτέρως
καὶ τελειοτέρως νοεῖται ὑφ' ἑαυτοῦ ἢ ὑπὸ τοῦ υἱοῦ : *In Joann.* xxxii. 18 the
glory which the Father has in Himself is greater than that which He has in
His Son. On the other hand, *In Joann.* i. 27 the Son's knowledge is equal
to that of the Father. Redepenning, ii. 277 sqq.; Denis, 111 sqq.; *Origeniana*, ii. 2. 19 (Lom. xxii. p. 172); Bull, ii. 9. At any rate Origen
did not think himself debarred from considering the question.

angels understand, much less thou[1].' It is a wise
admonition, but it is double-edged, and must not be so
applied as to smite Origen alone. Nor indeed is it just
to blame him here for presumption. He could not, he
dared not, shrink back where the word of God led him
on. He could not think that a truth three times at
least pressed upon the Church by Christ Himself might
safely be ignored. To his dauntless spirit these words
of the Master seemed to be not a scandal but a flash of
light. They spoke of the supreme anchor of all our
hopes, the transcendental Goodness of Him from whom
all things ultimately proceed, of that day when Christ
shall render up His Kingdom to the Father, and God,
the Good, shall be all in all. Lastly, let us remember, he
is speaking, though more emphatically than others, the
belief of his time[2]. He was condemned by Jerome and
Justinian; but he has been acquitted by Athanasius and
theologians of every school to whom history and Scripture
do not speak in vain.

The objections urged in ancient times against Origen's
Subordinationism, objections resting in' many cases on
the most serious misapprehension, may for the present
be dismissed[3]. But there is one true consequence of his
view so momentous that it must not be passed over.
I refer to his teaching on the subject of prayer offered to
the Son.

He has declared himself upon this point many times,

---

[1] Orat. xxxv. 29. 30; in Migne, xxix. 8.

[2] See the catena of patristic explanations of John xiv. 28 given by Dr.
Westcott, *Gospel of St. John*, p. 213, ed. 1882. 'Towards the close of the
fourth century the opinion began to gain currency that the superior greatness
of the Father was referred to the human life of the Son.'

[3] The curious reader will find them in the *Origeniana*.

especially in the *Celsus.* 'Away with the advice of Celsus that we should pray to demons. For we must pray only to the Supreme God, yes, and we must pray to the Only-Begotten and Firstborn of every creature, and beseech Him as our High Priest to offer to His God and our God, to His Father and the Father of all that live, our prayers as they come first to Him.' The meaning of these words is explained at large in the *Treatise upon Prayer.* Starting from the text of St. Paul, 'I exhort therefore that first of all supplications, prayers, intercessions and giving of thanks be made for all men[1],' he proceeds to draw a distinction between these four terms. Prayer in its proper sense, he concludes, is that which the soul sends up with clearest

[1] 1 Tim. ii. 1: παρακαλῶ οὖν πρῶτον πάντων ποιεῖσθαι δεήσεις, προσευχάς, ἐντεύξεις, εὐχαριστίας ὑπὲρ πάντων ἀνθρώπων. There is a difficulty in explaining Origen's meaning because 'prayer' must be used as the equivalent both of εὐχή and of προσευχή. Εὐχή seems to be regarded as the genus including these four species. Δέησις is defined τὴν περὶ (so the English editor) ἐλλείποντός τινι μεθ' ἱκεσίας περὶ τοῦ ἐκείνου τυχεῖν ἀναπεμπομένην εὐχήν. It is prayer without worship (προσκύνησις). Intercession is a confident appeal for benefits to oneself or to others, τὴν ὑπὸ παρρησίαν τινὰ πλείονα ἔχοντος περί τινων ἀξίωσιν πρὸς θεόν: the difference here lies in the character of the speaker, it is the address of a son to his father. It should be added that Origen lays down not only that we must pray to God through Christ, but that we must not pray to Him in any other way. In the opening of the eighth book *Contra Celsum* where Origen is replying to the reproach of Celsus that the Christian served two Masters and so introduced στάσις, hostile division, between the old Deity and the new, he uses of Christ not merely τιμᾶν and θεραπεύειν, but σέβειν, θρησκεύειν, δουλεύειν, referring to John v. 23; x. 30; xiv. 11; xvii. 22. *Ibid.* i. 51 Christ is ὁ ὑπὸ Χριστιανῶν προσκυνούμενος. Worship, the highest adoration, is offered to God through Christ, and to Christ as He is in, as He is One with the Father. This will explain the language of the *De Oratione* where it is said that worship (προσκύνησις) belongs to Christ only in a figurative sense, not absolutely or in His own right. Everywhere Origen's language is the same. With the fullest recognition of the Divinity of the Son there is the constant warning that we must not forget that God is our Father and the Father of all that is.

insight for the higher spiritual gifts, and is accompanied by a Doxology. The three lower forms of petition may be addressed to men for help or pardon, or to saints or angels, or to the Holy Spirit or Christ, the last and highest only to the Father in the Son's name ¹. He does not, it will be observed, forbid the Christian to pray to Christ as God. He refers to the prayers of the Penitent Thief, of Stephen, of the father of the lunatic child, all addressed to the Son and the Son alone, and he himself prays to the Son in the same way ². We may throw light upon his meaning by refer-

---

¹ *Contra Celsum*, v. 4 ; viii. 13, 26 ; *De Orat.* 14, 15. The words 'with clearest insight' are given as a translation of μεγαλοφνέστερον in *De Orat.* 14 (Lom. xvii. 142). It is justified by the observation that μεγαλοφυές is frequently used of the mystic spiritual sense. Prayer in the sense of supplication, δέησις, to saints, *ibid.* (Lom. xvii. 146), τὴν δὲ δέησιν μόνοις ἁγίοις, εἴ τις εὑρεθείη Παῦλος ἢ Πέτρος, ἵνα ὠφελήσωσιν ἡμᾶς ἀξίους ποιοῦντες τοῦ τυχεῖν τῆς δεδομένης αὐτοῖς ἐξουσίας πρὸς τὸ ἁμαρτήματα ἀφιέναι. Origen no doubt regarded this kind of prayer as lawfully offered to saints, whether on earth or in heaven. As regards the Angels see *Contra Celsum*, v. 4 ; viii. 57, but especially viii. 13, where Origen says that a sort of θεραπεία may be offered to the angels if we understand exactly what we mean by the word. In *De Mart.* 6, 7 he denies that either λατρεία or προσκύνησις could be offered to Angels, but this language does not exclude prayer provided that in prayer we do not confound these high servants of the Almighty with their Maker and Master. In this sense Origen may be said to pray to the guardian Angel of the newly baptized, *In Ezech.* Hom. i. 7 (Lom. xiv. 20), Omnia angelis plena sunt, veni Angele, suscipe sermone conversum ab errore pristino.

² *Contra Celsum*, v. 4, δεησόμεθα δὲ καὶ αὐτοῦ τοῦ λόγου καὶ ἐντευξόμεθα αὐτῷ καὶ εὐχαριστήσομεν καὶ προσευξόμεθα δέ, ἐὰν δυνώμεθα κατακούειν τῆς περὶ προσευχῆς κυριολεξίας καὶ καταχρήσεως : explained ibid. viii. 26, μόνῳ γὰρ προσευκ-τέον τῷ ἐπὶ πᾶσι θεῷ καὶ προσευκτέον γε τῷ μονογενεῖ καὶ πρωτοτόκῳ πάσης κτίσεως, λόγῳ θεοῦ, καὶ ἀξιωτέον αὐτὸν ὡς ἀρχιερέα τὴν ἐπ' αὐτὸν φθάσασαν ἡμῶν εὐχὴν ἀναφέρειν ἐπὶ τὸν θεὸν αὐτοῦ καὶ θεὸν ἡμῶν, καὶ πατέρα αὐτοῦ καὶ πατέρα τῶν βιούντων κατὰ τὸν λόγον τοῦ θεοῦ. Hymns were sung to the Father and to Christ, *Ibid.* viii. 67. See also *In Exodum*, Hom. xiii. 3, Domine Jesu, praesta mihi ut aliquid monumenti habere merear in tabernaculo tuo : *In Levit.* Hom. i. 1, ipse igitur nobis Dominus, ipse Spiritus Sanctus depre-

ence to his favourite idea of the *Epinoiai.* We may address the Saviour, in immediate supplication, for those boons which it is His special province to bestow. But in the supreme moment of adoration, when the soul strains upwards to lay itself as a sacrifice before the highest object of thought, we must not stop short of Him who is above all. Such prayer is necessarily attended by a 'doxology,' a clear recognition of the Nature of Him before whom we stand, and in the doxology the Father's Name is first. Origen appeals to the express command of Jesus, 'Whatsoever ye shall ask the Father He will give it in My name,' to the usage of Scripture, and lastly to the usage of the Church. It is probable that at this very time a change was creeping into the language of worship. 'Are we not

candus est, ut omnem nebulam, omnemque caliginem, quae peccatorum sordibus concreta visum nostri cordis obscurat, auferre dignetur : *In Levit.* Hom. v. 5, Dominum meum Jesum invocare me oportet ut quaerentem me faciat invenire et pulsanti aperiat : *In Num.* Hom. xxv. 3, nos autem oremus ex corde Verbum Dei, qui est unigenitus eius, et qui revelat Patrem quibus vult, ut et nobis haec revelare dignetur : *In Ezech.* Hom. iii. 4, Praesta mihi, Christe, ut disrumpam cervicalia in animarum consuta luxuriam : *In Rom.* viii. 4, Sed et in principio Epistolae, quam ad Corinthios scribit, ubi dicit 'cum omnibus qui invocant nomen Domini nostri Jesu Christi, in omni loco ipsorum et nostro,' eum cuius nomen invocatur Dominum (al. Deum) Jesum Christum esse pronuntiat. Si ergo et Enos et Moses et Aaron et Samuel 'invocabant Dominum et ipse exaudiebat eos,' sine dubio Christum Jesum Dominum invocabant : et si invocare nomen Domini et orare Dominum unum atque idem est, sicut invocatur Deus invocandus est Christus, et sicut oratur Deus ita et orandus est Christus . . . Unum namque utrique honorem deferendum, id est Patri et Filio, divinus edocet sermo, cum dicit ' ut omnes honorificent Filium sicut honorificant Patrem.' But this last passage goes beyond Origen's usual language and may have been amended by Rufinus. It will be observed that he insists upon the difference between the κυριολεξία and κατάχρησις, the absolute and relative sense, of Prayer, and that his own Prayers to the Son are ejaculatory and brief. The reader may consult Lücke, *De Invocatione Jesu Christi in precibus Christianorum accuratius definienda,* Gottingae, 1843; Redepenning, *Origenes,* ii. 38 sqq. ; Bingham, xiii. 2. 3.

divided,' he asks, 'if we pray some to the Father, some
to the Son, falling into the error of ignorant men because
we have never enquired into the real nature of what we
are doing [1]?' Strange and innovating as his words may
seem to us, they are really the very opposite of this.
They are a plea for ancient usage in a time of change.
It has been thought that his protest refers specially to
the Eucharist, the Anaphora or Missa Fidelium, in which
for long after this time there was no direct address to
the Son [2]. But in truth it has a wider scope. He is
warning his readers not against excessive devotion to
'the Lord and Saviour Jesus,' for in this Origen himself
yields to none, nor against the fullest belief in Christ's
Divinity, for here also Origen's doctrine, in the judgment
of those most worthy of our deference, stands above
suspicion, but against the language, if I may risk the

---

[1] *De Orat.* 16.

[2] At the time when Gregory the Great introduced the Christe Eleison into
the Roman Mass it was not found in the Greek Liturgies. Greg. *Epp.* ix.
12, *Ad Joannem Syracusanum Episcopum* : 'Kyrie Eleison autem nos neque
diximus neque dicimus sicut a Graecis dicitur, quia in Graecis simul omnes
dicunt, apud nos autem a clericis dicitur et a populo respondetur, et totidem
vicibus etiam Christe Eleison dicitur, quod apud Graecos nullo modo dicitur.'
The Kyrie Eleison had been introduced into the Western Mass about the beginning of the sixth century ; see Canon 3 of Conc. Vasense III. in Mansi, viii.
727. In the Church of Africa a protest was made at the end of the fourth
century against the insertion of prayers to the Son in the Mass. See the 21st
of the second series of Canons of the Synod of Hippo held in 393 (Hefele,
vol. ii. p. 398, Eng. trans.) : ' In prayers no one shall address the Son instead
of the Father or the Father instead of the Son, except at the altar, when
prayer shall always be addressed to the Father. No one shall make use of
strange forms of prayer without having first consulted well-instructed brethren.'
Probst, *Liturgie*, pp. 141 sqq., finds in the four words defined by Origen an
outline of the whole Liturgy. Δέησις, he thinks, means the prayers of the
Catechumens and Penitents ; προσευχή, the Thanksgiving, Trisagion, and
Confession ; ἔντευξις, the Memento ; and εὐχαριστία, the Thanksgiving after
Communion. His view is too ingenious, but it seems not unlikely that by
προσευχή Origen means particularly the prayers that accompanied the
Eucharist.

phrase, of partial adoration, which verges on the one hand towards Noetianism, on the other towards some form of Gnosticism, that is of moral opposition. Is it too much to assert that the latter and graver danger has more than once been perilously near at hand, that the Father has, in appearance at any rate, been obscured behind the Son, as the Son in turn behind the Virgin and the Saints?

It is curious to observe that Origen himself contributed, perhaps more than any one else, to direct and feed this movement by his Commentary and Homilies on the Song of Songs. He undertook the work with many misgivings, for he was startled at finding the Greek word which denotes sexual affection used, as he thought, of the love between Christ and His mystical Bride. But he persuaded himself that there is no real difference between the *Eros* of poetry and the *Agape* of the New Testament. 'It matters not therefore which word we use of God. Nor do I think any one can be blamed if he calls God *Eros*, as John called Him *Agape*. Lastly, I remember that one of the Saints, Ignatius by name, said of Christ, "My *Eros* is crucified;" nor do I think he should be censured.' Jerome said of the Homilies on the Canticles that Origen, who had surpassed all other writers in his other books, had in this surpassed himself. It gave welcome expression to what after the triumph of Athanasius was the dominant feeling, and redeemed in some degree the fame of its author, damaged by his supposed inclination to Arianism. And thus Origen, the first pioneer in so many fields of Christian thought, the father in one of his many aspects of the English Latitudinarians, became also the spiritual ancestor of Bernard, the Victorines, and the author of the *De Imitatione*, of Tauler and Molinos and Madame de Guyon [1].

In Subordinationism, in the theory of the Two Lives, above all in Allegorism, we may still discern the hand of Philo. But the influence of the illustrious Jew was far weaker on Origen than it had been on Clement. Nowhere is this emancipation so visible as in the doctrine of the Incarnation. Greatest of all miracles is this, that the Very Word and Wisdom of God should have dwelt within the frame of that Man who appeared in Judaea, should have been born and wailed as an infant, should have died and risen again. The understanding of man is stupefied and knows not whither to turn. If we think of Him as God, behold He is Man; if as Man, we see Him returning from the grave, bearing in triumph the spoils of conquered death [2].

Origen's view of the God-Man—a term which he first employed—differs from the ordinary view, generally speaking, only in so far as it is conditioned by his opinions of the preexistence of the Soul and of the nature of the resurrection body.

He is the first to speak at large of the Human Soul of Jesus. Like other souls, it was eternal and eternally

[1] See the Prologue to the Commentary on the Song of Songs, and Jerome's Preface to his translation of the Homilies on the same book. It need hardly be said that Origen himself remains faithful to the ideal point of view, and is never betrayed into the imagery of earthly passion used by the monastic writers on the subject of 'the Bridegroom's Kiss' and similar phrases. These widowed spirits transferred to Jesus that 'mortal yearning' which they were forbidden to indulge towards wife or husband. Hence the Mysticism of the Middle Ages, so alluring in its finer manifestations, so revolting, so nearly allied to the most frightful form of hypocrisy in its coarser shapes.

[2] *De Princ.* ii. 6. 2.

united with the Word. From the first it received Him wholly, and clove to Him inseparably. It was like in all things to all other human souls, free as they, but the perfection of love, the singleness of worthiness bound it so closely to the Godhead, that the union of the two may be compared to a mass of iron glowing for ever with a white heat. He who should touch the iron would feel not the iron but the fire. Hence in Scripture we commonly find the titles proper to the Humanity of our Lord transferred to His Divinity and conversely. It is the *Communicatio Idiomatum* [1].

The flesh of Jesus was pure from all birth stain, from all defilement of every kind [2]. It was real flesh. His

---

[1] *De Princ.* ii. 6. 4 sqq. ; *In Joann.* i. 37 ; xx. 17 ; *Contra Celsum*, i. 32, 33. Nevertheless the properties of the Two Natures remain in truth distinct, *Contra Celsum*, iv. 15 ; vii. 16. Redepenning, ii. 387, points out that the soul of Christ being sinless was in Origen's theory not a soul at all. For the word ψυχή is derived fancifully from ψύχω, and explained to mean 'the spirits whose love had grown cold' through their defection from God. There is certainly an inconsistency here ; but Origen held, as we shall see in the next Lecture, that many sinless or nearly sinless spirits had assumed flesh to aid in our redemption. Other difficulties have been raised by those who are determined to see something unsound in all that Origen wrote. If the soul of Christ existed before the union, can it be said to have *deserved* the union ? Again, ' ex unione hypostatica Verbi cum anima aut peccatrice aut quae peccare et damnari potuisset sequereter de Verbo sic ei unito idem ob communionem idiomatum dici posse,' see the *Origeniana*. This how-ever is absurd. According to Origen the soul of Christ was created sinless but free. It was in the same position as the soul of Adam before the Fall, and by its union with the Word was removed for ever from the possibility of sin. Origen proves the existence of Christ's human soul partly by Scripture, e. g. Matth. xxvi. 38, 'My soul is exceeding sorrowful,' partly by the con-sideration that it was necessary as a link of connection between the Godhead and the Flesh, see *De Princ.* ii. 6.

[2] *In Levit.* Hom. xii. 4. Hence when, as *In Levit.* Hom. ix. 6, Origen regards the High Priest Joshua ' clothed in filthy garments ' (Zech. iii. 3) as a type of the Incarnation, we must understand him to be speaking merely of the Saviour's humiliation. This is expressly stated *In Lucam*, Hom. xiv, ' ut autem scias Jesum quoque sordidatum sentiendum secundum ignominiam

Life, His Passion were in no sense fantastic[1]. So real
was His Body that we cannot accept in the literal sense
the story of His being carried up into a mountain by the
Tempter[2]. But as the pellucent alabaster vase shows
the fire within, so the flesh of Jesus was at times suffused
by the glory of the indwelling Deity. So it was especially at the Transfiguration, so it was according to an
ancient tradition throughout the year of His ministry.
Some saw but the figure without grace or comeliness of
the carpenter's son, but those whose eyes were opened
by the Spirit discerned the beauty of the Word flashing
through the veil of matter. Hence it came to pass that
the followers of Judas at the Betrayal knew not who He
was; the darkness of their own souls was projected
upon the features of Him they sought. In this beautiful
fancy we may perhaps recognise the last faint trace of
Docetism[3].

crucis, non secundum ipsam quam assumpsit sanctam carnem.' So again, *In
Levit.* Hom. viii. 2, the law of purification applies to every woman 'quae
susceperit semen et pepererit.' The last words are intended to exclude the
Virgin. See also *In Rom.* vi. 12.

[1] *Contra Celsum*, iii. 23 ; iv. 19. As Man He was not ἀπαξαπλῶς ἀπαθής,
as Clement taught : καθὸ δὲ ἄνθρωπος ἦν, παντὸς μᾶλλον ἀνθρώπου κεκοσμημένος
τῇ ἄκρᾳ μετοχῇ τοῦ αὐτολόγου καὶ τῆς αὐτοσοφίας, ὑπέμεινεν ὡς σοφὸς καὶ
τέλειος ἅπερ ἐχρῆν ὑπομεῖναι τὸν ὑπὲρ παντὸς τοῦ γένους τῶν ἀνθρώπων, ἢ καὶ
τῶν λογικῶν, πάντα πράττοντα, *Contra Celsum*, vii. 17. He suffered sorrow
at Gethsemane, *In Matth. Comm. Series*, 92 ; temptation, *In Luc.* Hom.
xxix.

[2] *De Princ.* iv. 16, Quod secundum literam quomodo fieri potuisse
videbitur, ut vel in excelsum montem educeretur a diabolo Jesus, vel etiam
carnalibus oculis eius tanquam subiecta, et adiacentia uni monti omnia
mundi ostenderet regna.

[3] *In Matth. Com. Series*, 100 ; *Contra Celsum*, ii. 64. Connected with
this perhaps is his refusal to accept the ancient view that the human form of
Jesus was wanting in beauty or dignity. See *Contra Celsum*, vi. 75, where
he contrasts Is. liii. 1–3 with Psalm xlv. 3, 4, περίζωσαι τὴν ῥομφαίαν σου
ἐπὶ τὸν μηρόν σου, δυνατέ, τῇ ὡραιότητι σου καὶ τῷ κάλλει σου. Origen
appears to have thought that Jesus resembled John the Baptist in features,

Jesus truly rose from the dead, not in this flesh but in that glorified Body of which St. Paul speaks. Pure as it is, as it was, it is the Body of our Brother, and our High Priest may be said to need purification for the sins of the people that are laid upon Him[1]. Hence the mysterious 'Touch Me not.' 'At even He washed His garment in wine, that is His blood.' 'It was necessary that my Lord and Saviour should not only be born among men but also descend into hell, that as a man prepared He might lead the scapegoat into the wilderness, and returning thence, His work being now achieved, might ascend to the Father, and there be purified more fully at that heavenly altar, that He might endow with perpetual purity the pledge of our flesh which He had carried up with Him.'

hence the mistake of Herod, Matth. xiv. 2; *In Joann.* vi. 30. He was baptized in the month of January; *In Ezech.* Hom. i. 4.

[1] *In Levit.* Hom. ix. 5; *In Joann.* vi. 37. Redepenning therefore is wrong in speaking of Origen's 'Auflösung der menschlichen Natur des Herrn bei der Erhöhung desselben.' Whatever criticisms attach to Origen's view of the Resurrection of men attach also to his view of the Resurrection of Jesus, but no others.

LECTURE VI.

That God may be all in all.—I COR. xv. 28.

CREATION, as the word is commonly understood, was in Origen's views not the beginning, but an intermediate phase in human history. Aeons rolled away before this world was made; aeons upon aeons, days, weeks, months and years, sabbatical years, jubilee years of aeons will run their course, before the end is attained. The one fixed point in this gigantic drama is the end, for this alone has been clearly revealed, 'God shall be all in all.' There will come a time when man, completely subjected to Christ by the operation of the Holy Ghost, shall in Christ be completely subjected to the Father. But now, he adds, the end is always like the beginning[1]. The manifold diversity of the world is to close in unity, it must then have sprung from unity.

[1] *De Princ.* i. 6. 2, Semper enim similis est finis initiis, et ideo sicut unus omnium finis, ita unus omnium intelligi debet initium. The end of all intelligent work is perfection ; it cannot be regarded as ended till perfection is attained. 'Finis vel consummatio rerum perfectarum consummatarumque esse videtur indicium.' But the beginning is the desire of perfection, and though absolute Wisdom plans the beginning in such a way that it carries within itself the means of its own fulfilment, each stage in the development is preparatory to all that follow, and in this sense inferior to them, and in this sense evil, relatively evil and relatively good. Even in God's work then it is not strictly true that the end is always like the beginning. The caution given by Origen at the commencement of this chapter applies to all his speculations outside the letter of the Creed and must never be forgotten : 'Nunc autem disputandi specie, magis quam definiendi, prout possumus, exercemur.' Compare i. 6. 4, Certius tamen qualiter se habitura sit res, scit solus Deus, et si qui eius per Christum et Spiritum Sanctum amici sunt; ii. 6. 6, Si quis sane melius aliquid poterit invenire, et evidentioribus de Scripturis sanctis assertionibus confirmare quae dicit, illa potius quam haec recipiantur. Innumerable passages of the same

O

His expansion of this theory is in fact an elaborate commentary upon the eighth chapter of the Epistle to the Romans and the fifteenth chapter of the First Epistle to the Corinthians. These he felt were the two keys, the one to the eternity before, the other to the eternity after.

What is it that we see? A vast creation orderly and beautiful, yet manifestly out of joint. Everywhere the order is crossed and marred, yet the disorder is not intentional. It is that of an organism striving to shake off a mortal disease. The soul wrestles with the body, and the thrill of man's agony is felt by the great system of which he is a member. 'The whole creation groaneth and travaileth together in pain until now.' What do these words mean? If we look upwards, we see Sun, Moon and Stars, intelligent creatures like ourselves, condemned to minister to our needs, nourishing the fruits of earth for our subsistence, marking the seasons for our direction. If we search the Scriptures, we read of Angels and Archangels, who are all of them 'ministering spirits.' So 'the creature was made subject unto vanity,' ordained to help the vain and corruptible body of man, not willingly, but by reason of God who hath subjected the same in hope. And the hope is 'the manifestation of the sons of God,' the day when those things shall be revealed, which God has prepared for those who shall deserve to be His Sons, or when, the veil being taken away, it shall be known that they are His Sons. Nay the trouble of sin reaches higher still.

kind might be cited, but these will suffice. The reader will understand that Origen never dogmatises. This point is insisted upon by Pamphilus in the *Apologia.*

As yet even the Saviour will not 'drink wine' in the kingdom of God. He will not drink it, for He is alone. He waits for us. He will not receive His perfect glory without thee, that is without His people, which is His Body. Thus all evil is resolved into sin. And sin is not isolated or individual. For all intelligent creatures are knit together in a solidarity so close, that the defect of one clouds the felicity and impedes the energies of all. But again, we see apparent injustice. Everywhere there is inequality. Star differeth from star in glory. Among the angels themselves there are grades—thrones, dominations, princedoms, powers—there are even those who have fallen wholly from their high estate. On earth it is the same. One man is born within the fold of God's Church, another in polished Athens, a third is a lawless Scythian or a cannibal Ethiope. There are the wise man and the fool, the rich and the poor, the civilised and the squalid savage. Everywhere Jacob is chosen, while Esau is cast out. The facts of life led the Gnostics to predestination, the sense of violated justice to the belief in conditional immortality. But it appeared to Origen, that the equity of God was imperfectly vindicated by a theory, which assigned to the majority of mankind a life of misery rounded off by annihilation. Thus opposition to Gnosticism becomes the motive of his practical theology, as it was also of his exegesis. Yet on one main point he is in agreement with the great Gnostic chief Basilides. Evil flows from precedent evil. But, as differences of circumstance and faculty are congenital, it follows that this life must be regarded as the continuation of one that has gone before [1].

---

[1] For the foundation of the preceding sections, see *De Princ.* ii. 9; *In*

Whence then comes Evil? Not from God, for God
would then not be God. Not from Matter, for this is
another form of fatalism, leading directly to the hope-
less Stoic doctrine, that the quantity of evil is fixed and
unalterable. It must then be the work of man [1].
In the beginning God created the heavens and the
earth, that is the perfect heavens and earth, and peopled
this world with Intelligences, forming in the Son the

Rom. vii. 4 sqq.; *In Num.* Hom. xxiii. 2; *In Lev.* Hom. vii. 2; Denis,
Philosophie d'Origène, chapter on *Cosmologie;* Redepenning, ii. 315 sqq.;
Guerike, ii. 185 sqq.; Harnack, pp. 539 sqq.

[1] On the Stoic doctrine, see Lecture vii. It was held also by some at
any rate of the Platonists, as for instance Celsus. So *Contra Celsum,* iv. 62,
κακὰ δ' ἐν τοῖς οὖσιν οὔτε πρόσθεν, οὔτε νῦν, οὔτε αὖθις ἥττω καὶ πλείω γένοιτ'
ἄν. Μία γὰρ ἡ τῶν ὅλων φύσις καὶ ἡ αὐτή, καὶ κακῶν γένεσις ἀεὶ ἡ αὐτή. The
same fatal notion is at the bottom of the smiling toleration of M. Aurelius.
To philosophers of this school nothing is intolerable but enthusiasm.
Celsus continues, 'It is not easy for any one but a philosopher to understand
the nature of evil;' *Ibid.* 65. Origen replies, 'It is not easy even for the
philosopher, nor perhaps possible ἐὰν μὴ θεοῦ ἐπινοίᾳ. Evil is not of God,
nor yet of matter, τὸ γὰρ ἑκάστου ἡγεμονικὸν αἴτιον τῆς ὑποστάσης ἐν αὐτῷ
κακίας ἐστίν, ἥτις ἐστὶ τὸ κακόν,' *Ibid.* 66. The subject is recurred to *Ibid.*
vi. 54 sqq. Virtue and Vice are good and evil κυρίως. Bodily goods or
ills, τὰ προηγμένα, ἀποπροηγμένα, are good or evil καταχρηστικώτερον. To
these latter refers Isaiah xlv. 7. 'Evil then, if by the word we understand
that which is essentially evil, God did not create, though some evils, few in
number if compared with the order of the whole world, followed as a consequence upon the plan of His work, just as spiral shavings and sawdust
follow as a consequence upon the plan of a carpenter's work, just as builders
seem to "make" the heaps of broken stone and mortar that are left lying by
the side of their buildings.' As to evils then in the secondary sense, we may
admit that God is their author, ἵνα διὰ τούτων ἐπιστρέψῃ τινάς, as similar
so-called evils are caused by fathers, teachers, surgeons, for corrective purposes. Of moral evil Origen speaks sometimes as if it were positive, sometimes as if it were negative. *De Princ.* ii. 9. 2, Certum namque est malum
esse bono carere; but again just below, in contrarium boni, quod sine
dubio malum est, trahebatur. But God does not know evil or the evil man.
This is illustrated by the words, 'Adam, where art thou?' of Gen. iii. 9.
This is from Philo, cf. *In Psalm.* i. 6 (Lom. xi. 392) with *Leg. Alleg.* iii. 17
(i. 97). See also below, p. 200. For the mode in which God brings good
out of evil the reader should turn to *In Num.* Hom. xiv. 2, one of the finest
passages in all Origen.

ideas, which were then realised by the Son as Agent [1]. The Intelligences were limited in number, for Wisdom is finite, and cannot comprehend the infinite. Except the Holy Trinity nothing is incorporeal. Each of the created spirits had from the first an envelope, a principle of differentiation, a body, adapted to the nature of its environment, at first then of fine ethereal texture fitted in all respects for its celestial habitation. The spirits were equal and like, but they were free. Some sinned and fell, some remained stedfast in their first estate, or rose to higher levels of power and goodness. The latter are the stars, the angels in the various degrees of their hierarchy. Of those who rebelled some became devils, fiends or archfiends, according to the manifold proportions of their transgression. But those whose error was less, whose love of God is cold yet not extinct (it is one of Origen's fanciful etymologies[2]), turned into 'souls,' better or worse according as the faculties of sense and desire gained the upper hand over the intelligence. For these at any rate there is hope of restitution, yet only through chastisement. The appointed scene of their discipline is this world, a later and grosser model of the first. It is infinitely various, to afford scope for the treatment proper to every phase of character, 'like a great house, in which are vessels of gold and silver, of wood and clay, some to honour and some to dishonour.' 'Wherefore neither will the Creator seem

---

[1] *De Princ.* ii. 9. Philo and Clement explained the first verse of Genesis of the creation of the Ideal World. To Origen it denotes the creation of the first, the perfect, but still material world. Thus he tells us of two creations, and if we may add the creation of Ideas in the Son (see above, p. 169), of three.

[2] Ψυχή, from ψύχω, to make cold. Plato, *Cratylus,* 399 E, suggests the same derivation in a different sense. It is called ψυχή because it ἀναψύχει τὸ σῶμα.

unjust, when He distributes to each his earthly lot, nor will any one think, that birth happy or unhappy is ruled by chance, nor that there are different creators, nor that souls have different natures.'

Origen rejected the Platonic doctrine of Metempsychosis[1], but he adopted that of pre-existence, and that which ascribes a soul to the stars. Both he found in Philo, and both were regarded as open questions in the Church[2]. It is not necessary to dwell at any length upon the philosophic difficulties attending his theory. He has not attempted to get rid of the break of con-

[1] Origen no doubt held that at the Resurrection the soul passes from one body into another. He himself insisted that the Resurrection body was in a true sense the same as the body of this life, but it is open to any one to argue that he has not proved the identity. See further on in this Lecture. But Metempsychosis in the sense of a migration of the soul into another human body or into the body of a beast, a plant, and so forth in another life on this same earth (and this is the only meaning of the word) he certainly did not hold; see *Contra Celsum*, iv. 7 ; v. 49; viii. 30 ; *In Rom.* v. 1 ; vi. 8 ; *In Mat.* x. 20 ; xi. 17; xiii. 1 ; *In Joan.* vi. 7. Yet Justinian and Jerome charged him with asserting it. Unfortunately the passage on which their accusation is based, *De Princ.* i. 8. 4 *ad fin.*, has been modified by Rufinus. A fragment of the Greek will be found in the *Ad Menam*, a Latin abstract in Jerome's *Ep. ad Avitum*. Both are given in the footnote in Lommatzsch. Jerome himself allows that Origen concluded his discussion with the words ' haec iuxta nostram sententiam non sint dogmata, sed quaesita tantum atque proiecta, ne penitus intractata viderentur.' Proiecta here means ' rejected ;' ' discussionis gratia dicta sint, et abiiciantur' is the version of Pamphilus, *Apologia*, ix. *ad fin.* Pamphilus adds that the words objected to were not Origen's own but were put into the mouth of an adversary or interlocutor. See *Origeniana*, ii. 6. 17 sqq. ; Denis, pp. 190 sqq.

[2] He found them also in Scripture. Psalm cxlviii. 3, ' Praise Him, all ye stars of light ;' Job xxv. 5, ' The stars are not pure in his sight.' Neither Jerome nor Augustine ventures to deny that the stars may have souls. Ambrosius agrees with Origen, and even Aquinas regards the question as open ; *Origeniana*, ii. 8. 2 sqq. The great support of the pre-existence doctrine was John ix. 2, ' Master, who did sin, this man or his parents, that he was born blind ?' Jerome himself at one time held pre-existence. Augustine did not deny it, and down to the time of Gregory the Great the

sciousness between the two lives, as Plato did, by the idea of partial reminiscence[1]. Yet if in this life we have no recollection of what happened to us before our birth, why it may be asked should we have any knowledge, in a future existence, of what befell us here on earth? What is the value of a schooling, in which each lesson is forgotten as soon as learned? Again, if the soul according to his fanciful etymology is the 'cold' sensualised intelligence, how does this agree with what he tells us about the sinless soul of Jesus? These are minor flaws, but there is one of a far more serious kind. If the spirits were all alike, all subject to precisely the same conditions, why did any fall away? Because, he tells us, they were free. But this is no answer. What is the faculty, which can thus oscillate between perfect virtue and vice? What is this mysterious paralysis, but the very fatalism he is struggling to avoid? In the *Phaedrus* myth the souls are neither pure·nor equal; the unruly steed Desire is yoked from the first by the side of Reason, and the charioteer who cannot curb his wanton plunges, is flung down from the cope of heaven. This did not satisfy Origen's craving for justice. But all he could accomplish by his departure from Plato was to push the insoluble problem a step farther back, and to stereotype Clement's vicious theory of the indifferentism of the Will.

But there were other difficulties arising out of the

question remained undecided. See his *Epistles*, vii. 53 ; *Origeniana*, ii. 6. 8 sqq. Mr. Neale, *Holy Eastern Church*, i. p. 36, regards the belief in pre-existence as erroneous but not heretical.

[1] The only passage, so far as I know, where Origen hints at the doctrine of Anamnesis is *De Orat.* 24 (Lom. xvii. p. 186), πᾶς τε τρανῶν καὶ τὰ περὶ τοῦ θεοῦ ὑπομιμνήσκεται μᾶλλον ἢ μανθάνει, κἂν ἀπό τινος ἀκούειν δοκῇ, ἢ εὑρίσκειν νομίζῃ τὰ τῆς θεοσεβείας μυστήρια.

language of Scripture itself. Most perplexing, in view
of the Alexandrine theory of Freedom, were the words
of St. Paul, 'Whom He did foreknow He did also predestinate.' The passage was at this time the sword
of Gnosticism, as at a later date, by one of those singular exchanges of weapons that have often occurred in
the chance medley of controversy, it became the sword
of Augustinianism. But Origen could admit neither
election nor reprobation. If, he argues, God predestines
only those whom He foreknows, it follows that He does
not foreknow those whom He does not predestine. This
is absurd. We are compelled therefore to drop the
preposition. Foreknow is the same as know, know in
countless passages of Scripture is equivalent to love.
God knows only the good, whom He loves ; of evil He
has no knowledge. Again, 'whom He did predestinate
them He also called according to purpose.' According,
that is, to their own purpose ; or if according to the
purpose of God, then because He knew that they
desired salvation. Origen in fact held that man is
free in such a sense that God Himself cannot foresee
what he may choose to do [1].

---

[1] The passage cited in the text is *In Rom.* vii. 8, with which should be
read the preceding chapter. Here Origen expressly denies foreknowledge
in the ordinary sense of the word. 'Non enim secundum communem vulgi
opinionem putandum est bona malaque praescire Deum, sed secundum
Scripturae sanctae consuetudinem sentiendum . . . "Novit enim Deus
eos qui sunt eius" . . . Caeteri autem praesciri non dicuntur ; non
quod aliquid latere possit illam naturam quae ubique est et nusquam
deest, sed quia omne quod malum est scientia eius vel praescientia ha-
betur indignum (see above, p. 196). Sed et hoc intuere si praescire et
praedestinare dici potest Deus de his qui nondum sunt, an de his qui sunt
quidem, nondum tamen conformes sunt imaginis Filii sui ; et si praesci-
entiam in hoc magis esse convenit, quam in eo quod futurum sit id quod
nondum est. In hoc enim voluntas magis est quam praescientia conditoris.
Nam praescientia in quo videbitur, cum id quod futurum est pendeat in

Another text which distressed him beyond measure was 'whom He will He hardeneth.' But even these terrible words he thought he could explain. Let us remember, he says, how the kindness of a lenient master makes the bad slave worse, how the same sunshine melts the wax but hardens the clay. God may be said to harden the sinner in this sense, that the contemptuous disregard of His goodness produces hardness. Or again, He hardens the wicked man, inasmuch as He abandons him, withdrawing from him His fatherly chastisements, and deferring the cure of his sins to the next life. And this is doubtless right, better for the sinner himself. For God alone knows both the disease and the remedy, and can measure out the time of healing [1].

The same considerations determine his view of Grace, which is that of Clement. God perpetually incites, surrounds, sustains, rewards, but does not constrain

factoris arbitrio?' Then follows the passage the sense of which is given in the text. Origen continues, 'Hoc ergo pacto neque in praescientia Dei vel salutis vel perditionis nostrae causa consistit, neque justificatio ex sola vocatione pendebit, neque glorificari de nostra penitus potestate sublatum est.' But, he adds, if foreknowledge be taken in the ordinary sense of the word, 'Non propterea erit aliquid quia id scit Deus futurum, sed quia futurum est scitur a Deo antequam fiat.' Language more in accordance with the general view is to be found *In Rom.* i. 2, 3, 18 sqq.; *De Orat.* 6. Jansen, who in his *Augustinus* vehemently attacked Origen's doctrine of predestination, complains that he makes election depend 'ex praevisis hominum meritis' and vocation proceed 'secundum propositum hominis non Dei.' Huet replies that the first proposition is still open in the Catholic Church, and that the second was maintained by Chrysostom and Theodoret, *Origeniana,* ii. 7. But neither Huet nor Jansen appears to grasp the full scope of Origen's teaching. Semi-Pelagianism was merely his δεύτερος πλοῦς, the second line of defence on which he fell back *if* foreknowledge was to be taken in the vulgar sense of the word.

[1] *De Princ.* iii. 1. 7 sqq.; Fragment from *Comm. in Exodum* in *Philocalia,* xxvii. It should be borne in mind that all these passages were Gnostic strongholds.

the will. To use the language of a later time, Grace is prevenient, concomitant, peculiar, but not efficacious. We must go to Christ, that He may open our eyes. 'As if,' retorts Bishop Huet, 'the will, that makes us go, were not given to us by God.' 'But,' replies Origen, 'he who does not know his sickness, cannot seek the physician, or, if healed, will not thank the physician.' And if pressed with the text 'God worketh in us both to will and to do,' he will answer, that the Apostle means the general faculty, not the special determination of volition[1].

A further and still more serious difficulty arises out of the doctrine of Original Sin. This tenet is found in Irenaeus and Tertullian, but not in Clement[2] or the *De Principiis*, and we may perhaps infer, that Origen did not seriously consider the question, or perceive its bearing upon his other views, till after his settlement at Caesarea. There he found the practice of Infant Baptism, with which the doctrine of birth-sin is closely connected, in general use, and the difficulty at once pressed upon his mind. The Church, he says, in obedience to a tradition received from the Apostles,

---

[1] *De Princ.* iii. 1. 19. I shall recur to the Alexandrine doctrine of Grace in Lecture viii, and it will therefore be sufficient here to refer to *Origeniana*, ii. 7, with the Excursus from De la Rue given in Lommatzsch, xxiii. p. 333.

[2] See Irenaeus, iii. 22 sq. ; Tertullian, *De Anima*, xli. Neither regarded the depravation consequent upon Original Sin as absolute. Justin is wrongly referred to by Bingham ; see the note in Otto's ed. p. 320, on *Trypho*, 88. Justin held that before Baptism men are children of necessity ; *Ap.* i. 61, Otto, p. 166. Theodotus and the *Homilies* also teach that before the birth of Christ men were creatures of Necessity. That is to say, being ignorant and weak, they were doomed to sin. But there is no connection between this frailty of nature and the sin of Adam. Fragment 5, Otto, vol. iii. 256, is wrongly ascribed to Justin. For Clement's doctrine, see Lecture iii.

baptizes even infants. 'For those, to whom are committed the secrets of the divine mysteries, know, that there is in every human being a real stain of sin, which must be washed away by water and the Spirit[1].'

But whence comes this stain? It is sufficiently accounted for by the doctrine of pre-existence, and at times Origen appears to rest in this explanation. But there are traces in Scripture, which point in a different direction, and when these are before his mind he stumbles and hesitates. Such was the Law of Purification. We see from this, that a certain impurity attaches to birth, though what this can be is a great mystery. So David says 'in sin hath my mother conceived me,' showing that every soul, that is born in the flesh, is polluted by the filth and iniquity of sin. Occasionally Origen seems to apply these words to the material uncleanness of the body, for in his system the flesh is more nearly akin to evil than in that of Clement. But the notion of physical pollution runs up into that of moral guilt. 'If there were nothing in little children to call for remission and indulgence, the grace of Baptism would seem superfluous[2].' And this is connected with the Fall. Our body is the 'body of sin,' because Adam's children were not born till after his disobedience[3].

Other passages again speak of heredity, of transmitted qualities of body and mind. There are 'families,' we read, in heaven and on earth. Souls have 'marks,' which

---

[1] *In Rom.* v. 9.

[2] *In Lev.* Hom. viii. 3. In this passage Origen makes the curious remark that in Scripture we read of none but wicked men celebrating their birthday. He regarded the body and its affections with fastidious disgust, *In Rom.* vii. 4, but he distinguishes the physical uncleanness of birth from sin, *In Lev.* Hom. xii. 1 ; *In Lucam*, Hom. xiv.

[3] *In Rom.* v. 9.

express themselves through the body in the face, in the handwriting [1]. The difference here thought of is one of texture rather than of kind. Peter and Paul are both good men, but the goodness of each has its own peculiar colour. But again, we read of the 'seed of Abraham [2].' The soul then has a pedigree as well as the body. As the latter reproduces the features of this or that of its countless ancestors, so the former comes into life bringing with it 'spermatic germs' of good and evil. It may be, that he conceived of the soul as waiting till a body like itself and fit for its reception should be born [3], but he has not cleared up this point. And probably heredity as regards the soul is a figure of speech, denoting merely affinities, which the soul creates for itself. For he refers us for its explanation to the doctrine of pre-existence. But it is evident, that we have here two radically incongruous trains of thought.

But there are places, where his vacillation is more conspicuous still. Writing against Celsus he treats the Fall as a pure allegory. Adam is Man. His sin is a mystical presentation of the defection of the souls, that fell away from God. The 'coats of skins' may perhaps be the bodies, in which they were clothed on their expulsion from Paradise [4]. Yet again, 'The Lord God expelled

[1] *In Num.* Hom. ii.

[2] *In Joan.* xx. 1 sqq.

[3] This is the opinion of Redepenning, ii. 21, but he rests it upon a wrong explanation of Origen's commentary on the Parable of the Labourers in the Vineyard, *In Matt.* xv. 31.

[4] *Contra Celsum*, iv. 40. He is replying to the scoff of Celsus that 'God made one man with his own hands and could not persuade that one to do right.' Again, *In Lev.* Hom. vi. 2, the 'coats of skins' are a symbol of mortality. Julius Casianus, a Gnostic teacher, gave this explanation; see Clement, *Strom.* iii. 14. 95. It is found also in the Kabbalah, Ginsburg, p. 30, and no doubt comes from a Rabbinical source.

Adam from Paradise, and planted him in this earth.
This was the punishment of his sin, which without doubt
has extended to all men. For all of us have been set in
this place of humiliation, this valley of tears, whether
because all Adam's descendants were in the first father's
loins and banished with him, or whether each one is
thrust out of Paradise in some other way ineffable and
known to God alone[1].' The latter words are a salvo,
but it is evident that Origen is here on the very point of
abandoning the belief in pre-existence with all its consequences.

Hence men are evil not only because they are 'the
sons and disciples of sinners[2],' but by the entailed sin of
the first father. Yet not all alike. Some stainless spirits,
like that of John the Baptist, have been sent down to
labour for us; some not wholly pure have descended for
our sakes lower than the law of their own purification
required[3]. And even in ordinary men Origen was far
from admitting a complete depravation. By Adam's sin
death, that is spiritual death, entered into the world and
'passed upon' all, affected that is with some touch of its
contagion even the just. But it 'reigned' over none but
those, who sinned after the similitude of Adam's transgression. The sense of the last words is doubtful. They
may have a mystical meaning, that is they may refer to
the character of the antenatal sin. Or they may denote

---

[1] *In Rom.* v. 4 *ad fin.* Compare *In Joan.* xx. 21 (Lom. ii. p. 257).
But *In Joan.* xx. 3, it is still a question among some whether Adam is to be
reckoned among the righteous or the unrighteous. The author of the
Homilies vehemently asserts the former. *In Jerem.* Hom. xvi. 4, the sin of
Adam was not so grave as the sin of Cain.

[2] *In Rom.* v. 1 (Lom. vi. 342).

[3] The κάθοδος τῶν εὐγενεστέρων ψυχῶν, *In Joan.* xiii. 43 *ad fin.*; cp.
Ibid. ii. 24, 25; *In Matt.* xii. 30; *Origeniana,* ii. 5. 24.

our inherited wickedness, or the evil imprinted on us by
bad education. 'In any case Christ has provided a
remedy. Our mortal generation is changed by the
regeneration of Baptism, and the doctrine of piety shuts
out the doctrine of impiety [1].'
Thus Theology finally triumphs over Ethics. Clement's
Apathy is a Stoic phantasm; his language is loose and
presumptuous, but it breathes a joyous confidence in the
assured victory of good over evil even in this world.
Origen looks habitually on the darker side. Life is an
expiation. Earth is a prison house. Man may be just
and holy compared with his fellow-men or even with
angels, but never in comparison with God. The son of
God indeed is not the servant of sin; he sins, but he is
not a sinner. Or again, 'he that believes sins not, that is
to say falls not into sins unto death.' But 'if any man
say that he has no sin, he is a liar, and the truth is not
in him.' 'I do not think any one's heart can become so
pure, that thoughts of evil never stain it.' There will
come a time, when Jesus will 'wash our heads,' but the
time is not yet. Such thoughts necessarily colour his
view of Grace and Redemption, even where his language
seems to be the same as that of Clement [2].

---

[1] *In Rom.* v. 1. Origen, it should be observed, omitted the negative in
Rom. v. 14. But he remarks that the reading ἐπὶ τοὺς μὴ ἁμαρτήσαντας
was found in some copies. In the *Commentary on Romans* Origen appears
to accept almost without reserve the literal sense of the story of the Fall.
On the question of Original Sin, see *Origeniana*, ii. 7. 24.

[2] *In Joan.* xix. 6, τίς οὖν ἄρα ἐστὶν ὁ πιστεύων, ἢ ὁ πεπονθὼς ἐκ τοῦ διακεῖσθαι
κατὰ τὸν λόγον καὶ συμπεφυκέναι αὐτῷ τὸ μὴ ἐμπεσεῖσθαι ἄν, ὅσον ἐπὶ τούτοις
τοῖς ῥητοῖς, εἰς τὰ λεγόμενα πρὸς θάνατον εἶναι ἁμαρτήματα. So *In Rom.* he
distinguishes 'peccatorem esse' from 'peccare.' *In Rom.* i. 1, Qui etenim in
carne quis positus adipisci integram libertatem ut in nullo iam serviat carni !
sicut nec adoptionem filiorum quis in corpore positus habere ex integro
potest; *Ibid.* v. 9, Nam omnino ex integro nescire peccatum solius Christi

Looking back over history Origen distinguished three separate progressive revelations of God, the Natural Law, the Law of Moses, and the Gospel. A fourth is still to come. It is the Eternal Gospel. The first two we may pass over with brief notice. His view is substantially that of Clement, though with a sweep of imagination reminding us of Hooker and Wordsworth he regards the Natural Law, the 'stern daughter of the voice of God,' as swaying not men only, but angels and stars. But he places the Gentile[1] and even the Jew

est; *In Jesu Nave,* Hom. xxi. 2, Non puto cuiquam tantum in corde puritatis evenire ut nunquam adversae cogitationis contagione maculetur. See also the commentary on Jesus washing the disciples' feet, *In Joan.* xxxii. *ad in.* The passages referred to by Huet, *Orig.* ii. 7. 18, where sinlessness is attributed to the perfect Christian, are all to be understood in this light.

[1] The Natural Law, the Law of Conscience, is Νόμος opposed to ὁ Νόμος, the Mosaic Law, *In Rom.* iii. 7; it is the Law which binds men, angels and all reasonable creatures, *In Rom.* v. 1. Commenting on the words 'there is none that doeth good, no, not one,' 'What none,' he asks, 'who sheltered a stranger, or gave bread to the hungry, or clothed the naked, or rescued the innocent from the gripe of the oppressor? I do not think that Paul the Apostle wished to make so incredible a statement.' But a man is said ποιεῖν χρηστότητα, as he might be said to build a house. If he has only got together material, or laid the foundations, or built a room or two, he has not built a house. 'Ita arbitror et hic Apostolum dicere neminem fecisse bonitatem, hoc est a nullo eam ad perfectum et ad integrum consummatam,' *In Rom.* iii. 3. Again, the Gentile who has followed the guidance of the law of reason, 'licet alienus a vita videatur aeterna, quia non credit Christo, et intrare non possit in regnum coelorum, quia renatus non est ex aqua et Spiritu, videtur tamen quod per haec quae dicuntur ab Apostolo bonorum operum gloriam et honorem et pacem perdere penitus non possit,' *In Rom.* ii. 7. There is a reward for him, then, though not the highest. See also iii. 6. Jansen, who held the absolute reprobation of the heathen, found great fault with Origen here. In the passage quoted above the Gentiles are excluded from the 'kingdom of Heaven,' the Beatific Vision, because they do not believe in Christ. This is modified, though it is doubtful to what precise extent, by what we read elsewhere. Thus, *In Matt. Comm. Series,* 39 (Lom. iv. 271), Quid autem dicamus de Britannis aut Germanis qui sunt circa Oceanum, vel apud Barbaros Dacas et Sarmatas et Scythas, quorum plurimi nondum audierunt evangelii verbum, audituri sunt

decidedly lower in the scale of God's favour. We may say that his idea of development is not so clear or serene. 'History tells us,' he says, 'that the wickedness of the world is greater than it was[1].' He would not go so far as to allow that the Greek was 'justified' by his philosophy. To his mind there is a certain breach of continuity, though probably he would not have admitted this. The Gospel is not the natural crown of Reason and the Law, but rather a remedy for their failure[2].

Again, as regards the Gospel itself there are numerous differences. On one side Origen is far more evangelical, on another far more ecclesiastical than his master. He speaks like Clement of the Two Lives, but as we have already noticed in a very different way; he no longer

autem in ipsa saeculi consummatione? This was proved by Matth. xxiv. 14.

[1] *Contra Celsum*, iv. 63.

[2] *In Rom.* v. 6, 'Law (there is no article) which entered that offence might abound' (Rom. v. 20) is the law of our members which rises up to resist the natural law. So too is the 'law which worketh wrath,' though it may be the Law of Moses, inasmuch as it fixes definite punishments for sins. Again, in chap. vii. 7, 'I had not known sin but by law,' law is the natural law. Origen will not admit that *the* Law is in any sense the cause of sin. On the contrary, it struck the first effective blow at the power of sin. The *locus classicus* for this is *In Rom.* v. 1, 'Per legem enim purificatio peccatorum coepit aperiri et ex parte aliqua tyrannidi eius obsisti per hostias, per expiationes varias, per sacrificia varia, per praecepta.' Being insufficient it was supplemented by the Prophets, by Christ. But it is not abolished so much as absorbed into the Gospel, *In Rom.* iii. 11 ; *In Lev.* Hom. vi. 2, 'Lavet te igitur Moses.' The works of the Law by which no flesh could be saved are not works of justice, but circumcision, sacrifice, keeping of new moons and sabbaths, *In Rom.* viii. 6. The Faith of Law and Gospel is One, *In Jesu Nave*, Hom. xvii. 2 ; cp. *In Joan.* xx. 12, but the Law is inferior, because to the Jews, except a few, God was known only as Lord, that is to say, was obeyed through fear, *In Joan.* xix. 1 ; again, because 'legis observantia poenam tantummodo effugit, fidei vero meritum spem repromissionis expectat,' *In Rom.* iv. 3. The Law is the clay figure which the artist afterwards casts in bronze, *In Lev.* Hom. x. 1 ; it is 'the lantern' opposed to 'the light,' *In Lev.* Hom. xiii. 2. M. Denis, p. 41 sqq., lays too much stress on the inferiority of the Law.

clings to the primitive belief, that all members of the Church are *ipso facto* in a state of salvation. The general relation of Faith and Conduct is the same, but in Origen Knowledge, or as he prefers to call it Wisdom, is only a deeper and fuller faith [1]. We hear no more of Apathy or of Disinterested Love [2]. There is a difference also in the object of Faith. To Clement Christ is principally

[1] Faith in Origen, as in Clement, means Belief determining Action and leading up through Obedience to Love. A leading passage is *In Joan.* xxxii. 9, where taking his start from the words 'Increase our Faith,' 'Though I have all Faith,' Origen distinguishes between perfect and imperfect Faith. They are different in extension, not in intensity. The contents of Faith are the articles of the Creed, to which we may add the Epinoiai of Christ. The distinction between Knowledge and Faith in Origen is evanescent. *In Rom.* iv. 5 he speaks of Two Faiths, a human and a divine. The addition of the latter makes perfect justifying faith. The one is of reason, the other of grace, the special gift of God, and both must coexist. As to the relation of Faith and Conduct, we know that men are justified by Faith without the works of the Law, for instance the Penitent Thief; and works without Faith justify no man, for instance the Pharisee of Luke xviii. 10; *In Rom.* iii. 9. This point is not brought out by Clement. But there are two justifications, one by faith, one by works. The former makes man just in the sight of God, it is forgiveness, known to God alone; the latter makes him just also in the sight of saints and angels. The former is strictly only the 'initium iustificari;' it is imperfect faith. The faith which was imputed to Abraham for righteousness was perfect faith, which had already manifested itself in obedience. This is 'justified by God,' the man is made really and truly righteous. Then his faith is no longer 'imputed to him for righteousness,' for he *is* righteous. This is further illustrated from Ps. xxxii. 1, 2, 'Blessed is he whose transgression is forgiven, whose sin is covered. Blessed is the man unto whom the Lord imputeth not iniquity.' First the soul leaves its evil and obtains pardon. Next by good deeds it covers its sins. Ubi vero iam ad perfectum venerit, ita ut omnis de ea malitiae radix penitus amputetur, eo usque ut nullum in ea vestigium possit inveniri nequitiae, ibi iam summa perfectae beatitudinis promittitur, cum nullum possit Dominus imputare peccatum; *In Rom.* iv. 1 sqq.

[2] *In Jesu Nave,* Hom. ix. 6, the six tribes who stood on Ebal are those who only desire to escape punishment, the six on Garizin are those who long for the blessing and the promises. Otherwise he speaks of the three degrees of perfection, the two classes of hearers, the milk and solid food much in the same way as Clement; *In Jesu Nave,* Hom. xxii. 2.

P

the Word and the Light; to Origen He is more emphatically 'my Lord and Saviour Jesus.' The life of the Christian is a growing receptivity of the Incarnate Son in His successive *Epinoiai*. But we cannot attain beyond the lower *Epinoiai*, those of Redemption and Mediation, in this world, nor for aeons yet to come. The Cross in all its wonder, its bounty, its power, is always before the eyes of Origen. 'We are justified,' he says, 'by faith, but far more by the blood of Jesus[1].' Those mysteries, which Clement scarcely dared to gaze upon, Origen has endeavoured to explain. He is the first to attempt a philosophy of the Atonement. Christ is our Teacher and Example, but above all He is our Sacrifice, and under the touch of Allegory the whole ritual of Leviticus becomes eloquent of Him, who bore our sins upon the tree.

Christ is our Ransom, our Redemption. By His precious Blood, that is not by His body but by His human soul, which the God within the Man, the Great High Priest, laid as a lamb upon the altar, He bought us from the powers of sin. His Death in some mystic way broke the powers of sin, as even now martyrs by Christlike self-surrender daunt and diminish the army of Satan. The spirits of evil were terrified and conscience stricken, some of them were even converted, by that immeasurable defiance[2].

---

[1] *In Rom.* iv. 11 (on Rom. v. 8, 9), Ex quo ostendit quod neque fides nostra sine Christi sanguine, neque sanguis Christi nos sine fide nostra iustificat ; ex utroque tamen multo magis sanguis Christi nos quam fides nostra iustificat. See also the passage quoted below, p. 221.

[2] *In Matt.* xvi. 8 (Lom. iv. 28), Δέδοται δὲ λύτρον ὑπὲρ ἡμῶν ἡ ψυχὴ τοῦ υἱοῦ τοῦ θεοῦ καὶ οὔτε τὸ πνεῦμα αὐτοῦ . . . οὔτε τὸ σῶμα, οὐδὲν γὰρ εὕρομέν πω τοιοῦτον περὶ αὐτοῦ γεγραμμένον. The ψυχή would include the Blood which is its οὐσία, *De Princ.* ii. 8. 2. *In Joan.* vi. 35 the Victim is

Again, He is our Propitiation. 'The true High Priest, He hath made God propitious to thee by His Blood, and reconciled thee to the Father.' 'For God,' says Origen in language that seems, but only seems, to anticipate Anselm, 'is just, and the just cannot justify the unjust. Therefore He willed the intervention of a Propitiator, that those might be justified by faith in Him, who could not be justified by their own works[1].'

the Man which is laid upon the altar by the God the great High Priest, but this does not contradict the former passage. *In Rom.* iii. 7 Christ paid his own Life as a Ransom to the powers of evil by whom man was held in captivity; *Ibid.* iv. 11, Tradens sanguinem suum principi huius mundi, secundum sapientiam Dei, quam nemo principum huius mundi cognovit; si enim cognovissent nunquam Dominum maiestatis crucifixissent, ne sanguis ille quem sitierant, non tam sitim quam vires eorum exstingueret regnumque destrueret. See also *In Matt.* xvi. 8. Some of the Guardian Angels of Nations were converted at the sight of Jesus, and this may account for the rapid spread of the Gospel in those regions over which they presided, *In Joan.* xiii. 58. But *In Lucam*, Hom. xii, this is put differently. Each Nation, like each individual, has two Angels who watch over it, one good, the other evil. The Incarnation strengthened the hands of the good Angels. For the manner in which Christ's Death broke the power of the evil spirits, see especially the grand passage *In Joan.* xxviii. 14. Origen attributes the same power to all acts of self-sacrifice, especially to the martyr's death; *In Jesu Nave*, Hom. xv. 6, Puto sane quia sancti . . . imminuant exercitum daemonum; cp. *In Num.* Hom. x. 2; xxiv. 1; *In Levit.* Hom. ix. 3; *In Joan.* vi. 35. 36; *In Matt.* xv. 34; *Contra Celsum*, viii. 44; *De Mart.* 30. 50. But while the sacrifice of Christ is the one sufficient atonement for all the sins of the whole world, the benefit of the martyr's example extends but to a few, and owes its efficacy to the Cross of Jesus. The merits of Christ's Death are conveyed through seven channels of remission, Baptism, Martyrdom, Almsgiving, Forgiveness, Conversion of a Sinner, Charity, Penitence; *In Lev.* Hom. ii. 4. To these must be added the Eucharist; *In Matt. Comm. Series*, 86. Nevertheless Origen's view coincides with that of Clement, that the only free forgiveness is that conveyed in Baptism; *In Lev.* Hom. ii. 4, Apud nos una tantummodo venia est peccatorum quae per lavacri gratiam in initiis datur. For though these words are put into the mouth of an interlocutor, Origen appears to adopt them. We are to distinguish free 'venia' from purchased 'remissio.'

[1] See especially *In Rom.* iii. 8; iv. 8. In the former passage will be found the fine allegory on the Mercy Seat. Here God is spoken of as reconciled to man. But 'God declares His righteousness' (Rom. iii. 25) is

Nay the salvation of man seems to be an inadequate
object for that unspeakable effort of Divine Goodness.
To Origen as to the Gnostics, as to Ignatius, the death
of Jesus is a world-sacrifice[1]. ' Christ was a double
Victim, meet for those in heaven, as for those on earth.'
The blood, which was shed in Jerusalem, was mystically
sprinkled on the altar above, where the Saviour pleads
His Atonement, till sin shall be no more. Wide as the
violated order of God is the healing influence of His
Love. All creation groaning and travailing in sympathy
with man's distress is soothed and strengthened, and will
be restored to perfect harmony, by Him, who in the blood
of Jesus reconciles all things unto Himself, whether they
be things in earth or things in heaven[2].

explained to mean, manifests, confers upon man His righteousness. In
the second passage the reconciliation is of man to God. Jesus Christus
nos per hostiam sanguinis sui reconciliavit Deo, sicut scriptum est, ' cum
essemus inimici Dei, reconciliati sumus Deo per sanguinem crucis Filii
eius (Rom. v. 10).' Et alibi idem Paulus addidit his dicens ' rogamus pro
Christo, reconciliamini Deo (2 Cor. v. 20).' Christ is our Peace because
He breaks down the hedge ' quam peccando texuimus.' The idea seems
to be that prior to the Atonement of Christ God could not pardon, not
because He had not received a sufficient price for His forgiveness, but
because man could only be made good enough to receive pardon through
faith in a crucified Saviour.

[1] *Ignatius, Ad Smyrn.* vi; *Ad Trall.* ix. 1; Dorner, i. 1. p. 113, Eng.
trans.

[2] *In Lev.* Hom. i. 3, Nisi quia forte hoc intellegi voluit, quod sanguis
Jesu non solum in Jerusalem effusus est, ubi erat altare . . . sed et quod
supernum altare quod est in coelis, ubi et ecclesia primitivorum est, idem
ipse sanguis adsperserit; sicut et apostolus dicit, quia ' pacificavit per sanguinem crucis suae sive quae in terris sunt sive quae in coelis' (Col. i. 20) . . .
Vis autem scire quia duplex hostia in eo fuit conveniens terrestribus et apta
coelestibus? But *In Lev.* Hom. ii. 3 on earth He is offered 'pro peccato,'
in heaven ' pro munere.' That the Passion of Christ ' profuisse coelestibus '
is stated also *In Luc.* Hom. x; *In Rom.* v. 10; *In Matt.* xiii. 8. It was
proved not only by Col. i. 20 but by Hebr. ii. 9, where Origen preferred the
reading χωρὶς γὰρ θεοῦ ὑπὲρ παντὸς ἐγεύσατο θανάτου, He tasted death for
all except God, *In Joan.* i. 40. Eph. iii. 10 was held by many of the early

In discipline as in doctrine Origen is the exponent of a later age than Clement. The Catholic Church is one, but still with a spiritual, not an administrative unity. Hence Origen speaks of ' the Churches ' as often as of 'the Church.' The famous words of Christ to Peter, ' whatsoever thou shalt bind on earth shall be bound in heaven, and whatsoever thou shalt loose on earth shall be loosed in heaven,' are spoken also to all Christians, whose faith is like that of Peter [1]. But the majesty of the ' most ancient Church ' of Rome exercised a certain fascination upon his mind. He did not think his education complete, till he had seen with his own eyes and heard with his own ears the ritual and the doctrine of

Fathers to mean that the Angels received some benefit from the Incarnation. Origen thought that in His descent Christ actually took upon Himself the form of an Angel; *In Gen.* Hom. viii. 8, Unde puto quod sicut inter homines habitu repertus est ut homo, ita et inter angelos habitu est repertus ut angelus. So also *In Matt.* xiv. 7; *In Joan.* i. 34; *In Rom.* i. 4, Si ergo cum apparuit nobis hominibus non sine Evangelio apparuit, consequentia videtur ostendere, quod etiam angelico ordini non sine Evangelio apparuerit, illo fortassis quod aeternum Evangelium a Joanne memoratum supra edocuimus. Huet comments, Singulis angelorum ordinibus in sua unicuique forma apparuisse, Evangelium praedicasse *et in coelo denique mortem pro iis obiisse* sciscere videtur aliquando. I can find no authority for the words italicised. All benefits to whatever recipients flow from the one death of Christ upon Calvary; see *In Rom.* v. 10. But Jerome and Justinian allege that according to Origen Christ was to be crucified again for the sins of the Demons, not once but many times. They refer to *De Princ.* iv. 25, where again Rufinus has altered his text. But Origen there (see Jerome's translation and the Greek fragment given by Justinian, both in Lom.) seems to mean that the Passion of Christ in a sense endures to the Consummation of All, referring no doubt to the altar on which stood ' a Lamb as it had been slain.' *Origeniana,* ii. 3. 23 sq. The difficult words *In Lev.* Hom. i. 3, 'et hic quidem pro hominibus ipsam corporalem materiam sanguinis sui fudit, in coelestibus vero ministrantibus, si qui illi inibi sunt, sacerdotibus vitalem corporis sui virtutem, velut spirituale quoddam sacrificium immolavit,' whatever they may mean precisely, do not refer to a sacrifice numerically different. See Redepenning, ii. 400; Höfling, ii. 25.

[1] *In Matt.* xiii. 31; *De Orat.* 14 (Lom. xvii. 146).

the great Italian see, which was already designated by its wealth and splendour, its authority and orthodoxy, as the leader, the champion, the arbiter of Christendom. He seems to have felt the acquiescence of Rome in the sentence of Demetrius as a heavy addition to his misfortune, and somewhere about the year 246 despatched a letter to Fabian, the reigning Pope, in which he protested his orthodoxy[1], and solicited readmission to communion. We must not however lay too much stress upon this fact. The same letter appears to have been addressed to the Bishops of all the Churches, which had ratified his condemnation. It was written after the accession of his pupil and friend Dionysius to the Patriarchate of Alexandria towards the end of Origen's life, when for the first time he felt it possible to make overtures towards reconciliation without disparagement to his self-respect.

The history of his career shows how little he thought the judgment of one Bishop ought to influence the action of another. Nor does he appear to have felt his disgrace as a bar to his activity or a burden on his conscience. Yet, rebel as he was, he ranked far higher than Clement the authority and privileges of the clergy. The analogy between the Christian and the Mosaic hierarchy is con-

---

[1] Eus. *H.E.* vi. 36. 4, γράφει δὲ καὶ Φαβιανῷ τῷ κατὰ Ῥώμην ἐπισκόπῳ, ἑτέροις τε πλείστοις ἄρχουσιν ἐκκλησιῶν, περὶ τῆς κατ᾽ αὐτὸν ὀρθοδοξίας. Jerome, *Ep.* lxv. *ad Pammachium* (in Migne, lxxxiv), Ipse Origenes in epistola quam scribit ad Fabianum Romanae urbis episcopum, poenitentiam agit cur talia scripserit, et causam temeritatis in Ambrosium confert, quod secreto edita in publicum protulerit. *Origeniana*, i. 3. 13. That Origen in this letter recanted doctrines which he continued to teach to the end of his life, or that he endeavoured to throw the blame of his heterodoxy on his friend and benefactor is not to be believed on the unsupported testimony of Jerome. See, however, Dr. Westcott's article on *Ambrosius*, Dict. Christ. Biog.

stantly in his mind, and if he does not draw from it all
the consequences that have been supposed, it is no less
true that in his view the priest is no longer the minister
of the congregation, but the vicar of God. The ordinary
Christian is indeed a priest, but only in the moral or
spiritual sense, that is to say only in a figure, inasmuch
as he offers to God the sacrifice of his own heart and
mind[1]. We still trace the working of the ancient mode
of thought in the emphasis laid by Origen upon the
moral and spiritual qualifications of the minister. His
doctrine of clerical authority is not unlike that of Wiclif.
The power to bind and loose depends upon the spiritual
worthiness of him who wields it[2]. He who is not holy

---

[1] Origen constantly speaks of the true Christian as a Priest, *In Lev.* Hom.
iv. 6; vi. 5; ix. 1. 8; xiii. 5. But the layman is a priest only 'secundum
moralem locum;' *In Lev.* Hom. i. 5; ii. 4; ix. 6; or 'secundum spiritualem
intelligentiam,' *In Lev.* Hom. xv. 3. A very modern sounding phrase may
be noticed, *In Num.* Hom. ii. 1, where it is said of priests, virgins, ascetics,
that they are *in professione religionis*. *In Jesu Nave,* Hom. xvii. 2, shows
that there was a strong tendency in Origen's mind to restrict the language
concerning the Priesthood of the Christian to these 'religious.'

[2] The *locus classicus* is *In Lev.* Hom. v. 3. The Priest 'eats the sins of
the people,' that is, takes them upon himself and remits them, 'secundum
imaginem eius qui sacerdotium ecclesiae dedit.' But he must 'eat the sin'
in a clean place, that is, he must have charity, faith, and a good conscience.
He is said again 'repropitiare delictum,' and this phrase is explained to
mean the moral amendment which the good Priest works in the sinner.
Probst, *Sakramente,* p. 267, argues that Origen means only that the sin
destroys the force of the priestly judgment if it affects him in respect of
the particular act. If the Priest was generally speaking a good man,
but absolved a particular penitent from personal affection, his absolution
would be of no avail. But if, though generally speaking a bad man, he
condemned a particular sinner after conscientious examination of his
case, the condemnation would hold good just as a secular judge may pronounce just and valid sentences though his private life may be thoroughly
vicious. This implies entire ignorance of the Alexandrine doctrine of
spiritual knowledge, and is refuted by the entire run of the Homily referred
to. The Priest is to have for himself 'the breast,' 'the right shoulder,' that
is to say, he must have a heart pure from sin, a hand fruitful of good works.
'Nisi habeat pectus ex omnibus membris electum *non est sacerdos* et nisi

is no priest, and his sentence has no effect at all. Nor is the priestly absolution in itself of force. The priest declares, but does not bestow forgiveness. Nevertheless he alone may teach. He has received judgment of souls. It is his office to stablish the sinner, who is converted from his sin. He is to invite confession both public and private, and to declare the conditions of absolution, the kind and degree of penance, by which the sinner may gåin his restoration to the peace of the Church [1].

How far this power extended was matter of grave doubt. The disputes, which afterward issued in the Novatian schism, were already smouldering in the Church. In many communities the opinion prevailed, that for mortal sins, especially for unchastity, murder, and idolatry, committed after Baptism, there was no forgiveness on earth. Early in the second century Hermas at Rome pleads for a mitigation of this stern rule, and would allow of one absolution for even the worst offences. This was, as has been said, the opinion of Clement also. In the time of Origen even a more lenient practice appears to have been adopted in the Church of Rome. At first perhaps those guilty of sins of unchastity, but soon afterwards all offenders of every grade, were de-

---

habeat brachium dextrum non potest adscendere ad altare Dei *et sacerdos nominari.*' To this end he needs the priestly science (*De Orat.* 28 ; Probst wrongly explains it to mean *casuistry*), but this he cannot have unless he is spiritual and pure, 'et ita demum eruditionis capax fiat, si prius capax fuerit sanctitatis.' Compare *In Psalm.* xxxvii. Hom. ii. 6 (Lom. xii. 267), Tantummodo circumspice diligentius, cui debeas confiteri peccatum tuum. Proba prius medicum ; *In Matt.* xii. 14, if the gates of hell prevail against the Priest, in vain does he bind or loose.

[1] The Priest has 'iudicium animarum,' *In Lev.* Hom. v. 12. For confession see *In Lev.* Hom. ii. 4 ; *In Psalm.* xxxvii. Hom. ii. 6. The judgment of any righteous man has power to bind and loose, as was shown above, but not as regards the discipline of the Church.

clared capable of forgiveness on proper evidences of
contrition. Thus the gates of mercy were thrown wide
open, and the sin against the Holy Ghost, the unpar-
donable sin, was declared to be defiance of the Church,
obdurate refusal of the terms of pardon. It is possible
that in some communities this view had prevailed from
the first [1].

On this point, as on some others, Origen's views
underwent a modification. It may be that he was
softened by age; it may be that he was carried along
by the changing sentiment of the Church around him.
In his earlier writings [2] he gives unflinching expression

[1] See the letter of Dionysius of Corinth, circa A.D. 169, to the Churches
of Pontus, Eus. *H. E.* iv. 23. For the obscure and difficult history of the
Penance Controversy the student may consult Döllinger, *Hippolytus and
Callistus*, p. 117 sqq., Eng. trans.; Probst, *Sakramente*, p. 296 sqq.; Harnack, article *Novatian* in Herzog, ed. 1882, *Dogmengeschichte*, p. 331 sqq.
An interesting monument of the triumph of the more merciful view is to be
found in the Jonah pictures in the Chapel of the Sacraments in the Cemetery
of Callistus ; Probst, *Kirchliche Disciplin*, p. 239.

[2] In *De Orat.* 28 (written about A.D. 236) idolatry, adultery, forni-
cation and wilful murder are death-sins. The distinction between mortal
and venial sins is based upon the Law of Moses, οἱ κατὰ νόμον ἱερεῖς
κωλύονται περί τινων προσφέρειν ἁμαρτημάτων θυσίαν, and on 1 Sam. ii. 25.
(Other texts appealed to by the severe party, and with good reason, were
1 John v. 16 ; Hebr. vi. 4 ; the precise meaning of Matt. xii. 31 is in
dispute.) For these sins there is no forgiveness in the Church, though
some ἑαυτοῖς ἐπιτρέψαντες τὰ ὑπὲρ τὴν ἱερατικὴν ἀξίαν, τάχα μηδὲ ἀκριβοῦντες
τὴν ἱερατικὴν ἐπιστήμην, presume to think they may be forgiven, διὰ τῆς
εὐχῆς αὐτῶν. De la Rue considered that Origen meant to blame the rashness of Priests who ventured to give absolution for mortal sins without
proper evidence of contrition, but the reader will see, I think, that he denies
the possibility of absolution for these sins on any terms. With this is to
be compared *In Ezech. Hom.* iv. 8, where Origen reproves 'nonnullorum
insipientiam, qui sensum animi sui Dei esse asserunt veritatem et frequenter
dicunt "futurum est ut unusquisque nostrum precibus suis eripiat quoscunque
voluerit de gehenna." ' These words may seem to refer to Prayers for the
Dead, but it is better to explain them in the same way as the passage of the
De Oratione. Origen goes on to reprove those who 'qui in sanctis fiduciam
habent.' The influence of confessors and martyrs was largely instrumental
in breaking down the antique rigour.

to the stern old rule. No death-sin can be forgiven, and those priests, who presume to pronounce absolution in cases of this nature, are ignorant of the priestly science. Not that the sinner is forbidden to hope. 'God alone knows,' he says, speaking of the crime of apostasy, 'what evils He will bring upon those who deny and do not repent, what upon those who deny and repent[1].' The Church cannot pardon them, but God may. The sin, which has no forgiveness in this aeon or the aeon to come, may be atoned for in some one of the countless aeons of the vast hereafter.

But in his later works he speaks with another voice. Even death-sins may be forgiven once—they may be forgiven a second and a third time—there are no limits to the Church's power of absolution. One crime alone, obdurate impenitence, has no forgiveness. The sinner who refuses to hear the Church, whether his offence be light or heavy, is cast forth, and when once expelled from the fold can never again re-enter. Yet even so it is better for him to repent, that he may have fewer sins to atone for in the Day of Judgment[2].

---

[1] *In Matt. Comm. Series*, 114. This passage belongs to those that express the later and more lenient view, but the particular words here quoted are applicable in either case.

[2] *In Lev.* Hom. xv. 2, In gravioribus enim criminibus semel tantum poenitentiae conceditur locus; ista vero communia quae frequenter incurrimus semper poenitentiam recipiunt; *In Lev.* Hom. xi. 2, Quod et si aliquis est qui forte praeventus est in huiuscemodi peccatis admonitus nunc verbo Dei, ad auxilium confugiat poenitentiae; ut si semel admisit, secundo non faciat, aut si et secundo, aut etiam tertio praeventus sit, ultra non addat. *Contra Celsum*, iii. 51, the sinner is readmitted to communion, after prolonged penance, but cannot be promoted to office in the Church. There are two remarkable passages in the Commentary on Matthew. In Tom. xiii. 30 Origen is explaining Matth. xviii. 15, 'If thy brother shall trespass against thee, &c.' Some, he says, take this to mean that even death-sins may be forgiven. Others that even the lightest sins are shut out from for-

On another important subject, the Eucharist[1], we observe a similar advance beyond the position of

giveness. Both have erred through not keeping closely to the text. Jesus says if the sinner repents on the first admonition, 'thou hast gained thy brother.' But what happens if he does not repent? This Jesus does not say. In that case then he is neither wholly gained nor wholly lost. We know not what he will suffer. God knows ; we judge not, that we be not judged. In the words that follow a superfluous negative appears to have crept into the text, ὅτι οὐκ ἔξεστι δὶς ἐξῆς μὴ ἀκούσαντα τὸ τρίτον ἀκοῦσαι. The οὐκ should surely be omitted. If, Origen says, this rule seems hard upon those who have committed only light sins, let us remember that they have three chances of amendment. He goes on to say that it is better in any case to repent, λυσιτελεῖ μεθ' ὁποσαοῦν ἁμαρτήματα μετανοεῖν, that we may have less to atone for at the Last Day. He certainly teaches here that if the sinner after three admonitions refused to submit to penance he was cut off from the Church, and this excommunication was final, whatever the gravity of the sin that had brought it about. But apparently there is no limit to the number of times that the sinner might be admitted to penance. In the *Comm. Series,* 114, Peter's apostasy was pardoned because he repented at the crowing of the cock, before the break of day, that is before the descent of the Holy Spirit. Since that time there is no remission of this sin for those who deny Christ ' in the day.' But, he adds, the denial itself proves that the day has not really dawned upon them. ' Forsitan autem et omnes homines quando denegant Jesum, ita ut peccatum denegationis eorum recipiat medicinam, ante galli cantum denegare eum videntur.' Origen appears in these last words to be defending with some reluctance the practice of granting absolution even to apostates. Hence even this passage belongs to those in which the more lenient view is maintained.

[1] The best account of Origen's doctrine on this subject is that given by Höfling, *Die Lehre der ältesten Kirche vom Opfer im Leben und Cultus der Christen,* 1851. The controversy on the subject between Romanists and Protestants in the Reformation times will be found in the *Origeniana.* Both parties claimed Origen as a friend. Against Höfling may be set Döllinger, *Die Eucharistie in den drei ersten Jahrhunderten,* 1826. The Alexandrines held a real but spiritual and in no sense material Presence of Christ in the Eucharist. But there was undoubtedly a party which believed in Transubstantiation, though probably there was as yet no set philosophical explanation of this belief. See *In Joan.* xxxii. 16, νοείσθω δὲ ὁ ἄρτος καὶ ποτήριον τοῖς μὲν ἁπλουστέροις κατὰ τὴν κοινοτέραν περὶ τῆς εὐχαριστίας ἐκδοχήν, τοῖς δὲ βαθύτερον ἀκούειν μεμαθηκόσιν κατὰ τὴν θειοτέραν καὶ περὶ τοῦ τροφίμου τῆς ἀληθείας λόγου ἐπαγγελίαν (Lom. ii. 459). Here the belief in a Corporal Presence is regarded as belonging to the Lower Life, the life of those who do not go beyond the letter. Transubstantiation rests upon Aristotelic or Stoic Realism, and is diametrically opposed to Platonism.

Clement, though here probably the difference is greater in language than in reality. The Church has its 'altar,' 'consecrated by the precious Blood of Christ[1].' The Bread is 'Sacerdotal Bread,' 'a kind of holy Body.' The communicant is said to 'receive the Body of the Lord,' 'the sacraments of the Lord's Body[2].' In these and similar phrases we trace the growing reverence and mystery attached to the material of this greatest of Christian rites. Yet we must not be carried too far. The Eucharist is a Mystery, one of the chiefest Mysteries, for here too there is a letter that killeth, a spirit that giveth life[3]. The Bread and Wine are an allegory,

Leading passages on the subject of the Eucharist are, *In Matt.*'xi. 14 (Lom. iii. 106 ; quite decisive as to the *opus operatum* and the value of the ὕλη) ; *Comm. Series*, 85 ; *In Lev.* Hom. xiii (the whole Homily should be read); *In Num.* Hom. xxiii. 6. It has been observed above, p. 143, that the Eucharist is a mystery in a double sense, firstly as regards its ritual, secondly as regards its doctrinal explanation.

[1] *In Jesu Nave*, Hom. ii. 1 ; x. 3 ; *In Jud.* Hom. iii. 2 ; Probst, *Kirchliche Disciplin*, p. 212. *In Jesu Nave*, Hom. viii. 6, Christ is Priest, Victim, Altar. *Ibid.* Hom. ix. Origen uses the language of Clement. The believers are the altar on which Christ offers His sacrifice to the Father. The 'ornatus altaris' is the Law in the type engraved by Joshua on stones, in the antitype by Christ on the heart ; and all true Christians are Priests and Levites. Compare *Contra Celsum*, viii. 17.

[2] *In Exodum*, Hom. xiii. 3, Cum suscipitis corpus Domini, cum omni cautela et veneratione servatis, ne ex eo parum quid decidat, ne consecrati muneris aliquid dilabatur ; *Contra Celsum*, viii. 33, ἄρτους ἐσθίομεν σῶμα γενομένους διὰ τὴν εὐχὴν ἅγιόν τι καὶ ἁγιάζον τοὺς μεθ᾽ ὑγιοῦς προθέσεως αὐτῷ χρωμένους ; *In Lev.* Hom. xiii. 6, Ille sacerdotalis panis qui est secretus et mysticus sermo.

[3] *In Lev.* Hom. vii. 5. The whole passage is one of the most important : Jesus ergo quia totus ex toto mundus est, tota eius caro cibus est, et totus sanguis eius potus est, quia omne opus eius sanctum est, et omnis sermo eius verus est. Propterea ergo et caro eius verus est cibus et sanguis eius verus est potus. Carnibus enim et sanguine verbi sui tanquam mundo cibo ac potu, potat et reficit omne hominum genus. Secundo in hoc loco post illius carnem mundus cibus est Petrus et Paulus et omnes Apostoli. Tertio loco discipuli eorum. 'Das Wort, die Verheissung des Herrn ist der heilskräftige Leib und das heilskräftige Blut, das wir sowohl innerhalb als

a symbol. 'For it was not that visible bread, which He was holding in His hand, that God the Word called His Body; it was the word as a symbol whereof that bread was to be broken. Nor was it that visible cup, that He called His Blood, but the word as a symbol whereof that wine was to be poured out . . . Why did He not say, this is the Bread of the New Testament, as He said, this is My Blood of the New Testament? Because the bread is the word of righteousness, but the wine is the word of the knowledge of Christ. Since then the covenant of God is placed in the blood of the passion of Christ, so that we are saved by faith and not by righteousness, it is said of the chalice alone, this is the cup of the New Testament [1].' There is a sacrifice in the Eucharist, and there is a commemoration of a sacrifice, the first is that of the believer himself, the second is that of Christ [2]. There is a Presence of Christ, but it is a spiritual, and therefore in Origen's view the only real, Presence, real precisely because in nowise material. It is worth while to

ausserhalb des Sakramentes empfangen und geniessen sollen.' Hence it is sometimes difficult to decide when Origen is speaking of the Eucharist and when of general spiritual communion with Christ, as *In Matt. Comm. Series,* 86 ; *Cels.* viii. 22 ; *De Orat.* 27 ; *In Jer.* Hom. xii. 2. Höfling.

[1] *In Matt. Comm. Series,* 85.

[2] *In Lev.* Hom. ix. 8. 9, at the heavenly altar, till the end of this world, Christ offers the incense which we must put into His Hands. Our sacrifices can have no propitiatory value unless He thus takes them, receiving from us both the incense and the coals, the fire of love. For the Christian's sacrifice, see *In Num.* Hom. xii. 3 ; xxiv. 2 ; *In Exod.* Hom. xiii. 2 ; *De Orat.* 12. But *In Lev.* Hom. v. 3, Ipse Christus solus est hostia pro peccatis et ipse est hostia sancta sanctorum. He is the only sacrifice in the sense of sin-offering. *In Lev.* Hom. iii. 5, Omnis quidem paene hostia quae offertur habet aliquid formae et imaginis Christi. Especially the young bullock of Lev. iv. 3, the ram of the trespass-offering, and the Paschal Lamb. But not the scape-goat. In the Eucharist we plead the death of Christ; *In Lev.* Hom. xiii. 3, Quod ista est commemoratio sola quae propitium facit hominibus Deum.

repeat that Origen held the Sacrifice of Christ to have consisted not of His Body but of His Soul. The Soul answers to the Wine, for according to the book of Genesis the blood is the soul or life. This one fact is enough to prove that, as regards the bread at any rate, Origen cannot have held the doctrine of transubstantiation in any shape whatever.

But the thoughts of Origen turn with constant hope and longing from the Church on earth, where tares grow side by side with the wheat, to the spiritual invisible Church, the Church of the faithful and true, which has neither spot nor blemish nor wrinkle. It is linked in close and vital union to the Church above, the Church of the first-born, of saints and martyrs and angels. These two form the Body, the Temple of the Lord, older in the counsels of God than creation itself. This is the saving Ark, the Church outside of which is no salvation. Men might belong to the visible Church, and yet be dead in trespasses and sins; they might be cut off from the visible Church, and yet be true brothers of Christ. So different is the view of Origen from that of the organising law-loving West [1].

[1] Church buildings, *In Jesu Nave*, Hom. ii. 1, Cum videris . . . ecclesias extrui; their disposition, *Ibid.*, Hom. x. 3; *In Jud.* Hom. iii. 2. The Church had been corrupted by prosperity, *In Jer.* Hom. iv. 3 (Lom. xv. 140) : ' If we judge things by truth and not by numbers we shall see now that we are no longer faithful. But in bygone times we were faithful when the people suffered martyrdom, when from the cemeteries to which we had escorted the bodies of the martyrs we returned to our places of meeting, and the whole church was gathered together, none falling away, and the catechumens were instructed in martyrdom and in the deaths of those who confessed the truth even unto blood, not yielding to temptation or being confounded before the living God. Then we know they saw signs and wonders ; then few were faithful, but they were faithful indeed, treading the strait and narrow path that leadeth unto life. But now when we have become many—for it is not possible that there should be many elect, for Jesus truly said many are called

To the Spiritual Church belongs the Eternal Gospel, a phrase taken from the Book of Revelation[1]. The Eternal Gospel bears the same relation to the actual Gospel, as this to the Law, or as Deuteronomy to the rest of the Pentateuch. It is that full disclosure of the purposes of God, which could not be given in the New Testament because of the nature of human language and the limitations of the flesh-bound mind. Yet there are hints, fragments, shadows, which he, who understands the reading of the Mystic Sense, can seize and interpret. These hints, these ' crannies in the wall,' Origen finds abundantly in the Books of Joshua and Leviticus; the earthly altar is a type of the heavenly altar; the earthly Canaan is a model of the Promised

but few chosen—out of the multitude of them that profess godliness there are very few that attain to the election of God and blessedness.' Compare *In Jesu Nave*, Hom. xxi. The true Church, ἡ κυρίως ἐκκλησία, is holy and undefiled, *De Orat.* 20 *ad in.* Outside the Church is no salvation, *In Jesu Nave*, iii. 5, Nemo semet ipsum decipiat ; extra hanc domum, id est extra ecclesiam nemo salvatur. Contrast however with this *In Jer.* Hom. xx. 3, Qui extra ecclesiam est neque vas misericordiae est neque irae . . . sed vas in aliud quiddam reservatum (see above, p. 207,note). But there are those within the Church who do not belong to it, there are those who have been driven forth wrongfully and yet remain members ; *In Lev.* Hom. xiv. 3. Christ, the Angels, the holy dead are all present at the public worship of the Church ; *In Lucam,* Hom. xxiii, Duplex hic adest ecclesia una hominum altera angelorum; cp. *De Orat.* 31. *In Lev.* Hom. ix. 8. 9, there are two Temples, the Holy Place and the Holy of Holies, the Church on earth, the Church in heaven. The former is the παράδεισος τρυφῆς, 'paradisus deliciarum,' a phrase borrowed from Philo, *Leg. All.* i. 14 (i. 52), *In Cant. Cant.* III (Lom. xv. 29), but this term expresses the Holy Church as a whole on earth or in heaven ; see *In Ezech.* Hom. xiii. 2. The Church in Heaven is the 'ecclesia primitivorum' (from Heb. xii. 23), *In Jesu Nave*, Hom. ix. 4. We find the phrases ecclesia catholica, catholice, doctores catholici, and even catholicus, a Catholic, the last *In Lev.* Hom. xiv. 2.

[1] Rev. xiv. 6. See *De Princ.* iv. 25 ; *In Joan.* i. 9. 10; *In Rom.* i. 4 ; ii. 5 ; *In Lev.* Hom. xiii. 2. The imperfection of Revelation in the usual sense of the word, the αἰσθητὸν εὐαγγέλιον, appeared to be proved, especially by 1 Cor. xiii. 9, 10, and John xxi. 25.

Land above. But the most significant are furnished by St. Paul. Pieced together by his cunning hand they form what is called his Eschatology, his vision of the life to come. He differs from Clement mainly in detail and the anxious care with which he discussed, debated, explained away the language of Scripture.

He learned from the Bible that the soul passes at death into one of two abodes, which in accordance with the general belief of his time he regarded as situated beneath the earth. The first is Hades, the prison of the imperfect. It is guarded by the Cherubim, who with their fiery sword keep the way of the Tree of Life. Nor had any been suffered to pass these stern sentinels, till Christ descended, and carried the souls of the Patriarchs and Prophets in His train to Paradise, the mansion of the blessed. Since that day the true believer passes at once into Paradise, unharmed by the fiery sword[1]. Even in this place of rest the soul still has a bodily form, such as that which clothed it before its entry into life.

At the close of this present Aeon will come the Great Day, when Christ will return to judgment. As in Clement, we hear nothing of the imminence of this catastrophe; what the more refined minds are pondering is not the time, but the manner of the great change, the

---

[1] *In libr. I Sam.* Hom. 2 (Lom. xi. 331); *De Princ.* ii. 11. 6, Puto enim quod sancti quique discedentes de hac vita permanebunt in loco aliquo in terra posito, quem Paradisum dicit Scriptura divina, velut in quodam eruditionis loco, et, ut ita dixerim, auditorio vel schola animarum. 'In terra,' I presume, is 'within the earth,' 'under the earth.' Compare also *In Lucam,* Hom. xxiv; *De Mart.* 36. All pass 'the fiery sword,' 'the fire,' but the righteous are not harmed nor stopped by the screen of flame because there is in them no fuel for it to fasten upon. That the soul in Hades or Paradise has a body was proved by the Parable of Dives and Lazarus; Redepenning, ii. 126.

meaning of the Resurrection, the nature of the reward[1]. The first of these questions Origen passes over, content to warn his readers that the Gospel prophecy must not be taken in its literal sense[2]. Enough that there will be a new heaven and a new earth. And yet it is but 'the fashion' of this world that passeth away. The new universe will still be material, still infinite in variety, and apt as this for the discipline of those that dwell therein[3]. In that Great Day men will be reunited to their bodies. This is the undoubted assurance of Scripture. But it constituted one of the great difficulties of the time. Christians were perplexed by it; heathen controversialists poured upon it unmixed ridicule and scorn. Origen like Clement found a solution of all his doubts in the teaching of St. Paul, but he refined upon this in a way peculiar to himself. The resurrection body will be the same as that we now inhabit, and yet not the same. Not the same because spiritual and glorious, because again its material substance will be entirely different. Yet the same, as our body of to-day is the same with our body of twenty years ago; every particle is changed, yet the body as a whole is not changed. Origen found an explanation of this identity in difference in what he calls the 'germinative principle,' a power similar to that, by which the ear of corn is evolved from the seed. The soul has a vital assimilative 'spark,' or 'principle,' which lays hold of fitting matter, and shapes

[1] Chiliasm is emphatically condemned, *De Princ.* ii. 11. 2. The First and Second Resurrection are distinguished, *Sel. in Psalm.* i. (Lom. xi. 392), as that of righteous and that of wicked. But *In Joan.* xx. 21 (Lom. ii. 259) the First Resurrection is for the ' dead in Christ,' the imperfectly righteous, who need resurrection most.

[2] *In Matt. Comm. Series,* 49.

[3] *De Princ.* i. 6. 4; ii. 1. 3.

it into a habitation suited to its needs. The same process, by which it repairs the daily waste of our organism now, will enable it then to construct a wholly new tenement for itself[1].

It has been urged that Origen's system leaves no real place for the Resurrection[2]. This he would most strenuously have denied. And it is in fact untrue. The body of the soul in Paradise, though different from that which it inhabited in life, is still a body belonging to this Aeon, this world; the resurrection body is the body of another Aeon, another world. Hence though its features are the same, because these are the natural outward expression of its abiding individuality, its texture is far different, because adapted on the one hand to its new element, on the other to the varying degrees of the soul's purity or impurity[3]. Man, he tells us, will

---

[1] *De Princ.* ii. 10. 3; iii. 6. 4 sqq.; *Sel. in Psal.* i. 5 (Lom. xi. 392); *Contra Celsum,* v. 22 sqq. The 'germinative principle' is the λόγος, substantiae ratio, σπινθηρισμός, ἐντεριώνη.

[2] Redepenning, ii. 127; Denis, 325.

[3] The principles laid down by Origen are four. The Resurrection body will be infinitely more beautiful; it will retain its general type and be recognisable; it will be adapted to the requirements of its new environment; it will have no superfluous organs. In consequence of the latter rule the 'gnashing of teeth' is not to be literally understood. The Resurrection body of the wicked will differ from that of the righteous, *De Princ.* ii. 3; 10. 2 sq.; iii. 6. 4. Origen taught the Resurrection of 'this body,' and even of 'the flesh' (Pamphilus insists upon this point, *Apol.* 7), but not of 'this flesh.' Even in his own time many were offended at his doctrine, *De Princ.* ii. 10. 1, and Jerome and others attacked him with great vehemence. The Origenist monks are said to have believed that the Resurrection body would be spherical, and this opinion is charged upon Origen by Justinian. The accusation rests probably upon *De Orat.* 31 (Lom. xvii. 278), where this shape is attributed to the bodies of the stars. The same general principles applied to the Body of our Lord as to that of man; see *Contra Celsum,* ii. 62; iii. 41, and passages referred to at end of last Lecture. Some charged Origen with asserting that the Saviour laid aside His Body in the Sun. Some Christians, according to

eventually cease to be 'a soul' at all. When his re-demption is complete, his love will be no longer 'cold;' he will become a pure Intelligence, as he was before he lapsed from his first estate. But even so he will still be corporeal, for except the Trinity no spirit can exist without a shroud. The same law will apply to the Saviour, in so far as He is perfect Man.

Clement figured the future life as an upward pro-gress of the soul through seven heavens to rest in the Ogdoad. But Origen doubted whether this Gnostic conception had sufficient Scripture warrant. Hence, following the hint conveyed in the phrase 'aeons of aeons,' he speaks of a vast stretch of cycles reaching onwards in almost illimitable extension to the Consum-mation of All. There is in this a certain resemblance to Stoicism, but it is merely superficial [1].

In that future life the soul is still free, is still tested by its use of freedom, rises and falls, is punished or

Pamphilus, *Apol.* 7, actually held this strange tenet, interpreting in this way Psalm xix. 4, in sole posuit tabernaculum suum. It is perhaps a Gnostic idea; see the account of Theodotus in Lecture i. Any stone was good enough to fling at Origen. See for the whole subject, *Origeniana*, ii. 9; Denis, p. 297 sqq.; Redepenning, places cited in Index. De la Rue con-sidered that there was nothing in Origen's speculations opposed to the Catholic faith, 'si modo quasdam exceperis quaestiunculas quas luxurians Origenis ingenium curiosius persequens paullo longius prosequitur.' The reader should also bear in mind *De Princ.* i. 5. 4, Certius tamen qualiter se habitura sit res scit solus Deus et si qui eius per Christum et Spiritum Sanctum amici sunt.

[1] *Contra Celsum*, vi. 21, the canonical scriptures do not speak of seven or any definite number of heavens, yet do speak of heavens in the plural, whether these are to be identified with the Greek spheres or understood in a mystical sense. *De Princ.* ii. 3. 7, the eighth heaven, the ἀπλανὴς σφαῖρα. There are three heavens, *In Matt.* xxx. 51; *In Psalm.* xxxix. Hom. i. 8; *De Mart.* 13. *De Princ.* ii. 3. 5, Multorum saeculorum finis dicitur esse hic mundus qui et ipse saeculum dicitur: compare *De Orat.* 27 (Lom. xvii. 226); *In Matt.* xv. 31.

rewarded, according to its works[1]. All punishment is medicinal, at least in the purpose of the good God[2]. And the reward is not payment like that of an earthly master, who gives money in return for toil. The Kingdom of God is within us, and what He promises is not happiness, still less pleasure, but the full satisfaction of that restless love of truth which He has implanted in thę soul, most surely not in vain[3]. But all revelation must be gradual, must be willingly received. Hence

---

[1] *De Princ.* i. 6. 3, Ex quo, ut opinor, hoc consequentia ipsa videtur ostendere, unamquamque rationabilem naturam posse ab uno in alterum ordinem transeuntem per singulos in omnes, et ab omnibus in singulos pervenire, dum accessus profectuum defectuumve varios pro motibus vel conatibus propriis unusquisque pro liberi arbitrii facultate perpetitur. The drift of the passage compels us to apply these words to the future as well as to the past and present life. Still more distinct is *De Princ.* iii. 1. 21, Ex quo opinamur quoniam quidem, ut frequenter diximus, immortalis est anima et aeterna, quod in multis et sine fine spatiis per immensa et diversa saecula possibile est, ut vel a summo bono ad infima mala descendat, vel ab ultimis malis ad summa bona reparetur : and more explicit still are *De Princ.* ii. 3. 3 *ad fin.*, and the Fragment from Jerome's translation of *De Princ.* in the *Ad Avitum* (Lom. xxi. 133). The possibility of a fall in the future life is the special characteristic of Origen's view. It appeared to flow necessarily from the doctrine of Free Will, on the other hand it is limited by the doctrine of Grace ; see below at the end of this Lecture. But I have not noticed any passage where Origen affirms this possibility outside of the *De Principiis*, and it is expressly denied *In Rom.* v. 10.

[2] The best passage for the curative nature of all punishment is to be found in the *Selecta in Exodum* on the hardening of Pharaoh's heart. Origen's belief is summed up very forcibly in the words ἕκαστος οὖν συνειδὼς ἁμαρτίας ἑαυτῷ εὐχέσθω κολασθῆναι (Lom. viii. 328). Compare also *De Princ.* i. 6. 3. The weak part of his doctrine is the tendency to regard the relation between vice and punishment as quantitative. *In Lev.* Hom. xiv. 3 there are three degrees of sinfulness, denoted by the 'wood, hay, straw' of 1 Cor. iii. 12, which the fire burns up in a longer or shorter time. *In Lev.* Hom. xi. 2 ; xiv. 4 the death, which was the punishment of certain sins under the Law, wiped out the sin. The Christian must make atonement either by penance ; this is the 'tradidi in interitum carnis' of 1 Cor. v. 5; or by fire in the next world. Here, as often, Origen is drawn in different directions by three irreconcileable principles—discipline, literalism, and spiritualism.

[3] *De Princ.* ii. 11. 4 sqq.

the future life is to be looked upon as one of progress through discipline.

'The Lord is like a refiner's fire.' 'It is certain that the fire which is prepared for sinners awaits us, and we shall go into that fire, wherein God will try each man's work of what kind it is .... Even if it be a Paul or a Peter, he shall come into that fire, but such are they of whom it is written, "though thou pass through the fire, the flame shall not scorch thee."' The holy and the just are cleansed, like Aaron and Isaiah, with coals from off the altar. But sinners, 'among whom I count myself,' must be purged with another fire. This is not of the altar, it is not the Lord's, but is kindled by the sinner himself within his own heart. Its fuel is our own evil, the wood, the hay, the straw, sins graver or lighter, which we have built upon the foundation laid by Christ. Anger, envy, remorse, these rack men even in this life with anguish so intolerable, that many. perish by their own hand rather than bear their torments longer. How much fiercer will be the smart, when the soul in the light of eternity surveys the history of all its wickedness written in indelible characters upon its own texture [1]; when it is 'sawn asunder' by the pangs which attend the separation of the guilty passions from the pure spirit; when it bewails in 'outer darkness' its banishment from Him, who is the Light and the Life [2].

---

[1] The soul never really forgets anything, but retains within itself 'signa quaedam et formas' of all its misdeeds, *De Princ.* ii. 10. 4. The same idea, that sin leaves an imprint on the soul, is expressed by the χειρόγραφον of *De Orat.* 28; the cicatrix of *In Lev.* Hom. viii. 5; the τύπος written on the heart with iron pen and nail of adamant, *In Jer.* Hom. xvi. 10.

[2] *In Psal.* xxxvii. Hom. iii. 1; *In Lev.* Hom. ix. 8; *In Lucam*, Hom. xiv, Ego puto quod et post resurrectionem ex mortuis indigeamus sacramento eluente nos atque purgante; nemo enim absque sordibus resurgere poterit;

Origen's view—we must not say his doctrine—rests largely upon general principles: that justice and goodness are in their highest manifestation identical; that God does not punish, but has made man so, that in virtue only can he find peace and happiness, because He has made him like Himself; that suffering is not a tax upon sin, but the wholesome reaction, by which the diseased soul struggles to cast out the poison of its malady; that therefore, if we have done wrong, it is good to suffer, because the anguish is returning health, will cease when health is restored, and cannot cease till then. Again, that evil is against the plan of God, is created not by Him but by ourselves; is therefore properly speaking a negation, and as such cannot be eternal. These are in the main Greek thoughts; their chief source is the *Gorgias* of Plato. But his final appeal is always to Scripture. The texts on which he mainly relies are those of St. Paul, 'He shall be saved yet so as by fire,' 'God shall be all in all.' But starting from these he finds a thousand hints and 'crannies,' especially in the Old Testament[1]. He laboured to answer objections.

nec ullam posse animam reperiri quae universis statim vitiis careat ; *De Princ.* ii. 10. 4 sqq. *In Jerem.* Hom. ii. 3 Origen speaks as if the saints do not need this baptism of fire. But this must be understood in the light of the above passages.

[1] Besides the famous texts Luke iii. 16, 1 Cor. iii. 15, Is. iv. 4, Origen quotes Is. xii. 1, 'Though Thou wast angry with me, Thine anger is turned away;' xxiv. 22, 'And they shall be gathered together as prisoners are gathered in the pit, and shall be shut up in the prison, and after many days shall they be visited;' xlvii. 14, 15, ὅτι ἔχεις ἄνθρακας πυρός, καθίσαι ἐπ' αὐτοῖς· οὗτοι ἔσονταί σοι βοήθεια : Micah vii. 9, 'I will bear the indignation of the Lord, because I have sinned against Him . . . He will bring me forth to the light ;' Ezekiel xvi. 53, 55, Restituetur Sodoma in antiquum ; Jerem. xxv. 15, 16, Per Hieremiam prophetam iubetur calix furoris Dei propinari omnibus gentibus ut bibant et insaniant et evomant. In quo comminatur dicens quia si quis noluerit bibere non mundabitur ; Matth. xviii. 30, 'Went and cast him into prison till he should pay the debt;' John x. 16, 'There shall

The word 'eternal' as applied to death does not necessarily mean 'endless[1].' The sin, which is not forgiven
in this aeon or the aeon to come, might yet be blotted
out in some one of the aeons beyond[2]. But he could
not be blind to the fact, that there are in Scripture
passages that make directly against him. Hence Restitution is a great and terrible mystery. It is taught in
Scripture not explicitly but in allegories. And there is
a reason for this, because many men are so vile, that
even the dread of endless torments will scarcely curb
their evil passions. Considerations such as these lay
heavy upon his candid spirit. Hence though undoubtedly his prevailing hope is, that all men shall be
healed in that far-off day, when there shall be one flock
and one shepherd, and even Sodom, as Ezekiel prophesied, shall be restored, at times his vision fails. 'Who

be one fold and one shepherd;' Rom. xi. 25, 26, 'Blindness in part is happened to Israel until the fulness of the Gentiles be come in, and so all Israel
shall be saved;' Rom. xi. 32, 'God hath concluded them all in unbelief that
He might have mercy upon all;' 1 Peter iii. 18-21, 'Christ went and
preached to those who perished in the Flood;' Ps. lxxviii. 34, 'When He
slew them then they sought Him.' Other texts are given by Huet, *Origeniana*, ii. 11. 20.

[1] *In Exodum*, Hom. vi. 13, Domine qui regnas in saeculum et in saeculum
et adhuc; *De Princ.* ii. 3. 5; *In Lev.* Hom. xiii. 6, Legitimum namque
et aeternum est omne quod mysticum est. *Contra Celsum*, vi. 26, Origen
seems to allow that αἰώνιος implies endless duration, but argues that the
word is used διὰ τοὺς μόγις φόβῳ τῆς αἰωνίου κολάσεως κἂν συστέλλοντας
ἐπί ποσον τῆς κακίας καὶ τῶν ἀπ' αὐτῆς ἁμαρτανομένων χύσιν. The word
αἰών in the usage of the Platonists of the time, certainly included the idea
of endless, changeless duration, see Plutarch, *De Ei apud Delphos*, 20;
and it must be admitted that the arguments employed in the passages quoted
above are not sufficient to prove Origen's point. Origen speaks of eternal
punishments in many passages. Vincenzi, *In S. Greg. Nyss. et Origenis
Scripta et Doctrinam*, Rome, 1865, refers to *In Lev.* Hom. ix. 4. 5; xiv. 4;
In Jesu Nave, Hom. xvi. 3; *In Ezech.* Hom. vi. 26; *In Matt. Com.* xvi.
22; *De Mart.* 25, and others, but he endeavours to prove far too much.
See *Origeniana*, ii. 11.

[2] *In Matt. Com.* xv. 21.

is that guest who is bound hand and foot, and cast into outer darkness? You will ask whether he remains bound in the outer darkness for ever?—for the words ' for this aeon,' or ' for the aeons,' are not added—or whether he will in the end be loosed?—for it does not appear that anything is written about his future release. It does not seem to me to be safe, seeing I have no full understanding, to pronounce an opinion, especially in a case where Scripture is silent[1].' The same hesitation is apparent, where he is led to speak of the final doom of the evil spirits[2].

Indeed the Alexandrine doctrine of Volition is such, that it is hard to reconcile with the hope of final unity. If the will is wholly free, unconditioned, indifferent, what after all is the use of these long ages of discipline? What can they produce, but an eternity of sterile change, in which each rise is balanced by a fall, and after the lapse of a million ages the end is no nearer than it was[3].

---

[1] *In Joan.* xxviii. 7 ; see also *In Rom.* viii. 12 ; *In Jer.* Hom. xviii. 15.

[2] *De Princ.* i. 6. 3, the salvability of some of the evil spirits is an open question. *Ibid.* i. 8. 4, the 'adversariae virtutes' are divided into two classes, 1. 'principatus, potestates mundi rectores ;' of these he only says that they are not essentially evil: 2. another class has sunk so deep ' ut revocari nolit magis quam non possit.' *Ibid.* iii. 6. 5, ' The last enemy that shall be destroyed is Death.' That is to say, not the substance but the wicked will of the Devil will at last be annihilated. He will cease to be an enemy. But this is denied, *In Rom.* viii. 9, Istius autem qui de coelo cecidisse dicitur nec in fine saeculi erit ulla conversio. In the *Epistola ad Amicos* (Lom. xvii. 8) according to the version of Jerome certain of Origen's adversaries taught that the Devil ' posse salvari,' according to that of Rufinus they affirmed that Origen taught 'diabolum esse salvandum.' Both translators agree in the sense of the following words, ' quod ne mente quidem quis captus dicere potest.'

[3] Jerome, *Ad Avitum*, considers that the result of Origen's speculations is ' rursum nasci ex fine principium et ex principio finem.' But Origen expressly denies this, *De Princ.* iii. 6. 6. See Denis, pp. 176, 328, 347. Redepenning raises other difficulties on which it is unnecessary to enter.

This is Jerome's criticism, and it has been pressed by later writers. It may be a logical sequence, but it is certainly not the meaning of Origen. Some spirits may be rebellious to the last, and it is certain that God Himself can constrain no man to goodness. But who shall presume to say from observation of this life, which is but a pin-point in the boundless ocean, that the soul will always be obdurate. Great is the truth and it will prevail, if it have but time to work in. Slowly yet certainly the blessed change must come, the purifying fire must eat up the dross, and leave the pure gold. Perhaps not till after many ages, not till after discipline prolonged through geologic cycles, the sinner will learn to kiss the rod, and submit to be healed. But at last his eyes will be opened, the prodigal will fall on the Father's bosom, and becoming ' one spirit with the Lord' will thenceforth sin no more. One by one we shall enter into rest never to stray again. Then when Death the last enemy is destroyed, when the tale of His children is complete, Christ will ' drink wine in the Kingdom of His Father.' This is the End, when 'all shall be one, as Christ and the Father are One,' when 'God shall be all in all.'

From this time forth there is no further change, but the soul remains secure in the fulness of intellectual fruition. Yet not all alike. To the Beatific Vision none can be admitted save the pure in heart. Though all other chastisements cease, when their object is fulfilled, the *poena damni* may still endure. Star differeth from star in glory. There are many mansions, many degrees[1]

---

[1] The many mansions are typified by the stages on the march of the Israelites from Egypt to the Promised Land. The end of the journey is

There are those, who bring forth thirty-, sixty-, a hundred-fold. 'The righteous shall shine as the sun. And upon whom shall they shine but on those beneath them?' If we do not misinterpret these expressions, they appear to mean, that the soul by sin may lose capacities, which can never be wholly regained, and in this sense at least Origen teaches the eternity of punishment.

the 'river which makes glad the city of God,' *In Num.* Hom. xxvi. 4. 5; xxviii. 2. 3. But again, *In Jesu Nave,* xxv. 4, there are different abodes even in the last degree figured by the final settlements of the tribes in East, West, South and North. Again, *In Num.* Hom. xi. 4. 5, as in this world the Gentile races are under the care of Guardian Angels, while Israel is the special portion of God, 'ita credo et in fine huius mundi atque in initio saeculi alterius futurum ut iterum dividat excelsus filios Adam, et qui non potuerint ita mundi esse corde ut ipsum videant Dominum et esse portio Domini videant sanctos angelos et sint secundum numerum angelorum Dei. It may be doubted here whether Origen is speaking of the Day of Judgment or of the Consummation, but *In Num.* Hom. xxi. 1 he is certainly speaking of the latter. The same uncertainty attaches to *In Luc.* Hom. iii, where it is said that though all the redeemed will be in one place, only the pure in heart will be able to see God. But here again I think he refers to the End. So again, *Ibid.* xvii, the δίγαμος is excluded from the church of the firstborn, 'non quo in aeternum mittatur incendium sed quo partem non habeat in regno Dei.' He may be saved but is not crowned. So again, *In Lev.* Hom. xiv. 3, he who is spotted with vices not of a mortal kind, 'huic etiamsi secundum Apostoli sententiam negantur regna coelorum non tamen alterius beatitudinis abscinditur locus.' Similar language is used of the Gentiles (see above, p. 207). To these passages may be added *De Mart.* 13. 14; *In Matt.* x. 3. The point is of importance because it is the only ground on which Jerome attacks Origen's doctrine of the Restitution of Man, alleging (*Ep.* lxxxiv. Migne, *Ad Pammachium et Oceanum*) that he taught 'post multa saecula atque unam omnium restitutionem id ipsum fore Gabrielem quod diabolum, Paulum quod Caipham, virgines quod prostibulas.' See *Origeniana,* ii. 11. 21.

LECTURE VII.

No man can serve two Masters.—ST. MATT. vi. 24.

OUR account of Origen would be essentially defective without a notice of his controversy with Celsus. We have seen how the Church utilised philosophy; we must now reverse the picture, and consider what the philosophers had to say on their side. It will be interesting to observe the attitude they took with regard to Christianity, the points they conceded, the points they denied, and to ascertain, as clearly as we can, what they treated as the vital issues of the great debate. But we shall be enabled to do this better, if we permit ourselves a wider scope, and review not the controversy with Celsus alone, but the mutual action and reaction of Christianity and Paganism during this period.

It would be a serious error to regard the Second Century as a time of irreligion. On the contrary it was an age of revival. Everywhere men were seeking with restless eagerness for deeper, more positive, more vital beliefs. The ancient mythology had perished with the Republic, and the old Greek and Roman deities appear henceforth for the most part as intermediate beings, angels or demons, who people the spaces of air between man and the supreme object of his worship. This is no longer Zeus or Jupiter, but a God of Syrian, or Persian, or Egyptian nationality. The altars of the Great Mother, of Isis and Serapis, of Mithra, are to be found all over the world, from Bactria to Gaul, in Northumberland, on the Rhine, in Numidia, wherever the Roman eagles flew, in the provinces, in Rome, in Caesar's palace. The change is significant in many ways. It shows, firstly, the irresistible tendency of the times towards a Monotheistic worship. For these Oriental Gods, though many in name, are in reality but one. As we gaze upon them they seem to melt into one another. Who is the Syrian Goddess? She is the Aramaic Astarte, the Babylonian Mylitta, she is the Great Mother, she is Isis, Universal Nature, the maternal feminine aspect of God. And God is the Sun, whose ray-crowned head is to be seen on Roman coins from the reign of Commodus to that of Constantine. Osiris, Mithra, Elagabalus, are all the same. They are the fatherly, fostering, masculine side of the Divine, aptly figured by the orb of day[1].

---

[1] The same idea, that of the substantial identity of deities, regarded by the vulgar as distinct, is found in Aeschylus, *Prom. Vinc.* 210, Θέμις καὶ Γαῖα πολλῶν ὀνομάτων μορφὴ μία. This mode of conception—it has been called Henotheism—is an intermediate stage between Polytheism and Monotheism. It had prevailed from very early times in Egypt (see M. Le Page Renouf, *Hibbert Lectures* for 1879 ; G. Maspero, *Histoire Ancienne des Peuples de l'Orient*, 4th ed., Paris, 1886) and obtains full expression in the *De Iside et Osiride* of Plutarch, the *De Dea Syria* of Lucian. See also Mommsen, v. 454. It is the chief reason for the great fascination exercised by the Egyptian religion, notwithstanding its zoolatry, upon Greek minds. Henotheism, however, preserves in a confused way the personality of the different deities, and does not go so far as to assert that the different names only mark more or less perfect or imperfect ideas of the same God. This was asserted in one passage by Clement, *Strom.* v. 14. 101, where he affirms that God is meant by the Zeus of the poets. Origen would not admit this. When Celsus insists that all mankind worship the same Father, whether they call Him ' Jehovah, Jove or Lord,' he replies that words have a natural affinity to things, that language is φύσει not θέσει, that the different names of the pagan gods have a real connection with demon-worship, as is

But besides this striving after unity, so natural to all civilised men, there were other motives at work. What these were we shall best see by a brief account of Mithra, the most popular and powerful of all the new order of deities. Mithra was a God of the world-old Arian stock [1] In the Vedas he is the giver of light, life, and truth, the assessor, almost the double of Varuna, the Lord of Heaven. In the new dualism of the Iranian peoples he is degraded to a subordinate place, and becomes, as Plutarch says, a mediator between Ormuzd the good and Ahriman the evil spirit, or between God and Man.

proved by their efficacy in magical incantations, and finally quotes Plato, τὸ δ' ἐμὸν δέος, ὦ Πρώταχε, περὶ τὰ ὀνόματα τῶν θεῶν οὐκ ὀλίγον, *Contra Celsum*, i. 24; v. 44.

[1] The history of Mithra worship in its original home will be found in the admirable Introduction of Darmsteter to his translation of the Vendidad in *Sacred Books of the East*. Duncker also may be consulted. For the spread of Mithra worship in Europe, see Preller, *Römische Mythologie*; Renan, *Marc Aurèle*, 576; Döllinger, *The Gentile and the Jew*; Keim, *Rom und das Christenthum*. An account of Mithraic monuments in England will be found in the *C. I. L.* vol. vii; and Bruce, *Wallet Book of the Roman Wall*. Almost any volume of the *Inscriptions* will supply interesting information; see especially the account of the Mithraic cave at Constantine in Algeria, vol. viii. pt. 1. no. 6975. The Mithra monuments were erected mainly by Roman officers. This fact proves how worthless is the distinction between *licitae* and *illicitae religiones* which used to be regarded as explaining the Christian persecutions. The birthday of Mithra, the Sol Invictus, was December 25, on which day the festival of the Nativity of Christ, the Sun of Righteousness, began to be celebrated not long before the time of Chrysostom. It may be that the heathen festival was retained under a Christian name from a politic desire to soften the change from the old order of things to the new, though the positive evidence for this rests upon a Homily formerly attributed to Chrysostom but of doubtful date and authorship. See King, *The Gnostics and their Remains*, p. 47; and Mr. Sinker's article *Christmas* in Dict. Christ. Ant. The same motive may account for the fact that the figure of the Sun, with the legend ' To the Invincible Sun, my Companion,' is found upon copper coins of Constantine; though not after the year 323, when his victory over Licinius raised him above the necessity of dissimulation. See Eckhel, vol. viii. pp. 75, 79.

He is the Sun, who shoots his rays down into this world to fight for man against cold, darkness, and disease. Hence he was worshipped in caves, and depicted as a youth slaying a bull. The cave is this dim earth; the bull is the changing world or evil, whose death is the life of the soul. So Mithra is a Redeemer, and the blood of the slain bull is an Atonement. His monuments exhibit beneath these figures a dog, emblem of the purified soul, lapping up the blood; and beneath all is the legend 'A holy stream,' or 'The stream that is shed for all [1].'

Connected with Mithra worship, though properly belonging to that of the Great Mother, was the barbarous rite of the Taurobolium. The devotee was seated in a trench, so that the blood of the slaughtered bull gushed all over him. Monuments which commemorate this hideous baptism speak of him by whom it was received as 'regenerate'—*Renatus in aeternum Taurobolio* [2].

Mithraism had also its Messiah [3]. In the fulness of time shall come a Saviour, a divine son of Zarathustra, the lawgiver. He shall bring to a glorious close the aeonian strife between good and evil. Death and Hell shall be destroyed, and men shall live in blessedness

---

[1] Νᾶμα σεβήσιον : nama cunctis; Preller, p. 761. .

[2] 'Der Einzuweihende wurde mit einem ärmlichen Gewande bekleidet, um so recht eigentlich als "armer Sünder" die reinigende Bluttaufe über sich ergehen zu lassen.' The oldest monument in commemoration of the Taurobolium is at Naples and dated 133, the most recent is at Rome and belongs to 390. Preller thinks the word *renatus* is borrowed from Christianity. It was in common use in the Isis mysteries; Apuleius, *Metam.* xi. 21.

[3] He was known by the name of Saoshyant. A tolerably precise outline of the doctrine is given by Theopompus, Fragments 71, 72 in Müller's *Frag. Hist. Graec.*

for evermore, 'casting no shadow,' children, as we say, of light. Even before that consummation there is a heaven for the righteous. It is figured as a staircase with seven portals[1]. These are the seven heavens, the abode of the six great Emanations and of Mithra. Through these the soul ascends, protected by its guardian angel, into the eighth, where it rests in the presence of Ormuzd.

It is peculiar to the religion of Mithra and to that of Serapis, which is in other respects very similar, that the guardian angel is the intelligence, the better and purer half of human nature, which becomes after death the champion, or spiritual bride, of the lower soul.

How closely all this resembles the ideas derived by Clement from the Valentinian Theodotus will be discerned without further comment.

---

[1] *Contra Celsum*, vi. 22. 'The priests held that only the pure and bright part of the soul could live on after death. Hence even in the living they distinguished this part from the polluted part, and in the purè immortal half they saw the side created by the good gods, its true being, the Fravashi, or protecting spirit allotted to each man;' Duncker, v. p. 180, Eng. trans. So in the Egyptian Mysteries, 'At death the intellect (Khu or Ka) becomes a demon; the soul passes into the under world and appears at the judgment bar of Osiris-Khent-Ament, and his thirty-two assessors. Its conscience, or as the Egyptians say its heart, accuses it. It is weighed in the balance of truth and justice. According as it is found light or heavy the righteous doom is pronounced, and the intellect, the demon, becomes the executioner. It reminds the soul how it neglected its warning and would none of its reproof; it flogs it with the scourge of its sins, and delivers it up to the storm and the whirlwind;' Maspero, Germ. trans. of 1877, p. 39. The account is taken from the *Book of the Dead*, a copy of which was buried with every mummy. But I observe that in his last edition M. Maspero does not bring out this peculiar relation of the intellect to the soul as its guardian angel or avenging demon. Compare p. 33 above, and Le Page Renouf, p. 147. Serapis or Sarapis (both spellings are found in inscriptions) is Osiris-Apis, that is, 'the dead Apis.' All men after death were regarded as entering into union with, as becoming Osiris. 'À partir de la xii⁰ dynastie le défunt est nommé couramment l'Osiris *N* ;' Maspero, pp. 31, 35, 38, ed. Paris, 1886.

The disciples of Mithra formed an organised church with a developed hierarchy. They possessed the ideas of Mediation, Atonement, and a Saviour, who is human and yet divine, and not only the idea, but a doctrine of the Future Life. They had a Eucharist, and a Baptism, and other curious analogies might be pointed out between their system and the Church of Christ[1]. Most of these conceptions, no doubt, are integral parts of a religion much older than Christianity. But when we consider how strange they are to the older polytheism of Greece and Rome, and when we observe further that Mithraism did not come into full vogue till the time of Hadrian, that is to say till the age of Gnosticism, we shall hardly be wrong in judging that resemblances were pushed forward, exaggerated, modified, with a special view to the necessities of the conflict with the new faith, and that differences, such as the barbarous superstitions of the *Avesta*, were kept sedulously in the background with the same object. Paganism was copying Christianity, and by that very act was lowering her arms.

This process of approximation, so visible in the popular religions, was carried to even greater lengths in the region of philosophy. The old scepticism was still represented by the Stoics, who combined the worship of humanity with speculative doubt, and by the Epicureans, who were practically Atheists. But these were the creeds of a few rebellious intellects. The belief in a future life, which Cicero had ridiculed in a court

[1] Justin, *Apol.* i. 66 ; *Trypho*, 70 ; Tertullian, *De Bapt.* 5 ; *De praescr. Haer.* 40 ; Preller, p. 759 ; Döllinger, *The Gentile and the Jew*, i. 416, Eng. trans.

of law, and Caesar and Cato had repudiated in the open Senate, had become a test. At Athens one who like Demonax stood aloof from the Mysteries was a marked man, much as a non-communicant would have been in the last century. This was the chief reason why Stoicism, for all its noble morality and its high services to law and to humanity, was swept away by the rise of the Platonising schools [1].

We may divide the heathen Platonists into two main branches, according to the predominance in their cast of thought of the religious or the philosophic vein. To the former belong the Pythagoreans. These gave a general adherence to the teaching of Plato, but combined with it a high veneration for all 'philosophers, wise men, and inspired poets;' for the shadowy figures of Pythagoras, Orpheus, Linus, Abaris, Zamolxis; for the much talked of but little known Brahmins and Buddhists [2];

---

[1] The 'godless Epicureans' were not popular, hence Origen thinks that Celsus was afraid to come forward openly in his true character as a professed Epicurean, lest he should be regarded even by the Greeks as ἄθεος. For the denial of the future life by Cicero, see *Pro Cluentio*, 61 (in the *Tusculan Disputations* he professes to delight in the Platonic doctrine of immortality) ; by Caesar and Cato, Sallust, *Cat.* 51, 52. For Demonax, see § 11 of Lucian's charming sketch. When accused of Atheism on the ground that οὐκ ἐμυήθη μόνος ἁπάντων ταῖς Ἐλευσινίαις, he replied that if the mysteries were bad he should have denounced them, and if they were good he should have revealed them to all men ; a noble sentiment in which he agrees with Philo. Stoicism, the ancient Positivism, was always sceptical. Their prayer always begins, ' O God, if there be a God.' The hypothesis was not necessary to their system. See the *Meditations* of Marcus Aurelius, ix. 28. They did not absolutely deny the Future Life, though they were vague on the point, and admitted at most a possible immortality for a few illustrious souls ; so Tacitus, *Agricola*, 46. - Stoicism throve because, like Christianity, it is a philosophy of suffering ; it fell because, unlike Christianity, it is a philosophy of despair.

[2] There was no doubt a certain kind and degree of intercourse between the West and India by way of the Red Sea, and overland through the half Hellenised kingdom of Bactria (see Lassen, *Zur Geschichte der Griech. und*

for Magi, Thracians, Egyptians, Jews. They profess to distil an elixir from all religions, from all that is except Christianity, which they never name. Yet the Church, from which they avert their eyes as from the angel of doom, is really the prompter and guide of all their efforts. If their beloved Hellenism was to be saved, it must be by reforms borrowed from this hated rival. And so they set to work with the energy of despair to prove that so far as Christianity was true it was not new.

What was the secret, they asked, of the formidable growth of this new sect? They could not miss the external conditions. Christianity was a development of an ancient faith; it had been preached by a divine person, whose mission was accredited by miracles. It taught a pure morality, and kindled a zeal that was stronger than the fear of death. It had its sacred books, dictated or inspired by the Spirit of God. Were not similar weapons to be found in their own armoury?

If they were not to be found, at any rate they were easy to manufacture. There were books of Orpheus, Hermes, Zoroaster, Osthanes, which would serve for Gospels. If Christ was Son of God, so were Plato, Pythagoras, Apollonius. If Christ wrought signs and wonders, Pythagoras also caused a miraculous draught of fishes and fasted for forty days, Theosebius cast out devils, the death of Proclus was foreboded by a supernatural darkness so thick that the stars were seen at

Indo-skyth. Könige in Baktrien, Kabul und Indien, Bonn, 1838), but in default of accurate literary information it cannot have been of such a nature as seriously to affect the course of European thought. The merchant mariners brought back little knowledge, see Strabo, xv. 4. What knowledge there was appears to be derived chiefly from Megasthenes; see the fragments in Müller, *Frag. Hist. Graec.* ii. p. 437. But it is sufficient to refer to Bishop Lightfoot, *Colossians,* p. 151 sqq., ed. 1875.

noonday. If Christ taught in parables, so too did Pythagoras. If the Church had martyrs, philosophy could boast of Damon and Phintias, of Myllius and Timycha, and of Anaxarchus. It was Pythagoras who first proclaimed the golden rule 'thou shalt love thy friend as thyself,' and his morning and evening hymn were cited as models of devotion [1]. In all this we may surely discern the reflex of Christian ideas. On the other hand it must be conceded that the doctrinal Reserve and the severe Asceticism attributed by the Pythagoreans to their founder affected sensibly the practice of the Church.

Very little is really known of Pythagoras, and the twenty biographies which were current in the second century are little better than a mass of fiction [2]. The same thing is true of the *Life of Apollonius*, yet this extraordinary romance has a genuine historical interest of its own [3].

---

[1] The miraculous draught of fishes, Porphyry, *Vita Pyth.* 25 ; the fast of forty days, *Ibid.* 57 ; for Theosebius, see Damascius, *Vita Isidori*, 56 ; for Proclus, Marinus, *Vita Procli*, 37 ; the philosopher healed the daughter of Archiades when at the point of death, *Ibid.* 29. Porphyry also tells us that Pythagoras first taught τὸν φίλον ἄλλον ἑαυτὸν εἶναι, 33 ; that no one ever saw him weep (whereas Jesus wept), 35 ; that he taught all but his chosen disciples in parables, 37 ; and speaks of his morning and evening hymu, 40. For Damon and Phintias, Myllius and Timycha, see *Ibid.* 60, 61. Anaxarchus, *Contra Celsum*, viii. 53. The Platonists were very anxious to prove that all Christianity taught was better taught in their own books ; see Augustine's *Confessions*, vii. 9.

[2] More than a score of complete or partial biographies of Pythagoras are referred to by Clement, *Strom.* i. 14. 62 sqq., and Porphyry in the *Life*. The only documentary foundation for all this mass of literature was the brief account of their master's teaching said to have been drawn up by Lysis and Archippus, and certain ὑπομνήματα κεφαλαιώδη asserted to have been composed by anonymous individuals for their private edification and handed down from father to son ; Porph. *Vita*, 58.

[3] The Life of Apollonius has been dealt with by Gibbon, Neander, Meiners,

It was composed by the courtly sophist Philostratus at the command of Julia Domna, wife of Severus, mother of Caracalla, aunt of Elagabalus and Alexander Severus. This princess was well acquainted with the faith and practice of Christians, who abounded in the royal household. Nor was she hostilely disposed towards them. But she was deeply interested in the Syrian worship of the Sun, to which her family owed its consequence, and she presided over a coterie of lawyers and men of letters, which was ardent in the defence of Paganism. To a lady so learned and so august the settlement of ecclesiastical disputes was a tempting, and seemed an easy, task. Let paganism be set forth at its best, let it be shown that the old mythologies also carried in their bosom the germ of their own regeneration, and could provide rational satisfaction for all the cravings of heart and mind, and then the reformed Judaism would be compelled to renounce its exclusive pretensions, and fall at once into its proper place in the new Pantheon. The necessary ideas were already current in the imperial saloons. What was wanting was a Messiah, some personage, not too ancient and not too modern, who would inspire the system with the needful human interest and vitality. Such a figure was to be found in Apollonius, a sage, though some said a charlatan, of the first century, and Philostratus was

---

Buhle, Jacobs, Letronne, Baur. I have made much use of Aubé, *Histoire des Persécutions de l'Église,* to which I may refer the reader for further information. Of the three main authorities referred to by Philostratus, Damis the Ninevite is probably his own invention, Maximus of Aegae wrote an account only of such part of the life of Apollonius as was spent at Aegae, and Moeragenes (cp. *Contra Celsum,* vi. 41) appears to have treated the sage much as Lucian dealt with Alexander.

commissioned to employ his facile pen and his rhetorical tropes in the great cause.

The birth of Apollonius was announced by Proteus, the changing god of Nature, the World Spirit, or Platonic Holy Ghost. 'What is it that I shall bring forth?' asked the mother. The god replied 'Myself.' At the age of sixteen the divine child entered on his mission. He gave away his patrimony, vowed perpetual chastity, and submitted to the law of five years' silence. His flowing hair, his bare feet and white linen robe, his rigid abstinence from flesh, marked him as a Pythagorean. His speech was sententious and authoritative, his radiant beauty imposed awe upon the most profane, and he dwelt in temples, especially those of Aesculapius the Healer, like a child in his father's house. One further testimony was needed, and to obtain this he journeyed on foot to the land of the Brahmins, who dwell with the gods, and for their purity and wisdom have been dowered with miraculous gifts. Thence he returned to be the saviour of the Hellenic world. He is described as wandering from city to city, in East and farthest West, attended by disciples, who like those of Jesus are devoted yet slow of heart to understand, as possessing all languages even that of birds, as healing diseases, as raising the dead to life. The heathen priests oppose him, but the people hang upon his words. There were no bounds to his mysterious power; the downfall of Nero and Domitian, the elevation of the good emperors Vespasian and Nerva, were due to the influence of this holy man.

Hearing of the persecution of the philosophers by Domitian he resolves at once to offer himself as a volun-

tary sacrifice to the tyrant's rage, and gently reproving
the fears of his disciples makes his way to Rome.   There
he is charged with the crime that was so commonly
urged against the Christians, that of having immolated
a child in secret magic rites ; he is insulted, thrown into
chains, and mockingly invited to save himself, if he can,
by a miracle.   But the child of God suffers only so far
as is worthy of his Father.   From the very tribunal of
Domitian Apollonius vanishes away, and appears the
same day to two of his disciples, who are seated in a
grotto of the Nymphs at Puteoli, talking sadly about
their lost Master.   Damis, one of the two, cannot
believe his eyes, and is convinced by a grasp of the
hand.

   After this Apollonius renews his beneficent activity
for a time.   Where or when the end came no man knew,
but according to one story which Philostratus probably
intends his readers to accept, it befell in Crete.   The
priests of Dictynna had confined him in their temple.
But at midnight the sage arose before his gaoler's eyes,
the chains fell from his limbs, the great gate swung open,
and he went forth.   A choir of angels was heard to salute
him with the cry ' Away from earth to heaven, away ; '
and Apollonius was seen in the flesh no more.   Yet
once again after this translation he appeared to a mourn-
ing disciple, to confirm his faith and assure him of the
truth of immortality.

   It is the story of the Gospel corrected and improved.
Apollonius is what the enlightened circle of Julia Domna
thought Christ ought to have been.   His portrait is
copied with minute care from that of the Son of Mary,
but it has been adorned and dignified according to

heathen notions. It is interesting to notice the point
at which his passion ceases. To the Sun-worshipper,
as to the Gnostic, the details of the Crucifixion seemed
degrading. If Christ were what he professed to be, he
could not have fallen so low. This was, in the eyes of
Celsus also one of the gravest objections to Christianity.

We see from this curious romance precisely how far
the authorities, with whose sanction it was published,
were ready to advance on the path of concession.
Apollonius refuses to be present at a bloody sacrifice,
and contents himself with scattering incense on the altar
of the Sun. He preaches against image worship, and
against the barbarous shows of the amphitheatre. On
the other hand, he loyally accepts the Emperor as Head
of Church and State. At Alexandria, when the philosopher Euphrates exhorts Vespasian to restore the Republic, Apollonius replies that monarchy is the only
form of government suited to the times. ' For me all
constitutions are indifferent, for I depend upon God
alone, but I do not wish the flock to perish for want
of a good and faithful shepherd.' These were the terms
now offered to the Christians, and had they accepted
them they would have been protected against the hostility of the heathen priests, which Apollonius is represented as defying, a hostility just as bitterly irritated
against the new Imperial religion as against the Church.

Such was Pythagoreanism at its best. It is needless
to exhibit its lower forms, or to describe at length that
grovelling theurgy which represents with such startling
exactness the coarse impositions of modern spiritualism.
Sufficient to say that they are all there, the table-rapping,
the apparitions, the aerial music, the floating in the air,

the magic writing, the thought reading, the medium with his sham miracles. The same causes produced the same effects, and then as now the most determined enemies of the quack were, as the arch-quack Alexander complains, the Epicurean Agnostic, and the Christian [1]. But we must turn from the Pythagoreans to the more scientific family of Platonists. Of these there were two branches, the Trinitarian and the Unitarian. We may take as representatives of the first Numenius [2], of the second Celsus.

The genesis of the Platonic Trinity is one of the most perplexing questions in the history of philosophy. Like almost all the leading ideas of the time it had its roots

---

[1] ' The famous oracle which predicted the death of Valens was obtained by certain men who sat round a table and noted letters of the alphabet, which were spelt out for them by some automatic agency after a fashion which, from the description of Ammonius, we cannot precisely determine.' Mr. F. W. H. Myers, *Greek Oracles* in Hellenica, p. 467. The reference is to Ammon. Marc. xxix. 2 ; xxxi. 1. Compare for talking tables, Tertullian, *Apol.* 23 ; dancing furniture in the *Homilies*, ii. 32 ; ' levigation ' in the account of the Brahmins in Philostratus, *Vita Ap.*; magic writing in Macrobius, *Sat.* i. 23, and Lucian's *Alexander.* See also the *Philopseudes*, and Lobeck, *Aglaophamus.* ' Telepathy,' thought-reading, are very common ; there is a good story in the account of Sosipatra in the life of Aedesius ; Eunapius, p. 469, ed. Firmin-Didot. These ' miracles ' attracted the notice of the police magistrate, and ceased or were concealed after the accession of Constantine ; Eunapius, p. 461. The dislike of the famous impostor Alexander for the disciples of Christ was expressed with the most outspoken candour. He complained that ' Pontus was full of Christians and Atheists,' 25, and denounced them by solemn proclamation at the commencement of his mystic rites. ' First of all there was an expulsion of strangers, and Alexander cried aloud, " Out with the Christians," to which the congregation replied, " Out with the Epicureans ;" ' 38.

[2] For this philosopher, see Zeller, iii. p. 545 sqq. ; Vacherot, i. p. 319 sqq. ; Siegfried, p. 277; Ritter and Preller, § 525 sqq. ; and the fragments preserved by Eusebius, *Praep. Ev.*, by Porphyry and Iamblichus in Stobaeus, *Ecl.* i. 836 ; and by Nemesius, *De Nat. Hom.* ii. 69 ; iii. 129-137. There was also a school of Platonists who held by the *Timaeus* and spoke of Two Gods. It was represented in the second century by Alcinous (see below, p. 250), but is not of sufficient interest to call for separate notice.

in the manysided speculations of Plato himself, and was largely modified by influences from other quarters. In the *Republic* we have, beside or above God, the Idea of Good, the cause of truth, knowledge and existence, itself above existence in majesty and power. If God is good, his goodness must be derived from this source, and it would seem at first as if we had here two divinities, the Father and the Son. Yet again in the same dialogue God is the creator at least of the subordinate Ideas. In the *Timaeus* the Demiurge forms the World-Spirit according to the pattern of the Ideas, which appear to be independent eternal existences. We have here three conceptions, God, the Ideas, the World-Spirit. Plato has nowhere explained or harmonised this triad. This was done in some way by the author of the *Epistles*, who speaks, in obscure language and with much parade of mystery, of Three Gods. Unfortunately the authorship and date of the *Epistles* in general, and of this passage in particular, are highly uncertain [1].

[1] The passage is *Ep.* ii. p. 312 E. It is quoted by Athenagoras, *Suppl.* 23; Justin, *Apol.* i. 60; Clement, *Strom.* v. 14. 104; Eus. *Praep. Ev.* xi. 17. 20, and others. Karsten, *Commentatio Critica de Platonis quae feruntur Epistolis*, Traiecti ad Rhenum, 1864, gives a history of opinion as to the authenticity and date of the letters, and concludes that all are spurious, by different hands at different times, the Second being one of the latest and worst. Cobet, *Var. Lect.* ed. 1873, p. 235, says of *Ep.* vii, 'Platonis ipsius esse et argumentum et stilus clamant ;' and Dr. Thompson (*Gorgias*, p. xii) appears inclined to follow Mr. Grote in regarding all the Epistles as the work of Plato himself. Zeller thinks that their composition falls at latest in the second half of the first century before Christ, but regards their spuriousness as beyond all question. I find it impossible to believe that this particular passage, which, though containing a most remarkable and important doctrine, is unknown to Philo or any of the heathen Platonists before Numenius, is much earlier in date than the last-named philosopher. It is to be observed that in *Ep.* vi. 323 C, D, only two Gods are spoken of. The two Epistles represent different schools, for in Origen's time some of the Platonists believed in two Gods, some in three ; *Contra Celsum*, v. 7.

In the time of Plutarch many regarded the Ideas as thoughts existing in the divine Mind [1]. For those who held this view there were two principles, as they were called, God and the World; and the latter might be regarded as a divine Being or not. Others, like Moderatus [2] and Nicomachus, assigned to the Ideas a substantive existence outside the divine Mind. For these there were accordingly three principles. But, though the Ideas might doubtless be gathered up into one, none of the later Platonists had as yet personified the Arch-Idea, or spoken of it as a God. This was the work of Numenius, a Syrian of Apamea, whose date falls probably about the middle of the second century [3].

[1] Plutarch, *De Placitis Phil.* i. 10. 1, Σωκράτης καὶ Πλάτων χωριστὰς τῆς ὕλης οὐσίας τὰς ἰδέας ὑπολαμβάνει ἐν τοῖς νοήμασι καὶ ταῖς φαντασίαις τοῦ θεοῦ, τουτέστι τοῦ νοῦ ὑφεστώσας.

[2] See Zeller, iii. p. 514 note. Simp. *Phys.* f. 50 b, οὗτος γὰρ κατὰ τοὺς Πυθαγορείους τὸ μὲν πρῶτον ὑπὲρ τὸ εἶναι καὶ πᾶσαν οὐσίαν ὑποφαίνεται· τὸ δὲ δεύτερον ἕν, ὅπερ ἐστὶ τὸ ὄντως καὶ νοητόν, τὰ εἴδη φησὶν εἶναι· τὸ δὲ τρίτον, ὅπερ ἐστὶ ψυχικόν, μετέχειν τοῦ ἑνὸς καὶ τῶν εἰδῶν. Moderatus of Gades then (*temp.* Nero) summed up the Ideas in the one Idea of Good, but did not apparently personify them. Zeller insists that οὗτος is Plato, not Moderatus, but this makes no real difference, for Simplicius is describing what Moderatus held to be the doctrine of Plato. M. Vacherot has therefore no ground for regarding Moderatus as the first propagator of the Platonic Trinity. Nor is he better advised in attributing the same doctrine to Alcinous. For, though Alcinous speaks (chap. 10) of the οὐράνιος νοῦς and ἡ ψυχὴ τοῦ κόσμου as distinct from God, these are merely two parts of the one Anima Mundi, as appears from chap. 14, καὶ τὴν ψυχὴν τὴν ἀεὶ οὖσαν τοῦ κόσμου οὐχὶ ποιεῖ ὁ θεὸς ἀλλὰ κατακοσμεῖ· καὶ ταύτῃ λέγοιτ᾽ ἂν καὶ ποιεῖν, ἐγείρων καὶ ἐπιστρέφων πρὸς αὐτὸν τόν τε νοῦν αὐτῆς καὶ αὐτὴν ὥσπερ ἐκ κάρου τινὸς ἢ βαθέως ὕπνου· δῆλον οὖν ὅτι ζῷον ἂν εἴη ὁ κόσμος καὶ νοερόν . . . ἴσως οὐχ οἷον τε ὄντος νοῦ ἄνευ ψυχῆς ὑποστῆναι. The doctrine of Apuleius (*De Habit. Doctr. Plat.* i. p. 162 Bip. ; Ritter and Preller, § 530) appears to agree with that of Alcinous. The question is perplexed by the difficulty of the dates. All we know of Alcinous and Nicomachus is that they are older than Plotinus. But, with the exceedingly dubious exception of the Second Platonic Epistle, it may be confidently affirmed that no Trinity is to be found in any Pagan philosopher who was not well acquainted with Christianity.

[3] All we know as to his date is that he is older than Clement, who refers

That Numenius differed from all his predecessors in this article is clear from the fact that he claimed to be regarded as the regenerator of philosophy on this very account. He boasts that he has gone back to the fountain head, to Plato, Socrates and Pythagoras, to the ancient traditions of Brahmins, Magi, Egyptians and Jews, and has restored to the schools the forgotten doctrine of Three Gods¹. Of these the first is Mind, simple and changeless, good and wise². Being changeless he cannot create, hence there is derived from him a second God, the Creator³. The Son is no longer simple,

to him by name and borrows from him not only the well-known comparison of Truth to the body of Pentheus (above, p. 48), but probably that also of the Pilot, and the phrase about the Son of God never leaving his περιωπή; cp. Strom. vii. 2. 5; Eus. *Praep. Ev.* xi. 18. 10, 24. Apamea was one of the centres of Neo-Platonism. There lived Amelius, who quoted the Gospel of St. John in support of the doctrine of the Logos, Eus. *Praep. Ev.* xi. 19, and his adopted son Hostilianus Hesychius; Porphyry, *Vita Plotini*, 2, 3. Numenius was a foolish, gossiping man; see the long and absurd story about Lacydes, Eus. *Praep. Ev.* xiv. 7.

¹ Eus. *Praep. Ev.* xiv. 5. 5, αἴτιον δὲ ὅτι, τρεῖς θεοὺς τιθεμένου Σωκράτους καὶ φιλοσοφοῦντος αὐτοῖς ἐν τοῖς προσήκουσιν ἑκάστῳ ῥυθμοῖς, οἱ διακούσαντες τοῦτο μὲν ἠγνόουν, κ.τ.λ. Numenius is no doubt referring to the Second Platonic Epistle, the author of which not only makes Plato ascribe his Trinity to Socrates, but actually affirm that he himself had never written upon theological questions at all; 314 C, διὰ ταῦτα οὐδὲν πώποτ᾽ ἐγὼ περὶ τούτων γέγραφα, οὐδ᾽ ἐστι σύγγραμμα Πλάτωνος οὐδὲν οὐδ᾽ ἔσται, τὰ δὲ νῦν λεγόμενα Σωκράτους ἐστι καλοῦ καὶ νέου γεγονότος. I understand the author to mean not that Plato did not write the dialogues but that they are what they profess to be, mere verbatim reports of the teaching of Socrates.

² For the attributes of the Supreme God, see Eus. *Praep. Ev.* xi. 22. 3 sqq., and xi. 10. It will be observed that the Deity of Numenius still possesses moral and intellectual qualities. Richter thinks that his doctrine of the Absolute did not differ from that of Clement or Plotinus, *Neu-Platonische Studien*, p. 60; but see *Praep. Ev.* xi. 18. 20, where even 'movement' is attributed in some sense to the Supreme. The doctrine of Ecstasy, in a form not unlike the self-induced mesmerism of the Quietists, is to be found in the extract from the περὶ τἀγαθοῦ given by Eus. *Praep. Ev.* xi. 22. 1.

³ Zeller, iii. 547, note, thinks that Numenius derived his doctrine of the Son-Creator from the Gnostics. This is quite impossible, for there is no trace of hostility between the two Deities.

like the Father, but twofold. ' Condescending to Matter, which is multiple, he gives to it unity, but is himself divided.' Part of him is incorporated in the things that he has made, becomes in fact the World Spirit; part hovers over the world as its guide, 'riding on Matter as a pilot on his ship,' and maintaining it in harmony with the will of God. ' He touches the sensible and cares for it, drawing it up to his own nature, because he yearns for it[1].' Hence, as Proclus says, the Trinity of Numenius consists of the Father, the Creator, and the World.

Numenius is but repeating the fashionable language of his school when he talks of Brahmins, Magi and Egyptians. The real source of his doctrine is undoubtedly Jewish. We learn that he allegorised the Old Testament with some skill and success, and, when he called Plato an Attic Moses, he must have had Philo in his mind. But there is an element in his doctrine which is not Philonic. He speaks of Matter not as the cause of evil, but as something which the Son loves and cares for, so much so that in a peculiar sense he condescends to take its nature upon him. And in strict conformity with this he regarded sin as the result of a conflict not between Mind and Matter, but between the higher and lower spirit of man. This is the language of St. Paul; and, when we consider that he was well ac-

---

[1] Eus. *Praep. Ev.* xi. 18. 1, 24. It will be observed that even in Numenius the doctrine of the Trinity has not yet attained to clearness and consistency. Though he speaks of Three Gods, the Son is still in part the same as the Anima Mundi : ὁ θεὸς μέντοι ὁ δεύτερος καὶ τρίτος ἐστὶν εἷς· συμφερόμενος δὲ τῇ ὕλῃ δυάδι οὔσῃ, ἑνοῖ μὲν αὐτήν, σχίζεται δὲ ὑπ' αὐτῆς, ἐπιθυμητικὸν ἦθος ἐχούσης καὶ ῥεούσης. Matter is a dyad, I presume, because it has a ψυχή, that is θυμός and ἐπιθυμία, but no νοῦς till this regulative unifying principle is infused into it by union with the Son. Numenius then has Three Gods but not Three Hypostases. Plotinus speaks of τρεῖς ὑποστάσεις, but not till after this phrase was current among Christians.

quainted with the Gospels and possibly with the Epistles, it seems reasonable to conclude that in this peculiar view, on which he is in direct and violent contradiction with Philo and the heathen Platonists in a body, he is reflecting the ideas proper to Christianity [1]. The same thing is, I believe, true of his doctrine of the Trinity, which marks a distinct advance on the teaching of Philo, and an advance in the direction of the Church.

Numenius may not unfairly be regarded as the founder of Neo-Platonism, with the reservation already pointed out in favour of Clement [2]. But I should be carried far beyond my limits, if I were to attempt to define his relation to the great Plotinus. I must turn away from this tempting subject to the system of Unitarian Platonism as it is depicted in the extant fragments of Celsus [3].

[1] *Contra Celsum*, i. 15; iv. 51. The story of Jannes and Jambres he may have learned either from 2 Tim. iii. 8 or from pseudo-Jonathan; see Siegfried. In the latter case he must have had a very remarkable acquaintance with Rabbinical literature, and we can hardly avoid the suspicion that he was a Jew. For his doctrine of Evil as arising out of the strife between the two souls of man, see Zeller. No true Greek would have explained the theory of Ideas in so materialistic a way as Numenius. God, the Good, is the Idea of the Son, whom He consequently creates. Just so every sensible Kind has its Idea, and the concrete Man, Ox, Horse, are created by the Ideal Man, Ox, Horse; *Praep. Ev.* xi. 22. 9. This is the view also of Philo and Clement. I suspect that the motive of Numenius' treatise Περὶ Τόπου was given by Philo, in whose terminology Place is another name for the Son. Of the same school and about the same date are Cronius and Harpocration, who are known to us only by name.

[2] Porphyry (*Vita Plotini*, 21) would not admit that Plotinus was indebted to Numenius. Nevertheless there was a historical connection between the two teachers. Numenius was, as Longinus pronounced, far inferior in ἀκρίβεια to Amelius and Plotinus, but, as Zeller says, he pointed out the way for them.

[3] The author of the Ἀληθὴς Λόγος may or may not have been the Celsus to whom Lucian addressed his exposure of the tricks of Alexander of Abo-

Celsus wrote his *True Word against the Christians* amid the civil troubles that clouded the latter days of M. Aurelius. Half a century afterwards the treatise fell into the hands of Ambrosius, who sent it to Origen, with a request that he would reply to it. Origen was reluctant to undertake the task, thinking that the one effective answer to all opponents lay in the actual triumph of the Gospel. But as soon as he began to read the book he perceived the gravity of the attack, and threw himself heart and soul into the controversy. Like most of Origen's work the *Contra Celsum* is marred by the fiery impetuosity of its author. He alters and enlarges the plan of his defence. With such haste does he pour out the eager flood of dictation, following and combating his antagonist sentence by sentence, that he often does not catch the point of an argument till he has wandered round it for many a page, and even to

noteichos. The name was not uncommon. Nor perhaps is it necessary to suppose that the friend of Lucian was an Epicurean, though that is certainly the natural inference from the words τὸ πλέον δέ, ὅπερ καὶ σοὶ ἥδιον, Ἐπικούρῳ τιμωρῶν, ἀνδρὶ ὡς ἀληθῶς ἱερῷ καὶ θεσπεσίῳ τὴν φύσιν, *Alexander, ad fin.* The author of the *True Word* was undoubtedly a Platonist, though Origen charges him with masking atheism under the garb of Platonism, *Contra Celsum,* i. 8; ii. 13; iii. 35. 80; iv. 4. 54; v. 3. He seems to have jumped at this conclusion from the way in which Celsus spoke of the miracles of Jesus, admitting some of them to be true but ascribing them to vulgar magic; see *Contra Celsum,* i. 68, ὁρᾷς ὡς διὰ τούτων οἱονεὶ παραδέχεται μαγείαν εἶναι· οὐκ οἶδα εἰ ὁ αὐτὸς ὢν τῷ γράψαντι κατὰ μαγείας βιβλία πλείονα. Now the Celsus who was Lucian's friend had written κατὰ μάγων, *Alex.* 21. Origen no doubt identified the two, and took it for granted that Lucian's friend was an Epicurean. Keim shows good reason for supposing that he was right in the first inference and wrong in the second. The date of the *True Word* is about 178. Nearly the whole work is found embedded in the reply of Origen. The fragments have been collected, translated, and commented on by several hands, especially by Theodor Keim, *Celsus' Wahres Wort,* Zürich, 1873, and with less erudition but great clearness and an interesting criticism by B. Aubé in the *Histoire des Persécutions de l'Église,* Paris, 1878.

the last he does not clearly realise that Celsus was not an Epicurean but a Platonist.

Celsus is scarcely to be called a philosopher, for he is deficient in system, penetration and sympathy. But he is a favourable specimen of the highly cultivated man of the world, keen, positive and logical, sceptical and mocking, yet not without genuine moral convictions, a student of the science of religion, an enlightened advocate of the reformed Paganism. He was well armed for his task, for he had studied the four Gospels and the books of Genesis and Exodus, possessed some knowledge of the Prophets and Epistles, and had read more or less of Gnostic and Jewish, or Jewish-Christian, literature [1]. Besides he had travelled widely, and sought conversation with religious professors of every shade, especially with Christians. He had gained, as he thought, full knowledge of his subject before he took up the pen. Nor is he consciously unjust. He pours out his scorn with perfect impartiality upon the begging priests, and mountebanks, and gross superstitions of the popular religions. He does not repeat the old and not yet extinct slanders against the Church, and pays a grudging respect to the purity of Christian morals. Yet

---

[1] According to Tischendorf and Volkmar, Celsus used all the canonical and some uncanonical Gospels; according to Meyer and Zeller, the Synoptics but not John; according to Redepenning and Mosheim, no canonical Gospel at all but Jewish and Apocryphal documents. The question is discussed by Keim, p. 219 sqq., who concludes that Celsus was well acquainted with all four canonical Gospels, that he makes most use of that of Matthew, that the general colouring of the Christology known to him is Johannine, and that there is no certain trace of his employment of any apocryphal Gospel. Of the Pauline Epistles Keim thinks he knew only a few phrases picked up in conversation, and his acquaintance with Old Testament prophecy is general and vague. See also Dr. Westcott, *On the Canon*, p. 404.

when he charges the Christians with sorcery, want of
patriotism and disloyalty, when he asserts with emphasis
that every church is an illicit college, he is deliberately
giving a new edge to the most deadly of all the accusations under which the Christians suffered[1]. Well
did he know the fatal significance of these cruel in-
sinuations.

We need not follow in detail his criticism of the
Scriptures. He treats the Gospel from the point of

[1] Their churches are illicit colleges, i. 1. 7; the charge of magic is
made, i. 6. 68; vi. 39; that of want of patriotism, faction, viii. 2. 21.
The law against illicit clubs or colleges was severe and bore very hard
on the Christians. See the exceedingly interesting treatise of Mommsen, *De
Collegiis et Sodaliciis Romanorum*, Kiliae, 1843. A Senatus Consultum
passed probably under Augustus, while recognising the ancient collegia
opificum, rendered all other clubs except burial societies illegal. They
were allowed to meet once a month for business purposes, when the subscrip-
tion (the 'stips menstrua') was collected, but they had other unrestricted
meetings for the purpose of offering sacrifice in the temple of the patron God
and feasting together. The qualified toleration of benefit societies by the
Sctum of Augustus appears to have been confined to Rome, and was extended
to Italy and the Provinces by Severus (*Digest* xlvii. 22). Before this time
clubs of all kinds and denominations appear to have been illegal in Italy and
the Provinces without special authorisation from the Emperor, and this was
very grudgingly conferred (see the Rescript of Trajan in Pliny, *Ep.* x. 42, 43;
Tac. *Ann.* xiv. 17). The language of Tertullian, *Apol.* 39, shows how
easily the Christian Churches could be brought under this law. He does not
deny that each Church is a collegium; all he aims at proving is that its
objects are good, and its management exemplary. The very phrases that
are used of colleges occur in his description, and no doubt are used purposely—
'coimus in coetum—si quod *arcae* genus est,' the regular word for the treasure
chest of a collegium—'modicam unusquisque stipem menstrua die vel quum
velit et si modo velit et si modo possit apponit'—the money was applied
'egenis alendis *humandisque.*' They had coenae also, but how different
from those of the colleges! He concludes, 'quum probi quum boni
coeunt, quum casti congregantur, non est *factio* dicenda sed *curia.*' 'Curia' is
apparently equivalent to 'collegium licitum,' as 'factio' to 'collegium illicitum.'
The charge of factiousness, want of patriotism, brought the Christian under
the law of Maiestas, and magic was a capital crime. The subject of the
laws under which Christians suffered has been investigated by M. E. Le Blant,
Note sur les bases juridiques des poursuites dirigées contre les Martyrs,
Acad. des Inscr. Nouvelle Série, vol. 2 (1866), p. 358. It seems probable

view of the Jew, the Law from that of an educated Greek. This enabled him to insist upon the factious nature of the new faith, the Christians being renegade Jews as the Jews themselves were renegade Egyptians; and at the same time to set in the strongest and most repulsive light whatever had been or could be urged against their documents. He was under no inherited restraint, and whatever his biting wit could find to say he said. But what we are concerned with is the more serious part of his work, his own belief, his intellectual relation towards Christianity, his view of the general religious position of the time.

In the creed of Celsus there is one supreme God. He is good, beautiful and happy, but has no movement, attribute or name. He created all reasonable immortal beings, the soul of man and the lower deities, and the lower deities created the world. His work is perfect, so

that there never was any law against Christianity as such. But there were several Rescripts directing how the laws in point were to be enforced. Of these the most important were that of Trajan forbidding anonymous accusations, that of Hadrian ordering that Christians should not be condemned except for definite offences against the laws, and another or others unknown directing that when convicted they should be put to death by decapitation, and that torture should only be applied in the usual way to force confession. See Tertullian, *Ad Scapulam*, 4: Quid enim amplius tibi mandatur quam *nocentes* confessos damnare, negantes autem ad tormenta revocare . . . . . *sine accusatore* negans se auditurum hominem secundum mandata. . . . . Nam et nunc a praeside Legionis et a praeside Mauritaniae vexatur hoc nomen, sed *gladio tenus* sicut et a primordio mandatum est animadverti in huiusmodi. The same treatise shows how little these wise restrictions were regarded by many of the governors. Severus is said to have gone further. Iudaeos fieri sub grandi poena vetuit: idem etiam de Christianis sanxit; Spartian, *Vita Severi*, 17. That he made sharp enactments against conversion to Judaism seems to be certain; see Julius Paullus, *Sent.* v. 22. 3, in Huschke, *Jurisp. Antejust.*; the incident recorded in Spartian's *Life of Caracalla*, chap. i.; and Origen, *Contra Celsum*, ii. 13. But it is almost certain from Tertullian, *Apòl.* 5 and *Ad Scap.*, that he made no new and special enactment against Christianity.

that He never needs to interfere for its correction or improvement. And being absolutely just and good, He is untouched by pity. Man's relation to Him may alter, but His relation to man must ever be the same[1]. It is still the old conception of God as pure Intelligence. God is the supreme ruler of Nature, whose laws are the expression of His reason, and in this sense He may be considered as exercising a general providence. But something more than this was demanded by the conscience of the times in which Celsus lived. To satisfy this need he inserts between God and the world the hierarchy of the inferior gods or Demons. These subordinate powers fill a very remarkable place in all the Platonic systems of the time. They change philosophy into religion, they are the mediators between God and man, and, what is even still more important, they form the connecting link between the old and the reformed Paganism.

It is not indeed a novel conception, for the Demons are as old as the poems of Hesiod, and appear in the *Timaeus* and the *Symposium*. But in the modern Platonists, Plutarch, Maximus Tyrius, or Celsus, they are no longer a subordinate accidental feature. Like the Powers of Philo, they are the real creators of all except the soul of man. Some of them are demons in the lowest sense of the word, spirits of evil banished

---

[1] On this point it is worthy of notice that Origen does not contradict Celsus : μετὰ ταῦτα δ' ἑαυτῷ λαμβάνει τὸ μὴ διδόμενον ὑπὸ τῶν λογικώτερον πιστευόντων, τάχα ὑπό τινων ἀνοήτων νομιζόμενον, ὡς ἄρα ὁμοίως τοῖς οἴκτῳ δουλεύουσι δουλεύσας, οἴκτῳ τῶν οἰκτιζομένων ὁ θεὸς τοὺς κακοὺς κουφίζει, καὶ μηδὲν τοιοῦτο δρῶντας τοὺς ἀγαθοὺς ἀπορρίπτει· ὅπερ ἐστὶν ἀδικώτατον, iii. 71. But God, in the view of Celsus, is still moral and intelligent, though He has no name. For He knows what goes on upon earth ; iv. 3.

from the presence of God. But for the most part they are of mixed nature, some almost wholly divine, some little better than man. They exercise rule over special provinces of Nature, sending the lightning and the rain; they are the 'invisible farmers,' who make the crops to grow and the cattle to increase. They are the 'lords of the prison-house,' rulers of the darkness of this world in which the fallen spirit of man is confined for its purification. They are the gods of the old national mythologies, whom in times past men ignorantly worshipped as the Supreme. They give oracles, prophecies, revelations, send and cure diseases, work miracles. They claim honour and service from man, the lower delighting in the steam and blood of sacrifices, the higher accepting no offering but that of a pure and holy spirit. Thus the Platonist found still a way to believe in the personal loving care of God for His creatures. He who denies the Demons, says Plutarch, denies providence, and breaks the chain that unites the world to the throne of God[1].

[1] Plutarch, *De defectu Orac.* 13. Special Providence and Mediation were the two great religious needs supplied by the doctrine of Demons. Both are very clearly brought out by Maximus Tyrius. For the latter, see *Oration* xv. Without the Demons no relation could exist between God and man. Δύο γὰρ πραγμάτων κεχωρισμένων τῇ φύσει χωρισθήσεται καὶ ἡ ἐπιμιξία παντάπασιν, ἐὰν μή τις κοινὸς ὅρος ἀμφότερα ὑποδέξηται. It is necessary then that there should be a class of beings partaking of both natures, ἢ ἀπαθὲς θνητὸν ἢ ἀθάνατον ἐμπαθές. For the former see xvii. 12, where there is an elaborate picture of the world as the palace of God. 'There is the great King tranquil as Law, bestowing upon his subjects the salvation that exists in him. There are the partners of his rule, many visible gods, many invisible. Some wait at his threshold, as it were his ushers (εἰσαγγελεῖς); some are kinsmen of the king, who share his table and his hearth; some are ministers again of these, and some are still lower in degree. Thou seest the hierarchy and graduation of rule which stretches down from God to earth.' Maximus distinguishes Two Lives in almost exactly the same way as Philo. The lower is the knowledge of God in His works. For God is beautiful, and all

There are so many coincidences between the Pagan doctrine of the Demons and the Christian doctrine of Angels and demons, that we are justified in assuming a close historical connection between the two. But the relation of these discrowned gods to the life of the soul is Philonic or Gnostic rather than Christian. They are the Gods of the imperfect, the saviours of those who are capable of virtue but not of knowledge. Here again we have the theory of the Two Lives, but they are separated by an impassable gulf. All but the gifted few are debarred by the law of Nature from the higher.

This brings us to the first cardinal difference between Celsus and Origen. How can God be known? 'It is hard to find Him out,' replied the heathen, 'impossible to reveal Him to all.' The knowledge of God cannot be conveyed in words, but from much meditation and close personal converse with the wise a spark is kindled in the soul. Philosophy can give us 'some conception,' which the mind of the elect must develope for itself. The Christian replied, ' God is known to us, as far as He can be known, in the Incarnate Christ.'

that is beautiful will guide us to Him, the beauty of the human frame, of a flowering mead, of a fair-flowing river, of the sea and sky and the gods in the sky, that is the stars. 'If these are enough for thee, thou hast seen God.' But for higher minds there is higher knowledge. To them (xvi. 7) the sensible suggests the suprasensual; as the song of Demodocus suggested to Odysseus the siege of Troy, as the lyre suggests the beloved one who played on it, so the mind mounts up from lower to higher by a process resembling the thrill which vibrates through the slender shaft of a lance when you grasp the butt. The same ideas will be found in Plutarch, and indeed in Plato, *Symposium*, 202 E. But in Maximus and Celsus they have grown immensely in relative importance, and the reason for this is to be found no doubt in the conflict with Christianity. The doctrine of the Demons properly understood would, it was hoped, make the belief in Christ unnecessary.

This was the great rock of offence. Celsus flung
himself with all his force against the doctrine of the
Incarnation. He resisted it on *a priori* grounds. Why
should God come down to earth? Does He not already
know what is happening there, and can He not remedy
what is amiss without descending in person? How can
He forsake His proper abode, when, if you make the
least change in the order of Nature, all must go to
wreck? God is perfectly good, beautiful, happy; if He
descends into the world in human shape, He must
change, and suffer in the change an unutterable degradation. And why should He need like a bad workman
to correct what He has once made? Or if at all, why
not till after the lapse of so many ages, waking out of
sleep, as it were, and proceeding in unseemly haste to
amend the consequences of His long neglect?

The answer to all this from the Christian point of
view was easy. Celsus does not realise, as Origen with
truth insists, either the nature of God, or the value of
the human soul, or the necessary operation of its freedom. No Christian asserted that God 'came down,'
in such a sense as that His throne in heaven should be
left untenanted. Nor was it His own work that needed
correction, but the work of man. Nor was the resolve
a late and sudden one, for law-giver, priest, and prophet
had borne their part in the progressive revelation, and
the birth of Christ is but the crown of a long development[1]. Nor was God degraded by taking upon Him
the form of a servant. For He who knew no sin knew

---

[1] *Contra Celsum,* iv. 4. 7. But in the next chapter Origen goes on to say,
ἔχει δέ τι ὁ περὶ τούτων λόγος μυστικώτερον καὶ βαθύτερον. The full explanation, that is to say, depends on the doctrine of pre-existence and the varying
needs of purification entailed by the ante-natal sin.

no shame. But here the Christian and the heathen move in different planes, and their minds do not touch. To the one moral evil is the only pollution; to the other mere contact with matter is, in the case of God, inconceivable. Even the Christian is here betrayed into weakness by mental associations which he could not wholly shake off. Christ came 'out of condescension to those who cannot look upon the dazzling radiance of the Godhead; He becomes Man till he that has received Him in this guise, being little by little lifted up by the Word, is able to contemplate His proper shape [1].' Origen held, and it is, as we have seen, one of his characteristic thoughts, that the Incarnation was a weakening and obscuring of the divine glory. It is not with him the highest and profoundest revelation of the divine love.

In the historical argument of Celsus again we see this Platonic hatred of matter come out in strong relief. Jesus, he affirmed, making use of Jewish fables still to be found in the Talmud, was an impostor, who suffered the death he deserved. He was not the promised Messiah, for the Prophets spoke only of a King and Conqueror. He was not a Son of God, for then His mother would have been a queen like Semele or Andromeda. His person would have been beautiful; His flesh would not have been liable to pain; He would have vanished from the Cross, and appeared again in majesty to confound His enemies. His miracles, allowing them genuine, prove nothing, as He Himself admitted. His

[1] *Contra Celsum,* iv. 15. 19. In the latter passage we read the singular words, καὶ γὰρ οὐκ ἄτοπόν ἐστι τὸν ἰώμενον φίλους νοσοῦντας ἰάσασθαι τὸ φίλον τῶν ἀνθρώπων γένος τοῖς τοιοῖσδε οἷς οὐκ ἄν τις χρήσαιτο προηγουμένως ἀλλ' ἐκ περιστάσεως. The language is to be explained by Origen's view of the Epinoiai; see Lecture v.

Resurrection rests upon the testimony of 'a hysterical woman [1].' Above all He failed, for the Jews who were yearning for their Saviour rejected Him, and His own disciples abandoned and denied Him.

It did not occur to this singularly able man that, when the assigned cause is so inadequate to the manifest result, there must be some flaw in the calculation. Celsus dashes against the facts in passionate derision. 'He has failed,' he cries, 'and yet you believe Him.' The Christian's rejoinder was triumphant. He had but to point to the churches, springing up on all sides like grass after rain, and answer, ' He has not failed—because we believe Him.' This is in fact the chief of the external supports on which the faith of Origen reposed. He believed Scripture to be the Word of God, yet as we have seen he did not insist upon its literal truth. He believed in Miracles, and held that the power of working them was still bestowed upon the Church. Yet he confesses that, however powerful these signs and wonders had once been in calling forth faith, they had come to be regarded as myths, and themselves needed proof [2].

---

[1] Jesus warned His disciples that false Christs would work miracles; ii. 48. 49. 54. As pointed out above, Celsus did not wholly deny the miracles of Jesus, though he denied their significance. The ' hysterical woman ' is the Magdalene. See ii. 55, τίς τοῦτο εἶδε ; Γυνὴ πάροιστρος, ὡς φάτε, καὶ εἴ τις ἄλλος τῶν ἐκ τῆς αὐτῆς γοητείας, ἤτοι κατά τινα διάθεσιν ὀνειρώξας (the theory of Strauss) ἢ κατὰ τὴν αὐτοῦ βούλησιν δόξῃ πεπλανημένῃ φαντασιωθείς, ὅπερ δ' μυρίοις συμβέβηκεν· ἤ, ὅπερ μᾶλλον, ἐκπλῆξαι τοὺς λοιποὺς τῇ τερατείᾳ ταύτῃ θελήσας καὶ διὰ τοῦ τοιούτου ψεύσματος ἀφορμὴν ἄλλοις ἀγύρταις παρασχεῖν (the theory of deliberate imposition).

[2] *In Joan.* ii. 28 (Lom. i. 152), καὶ τοῦτο δὲ ἐπισκεπτέον, ὅτι αἱ μὲν τεράστιοι δυνάμεις τοὺς κατὰ τὸν χρόνον τοῦ Χριστοῦ γενομένους προκαλεῖσθαι ἐπὶ τὸ πιστεύειν ἐδύναντο· οὐκ ἔσωζον δὲ τὸ ἐμφατικὸν μετὰ χρόνους πλείονας, ἤδη καὶ μῦθοι εἶναι ὑπονοηθεῖσαι. Some miracles Origen doubted or explained away; the carrying of Christ up into a mountain by the Tempter he thought impossible, and (*Cels.* ii. 48) the daughter of the Ruler of the

The argument from the fulfilment of prophecy he considered as among the greatest of all the evidences [1]. But the one crowning proof of the truth of the Gospel, the miracle of all miracles, was the Christian life and the Christian society. To this he recurs again and again. He who questioned all things could doubt of nothing, when he fixed his eyes on the figure of the Church advancing swiftly onwards with the star of victory on her brow [2].

Other questions mooted in this famous debate, concerning the estate and destiny of man, are of secondary importance. Evil, Celsus held, was caused by the resistance of Matter to the moulding hand of God. Now, as the quantity of Matter is fixed and its resist-

Synagogue perhaps only slept. But the latter is accepted as a real instance of raising the dead, *In Galatas*. (Lom. v. 269), where it is said that Christ's miracles were historically true, and continue in the Church in a spiritual sense. *In Jerem.* Hom. iv. 3, the power of miracles has been lost by the Church because of her corruption. But this refers only to the greater miracles, and indeed only with some limitation even to these ; see *Contra Celsum*, ii. 8, ἴχνη ἐπὶ ποσὸν παρὰ Χριστιανοῖς εὑρίσκεται, καὶ τινά γε μείζονα, καὶ εἰ πιστοί ἐσμεν λέγοντες, ἑωράκαμεν καὶ ἡμεῖς. The ἴχνη are Exorcism, Healing, Prophecy, *Ibid.* i. 46. But the disciples of Jesus work even greater miracles in opening the eyes of the spiritually blind, *Ibid.* ii. 48. Miracles prove the divinity of Christ, and are themselves proved by prophecy, *Ibid.* viii. 9. The spread of Christianity was at first due to Miracles, *Ibid.* viii. 47. Chrysippus, Plutarch, Numenius tell of Pagan miracles, which even Celsus believed in. Why then are Christian miracles false? Care and study are requisite to distinguish true miracles from imposture, *Ibid.* v. 57. Miracles are ὑπὲρ φύσιν, not παρὰ φύσιν, *Ibid.* v. 23 ; see also the following chapter. Another great evidence was to be found in the voluntary sufferings of the Apostles, *Ibid.* i. 31 ; iii. 23.

[1] Prophecy is more important than Miracles, *In Joan.* ii. 28 ; cp. *In Joan.* xxxii. 9, *ad fin.* ; *Contra Celsum*, vi. 10 ; viii. 48.

[2] *Contra Celsum*, iii. 9 ; iv. 32 ; vii. 26 ; *In Cant. Cant.* iii. (Lom. xv. 43). There are many other passages of the same tenor. If we may rely upon *In Lucam*, Hom. vi. (Lom. v. 106), Christianity had already been preached in Britain, but this appears to be contradicted by the passage quoted above, p. 207. In *Contra Celsum*, iii. 65, Origen tells us that the converts were not as a rule drawn from the vicious classes.

ance is uniform, it follows that the quantity of Evil also
is capable neither of increase nor of diminution. Man
again, he taught, was by no means the chief object of
divine care, many of the animals being equal, or even
superior, to him in wisdom and in piety [1]. These two
ideas caused in him a cynical scorn of all endeavours to
raise the vulgar masses from their degradation, and here
again, surely from no truly philosophic reason, he was in
fierce antagonism to the active, and oftentimes doubtless
ignorant, Christian missionaries. His doctrine of a Future
Life was that of his school. The main point at issue
here was the belief in the Resurrection of the Body.
To the Platonist this was revolting. 'They say,' he
exclaims, 'that everything is possible to God. But
God cannot do what is shameful, and will not do
what is unnatural [2].' His arguments are levelled

[1] For the fixed quantity of Evil, see iv. 62. 69. 99; for its connection
with Matter, iv. 65; viii. 55. Keim maintains that Celsus departs from
Socrates and Plato in denying that God made the world for man any more
than for brutes; that man as regards his body is no better than the brutes;
that God is no more angry with man than with apes or flies, and that many
of the animals are better than man, iv. 52–99. It must be allowed that his
language on the subject of Evil is rather Stoic than Platonic. But all that
he says is a natural consequence of the doctrines of the independence of
Matter and of Metempsychosis. The Cynics, who were indefatigable street
preachers (and in other respects also bore a striking resemblance to the
Mendicant Friars), were in this honourably distinguished from their Stoic
cousins. See *Contra Celsum*, iii. 50. It was the Cynic Demonax who
advised the Athenians to destroy the altar of Pity if they persisted in their
plan of introducing gladiatorial shows into the city; Lucian, *Demonax*, 57.
To this love of souls rather than to the reason assigned by Augustine we
may ascribe the singular fact that Cynicism outlived Stoicism. See Aug.
Contra Academ. iii. 19: Nunc philosophos non fere vidimus nisi aut Cynicos
aut Peripateticos aut Platonicos. Et Cynicos quidem, quia eos vitae quaedam
delectat libertas atque licentia.

[2] The hope of the Resurrection is σκωλήκων ἐλπίς, v. 14; the Christians
are δειλὸν καὶ φιλοσώματον γένος, vii. 36, and παντελῶς τῇ σαρκὶ ἐνδεδεμένοι,
vii. 42. In vii. 36 again he says, οὐκ ἀνθρώπου μὲν οὐδὲ τῆς ψυχῆς ἀλλὰ
τῆς σαρκὸς ἡ φωνή. 'For this use of the word "flesh" by Stoics and

against the cruder forms of the belief, and we have
already seen what was Origen's reply.

Celsus was a bitter foe to Christianity, but he was
also a man of far-sighted practical vision, and his hostility
had its limits. He forgot philosophy, and even justice,
in his anger against these wilful sectaries, whose growth
threatened destruction to temple and school. But he
was the first of the governing classes who clearly discerned the rift that was beginning to divide society, and
he viewed with alarm the danger that might arise from
a large, intelligent, ill-used and alienated class, at a time
when the state was called upon to struggle for its existence against the barbarians of the Danube. And so
while Marcus Aurelius was lamenting in neatly turned
phrases the 'dogged obstinacy' of the martyrs of Vienna,
whom he had himself condemned to death on the most
ridiculous accusations, this unknown scholar was asking
whether it was already too late to heal the breach.

Changing his tone of angry mockery for one of stern
but not unfriendly remonstrance, he presses the Christians to consider whether after all it is impossible to
serve Two Masters. Every good citizen ought to respect
the worship of his fathers. And God gave to the Demons
the honour which they claimed. Why then should the
Christian refuse to eat at the Demons' table? They
give us corn and wine and the very air we breathe; we
must either submit to their benefits or quit the world

Platonists cp. Seneca, *Ep.* 65 ; *Consol. ad Mar.* 24 ; Persius, ii. 62 (pulpa).'
Zeller, *Theol. Jahrb.* 1852, pp. 293 sqq. It may perhaps be doubted whether
this word was borrowed from the Christian vocabulary. But this doubt
will hardly apply to the word 'angel.' Maximus Tyrius, xvii. 9, ὁ ἐξ
'Ακαδημίας ἡμῖν ἄγγελος of Plato. I have seen also the phrase 'angelic life,'
but cannot now recover the reference.

altogether. All that is really important in Christianity is the belief in the immortality of the soul, in the future blessedness of the good, the eternal punishment of the wicked. Better suffer any torments than deny this faith [1]. But why not swear by the Emperor, the dispenser of all temporal blessings, as God of all spiritual? Why not sing a paean to the bright Sun or Athena, and at any rate kiss the hand to those lower deities who can do us harm if neglected [2]? It cannot be supposed that the great Roman Empire will abandon its tried and ancient faith for a barbarous novelty. 'He who thinks this knows nothing [3].' If there is to be unity the Church must make concessions, and Christ must accept a place, as in the Lararium of Alexander Severus, side by side with Apollonius and the chief gods of Rome.

And so Celsus concludes with an almost pathetic exhortation to the injured Christians to have pity on their country, to rally round Caesar's eagles against the common foe, and not to refuse to serve in public offices, but in this way also to give their support to the laws and piety. The conclusion of the *True Word* is creditable both to the sagacity and to the temper of its author. But, when the persecutor thus found his weapons breaking in his grasp, and stooped to appeal to the generosity of his victim, it is evident that the battle was already lost.

---

[1] *Contra Celsum*, viii. 53. 66.

[2] Δεξιοῦσθαι, not θρησκεύειν or θεραπεύειν or δουλεύειν, is all the observance Celsus claims for those inferior demons, like the Egyptian Decani, whose influence was chiefly malefic ; viii. 58. Yet what a concession is this ! Gibbon might well have reckoned amongst the causes of the triumph of Christianity the immorality and absurdity of the best alternative that the best Pagans could offer. On kissing the hand to idols, see Dr. Holden's note to Minucius Felix, *Octavius*, 2.

[3] *Contra Celsum*, viii. 72.

'Did Celsus know,' says Origen in one place[1], 'what to think of the immortal soul, its nature, its destiny, he would not mock at the Incarnation which is due to the great love of God for man.' There is justice in this reproach as regards Celsus, but it is hardly applicable to the Platonists generally. The real root of the difficulty lay in their sharp antithesis of Form as good to Matter as evil. Had Philo ever considered the question, he must have rejected Christ on the same grounds as Celsus, though assuredly without denying, as Celsus did, the moral beauty of the Saviour's life. Connected with the abhorrence of Matter was the disapproval of all emotion, which was regarded as inseparably linked with the perishable body. Hence the ancient world, with all its noble and intelligent devotion to truth and justice and the masculine virtues generally, was unable to perceive that the one cure for moral evil is Love, and that, as Love is necessarily self-sacrificing, so vicarious suffering is the deepest and most universal law of Ethics. This was then, as it is now, the leading difference between the 'wisdom of the world' and the preaching of the Cross. Even the Church hardly realised the full meaning of the truth of which she was the custodian. But the truth was given to her not in a doctrine, nor in a tradition, but in a life. The love of Jesus, like the power of light, may be wrongly analysed, but its width and its potency are none the less for our failure to explain them. It is one of the powers of Nature; it is enough that it is there.

[1] *Contra Celsum*, iv. 17.

LECTURE VIII.

*Blame not before thou hast examined the truth : understand first
and then rebuke.*—ECCLESIASTICUS xi. 7.

WE have traced in the previous Lectures the rise of
the Eclectic Alexandrine Platonism and the mode of
its application to Christian life and doctrine. In the
latter sphere its effect is to be traced mainly in the
development of those articles of the Creed which treat
of the mystery of the Trinity; in the former in the
attempt to reconcile the peculiar teaching of St. Paul,
or, to employ a much abused word, Paulinism, with the
older disciplinary theory of the Church. We have seen
also how heathen Platonism borrowed light from the
Gospel. There can be little doubt that in all essential
points, especially as regards the doctrine of the Trinity,
the indebtedness lies not upon the Church, but upon the
School. It remains for us in the present Lecture to
pass in hasty review the later history of Alexandrinism,
and to estimate in some degree the permanent value of
their contribution to Christian thought.

Clement had no enemies in life or in death. He did
not, it is true, escape censure. Pope Gelasius is said to
have placed his writings in the first *Index librorum pro-
hibitorum*, but the statement probably refers to the
author of the Pseudo-Clementine *Homilies* and *Recognitions* [1]. More serious was the attack of Photius in the

---

[1] The decree of Gelasius will be found in A. Thiel's *Epistolae Pont. Rom.
Genuinae*, pt. i. p. 461. Gelasius amongst other books condemns ' Itinera-
rium nomine Petri Apostoli quod appellatur Sancti Clementis, libri numero

ninth century, though even this was temperate and not
unkindly. The censures of Photius were directed against
the *Hypotyposes*, a commentary on the Bible in eight
books, of which we now possess only a few Greek fragments, and an adulterated Latin version of the notes on
the Catholic Epistles. Some of his charges can rest
upon nothing but error. Others are accurate but insig-
nificant and uncritical [1]. In Egypt a certain suspicion

decem, apocryphum.' This probably refers to the *Recognitions.* Then
after a considerable number of other works, ' Opuscula alterius Clementis
Alexandrini apocrypha.' Benedict XIV considered this to refer to our
Clement ; the Bollandists to ' another,' the pseudo-Clement. Not less than
three words in this brief sentence are obscure, *opuscula, alterius,* and
apocrypha. The first can hardly refer to works of the bulk of the *Stromateis*
and *Hypotyposes ;* the second, standing as it does practically by itself, may
distinguish Clement of Alexandria from the author of the *Recognitions* or
our Clement from another Alexandrine Clement ; the third may refer to the
professions of mystery so common in the *Stromateis* and elsewhere, or may
refer to ' spurious ' works. Zahn (*Forsch.* iii. 140) is inclined to think that
the genuine works of our Clement are meant. But I doubt whether the
works of our Clement were known at Rome, seeing that the much more
famous Origen was wholly unknown to Pope Anastasius before the Rufinian
commotion, and almost wholly unknown to Augustine.

[1] Photius thought the *Stromateis* unsound in some points which he does
not specify (*Cod.* cxi), and enumerates several definite errors which he
detected in the *Hypotyposes.* Clement, he says, here taught the Eternity of
Matter, Metempsychosis, and the existence of several worlds before Adam,
that is to say Pre-existence. All these Clement in his extant works denies
(but the last with some uncertainty, see above, p. 76). Photius is right in
affirming that Clement held the doctrine of Ideas, but wrong if he means
that he attributed to the Ideas an independent existence outside of the Son.
He is probably right again in his statement that Clement applied the verb
κτίζειν to the Generation of the Son (see above, p. 69), and certainly right
in his statement that Clement interpreted Genesis vi. 2 of actual marriage
between the fallen angels and the daughters of men. Again, he asserts that
Clement described the creation of Eve from Adam in a manner that contradicted Tradition. To what this refers we do not know. Again, that he
taught μὴ σαρκωθῆναι τὸν λόγον ἀλλὰ δόξαι. This is a grave exaggeration.
It is incredible that Clement should have taught Docetism pure and simple
in the *Hypotyposes*, though there is that in the *Stromateis* which shows us
how the exaggeration might arise (see above, p. 71). Lastly, λόγους τοῦ
πατρὸς δύο τερατολογῶν ἀπελέγχεται. This most probably rests on some

appears to have fallen upon Clement, owing to his
personal connection with Origen [1]. But with these
exceptions his posthumous history has been like his
life, peaceful, honourable and obscure. Among Mystic
writers he has enjoyed a certain fame, but he has been
little read, and Bishop Potter is almost the only scholar
of note who has cared to spend much labour upon his
writings. Partly this is due to his antique cast of
thought; partly to his style, which elaborate as it is
does not lend itself to quotation; partly to the extreme
difficulty of the text. Yet his books are in many ways
the most valuable monument of the early Church, the
more precious to all intelligent students because he
lived, not like Origen in the full stream of events, but in
a quiet backwater, where primitive thoughts and habits
lingered longer than elsewhere. It is much to be desired
that some competent editor should present his writings
to the world in a less repulsive form than they bear
at present, overlaid as they are with the rust of long
neglect.

Down to the seventeenth century the learning, virtues

confusion between the universal logos, the νοῦς of man, and the hypostatic
Logos, the Son (see Zahn, *Forschungen*, iii. p. 144). The accusation is
especially based upon the *Hypotyposes*, otherwise we might suppose with
Dr. Westcott that it rests upon a misunderstanding of the *Excerpta*. Origen
also (see Pamphilus, *Apologia*, and Huet, *Origeniana*, ii. 3. 15) was charged
with preaching 'two Christs,' as afterwards was Nestorius. In all three
cases the accusation has no other root than an unreasoning bitterness of
which the most ardent controversialist would now feel ashamed. Photius
showed his kindly feeling towards Clement, not by trying to understand
him, but by supposing that his writings had been adulterated: καὶ ἄλλα δὲ
μυρία φλυαρεῖ καὶ βλασφημεῖ εἴτε αὐτός, εἴτε τις ἕτερος τὸ αὐτοῦ πρόσωπον
ὑποκριθείς.

[1] Dr. Zahn, *Forschungen*, iii. p. 141, refers to a Coptic Synaxarium in
which Clement, Origen, and Arius are said to have been excommunicated
by the Patriarch Demetrius.

and orthodoxy of Clement were held to merit for him the title of Saint. His name filled a place in the Martyrologies, and his festival was fixed for the fourth of December. But, when the Roman Martyrology was revised by Clement VIII, the name of the Alexandrine doctor was omitted from the roll on the advice of Cardinal Baronius. Benedict XIV maintained the decision of his predecessor, on the grounds that Clement's life was little known, that he had never obtained public cultus in the Church, and that some of his doctrines were, if not erroneous, at least suspect. The last article refers chiefly to the accusations of Photius[1]. But the Abbé Cognat does not hesitate to discuss the reasons upon which this verdict is based. It is not he urges an *ex cathedra* judgment, and therefore though valid may be reversed. Its effect is simply to banish the name of Clement from the Martyrology, and to refuse him the honour of *dulia*. But in his own mind the candid Roman Catholic priest still appears to regard as a saint the saintly advocate of Disinterested Love, and few deserve the title better than this most reasonable, humane, and sunny spirit[2].

---

[1] Benedict justified the omission of Clement's name in the course of his elaborate Letter to King John of Portugal, who had undertaken to bear the expense of a new edition of the Martyrology. The Letter will be found in the *Bullarium* of Benedict XIV published at Venice 1778, no. liv. in vol. ii. p. 195. Abbé Cognat refers to the Mechlin *Bullarium* of 1827, vol. vi. p. 122. Benedict rested his doubts upon the Decree of Gelasius, the remarks of Cassiodorus (or Cassiodorius) upon the *Adumbrationes* (see Zahn, iii. 133 sqq.), the criticisms of Barbeirac and Petavius, and those of Photius.

[2] See *Clément d'Alexandrie*, par l'Abbé J. Cognat, Paris, 1859. In France Clement has never lost his title. ' Ni l'autorité de Benoît XIV ni celle du Martyrologe Romain n'ont jamais empêché les Églises de France de célébrer sa fête le 4 décembre, suivant le martyrologe et l'autorité d'Usuard ; ' *Dictionnaire de Patrologie*, Migne. His name will be found in the popular lists of saints whose names may be given to French children at baptism (see

Very different has been the fate of Origen. Even before his death he was the mark of the most devoted affection and of the bitterest hostility [1], and for many ages the same stormy halo surrounded his name. Down to the end of the fourth century he retained upon the whole the high estimation to which his learning, his piety, and his sufferings entitled him. If portions of his doctrines were assailed by Methodius and Eustathius, Pamphilus and Eusebius cherished his memory with loyal veneration, and protested against the ignorant misrepresentations of those who could not understand the greatness they decried; Athanasius stamped with high approval his doctrine of the Trinity; Basil and Gregory Nazianzen edited the *Philocalia,* a selection from his works, including passages from the *De Principiis,* reputed the most dangerous of all; Gregory of Nyssa repeated a large portion of his speculations; Hilary of Poitiers, Eusebius of Vercellae, Ambrose translated into Latin certain of the Commentaries or Homilies. Even Jerome, in his earlier and better days, could find no language too strong to express his admiration for one who was 'a teacher of the Church second only to the great Apostle [2].'

for instance Bouillet's *Atlas d'Histoire et de Géographie,* Hachette, 1877). Bossuet speaks of him as St. Clement after his erasure from the Roman Martyrology.

[1] *In Lucam,* Hom. xxv: Quod quidem in ecclesia patimur; plerique enim dum plus nos diligunt quam meremur haec iactant et loquuntur sermones nostros doctrinamque laudantes, quae conscientia nostra non recipit. Alii vero tractatus nostros calumniantes, ea sentire nos criminantur quae nunquam sensisse nos novimus. *De Princ.* ii. 10. 1: Offenduntur quidam in ecclesiastica fide, quasi velut stulte et penitus insipienter de resurrectione credamus; praecipue haeretici: cp. *De Princ.* i. 16. 1, the *Epistola ad Amicos,* and the *Apologia* of Pamphilus. The foundation of the following sections will be found, where not otherwise specified in the notes, in Huet and Denis.

[2] In the Preface to his translation of the Homilies on Ezekiel. In the

But towards the end of the fourth century the clouds began to gather. The Church was distracted by a series of heresies, and though none of these could be traced directly to Origen, there were expressions in his endless discussions that might seem to favour them all. The Arians never appealed to him; yet he was called the father of Arianism. Pelagius considered that he was refuting Origen; yet Jerome, not without reason, treated the two doctrines as closely allied. The name of Origen again was brought into question by the Eutychian and Nestorian disputes. All this fostered a sense of uneasiness, which was aggravated by the growing but obscure popularity of his teaching on the subjects of Pre-existence and the Resurrection. Many of the monks in Egypt and Palestine brooded in the silence of their Lauras over the fascinating visions of the Eternal Gospel, and it became a question with the rulers of the Church whether books so dangerous ought not to be taken by force out of the hands of the faithful.

The commotions that ensued form one of the most painful episodes in ecclesiastical history. There was zeal for truth no doubt in the victors, but it was a base and cruel zeal. Origenism was laid under the ban in

Preface to his translation of the Homilies on the Song of Songs he applies to Origen the text, 'introduxit me rex in cubiculum suum.' In his later days Jerome pressed very unfairly upon Origen, and is not to be acquitted of inconsistency, sophistry, harshness, and duplicity. Yet let us notice here he always spoke with the profoundest respect of Origen's services: Hoc unum dico; vellem cum invidia nominis eius, habere etiam scientiam Scripturarum, flocci pendens imagines umbrasque larvarum, quarum natura esse dicitur terrere parvulos, et in angulis garrire tenebrosis; *Liber Hebraic. Quaest. in Gen.*, Preface. Again, in the *Letter to Pammachius and Oceanus*: Non imitemur eius vitia cuius virtutes non possumus sequi. . . . Sed dicas, Si multorum communis est error cur solum persequimini? Quia vos laudatis ut apostolum. Tollite amoris ὑπερβολήν et nos tollimus odii magnitudinem.

the synods of Alexandria and Cyprus [1]. In Italy, where Origen was as yet only known by versions of his exegetical writings, the translation of the *De Principiis* caused a storm that was only allayed by the condemnation of Origenism and the disgrace of Rufinus at the instigation of Jerome [2]. In the East the quarrel of the bad Theophilus with the Nitrian monks led to a far more deplorable catastrophe. Expelled from Egypt, the monks found shelter at Constantinople. Theophilus

[1] Matters were brought to a crisis by three disputes—that between Theophilus and the Nitrian monks; that between Epiphanius and Jerome on the one side and John of Jerusalem on the other; and that between Jerome and Rufinus. Origenism was condemned by Synods held at Alexandria and in Cyprus, and according to Jerome the sentence was adopted by the Bishops of Rome, Milan, Aquileia, 'et omnis tam Orientis quam Occidentis Catholicorum Synodus.' Jerome's statement is to some extent confirmed by the Letter of Pope Anastasius to John of Jerusalem, which will be found in Mansi, vol. iii. 943. Anastasius, who frankly confesses that he had never heard of Origen before the translation of the *De Principiis*, appears to have personally approved of the action of Theophilus. But he says nothing about Western Synods. And it is certain that Origen was not condemned as a heretic, though Jerome appears to assert this; *Adv. Ruf.* ii. 22 ; *Ad Pamm. et Marc.* 97 (Migne). For long after this in the deliberations which preceded the Fifth Council the question was debated whether anathema could be pronounced against the dead (Evagrius, iv. 38). The sentence applied only to his books, and to them with some restriction, whether some of these were condemned and some allowed, as afterwards by Pope Gelasius ; or whether all were directed to be read with caution by the learned. The latter is the more probable supposition ; see Jerome, *Ad Tranquillinum*, Ep. 62 (Migne). And there is a story that Theophilus himself was found reading the works of Origen after the downfall of Chrysostom, and defended himself by saying (Socrates, vi. 17), τὰ Ὠριγένους ἔοικε βιβλία λειμῶνι πάντων ἀνθέων. Εἴ τι οὖν ἐν αὐτοῖς ἐφεύρω καλόν, τοῦτο δρέπομαι· εἰ δέ τί μοι ἀκανθῶδες φανείη, τοῦτο ὡς κέντρον ὑπερβαίνω. Socrates however (vi. 10) and Sozomen (viii. 14) say that the reading of the books of Origen was absolutely forbidden. So also Anastasius, *Letter to Simplicianus*, Mansi, iii. 945.

[2] Pope Siricius supported Rufinus, but the next Pope, Anastasius, at the instance of Marcella, a disciple of Jerome, joined in the condemnation of Origen and censured Rufinus for his rashness in translating the *De Principiis*, but did not molest him any further. Jerome calls this ' a glorious victory.'

eagerly caught the opportunity of humbling the rival Patriarch, and, aided by the wounded vanity of the empress Eudoxia, drove the holy Chrysostom to exile and death. Of his two allies, one, Epiphanius, repented too late, when he learned from Eudoxia's own lips the nature of the service expected from him. But Jerome was not dismayed by the tragic issue. He exulted over the ruin of a great and good man, whose only fault was that he had extended the hand of charity to the hunted exiles, whose innocence Theophilus himself was not ashamed to acknowledge when once his vengeance was secured. 'Babylon,' Jerome wrote to his accomplice, 'is fallen, is fallen.' Babylon was Chrysostom[1].

The same excited state of feeling continued during the next century and a half. In 496 A.D. Origen was branded as a schismatic by Pope Gelasius[2]; and the fierce disputes of the Origenist and orthodox monks for possession of the convents of St. Saba in Palestine led to fresh condemnations in the reign of Justinian[3]. From

---

[1] Jerome, Ep. 88, *Ad Theophilum.* But in Migne this letter (numbered 113) is ascribed to Theophilus.

[2] Gelasius forbade the use of all those works of Origen which Jerome had not sanctioned by turning them into Latin. 'Item Origenis opuscula nonnulla quae vir beatissimus Hieronymus non repudiat legenda suscipimus. Reliqua autem omnia cum auctore suo dicimus renuenda.' In the next sentence the epithet schismaticus is applied to Origen ; Thiel, *Epistolae Rom. Pont. Genuinae*, pt. i. p. 461.

[3] What these condemnations precisely were is an intricate, thorny, and in part perhaps insoluble question. I. Huet refers to a Synod of Antioch ; *Origeniana*, ii. 3. 19 (Lom. xxiii. 328), Antiochena Ephraemii Synodus anathema dixit Origeni ; and again, ii. 4. 3. 6 (Lom. xxiv. 78), Qua circiter tempestate harum regionum Origenistas collecta ab Ephraemio Antiocheno praesule synodus anathemate damnavit, ut narrat auctor Synodici, quod nuper in *Bibliotheca Juris Canonici* recudi curavit eruditissimus et humanissimus Henricus Justellus. The reference is to the *Bibl. Jur. Can.*, Paris, 1661, vol. ii. p. 1202 ; and the notice runs thus, Ἐν ᾧ καιρῷ τὰ ὠριγένεια δόγματα ὑπό τινων τῶν Παλαιστίνης μοναχῶν ἐκρατύνετο· καθ'

that time throughout the Middle Ages the name of
Origen was a byword in the East, and the margins of

ὧν ὁ μέγας Εὐφραίμιος, 'Αντιοχείας Συρίας ἀρχιεπίσκοπος, θείαν σύνοδον καὶ
ἱερὰν συστησάμενος ἀναθέματι τοὺς προασπιστὰς αὐτῶν κατεδίκασε. Huet's
first notice then is incorrect ; the sentence of this Synod was launched not
against Origen but against the ringleaders of the turbulent Origenist monks
by name. II. In the *Epistle of Justinian to Menas* nine anathemas are
propounded by the Emperor, covering the whole list of Origen's 'errors.'
They will be found in Mansi, ix. 534. The nine anathemas given by
Nicephorus (*H. E.* xvii. 27) are these nine, which were framed by the
Emperor himself and never sanctioned by any ecclesiastical authority.
They appear to have been laid before the Home or Domestic Synod of
Bishops habitually resident in Constantinople, by Menas in 541, and the
Synod in reply enacted fifteen anathemas (they will be found in Mansi, ix.
395), embodying the substance of those of Justinian, but with considerable
difference, and far inferior accuracy, of expression. III. Origen's name
occurs also in the eleventh anathema of the Fifth General Council, though
in somewhat singular company and without reason given (Mansi, ix. 377).
This anathema was reaffirmed, as it stood, by the First Lateran Council
in 696 (Mansi, x. 1051). Origen's name is mentioned again in combination
with those of Evagrius and Didymus in the Imperial Edict recited at the
Sixth General Council (the Third Council of Constantinople, A.D. 680) :
Suscepimus quoque et quae in temporibus Justiniani divae memoriae in
praedicta a Deo conservanda nostra felicissima civitate complosa est synodus
contra Dei impugnatores Origenem, Didymum et Evagrium ; Mansi, xi. 710.
This probably is intended to repeat the sentence of the Fifth Council,
though it may refer to that of the Home Synod. It is difficult to suppose
that the theologians of the Lateran Council were imposed upon by a forgery,
yet it has been maintained upon very serious grounds that the name of
Origen was added to the anathema of the Fifth Council at a later date.
The point has been discussed at length by Walch, vol. vii ; Huet, *Origeniana*,
ii. 3. 14 ; Cave, *Hist. Lit.* i. 558 ; Garnerius, in Gallandi, xii. 168 ; Cardinal
Noris, *Diss. de Synodo V*, vol. i. p. 638, ed. Ballerini ; Hefele, *Concilien-
geschichte*, vol. ii. p. 834, ed. 1856 ; Dr. Pusey, *What is of Faith*, &c., p.
137 ; F. N. Oxenham, *What is the Truth as to Everlasting Punishment*,
part ii ; Vincenzi, *In S. Greg. Nyss. et Origenis scripta et doctrinam.* It
will be observed that the Fifth Council, though it probably denounced
Origen by name as a heretic, did not specify, and apparently did not discuss,
any one of his erroneous opinions. ' Allerdings hat die fünfte Synode auch
den Origenes anathematisirt, aber nicht in einer besondern Sitzung und
nicht in Folge von besondern Verhandlungen, sondern nur *transeundo* und
in cumulo, indem sie in ihrem XIten Anathematismus unter einer Anzahl
älterer Häretiker auch seinen Namen aufführte ;' Hefele. The documents
referred to, with the exception of the *Epistola ad Menam*, are given by

his MSS. are found scrawled over with fierce execrations of his heresies and his blasphemies [1]. But the Westerns, among whom the respect for learning never wholly died, took a more generous view. Leo III inserted passages from his works among the readings from the Fathers in the Roman breviary [2]. Mechtildis, a saintly woman of the fourteenth century, saw a vision in which she was assured that God had been merciful to his errors. Books were written to prove that his salvation might be believed in, notwithstanding the anathemas of the Church [3]. His works continued to be studied, and all that seemed unsound was charitably ascribed to heretical interpolation [4].

Denzinger, who, with others, still ascribes the Fifteen Anathemas to the Fifth Council.

[1] Βλασφημεῖς αἱρετικέ et similia. Even in the West fierce notes of the same kind are to be found. Thus in three MSS. of Jerome's *De Viris Illustribus* Martianaeus found the following scholion on the life of Origen : ' Haec laus Origenis et falsa est et deceptio plurimorum, qui in amorem eius provocantur, cum constet eum super omnes haereticos venenato ore inauditas et intolerabiles blasphemias spiritu diabolico in Dominum nostrum Jesum Christum locutum fuisse : quique a sanctis Patribus, episcopis et monachis anathematizatus, etiam bona illius minime legi debere.'

[2] Huet, *Origeniana*, ii. 3. 19 (Lom. xxiii. 331).

[3] Robert Curzon, an Englishman, wrote a book *De Salvatione Origenis* ; Bale, *Centur.* 3 : Picus Mirandulanus maintained in a printed treatise ' Rationabilius esse credere Origenem esse salvum quam credere ipsum esse damnatum :' Stephanus Binetus also wrote ' De Salute Origenis.' See Huet, *Origeniana*, ii. 4. 3. 18 sqq. (Lom. xxiv. 98 sqq.), where other interesting information on the same point will be found collected.

[4] The foundation for this mode of defence is to be found in the *Epistola ad Amicos*, where Origen complains that reports of public disputations between himself and Gnostic teachers had been manipulated by the latter, and in one case at least actually manufactured. There is no reason whatever for supposing that his works, as we have them, have been tampered with. But the theory furnished a convenient shelter for timid friends, as we have already seen in the case of Photius and Clement. It is found in Rufinus' Preface to his translation of the *De Principiis*, and though justly set aside by Jerome, *Adv. Rufinum*, ii. 4. 5, held its ground throughout the Middle Ages. So in the well-known passage of Vincentius Lirinensis, *Comm.* i. 17, which deserves quotation also as showing the strange problem which

Probably Luther, whose passionate phrase, *Origenem jam dudum diris devovi*, is one of many that lie heavy on the great Reformer's fame, is the only man of eminence that ever spoke of Origen in language like this; though the Augustinian divines of the sixteenth and seventeenth centuries were scarcely more just towards the great Alexandrine than the *Graeculi* of the Lower Empire[1]. Even Methodius, even Theophilus, were diligent students of his books. Augustine, Bede, Bernard, respect the memory of one with whom they had little in common but learning and greatness of soul. Origen's name has been a kind of touchstone. There has been no truly great man in the Church who did not love him a little.

In later times he has not missed the respect which is

Origen presented to a saintly and not unlearned man in uncritical times: 'Sed forte discipulis parum felix? Quis unquam felicior? Nempe innumeri ex sinu suo doctores, innumeri sacerdotes, confessores et martyres extiterunt ... Sed dicet aliquis corruptos esse Origenis libros. Non resisto; quin potius et malo. Nam id a quibusdam et traditum et scriptum est, non Catholicis tantum verum etiam Haereticis. Sed illud est quod nunc debemus animadvertere, etsi non illum, libros tamen sub nomine eius editos, magnae esse tentationi.' Others, as has been said (above, p. 116), had recourse to the hypothesis of two and even of three Origens.

[1] The quotation from Luther, which I have not been able to verify, I owe to Huet. Melanchthon (ed. Wittebergae, 1564, vol. iii. p. 1060) criticises Origen at some length; approves his doctrine of the Trinity, but rejects that of Faith and Justification. He says of Rom. viii, 'hoc totum caput Pauli sceleste contaminatum est ab Origene.' The Alexandrine teaching on the subject of Free Will, &c. was harshly criticised by Jansen in his *Augustinus*. On the other hand ·Erasmus writes (vol. iii. p. 99, ed. Basel, 1558), Quid aliis usu veniat nescio; in me certe comperio quod dicam; plus me docet Christianae philosophiae unica Origenis pagina quam decem Augustini: and again (vol. ix. p. 75), Nam Origenis exemplum fortassis reiecturi sunt, etiam si nemini plus tribuendum arbitror exceptis dogmatibus aliquot: and yet again (praef. in opera Origenis; this quotation also I borrow), 'He loved that of which he spoke, and we speak with delight of the things which we love.'

his due. He has had zealous friends, liberal critics, editors whose erudition and industry are beyond all praise. But only in recent times has it been possible to treat him with justice. For all depends upon the point of view. Those who judge him in the light of later opinion must either condemn him with reluctance, like Vincent of Lerins, or defend him as from a brief like Halloix and Vincenzi. But in no other field of knowledge would such a course be tolerated. Theology is the only ungrateful science. She crushes her builders with the very stones they helped to pile. Among the greatest of these builders were Clement and Origen. We must ask what they found to build with. We must throw ourselves back into the days when tradition was in the making, and beliefs, which afterwards seemed eternal truths, had as yet occurred to no man. We must compare them not with Anselm, or Augustine, or Basil, or Athanasius, but with Irenaeus, or Tertullian, or Hippolytus, or Justin; and where these disagree we must allow that there was as yet no definite creed.

If we compare the creed of the fourth century with that of the second, we cannot deny that there has been development. There has been no demonstrable change, if by change we mean shifting of ground or alteration of principle. Yet doctrine is not the same thing as sentiment, nor technical formularies as implicit belief. The Church of Origen is no more the Church of the Athanasian Creed, than the Parliament of Charles I is the Parliament of Queen Victoria.

Where does this process of expansion, governed as it is not by Scripture but by philosophy, cease to be wholesome and necessary? The problem of the earliest

Christians was to harmonise the Three Names of God with Monotheism, in such a way that they could justify their faith and live by it. That of later ages was the repression of error, a very different thing. At what point this later motive, in itself not indefensible, becomes purely mischievous, each party, each 'heresy,' will decide for itself. The Alexandrines were animated by the earlier purer motive. They did not see all that their successors saw; but the question arises whether they did not see all that there was to be seen. In any case the later faith passed through theirs, grew out of theirs. And certainly if sufficiency of knowledge is to be tested by fulness and purity of the moral life, they will not be found to fail.

It has been said that their Exegesis survived while their Philosophy perished[1]. This is true in a sense. They left behind them a strong influence, but they founded no school. Their spell was laid on Eusebius and his circle, on Didymus who, blind from his fifth year, became one of the leading scholars of his time and never dissembled his love for Origen, on Basil and the two Gregories. Their mode of thought may be traced far down into the sixth century, when it vanished, crushed out by tyranny and the leaden ignorance of the age. But in truth their exegesis was too closely wedded to their philosophy not to share its fortunes. Allegorism in a sense survived; so far, that is, as its object was to multiply types, symbols, Messianic prophecies, proof-texts[2]; or to give meaning to what in the

---

[1] By M. Denis; *Philosophie d'Origène,* p. 416.

[2] Basil rejected the theory of the Ideal world and accepted the history of Creation in the literal sense. What I have called the negative apologetic

prevailing oblivion of Hebrew, and in the West of Greek also, was unintelligible. But its great principles perished. Origen held that God can do nothing which is not just; Augustine that what God does must be just. The propositions are convertible, but they lead to very different interpretations of Scripture. To Origen again the 'letter which killeth' was the transient, mechanical, carnal, whether in the New Testament or in the Old. The Ceremonial Law was symbolical of Christ, but only in a very limited degree of the Christian hierarchy. Here his weapons were turned against him, and became the instrument, not of freedom, but of servitude.

In this last respect the Reformation divines recurred to the Alexandrine method without realising that they had done so. For the word Allegorism, like many others, has changed its meaning. When Clement explains the precept 'Sell all that thou hast and give to the poor' in such a way as to legitimatise the retention of wealth, when he says that the Christian altar is the congregation, when he defines spiritual death as alienation from God, or the Heavenly Bread as Gnosis, all these in his view are Allegories. We should call them by another name.

We need not pause on Origen's idea of Pre-existence,

use of Allegorism disappeared entirely, and thus the door which had been opened for the partial admission of philosophy and science was again closed. Those Allegorisms again by which Christian dogmas were discovered in the Old Testament came very early to be regarded as the indisputable literal sense of the several passages and not allegorisms at all. A remarkable instance of this is furnished by the decrees of the Council of Sirmium in 357 : Si quis *Faciamus hominem* non Patrem ad Filium dixisse, sed ipsum ad semetipsum dicat Deum locutum, anathema sit. See Rosenmüller, iii. p. 290. Thus the word Allegorism gradually drifted into its modern sense and came to mean loosely any metaphorical application of the language of Scripture to the purpose of edification.

on which time has delivered a sufficient verdict. It is enough to repeat that it was no mere arbitrary crotchet, but a serious and systematic attempt to explain and vindicate the distributive justice of God. Origen was the first to apply it in this way; but the belief itself was one that had an imposing array of authority, both Pagan and Jewish, in its favour, and might even claim support from the well-known passage in St. John's account of the healing of the man who was born blind.

But what we have called the Paulinism of the Alexandrines is far too important to be dismissed without further notice. It is here that we have to appreciate their contribution to religion, to the grasp of opinion upon conduct. They endeavoured to show that Christianity is not a doctrine but a life, not a law but a spirit. The Christian must be holy yet free, obedient yet intelligent, able to judge and act for himself, a true son of God, needing no earthly director because guided by his Father's eye.

This they achieved. They showed that, though Habit is good, Knowledge and Love are better. They taught how Freedom is to be harmonised with Reverence and Order; the spontaneity of individualism with unity through the trained and sanctified intelligence. They struck the golden mean between Anarchy and Despotism, a lesson which after times discarded, which even at this day is not sufficiently apprehended. It was not their fault, if they failed to grasp the true relation between the beginning and the end of the spiritual progress. Their errors were two, both given to them by the modes of thought in which they had been trained.

They regarded Habit as the cause, or rather as the indispensable condition, of Love; and Love as the Platonic love of the Ideal in itself, not of the Ideal as discerned in and through the perfect Humanity. The influence of St. Paul did not rise high enough to sweep away these misconceptions till the time of the Pelagian controversy. Even then the real lesson of the debate was obscured by the misplacement of the point. It was made to hinge on the insoluble problem of the Freedom of the Will. But this is in truth a side issue. The really fruitful question is the nature of the Motive, not the mode of its operation. Yet it will conduce to the justice of our estimate, if we compare the teaching of the Alexandrines with that of Augustine on both points.

The Alexandrines held, as we have seen, the theory of Indifferentism. The Will is a non-moral faculty, the power of choosing motives. They did not clearly see that the state of liberty, as they understood it, is a state of imperfection. Practically they admitted that at a certain point the soul, through union with Christ, becomes so pure that it can no longer sin. But generally and in this life they maintained that man can do what he likes. Thus they accounted for the fall of Adam. Since that lapse the whole world has been prone to sin. But men are still so far free that they can choose at any rate the beginnings of amendment. Beyond this the Alexandrines distinguished between Virtue and Salvation. To the former man could attain by reason, which is itself a gift, a general grace, of God. But goodness varies in direct relation to knowledge, and perfect knowledge is revealed in Christ alone. Hence salvation, spiritual health, life eternal, sonship, is in the fullest

sense a gift of God. For it is the union of the soul
with God, and that there may be this union God must
come to us. We cannot claim His coming. But we can
at least desire it. We can go to meet Him; we can
hold out our hand for His gift. This one point, the
initial desire of amendment, is all that Origen and even
Clement postulates; and even this, being reasonable, is,
let us repeat, a grace, inasmuch as it is the voice of that
word which God breathed into us at Creation[1].

Small as the postulate may seem, it involves an insu-
perable speculative difficulty. For it requires us to
admit that man can do not only what he likes, but
what *ex hypothesi* he does not like. Origen knew this.
It was not through failure of insight that he adopted a
theory, which, if scientifically imperfect, is consistent
with itself, is in harmony with the facts of experience
and involves no moral paradox.

The theory of Augustine is open to objection on all
these grounds. We may say indeed that he has no theory.
He approaches the subject from the side of Scripture,
which may be quoted with equal facility in either sense,
and his language varies with the point that he desires to
establish. He explained the Fall on the Alexandrine

---

[1] The difference between Origen and Augustine as to the necessity of the
Divine Grace is very like that between Law and Wesley. After his conversion Wesley wrote a somewhat petulant letter to Law, whose *Serious Call*
had for years been his model and guide. It had taught him, he says, that
the law of God is holy, but he had learned also that he had not the power
to fulfil it, and in this state he might have groaned till he died had not the
Moravian Bohler showed him the better way of salvation by Faith. Why
then, he asks, did you never give me this advice? Law replies, 'You have
had a great many conversations with me, and you never were with me for
half an hour without my being large upon that very doctrine which you
make me totally ignorant and silent of.' See Tyerman's *Life of Wesley*,
vol. i. p. 185.

view, though this is far more difficult for him, because
he regarded Adam as originally perfect. This is the
first terrible weakness in his position. He is driven into
it not only by the nature of the case, but by the supposed necessity of justifying the reprobation of the
entire world, which sinned in Adam[1]. Here again
there is another and even more startling breach of sequence. For, as he refuses to deny that each soul
comes fresh from the hand of God, the phrase that
' in Adam all die' cannot have the meaning that he
gives it[2].

But, as regards the actually existing race of men he
asserts a wholly different thesis. ' The Will,' he says,
' is always free, but it is not always good. It is either
free from Righteousness, and then it is evil; or it is free
from sin, and then it is good[3].' His sense is confused

---

[1] *De Corrept. et Gratia*, 10 : Quia vero (Adam) per liberum arbitrium
Deum deseruit, iustum iudicium Dei expertus est, ut cum tota sua stirpe,
quae in illo adhuc posita tota cum illo peccaverat, damnaretur. *Ibid.* 11 :
Posset enim perseverare si vellet: quod ut nollet de libero descendit arbitrio;
quod tunc ita liberum erat, ut bene velle posset et male.

[2] *Ep.* 169. § 13 : Scripsi etiam librum ad sanctum presbyterum Hierony-
mum de animae origine (*Ep.* 166) consulens eum, quomodo defendi possit
illa sententia, quam religiosae memoriae Marcellino suam esse scripsit, sin-
gulas animas novas nascentibus fieri, ut non labefactetur fundatissima ecclesiae
fides, qua inconcusse credimus quod in Adam omnes moriuntur, et nisi per
Christum liberentur, quod per suum Sacramentum etiam in parvulis operatur,
in condemnationem trahuntur. Augustine then was quite aware of the difficulty. But again, *Opus Imperf.* iv. 104, he writes, Argue de origine animarum
cunctationem meam, quia non audeo docere vel affirmare quod nescio.

[3] *De Gratia et Libero Arbitrio*, 15 : Semper est autem in nobis voluntas
libera, sed non semper est bona. Aut enim a iustitia libera est quando servit
peccato, et tunc est mala : aut a peccato libera est, quando servit iustitiae et
tunc est bona. Gratia vero Dei semper est bona, et per hanc fit ut sit homo
bonae voluntatis, qui prius fuit voluntatis malae. He ridiculed the ' balance '
theory of the Pelagians, *Opus Imperfect.* iii. 117 : Libra tua, quam conaris ex
utraque parte per aequalia momenta suspendere, ut voluntas quantum est
ad malum, tantum etiam sit ad bonum libera. But this is exactly what he
himself maintained as regards the First Parent. Nor does he get out of this

here by an inherited phrase, which to him has no meaning, which he ought to have rejected, and retains only for a purpose. What he says amounts in fact to this, that there is no such thing as Freedom of Will, but that the man himself is free when his energy is unimpeded. He can do what he likes, but never what he dislikes. It is a tenable view, but it carries with it obligations; and if these are disregarded, it becomes at once immoral. Augustine did disregard them. Action, he maintains, follows the strongest motive, and the strongest motive is given to us, either by the direct operation of God, or by Nature. But Nature is tainted; hence prior to Grace the strongest motive is invariably evil.

Thus Augustine explains with facility those dark and reluctant utterances of the Epistle to the Romans under which Origen writhes in vain. Yet even he has not exactly caught the meaning of the Apostle, who speaks of man as free when enabled by grace, and not free yet yearning for freedom while sold under sin. 'For to will is present with me, but how to perform that which is good I know not.' Nor can his view be made to fit his theology without additional machinery, like the Ptolemaic epicycles. For though Grace furnishes the stronger motive, and so constrains the will, it is in itself valueless. Man may fall away by Free Will, which here again has

difficulty by distinguishing two kinds of Grace of which the first only was given to Adam; *De Correptione et Gratia*, 11, Prima est enim qua fit ut habeat homo iustitiam si velit; secunda ergo plus potest, qua etiam fit ut velit. For what is the first except Free Will in the Alexandrine sense? No Greek and no philosopher could have written as Augustine wrote here. It would have been far better if he had made the same confession of ignorance as regards Free Will that he makes frankly as regards the origin of the soul. But then the Pelagians could not have been condemned.

to reappear. For upon this phantom phrase hangs nothing less than the Divine Justice. Hence above Grace Augustine is compelled to place the gift of Perseverance [1]; and this, and not Grace, is the cause of Salvation, which is here conceived of in the archaic fashion as something not to be attained till after death. Augustine has been called more logical than Origen. But surely on insufficient grounds.

But by far the more important question remains. What is Grace? According to the Alexandrines it is anything that makes men better. According to Augustine it is Love, the one and only thing that makes men better. 'For when it is asked,' he says, 'whether any one be a good man, it is not asked what he believes, or what he hopes, but what he loves. For he who loves rightly without doubt he rightly believes, and rightly hopes; but he who loves not believes in vain, hopes in vain [2].' 'Little love is little righteousness; great love is great righteousness; perfect love is perfect righteousness.' Here we have the full meaning of the Gospel. Such language is far in advance of the Alexandrines, who puzzle themselves and their hearers with their moral alchemy, seeking to distil love out of hope and fear, or to climb to it by the ladder of discipline, which without love has no ground to stand upon. The whole cumbrous structure of the Two Lives disappears at once. Henceforth except among the Mystics, who will be something more than Christians, there is but One.

---

[1] See especially the *De Dono Perseverantiae.*

[2] *Concerning Faith, Hope, and Charity,* i. 117 (I quote the *Enchiridion* here from Mr. de Romestin's Translation, Parker, 1885). The following passage is from *De Natura et Gratia,* 70 : Caritas inchoata inchoata iustitia est ; caritas provecta provecta iustitia est ; caritas magna magna iustitia est ; caritas perfecta perfecta iustitia est.

Had Augustine rested here all would have been well. For Determinism loses its terrors when we call it by its heavenly name of Charity. But here again his theology was too strong for his ethics. He has to combine his Determinism, not only with the terrible doctrine that all men are reprobate for a sin that was not their own, but with the scarcely less terrible doctrine that the healing love of God flows only through the ordinances of a Church, from which all but a fraction of humanity have been shut out by His own direct act. The unbaptised infant is doomed to eternal exclusion from the Beatific Vision [1]. Fabricius will be punished less than Catiline, not because he is good, but because Catiline is worse [2]. St. Paul never taught Augustine this. If he is asked, how then God is just, he replies, ' He is just; I know not how.'

It is not difficult to understand why his opponents asserted that Augustine had never ceased to be a Manichee. His system is in truth that of the Gnostics, the ancestors of the Manichees. For it makes no real

---

[1] This has been held to be the sole penalty of Original Sin as such. It implies no *poena sensus*, no suffering, and has been called 'a natural beatitude.' See the decree of Pope Innocent III (*Decr.* iii. 42. 3 in Denzinger, *Enchiridion*, p. 145, ed. 1865) : Poena originalis peccati est carentia visionis Dei, actualis vero poena peccati est gehennae perpetuae cruciatus. The same view is maintained by Thomas Aquinas. Before this time the state of unbaptised infants after death is spoken of as one of punishment, but of punishment in its most attenuated form. So Augustine, *Concerning Faith, Hope, and Charity*, i. 93 : ' The mildest punishment indeed of all will be theirs, who have added no sin further besides the sin of origin.' And even at a much later date the same language was used. See the *Professio Fidei Graecis praescripta a Gregorio XIII* (in Denzinger, *Enchiridion*, p. 295, ed. 1865) : Illorum autem animas qui in actuali mortali peccato, vel solo originali decedunt, mox in infernum descendere, poenis tamen disparibus puniendas. I might therefore have used a stronger phrase in my text.

[2] *Contra Julianum*, iv. 3 : Minus enim Fabricius quam Catilina punietur non quia iste bonus, sed quia ille magis malus.

difference whether our doom is stamped upon the nature
given to us by our Creator, or fixed by an arbitrary
decree. It is Gnosticism without the consolatory belief
in conditional immortality. He could never have written
as he did, had Gnosticism still borne as menacing a
front as in the days of Origen. As regards the doctrine
of Redemption he still occupies the ground of earlier
theology. It was reserved for Anselm, centuries afterwards, to array the Justice against the Goodness of God,
and thus to complete the resemblance of Christianity to
its ancient deadly foe [1].

---

[1] Anselm's doctrine rests upon the idea that sin constitutes a debt to
God. God has been defrauded and must be repaid, The obligation is so
huge that man cannot satisfy it. Christ pays it for him; and receives from
God Forgiveness, which, as He does not need it Himself, He bestows upon
man. *Cur Deus Homo,* i. 23: Quid abstulit homo Deo cum vinci se
permisit a diabolo? ... Nonne abstulit Deo quidquid de humana natura
facere proposuerat?—Non potest negari.—Intende in districtam iustitiam;
et iudica secundum illam, utrum ad aequalitatem peccati homo satisfaciat
Deo; nisi id ipsum quod, permittendo se vinci a diabolo, Deo abstulit,
diabolum vincendo restituat; ut quemadmodum, per hoc quod victus est,
rapuit diabolus quod Dei erat, et Deus perdidit; ita per hoc quod vincat,
perdat diabolus et Deus recuperet. *Ibid.* ii. 20 (Migne): Quantum autem
sit quod Filius sponte dedit non est opus exponere.—Sufficienter patet.—
Eum autem qui tantum donum sponte dedit Deo sine retributione debere
esse non iudicabis.—Immo necesse esse video ut Pater Filio retribuat;
alioquin aut iniustus esse videtur, si nollet, aut impotens si non posset;
quae aliena sunt a Deo. ... Si voluerit Filius quod sibi debetur alii dare,
poteritne Pater iure illum prohibere aut alii cui dabit negare?—Immo et
iustum et necessarium intellego, ut cui voluerit dare Filius a Patre reddatur;
quia et Filio quod suum est dare licet, et Pater quod debet non nisi alii
reddere potest. According to Anselm, then, Christ redeems mankind from
God. Redemption is thus conceived of as a kind of mercantile transaction;
its moral and spiritual significance is thrown into the background. Again,
it is impossible, on this mode of statement, to avoid the suspicion of moral
opposition between Him who exacts and Him who pays the debt. This is
of course not so violently expressed by a pure Trinitarian like Anselm as by a
Gnostic, in whose idea the God from whom man was redeemed was the
Demiurge, an imperfect Being and not a member of the Trinity. Nevertheless the difficulty is inherent in Anselm's theory, and has often led to the use

The Alexandrines were blamed also for their view of the nature of that body which the soul will receive at the Resurrection. It may still be doubted whether Origen does not offer a fair explanation of the words 'flesh and blood shall not inherit the kingdom of God.' As on the question of the Will so here Augustine, before he became Bishop. held an opinion undistinguishable from that of the Alexandrine. Even his later revised belief is more like that of Origen than it is like that of Athenagoras[1]; and it is probable that Origen's speculations would have escaped rebuke, had they not been

of language that is most earnestly to be deprecated. The old view was that Christ redeemed man from the Powers of Evil. This again is capable of being understood in two very different ways. According to Origen the death of Christ partly daunts and weakens the Powers of Evil conceived as external entities, partly breaks the grasp of evil conceived as a moral force existing in the soul; and thus by making man better reconciles him to God. See in addition to passages quoted above (p. 210) *In Rom.* v. 10 (Lom. vi. 406). But here also the mercantile theory obtruded itself. By Augustine God is regarded as buying man from the Devil by the sacrifice of Christ. *De Trinitate,* xiii. 12: Quadam iustitia Dei in potestatem diaboli traditum est genus humanum. ... Si ergo commissio peccatorum per iram Dei iustam hominem subdidit diabolo, profecto remissio peccatorum per reconciliationem Dei benignam emit hominem a diabolo. And again, *Ibid.* 14: Quae est ergo iustitia qua victus est diabolus? Quae nisi iustitia Christi? Et quomodo victus est? Quia cum in Illo nihil dignum morte inveniret, occidit tamen. Et utique iustum est ut debitores quos tenebat liberi dimittantur, in eum credentes quem sine ullo debito occidit. Hoc est quod iustificari dicimur in Christi sanguine. Augustine was still keenly alive to the danger of introducing any shadow of antagonism into the relation between Father and Son. So *Ibid.* 11: Sed quid est *iustificati in sanguine ipsius?* Quae vis est sanguinis huius, obsecro, ut in ea iustificentur credentes? Et quid est *reconciliati per mortem Filii eius?* Itane vero, cum irasceretur nobis Deus Pater, vidit mortem Filii sui pro nobis et placatus est nobis? This cannot be, for omnia simul et Pater et Filius et amborum Spiritus pariter et concorditer operantur. The ancient view also, like its successor, is capable of degradation and caricature. But, if understood as it is meant, it is far profounder than that of Anselm.

[1] *Retractationes,* i. 17; *Concerning Faith, Hope, and Charity,* i. 84 sqq. (Trans. of Mr. de Romestin.)

seized upon and caricatured by the ignorant Eastern monks. Far greater is the interest that attaches to the doctrine of Restitution or Catharsis. Here again Augustine is in opposition to Origen. Yet let us observe his opposition is managed with forbearance. If in one passage he speaks of this tenet as one ' which the Church rightly detests,' in another he regards those who hold it as yet Catholics, and ' deceived by a certain human kindness [1].'

Neither Clement nor Origen is properly speaking a Universalist. Nor is Universalism the logical result of their principles. For if the goodness of God drew them in one direction, the Freedom of the Will, their negative pole, drove them with equal force in the other. Neither denied the eternity of punishment. What is known as the *Poena Damni*—exclusion that is from the sight of God—they held would never cease. The soul that

---

[1] Hoc in Origene dignissime detestatur Ecclesia ; *De gestis Pelagii*, iii. 10. Nevertheless Augustine always treated Origen with great respect and forbearance. He refused to be entangled by Jerome in the controversy with John of Jerusalem. In *Ep.* 8 he expresses the wish of the African Church that Jerome would continue his work of interpreting the Greek divines, especially Origen, and when warned by Jerome that he should be careful how he read Origen, merely begged to be informed what the errors of Origen were ; *Origeniana*, ii. 4. 1. 14. In the *De Civitate Dei*, xxi. 17, it is noticeable that he does not attribute Universalism to Origen : Qua in re misericordior profecto fuit Origenes, qui et ipsum diabolum atque angelos eius post graviora pro meritis et diuturniora supplicia ex illis cruciatibus eruendos atque sociandos sanctis Angelis credidit. Sed illum et propter hoc, et propter alia nonnulla, et maxime propter alternantes sine cessatione beatitudines et miserias, et statutis seculorum intervallis ab istis ad illas atque ab illis ad istas itus ac reditus interminabiles, non immerito reprobavit Ecclesia. . . . Longe autem aliter istorum misericordia humano erat affectu, qui hominum illo iudicio damnatorum miserias temporales, omnium vero, qui vel citius vel tardius liberantur, aeternam felicitatem putant. Of these last he says (*Concerning Faith, Hope, and Charity*, i. 67), ' But they who believe this and yet are Catholics seem to me to be deceived by a certain human kindness.'

has sinned beyond a certain point can never again become what once it might have been. The 'wise fire' will consume its evil fuel; anguish, remorse, shame, distraction, all torment will end when 'the wood, the hay, the straw' are burnt up. The purified spirit will be brought home; it will no longer rebel; it will acquiesce in its lot; but it may never be admitted within that holy circle where the pure in heart see face to face. Even this general cessation of 'the pain of sense' they hoped, but did not venture to affirm. Man tramples on God's goodness here; he may scorn and defy it for ever. And so long as he answers 'I will not' to the eternal 'Thou shalt,' so long must his agony endure.

The hope of a general Restitution of all souls through suffering to purity and blessedness lingered on in the East for some time[1]. It was widely diffused among the monasteries of Egypt and Palestine. It was taught by Diodorus and Theodore[2]. The names of these liberal theologians are regarded with suspicion. But there is no stain on the orthodoxy of the two Gregories. Yet Gregory Nazianzen regarded it as an open question[3]; while Gregory of Nyssa, one of the most revered leaders in the Church of the fourth century, proclaims it more

---

[1] See M. Denis, *Philosophie d' Origène*, pp. 535 sqq.

[2] The opinion is attributed to Theodore of Mopsuestia and Diodorus of Tarsus by Salomon, Metropolitan of Bassora in A.D. 1222. See Assemanni, *Bibl. Orient.* iii. 323.

[3] *Oratio* 40. § 36: Οἶδα καὶ πῦρ καθαρτήριον ... οἶδα καὶ πῦρ οὐ καθαρτήριον ἀλλὰ κολαστήριον. ... πάντα γὰρ ταῦτα τῆς ἀφανιστικῆς ἐστι δυνάμεως· εἰ μή τῳ φίλον κἀνταῦθα νοεῖν τοῦτο φιλανθρωπότερον, καὶ τοῦ κολάζοντος ἐπαξίως. *Poemata de Seipso*, i. 543 (Migne, xxxvii. 1010) he says of God, Ὅς ῥα καὶ οὐδὲν ἐόντας ἐπήξατο καὶ μετέπειτα λυομένους πήξει τε καὶ ἐς βίον ἄλλον ἐρύσσει, ἢ πυρός, ἠὲ Θεοῖο φαεσφόρου ἀντιάσοντας. εἰ δὲ Θεοῦ καὶ ἅπαντας ἐσύστερον; ἄλλοθι κείσθω. It is evident that Nazianzen regarded the doctrine as tenable, if he did not hold it himself.

emphatically and absolutely than the Alexandrines[1]. Even Epiphanius and Theophilus, the fierce antagonists of Origenism, appear to have regarded this particular article with indifference, except in so far as it embraced the fallen angels. The attitude of Jerome is highly ambiguous[2]. Origen's speculations on the subject of Catharsis were drowned in the general condemnation of

---

[1] *Or. in I Cor. xv.* 28 (*Opp.* ii. 6, ed. Paris, 1638): 'What then is the scope of the word which the Apostle authoritatively uses in this passage? That one day the nature of evil shall pass into nothingness, being altogether destroyed from among things that are; and that the divine and unsullied goodness shall embrace within itself all intelligent natures, none of those whom God hath made being exiled from the kingdom of God; when, all the alloy of evil that has been mixed up in things that are having been separated by the refining action of the purgatorial fire, everything that was created by God shall have become such as it was at the beginning, when as yet it had not admitted evil. . . . This is the end of our hope, that nothing shall be left contrary to the good, but that the divine life penetrating all things shall absolutely destroy death from among things that are; sin having been destroyed before him, by means of which, as has been said, death held his kingdom over men.' *De Anima et Resurrectione* (*Opp.* ii. pp. 226-229, ed. Paris, 1638) is equally strong. St. Germanus, Patriarch of Constantinople, in his *Retribuens et Legitimus* maintained that the latter treatise had been interpolated by heretics. We have seen the same subterfuge adopted in the case of Origen. Dr. Pusey and Vincenzi quote numerous passages in which the Nyssen speaks very clearly and strongly of eternal punishments. This again is true of Origen.

[2] Jerome at one time asserted (see Rufin. *Apol.* ii. 20) that Origen had been banished and degraded out of mere envy, 'non propter dogmatum gravitatem, non propter haeresim, ut nunc contra eum rabidi canes simulant, sed quia gloriam eloquentiae eius et scientiae ferre non poterant, et illo dicente omnes muti putabantur.' In his preface to the translation of the Homilies on Ezekiel he called Origen 'alterum post Apostolum Ecclesiarum magistrum.' Yet in these Homilies Origen's doctrine of Restitution is very clearly expressed, and at the time when Jerome wrote these words he must have been familiar with the *De Principiis*. Afterwards he inveighed strongly against the belief of the salvability of the Demons and against that of the restitution of man so far as it implied or seemed to imply restitution of the best and worst to an identical grade of blessedness (see above, p. 234). His own doctrine is that the demons and *impii*, that is men who never knew God or, having known, abandoned Him, will be punished for ever, but that all 'Christians' will be cleansed by fire. Huet speaks of this view as unortho-

his name and teaching [1]; but their place was to a large extent supplied by the doctrine of Purgatory. This existed in germ in the days of the Alexandrines [2], and is found fully developed in the Church of Augustine. From that time the Greek and Latin communions, that is to say the great majority of Christians, have held the faith that some sinners are punished but for a time [3].

dox, but, if *impii* means those dying in mortal sin, it appears to coincide very nearly with the general doctrine of Purgatory, at any rate in its earlier form. For it was held by many that all Christians must pass through the Purgatorial flame. See especially Ambrose, *In Psalm.* xxxvi. 15 and cxviii. 153; Alexandre, *Oracula Sibyllina*, ii. p. 531; Huet, *Origeniana*, ii. 11. 25.

[1] The Greek Church holds that Origen was condemned by the Fifth Council principally on this ground. *Confessio Orthodoxa*, i. 66 (in Kimmel, *Monumenta Fidei Eccl. Orient.*): De Purgatorio autem igne quid nobis iudicandum? Nihil usquam de eo in sacris literis traditur, quod temporaria ulla poena, animorum expurgatrix, a morte exsistat. Imo vero eam praecipue ab causam in Secunda Synodo Constantinopolitana Origenis damnata est sententia. But, as has been pointed out above, it is doubtful whether he was condemned by the Fifth Council at all, and probable that if he was no reason was assigned. The only express condemnation of his Restitution theory is to be found in the Fifteen Anathemas ascribed to the Home Synod, of which the first runs, εἴ τις τὴν μυθώδη προύπαρξιν τῶν ψυχῶν καὶ τὴν ταύτῃ ἑπομένην τερατώδη ἀποκατάστασιν πρεσβεύει, ἀνάθεμα ἔστω: and the fifteenth, εἴ τις λέγει ὅτι ἡ ἀγωγὴ τῶν νοῶν ἡ αὐτὴ ἔσται τῇ προτέρᾳ, ὅτε οὔπω ὑποβεβήκεσαν ἢ καταπεπτώκεισαν, ὡς τὴν ἀρχὴν τὴν αὐτὴν εἶναι τῷ τέλει καὶ τὸ τέλος τῆς ἀρχῆς μέτρον εἶναι, ἀνάθεμα ἔστω. But the Home Synod consisted only of a handful of Bishops resident in the capital, and has no claim to be regarded as the mouth-piece of the Church at large. As to the condemnation by the Fifth Council (if it was really pronounced), our sense of its gravity must be profoundly modified by the fact that it was pronounced not less than three hundred years after the death of Origen.

[2] In the Montanist treatises of Tertullian see above, p. 110. For Augustine's view see *Enchirid. ad Laur.* 67; *De Civ. Dei*, xx. 18; *De gestis Pelagii*, iii. 10.

[3] Mr. H. N. Oxenham (*Catholic Eschatology and Universalism*) regards the teaching of the two Churches as identical. There is however considerable difference in detail. The Greeks have no word for Purgatory, and certainly do not admit the existence of Purgatory as a distinct state. So *Confessio Orthodoxa*, i. 64: Annon et aliqui sic diem suum obeunt ut beatorum damnatorumque medii sint? Huiusmodi homines nulli reperiuntur. Again, the Greek belief rests upon a different foundation. They make no

What then is the true difference between this ancient and all but universal belief and that of the Alexandrines? It is by no means easy to define. For this question lies so near the roots of life, it is united by such tender fibres to our dearest hopes and fears, that it cannot be touched without a thrill. Hence it is seen through the mist of love and horror, and these two emotions intensify one another. The thought of the City of Destruction adds wings to the pilgrim's feet; and while he rejoices with trembling over his own salvation, he cannot wish that the pursuing fury should seem less vengeful to others. Hence there has been much diversity. Words have been employed in very different senses. Points, upon which high authorities have insisted as vital, are treated by other authorities not less high as subordinate and immaterial. Yet if we fix our attention upon the

---

use of the texts 1 Cor. iii. 15, Matth. iii. 11, on which according to Cardinal Newman the Roman doctrine reposes. They find no mention in Scripture of any 'purgatorial fire' or of any punishments that are not eternal. On the other hand, they attach great importance to Luke xii. 5, 'Fear Him which after He hath killed hath power to cast into hell.' It is to be inferred from this that God does not in all cases use this power; that there are some souls whom He releases from torment. Nor does the Greek Church attempt to ascertain who these souls are. This lies entirely in the hand of God; *Conf. Orthod.* i. 65. Whereas the Roman Church defines that none are admitted to Purgatory except those 'qui vere poenitentes in Dei caritate decesserint, antequam dignis poenitentiae fructibus de commissis satisfecerint et omissis.' Both Churches believe in the efficacy of prayers and sacrifices for the dead, but the indefiniteness of the Greek doctrine has saved it from the practical abuses that have arisen out of the Roman view. So indefinite is the Greek doctrine that it was possible for Cyril Lucar to deny that his Church believed in Purgatory; and Gerganus declared that 'the Popish Purgatory was the invention of Virgil.' The Greek view will be found in the *Confessio Orthodoxa* in Kimmel or Schaff; Cyrilli Lucaris Patr. Const. *Confessio Christianae fidei cui adiuncta est gemina eiusdem confessionis censura*, 1645; Hofmann, *Symbolik*, p. 186, and article *Fegfeuer* in Herzog; Loch, *Das Dogma der Gr. Kirche vom Purgatorium*. The Roman doctrine will be found most conveniently in Denzinger's *Enchiridion.*

language of the wisest teachers, there is also considerable
agreement. As to the instruments of the Divine Retribution [1], there is no longer any serious dispute. Nor
perhaps will any one now deny, that the first object of
chastisement is the amendment of the sinner, and that if
in any case it appears to lead to a different issue, the
cause is in the sinner himself.

But if we compare the teaching of Origen or Clement
with that of Augustine or Aquinas, we shall find two
points of antagonism, of which the first is real, the
second verbal only.

Both would agree that, if the grace of God is dead
within the soul, hope can shine no more. But to the
Alexandrines every man that lives is a child of God,
a possessor of the divine grace, inasmuch as he bears
within him, in his reason and his conscience, the image
of the Divine Word. It may be that he has cast down
and broken the image, that he has wholly embruted
himself. But unless he has sunk to this frightful depth
by his own free will, unless he has ceased to be a man,
the Alexandrines held that we may leave him with fear-
ful hope to the judgment of God. The later theologians
took a far more sombre view. They who are in the
Church and they only are within the pale of the Divine
Love. Upon the excommunicate, the unbaptised, the
heathen, the door is shut [2]. This is the real distinction
between the two.

---

[1] The Greek Church believes only in mental, spiritual punishment. The
Roman Church does not define this point; but what her best minds think
may be seen in the *Dream of Gerontius* or the meditations of St. Katharine
of Genoa (in Loch, p. 150).

[2] The Council of Trent mitigated this. Quae quidem translatio (in
statum gratiae) post Evangelium promulgatum sine lavacro regenerationis
aut eius voto fieri non potest; Sess. vi. c. 4. We may observe here that

The other, though it has been regarded as of the essence of the question, is in reality a purely verbal difference. It is this, whether the soul that is admitted to purgation can be said to repent or not? This Origen affirmed, this the Roman and the Greek deny. But it matters little what language we employ, so long as the thing signified is the same. As the stress of its anguish passes, so the soul is braced to completer submission; so it wakes to more fervent love, to deeper knowledge; so it turns from its evil, and fixes its gaze with intenser faith upon its Judge and Saviour. Origen meant no more than this; nor do the Roman and the Greek mean less [1].

With respect to the bearing of Origenism on the teaching of our own Church I may venture to observe

there are several expressions (chiefly Eastern) of a belief that great power attached to the prayers of persons eminent for sanctity. Thus Perpetua (above, p. 110) is said to have rescued the soul of her unbaptised brother Dinocrates; Gregory the Great to have obtained pardon for the Emperor Trajan; Thecla for her heathen mother Falconilla; and Johannes Damascenus for his Mahometan father. See Loch, p. 79, and the Bishop of Durham, *Apostolic Fathers*, part ii. vol. i. p. 3.

[1] The Greek Church has defined this point strictly and repeatedly. *Confessio Orthodoxa*, i. 64: Quibus ex verbis clarum evadit ab excessu suo liberari per se animam poenitentiamque agere non posse, nihilque eiusmodi moliri quo infernis eximatur vinculis. The Roman Church does not appear to have decided it further than by condemning a proposition of Martin Luther, 'nec probatum est ullis aut rationibus aut Scripturis ipsas (animas in Purgatorio) esse extra statum merendi aut augendae charitatis' (Denzinger, § 662), and by the definition already quoted that the soul must have 'truly repented' in this life. Mr. H. N. Oxenham (*Catholic Eschatology and Universalism*) holds that the words 'repentance,' 'probation,' cannot be applied to the future life. 'The acts of the soul in Purgatory are moral, though they are not strictly speaking meritorious; they do not affect its final destiny which is already fixed.' 'We cannot admit that Purgatory includes the idea of a second probation for those who have already had their trial and failed.' All depends upon what we mean by 'repentance,' 'probation,' and especially 'failure.'

that here again there are two points involved. The first
is as before as to the nature, the scope, still more the
degree of saving grace. Few among us would desire to
bar the gates of heaven against the Unitarian Channing,
against the Buddhist ascetic, against even the naked
savage who on his sea-swept coral reef, forsaken as he
may seem of God and man, is yet just and grateful and
kind to wife and child. Yet few would think that for
these maimed souls no instruction is needed, that the
mere rending of the veil can make tolerable the splendour
which it reveals. We believe in the many stripes and
the few. We believe that star differeth from star in
glory, and in these words lies all that any sober-minded
man has ever maintained.

'God shall be all in all.' These words were never out
of Origen's mind. He looked upon the hope that they
enshrine as the golden key to every doubt. Nor can his
hope, even in its fullest sweep, be thought unscriptural
so long as this text remains part of the Bible. For we
can hardly say that an explanation adopted by Origen
and by Gregory of Nyssa is wholly baseless.

It is not for me to defend the moral character of
Clement or of Origen. Yet, as it has been argued that
their teaching implies an inadequate conception of sin,
a few words may be permitted.

It is not possible to exaggerate the horrors of that
abyss, when we figure to ourselves all that it holds within
its dark recesses. Nor will any one who lifts up his eyes
to Him, in Whose sight the very heavens are not clean,
dare to extenuate the measure of his own transgressions.
But guilt may be exaggerated, our own and still more
easily our brother's. The mote is not as the beam. Is

it not an exaggeration to say, or to imply, or to dream, that because God is infinite all offences against His Holy Law are also infinite, or to think of Him as angry with sin, as losing by sin? The Alexandrines protested against such errors, but they regarded sin as spiritual death; as separating us from Him, who is the joy and glory and life of the soul; as needing, as doomed, to be eradicated by anguish sharper than a sword. They knew well 'the agony of seeing all past sins in the sight of Jesus[1].' But they believed above all things in the Father's love. They did not understand how His Creation could for ever groan and travail, or how the Saviour could 'drink wine' in the sight of endless misery and wrong.

Origen's view has been called a cruel view[2], because aeonian probation implies aeonian change, and so eternal hope seems to issue in never-ending fear. Neither Clement nor Gregory admitted the possibility of a fall from grace in the future life. Even Origen held that there is a point, here or hereafter, at which love takes complete possession of the will, and the spirit is secure in the bosom of God.

Space does not permit me to cast more than a flying glance upon the pathetic history of Quietism. The opinions which drew shame and ruin upon Molinos, Fénelon, Madame de Guyon, in a hypocritical court and

---

[1] The phrase is from Dr. Pusey, *What is of Faith*, p. 116.

[2] By Mr. H. N. Oxenham. *In Rom.* v. 10 (Lom. vi. 407 sqq.) Origen expressly denies the possibility of declension from grace in the future life, on the ground that 'charity never faileth' and that 'nothing can separate us from the love of God' (Rom. viii. 35, 39; 1 Cor. xiii. 8). And I do not feel sure that the passages quoted above, p. 228, are sufficiently clear to demonstrate that he ever held the opposite opinion. At any rate the love of God in Christ, when once kindled in the soul, is indefectible.

a timeserving Church, were in substance those of Clement. Again, we read of the Absolute Good, the Two
Lives, Apathy, Disinterested Love, Silent Prayer. But
that which in the Alexandrine was largely traditional
and academic has become personal and impassioned,
that which was intellectual and Platonic has passed over
into the emotional and even sensuous. It rests no
longer upon the *Phaedrus* or St. John, but on the
Song of Songs.

The Quietists were but lightly touched by the characteristic infirmities of Mysticism. They were guarded
from these not only by deep piety, but by their high
social standing and cultivated minds. Like all their
class they sought to ' antedate the peace of heaven '—
an impossible and to untutored spirits a perilous effort.
The moral dangers of this presumption were not far
distant when Madame de Guyon was pressing the doctrines of Silent Prayer and Disinterested Love upon a
bevy of school-girls at St. Cyr. But their real offence
was not this. Quietism is a form of spiritual liberty,
and this was a fatal blot in an age of directors and
confessors. But there is no need to dwell upon a subject
so fascinating in itself and so accessible to all. Those
who wish to know what Quietism really was can peruse
the *Maxims of the Saints*. Those who care to see how
readily it lends itself to perversion and ridicule may read
Bossuet or La Bruyère. A just and temperate censor
will be found in Bourdaloue, a sympathising critic in
Vaughan [1].

---

[1] The instruments condemnatory of Molinos and the doctrine of Disinterested Love will be found in Denzinger, pp. 333-348, ed. 1865. It is
impossible not to feel and express sympathy for the Quietists, who but for
political reasons would probably have been left unmolested, and were

As we turn the pages of the Alexandrines, it is, to use
a well-worn simile, as if we were walking through the
streets of some long-buried city. Only with effort, only
imperfectly, can we recall the vanished life. Even when
we succeed in reconstructing the image of the past our
first impulse is an ungenerous one—How different these
men were to ourselves, how different and how inferior!
A second and finer thought teaches us better. They
were as we are. We have drifted far away from them,
and experience has taught us many things. But our
horizon is no wider, and our light no fuller. We know
no more than they. The only way in which we can
hope to surpass them is by the renunciation of vain
endeavours, and the concentration of all our efforts on
the ideal of Duty.

They were too subtle, too inquisitive, but the good
sense of the world has already judged their presumptuous sallies. It has been urged that they are too intellectual and cramp the play of the emotions. This is
true, and it is a fault, but on the other hand they are
not effeminate. Their tone is bracing and salutary.
Their use of Scripture is often wild and fantastic, but
it has not the faults of the Middle Age; it is free, un-
prejudiced, reasonable in endeavour if not always in
result. The one point on which we may justly blame

certainly harshly used. Nevertheless the authorities who condemned them
were in the right. Beautiful as Quietism is in its highest expression, in
cultivated and truly saintly spirits, it is yet rooted in error; it is a revolt against
reason and the facts of life, as well as against the teaching of Revelation.
Hence in grosser natures it leads inevitably to moral depravation. Sufficient
proof of this will be found in the account of Wesley's struggle with Quietism
of the lower type given in Tyerman's *Life.* The *Dialogues on Quietism* referred to above will be found in M. Servois' edition of La Bruyère, but there
is some doubt as to their real author. They are written somewhat in the
style of Pascal, but with a far coarser touch.

them is their immoral doctrine of Reserve. Yet it is precisely this blot in their conduct which has most commonly escaped censure, because it was capable of being turned to profit.

But this is the stain of the age in which they lived and cannot obscure their great services to Christianity. His work upon the text of Scripture alone would entitle Origen to undying gratitude. It was he and his predecessor, more than any others, who saved the Church not only from Noetianism but from Gnosticism, Chiliasm, Montanism, that is from Paganism, Sensualism, Fanaticism. In that age so like our own, when the Church had not yet acquired that civil support, that prescriptive hold upon the imagination, which now again she is rapidly losing, they broke the power of the Stoïc Religion of Humanity, of Epicurean Agnosticism, of Platonic Spiritualism. Almost alone they strove to reconcile the revelation of God in Jesus with the older revelation of God in Nature. What could be done at that time they did, and their principles are of permanent value. They never wrestle with Science for a few inches of doubtful ground. For the ground of Science is not theirs, and that sense of Scripture, which alone can conflict with Science, is not the 'spirit that giveth life.'

Last and highest among their merits we must place their preaching of the Fatherhood of God. It may be that on some points they erred, like Fénelon, 'from excess of love,' but such errors, if they are really there, must be treated in the spirit from which they flow. Their teaching is associated, in Origen at least, with ideas on which most Christians fear to dwell, though they are impressed upon us by the authority of the

Saviour Himself. They taught that the Just One is Good, as few since have taught that highest and most lifegiving of all truths. Origen added that Goodness is the source of all that is, that in all the efforts of our soul we should strive through Christ to Him who is the First Source of Redemption as of all other blessings, that there will come a time when the work of Mediation and Salvation will be achieved, when Christ will present the Church, His Sanctified Body, to the Father, Whom we shall see 'face to face.'

It is the teaching of St. Paul.—' Then cometh the End when He shall have delivered up the Kingdom to God, even the Father . . . Then shall the Son also Himself be subject unto Him that put all things under Him, that God may be all in all [1].'

---

[1] In two passages, *Contra Celsum*, viii. 11 ; *De Oratione*, 25 (where he is commenting on 'Thy Kingdom come'), Origen speaks of the delivering up of Christ's Kingdom to the Father. There will come a time when the Church and each of its members, being purified from all stain of sin, will be 'governed by God alone.' These passages must be read in connection with those cited above (pp. 169–170) as to the cessation of the Mediatorial office of Christ, and *In Matth.* xiv. 7, where it is said that Christ is 'perhaps' αὐτοβασιλεία. Some light again may be thrown upon Origen's meaning by other passages where it is intimated that the Father Himself has *Epinoiai*—as 'consuming fire' and 'light,' and again as 'Lord' and 'Father'; not that He changes, but that we change in relation to Him. See M. Denis, p. 378. Christ does not cease to be the Head of the Church or the King of Heaven. But He brings man when sin is dead within him, when he is now capable of the highest revelation of all, into immediate contact with the Father, so that he may see Him 'face to face,' 'as He is.' This contact depends on our complete and eternal union with Christ, and this again on the complete and eternal union of Christ with His Father. We have here no doubt the final expression of Origen's Subordinationism. But it must be observed 'subjection' means absolute harmony with the Archetypal Will. At the End all will be one because the Father's Will isall in all and all in each. Each will fill the place which the Mystery of the Economy assigns to him.